NEGOTIATION

For my wife, Linda,
from whom I've learned a great deal about negotiation
and from whom my inspiration comes for teaching and writing.

M. S.

For my husband, Frank,
my supporter and partner in negotiating four decades of marriage.
And for our grandchildren, Hannah, Adeline, and Jesse,
who will hopefully use negotiation skills in making their world a more peaceful place.

M. W. I.

NEGOTIATION

Communication for Diverse Settings

MICHAEL L. SPANGLE
Regis University

MYRA WARREN ISENHART
President, Organizational Communication, Inc.

SAGE Publications
International Educational and Professional Publisher
Thousand Oaks ■ London ■ New Delhi

For information:

Sage Publications, Inc.
2455 Teller Road
Thousand Oaks, California 91320
E-mail: order@sagepub.com

Sage Publications Ltd.
6 Bonhill Street
London EC2A 4PU
United Kingdom

Sage Publications India Pvt. Ltd.
M-32 Market
Greater Kailash I
New Delhi 110 048 India

Printed in the United States of America

Library of Congress Cataloging-in-Publication Data

Spangle, Michael.
Negotiation: communication for diverse settings / by Michael Spangle and Myra Warren Isenhart.
    p. cm.
Includes bibliographical references and index.
ISBN 0-7619-2348-9 © — ISBN 0-7619-2349-7 (P)
    1. Conflict management. 2. Negotiation. I. Isenhart, Myra Warren.
II. Title.
HM1126 .S63 2002
303.6´ 9—dc21

2002010850

02 03 04 05 10 9 8 7 6 5 4 3 2 1

Acquiring Editor:	Margaret H. Seawell
Editorial Assistant:	Alicia Carter
Copy Editor:	Meredith L. Brittain
Production Editor:	Claudia A. Hoffman

CONTENTS

Part II

ACKNOWLEDGMENTS

Many people have contributed to the completion of this work. We wish to express our gratitude to our families, who assisted, encouraged, and waited patiently during the long months of research and writing required to produce this book. We wish to thank our editor, Margaret Seawell, who immediately grasped the concept of studying negotiation across contexts and supported our efforts in many ways. Our copy editor, Meredith Brittain, checked the work assiduously. Special appreciation goes to graduate students who assisted in various ways, including Laurie Zant and Jacqui Snow, who each conducted an interview in a subject area where she held significant expertise. Snow also contributed many hours proofreading, reference checking, and generally upgrading the accuracy of the text. Another graduate student, Beth Levin, assisted with compiling the index.

John Martin, a colleague and specialist in labor law at Qwest Communications, conducted interviews with both the labor and management negotiators, colleagues who sat across the table from each other for many negotiations. Stephen Reiquam and Nancy Erbe contributed valuable input regarding intercultural and international negotiation. We are grateful to Thanh-Chau Nguyen-Vu and Mohammed Lotfy for the graphics found in the chapters. In addition, our appreciation goes to Laura Buseman, a newspaper editor and former English professor who offered editorial suggestions for most of the chapters. Our anonymous reviewers offered suggestions that focused the material more closely. Finally, we are thankful for the many graduate students and faculty members at the University of Denver who provided feedback on the subject matter along the way. The book has been improved by all of their contributions.

PREFACE

This book compares the practice of negotiation across contexts. In teaching negotiation to adults in the workplace, we discovered that no single negotiation book covered the variety of environments in which our students conduct negotiation and addressed how negotiation practice changes as contexts change. There are excellent texts covering negotiation in interpersonal, consumer, organizational, community, and international arenas. However, we found that no single book addressed the multiple roles that we all engage in as students, partners, parents, employees, consumers, or citizens.

This writing was also inspired by the variety of organizational clients we serve. Both of us consult with organizations that seek assistance with conflict management, so we frequently advise and train in the area of negotiation. Should our advice to the staff of a software development company about negotiating sales be the same as that given to members of a customer service department? Should families be advised to negotiate problems in the same manner as managers negotiate with employees about job descriptions? Common sense dictates "no," but which elements of the negotiations change as the contexts change? Again, we found information in a number of different sources, but no single text that answers such questions for multiple contexts.

A third purpose for writing this book is to offer in an accessible manner an understanding of negotiation for readers from a variety of backgrounds or levels of education. We avoid academic jargon whenever possible and use many examples to illustrate major points. We provide a breadth of information drawn from negotiation research, along with clear applications of negotiation practices, without bogging down the reader in theory. Although depth is sacrificed in some instances in favor of breadth, we provide an extensive References section where readers can pursue specific areas in greater depth.

Although our goal is to educate a wide audience, we believe that the readers for whom this text will have greatest appeal include the following:

- Junior- and senior-level undergraduates studying negotiation, either as a required course or as an elective
- Graduate students studying negotiation in various programs, including communication, alternative dispute resolution, business, social work, organizational development, or law

■ Students in executive development programs, usually offered within a business school, whose leadership effectiveness will depend on skilled negotiations with clients, employees, and suppliers

■ Organizational development, training, and human resource practitioners who want an overview of negotiation practice and concrete strategies for application in the workplace

■ Students of conflict management who would benefit from a supplementary text on the contextual approach to negotiation

● STRUCTURE OF THE BOOK

This book is divided into two parts. Part I, which contains Chapters 1 through 6, provides the reader with background and fundamentals of negotiation. Part II, which contains six chapters, focuses on different contexts: interpersonal, consumer, organizational, community, and international. Although we are aware that many readers will not engage in international negotiation, they will undoubtedly have occasion to engage in problem solving with people from different cultures in their communities and professional careers. The final chapter identifies the similarities and differences uncovered in the interviews with negotiation scholars and researchers presented throughout the volume.

Because the ability to negotiate involves art as well as science, practitioner interviews follow Chapters 3 through 11. Twenty-five interviewees, known and respected in their fields, were invited to describe their experiences with negotiation. We chose scholars and practitioners of negotiation who represented different professional contexts and who could present different points of view about negotiation. Some of those interviewed conduct research, teach, and facilitate negotiation, such as Bill Ury, Larry Susskind, James Freund, and Linda Putnam. Others interviewed serve primarily as practitioners, such as Annie Hill, Karen Graves, Anthony Roisman, and Russel Turbeville. In each of the 60- to 90-minute interviews, we asked the practitioners and scholars:

1. How did you become involved in the practice of negotiation?

2. What skills are critical to your practice?

3. How do you prepare for a negotiation?

4. Describe a typical session from your negotiation practice.

5. What is essential for success?

6. What have been some of your toughest challenges as a negotiator?

7. What occurs when negotiation breaks down?

8. How does negotiation in this context differ from that of other contexts?

9. What are new or emerging trends in your area of work?

10. What are the topics about which practitioners in your field disagree?

OVERVIEW OF THE CONTENTS ●

Chapter 1, "Foundations of Negotiation," defines negotiation and places it in the context of problem solving, managing conflict, overcoming resistance, or achieving valued interests. A discussion of the economic and social-psychological dimensions of negotiation emphasizes the importance of both relational and substantive interests that are achieved during negotiation. This chapter points out that the substance of negotiation may involve any of seven factors, from perceptions to outcomes. Awareness about what you are negotiating can influence choice of tactics. The chapter includes important distinctions between integrative and distributive negotiations that influence both the process and outcome of negotiation.

Chapter 2, "Contextual Nature of Negotiation," addresses the six major contextual variables—structure, norms and values, relationship, communication, interdependence, and power—that cut across the five contexts included in our survey. *Structure* refers to factors such as the number of parties negotiating, the location and environment in which the negotiation takes place, how negotiators view time, and the level of formality or informality of communication. Discussion of *norms and values* includes both formal and informal norms that guide the course of discussion. *Relationship* can also be important; where relationship is strong, people demonstrate more willingness to collaborate and more willingness to find solutions. The *communication* variable—the way that information is sent and received—is critical. This variable involves perspective taking, framing, style, and degree of emotion expressed. In addition, understanding the levels of *interdependence* or the balance of *power* influences the choice of tactics for achieving objectives. Each of the factors may affect the others. The level of interdependence impacts the ability to influence the other party. The quality of relationship influences communication and the kind of norms found in the interactions. Awareness about each of the factors makes the negotiator much more attuned to how to adapt to a particular context.

Chapter 3, "Theoretical Perspectives," reminds the reader that, whether we apply theories about negotiation consciously or not, our behavior is based on a frame of reference and a set of assumptions about how best to achieve our goals. The chapter includes brief discussions of seven theories that explain many of the dynamics that often occur in negotiations. Here again, a broad sweep of the theories promotes understanding about the factors that influence negotiation without having to deal with many concepts of the theories that lack applications in negotiation. Our hope is that readers will become aware of the theories that guide them in their choices of tactics in negotiation and that greater awareness of theoretical principles will provide more understanding about why some negotiations succeed while others fail. The chapter is enlivened by the contrasting theories of William Ury, cofounder of The Program on Negotiation at Harvard Law School, and James Freund, an author, professor, and attorney who specializes in corporate mergers.

Chapter 4, "Negotiation Processes," walks the reader through five stages of negotiation: prenegotiation, opening, information sharing, problem solving, and agreement. It stresses the importance of the prenegotiation period. The chapter offers advice for the opening, including how to work with the group dynamics of multiparty disputes. The coverage of the information-sharing stage includes understanding problems, identifying issues, and prioritizing interests. The chapter presents problem solving as a series of phases: generate ideas and options, separate inventing from deciding, engage in tradeoffs, agree on criteria for acceptable settlement, and select the best package of options and tradeoffs. Agreement involves many activities, including summarizing what is expected of each party in the agreement, establishing a strategy for monitoring commitment to the agreement, having parties contribute to a working draft of agreement, and creating provisions and timing for review or revision. At the end of this chapter, you'll find profiles of Lawrence Susskind, Ford Professor of Urban and Environmental Planning at MIT; Marvin Johnson, founder and director of the Center for Alternative Dispute Resolution; and Edward Selig, environmental attorney and mediator for the United States District Court for Massachusetts.

Chapter 5, "Qualities and Skills of Effective Negotiators," identifies the traits of successful negotiators based on a review of 17 publications by scholars and practitioners of negotiation. The chapter breaks down these skills into qualities in three categories (borrowed from the attributes favored in the Wizard of Oz): brain (mind), heart, and courage. Effective negotiators use their minds in preparation for negotiation and ask good questions to uncover valuable information. Listening, managing emotion, and integrity describe qualities of the heart. Courage involves willingness to risk speaking clearly, engage in creative thinking, and build relationships. The chapter points out the similarities between communication competence in conflict management and the communication skills necessary in effective negotiation. Finally, the chapter ends with an investigation of variables such as personality style, experience, and gender in negotiation effectiveness. Interviews with Texas A & M professor Linda Putnam and Robert Waterman, coauthor of *In Search of Excellence,* complete this chapter.

Chapter 6, "When Negotiation Breaks Down," concludes Part I. This chapter assists the reader in anticipating and hopefully avoiding some of the barriers to successful negotiation. Barriers that create impasse are explained, as well as suggestions about how to overcome them. Brief descriptions of mediation and arbitration provide the reader with awareness about options to consider when negotiations stall or fail. This chapter ends with a brief section on ethics to inform the reader about why some negotiations may be impossible; it is not meant to be a compilation of all the ethical issues associated with negotiation. Three professional profiles follow the discussion: Elaine Taylor Freeman, founding director of the ETV Endowment of South Carolina; Robert Coulson, retired president of the American Arbitration Association; and Anthony Roisman, lead counsel for landmark environmental cases, such as the one featured in the movie *A Civil Action* (Hall, 1998).

Part II of the book examines five contexts where readers are likely to be involved in some kind of negotiation. In each of the contexts, it identifies similarities and differences across the six variables presented in Chapter 2: structure, norms and values, relationship, communication, interdependence, and power. (In Chapter 8, the headings differ slightly to accommodate the literature of consumer affairs.) Chapters 7 through 11 in Part II end with a set of interviews with negotiators who have considerable expertise in the context featured. The final chapter integrates the art of negotiation, as presented by practitioners, with principles found in the science of negotiation, as presented in the first six chapters.

Chapter 7, "Interpersonal Negotiation," covers negotiation by couples, families, and neighbors. It opens with attention to antecedents, a term recognizing that interpersonal disputes usually evolve out of a history of conflict. The discussion of contextual factors begins by noting that characteristics such as small numbers, privacy, and tacit understandings influence the course of interpersonal negotiations. The relationship factor describes how triangulation, lack of clear boundaries, and the captive-audience nature of this context influence how issues are talked about and what types of agreements are achieved. These discussions are followed by profiles that highlight settings in which a great deal of interpersonal negotiation occurs. Marjorie Bribitzer, family therapist, presents her perspective on how parents can best negotiate with teenagers; Christine Coates, family mediator, offers her experience in both conducting and coaching negotiation with divorcing parents; and Sam Keltner, professor emeritus in Speech Communication, author, mediator and consultant, speaks of his work with neighborhood disputes and his attempts to negotiate them.

Chapter 8, "Consumer Negotiation," is a unique and useful chapter because it covers seller tactics and buyer concerns, as well as typical problems that consumers encounter. A short discussion about e-negotiation provides insight about the challenges facing those who choose to negotiate using an electronic medium. The chapter concludes with advice about reading and writing contracts. Three professional profiles with experts in consumer negotiations follow. Barbara Opotowsky, the past president of the New York Better Business Bureau, lends her informed perspective about what, when, and how to negotiate. Christine Beard, owner of a travel agency, specifies advice to those of us who encounter difficult negotiations related to traveling by ship or plane. Russel Turbeville, district attorney for Harris County, Texas (Houston), describes the traps that scam artists set for unwary consumers and the increasing difficulties that law enforcement agencies have in apprehending and convicting the culprits.

Chapter 9, "Organizational Negotiation," explores the contextual factors as they affect this type of negotiation. In this setting, structure includes not only formal roles on the organizational chart, but also the decision-making procedures and designation of negotiation agents. Norms and values encompass both formal rules and tacit understandings. Relationships and communication in organizations are more politicized than in most other contexts. Our examination of the high interdependence of organizational units and individuals is accompanied by a discussion of the visible role of power in this context. The chapter ends with a brief overview of research on computer-aided negotiation and four profiles. Joseph Rice, chairman of a leveraged buyout firm in New York City, offers the reader an appreciation of how international, million-dollar deals are negotiated. Annie Hill, union negotiator for US West (now Qwest Communications), and her longtime counterpart, Karen Graves, management negotiator for the same company, give their insights on the same negotiation process. Finally, Judy Towers Reemstma, Emmy-winning producer of television documentaries, describes the negotiations required to assemble and coordinate all the resources for video production.

Chapter 10, "Community Negotiation," explores contextual factors that influence negotiation and problem solving in community groups. The most important variable in influencing the course of negotiation in this setting may be structure because of the many parties, multiple perspectives, and multiple conflicting interests that characterize this context. Distrust of community leaders and the influence of coalitions mark relationships. Communication is affected by many factors, including the skill levels of community representatives. Discussions of values are more common than in most contexts. Power imbalances are typical, as are disputes about data. The chapter concludes with recommendations about how to plan and conduct an effective community negotiation. Profiles illustrate how varied community negotiations may be. John Fiske, family mediator and former counsel for the city of Boston, recounts the emotional but eventually successful negotiations between police and protestors that permitted public demonstrations against the war in Vietnam to occur peacefully. Wayne Carle, retired superintendent of one of the largest public school districts in the United States, reflects on volatile contract negotiations between administrators and teacher representatives. Fr. Charles Currie, president of The Association of Jesuit Colleges and Universities, describes the process of trying to negotiate change in a value-intensive context with many stakeholders as "wall-to-wall toes waiting to be stepped on," a saying common in the university setting.

Chapter 11, "International Negotiation," comments on contexts that are cross-cultural and international. The structure of negotiations may be bilateral or multilateral and may involve decision makers who are not involved in the actual negotiation. Because norms and values differ among cultures and national boundaries, the most effective negotiators are sensitive to differences in communication styles, the level of autonomy that can be expected, the importance or lack of importance of relationship, how power is demonstrated, and the involvement of other entities who may be affected by agreements. The first profile is a conversation with Peter Adler, ADR consultant and past president of the Society for Professionals in Dispute Resolution (now Association for Conflict Resolution). Speaking from considerable overseas experience and a strong intercultural background, Adler notes that we do not have to travel to have cross-cultural negotiations. Next, Edward King, senior program manager for MCI WorldCom in Brazil, offers a practical businessperson's perspective on how to be an effective international negotiator.

The final chapter summarizes the insights of the 25 practitioners whose conversations appear at the ends of Chapters 3 through 11. We compare several aspects of their views: their insights across the six contextual factors, the abilities and skills they believe make negotiators successful, the barriers they've encountered in negotiations, professional differences of opinion, and new directions that they see in the field of negotiation. Because the same questions were asked of each of them, it is possible to compare and contrast their responses and the opinions of the researchers noted in the chapters. There is a great deal of consensus about effective negotiation processes, but there are also differences arising from the different expectations and needs of the contexts in which the researchers and practitioners work.

INTRODUCTION

The growth of advanced technologies, movement to more horizontally managed organizations, and greater equality in relationships introduces increasingly more people into discussions about decisions that affect their lives. Neighborhood organizations involve homeowners in discussions about policies that affect their community. Couples making decisions often must integrate two careers and two sets of expectations into their decision making. As the world community becomes more connected through faxes, cell phones, and the Internet, the ability to create understanding and manage differences becomes more important.

To be effective in all of these contexts, you need to master the techniques of negotiation. A more complex and connected world requires people who can engage in dialogue and who can fashion innovative solutions to seemingly unsolvable problems.

Negotiation occurs when two or more people engage in problem-solving discussions designed to promote shared understandings, resolve differences, or engage in tradeoffs that will be mutually beneficial. Sometimes, these discussions result in formal agreements; other times, the outcomes may be harder to measure but will be just as important, such as developing the ability to talk about problems together, building relationship, or achieving understanding. In our interview with Bill Ury, he points out that each of us "can serve as a container that gradually transforms serious conflict from violence to a more constructive form of negotiation." Linda Putnam proposes that negotiation provides parties with an opportunity to reframe some issues, allowing them to build their understanding of conflict as well as the relationship. And for some, negotiation can serve as a tool for overcoming resistance without resorting to demands, coercion, or forcing, which cost a great deal in terms of lost relationship.

In the course of our research and writing, we discovered that negotiation occurs far more often than most people realize. For example, negotiation occurs when a couple discuss how they will arrange their budget, when a supervisor changes an employee's job responsibilities, when consumers take purchases back to a store for a refund, or when project management groups discuss direction and priorities. The book's content addresses both the traditional kinds of negotiations (such as contracts, car buying, and business deals) as well as the nontraditional contexts (such as interpersonal, consumer, organizational, community, and international relationships). Because of the expanded range of discussion and examples, the book is relevant for both students of negotiation and professionals in the field.

Unfortunately, there is no single formula for negotiating in all of these contexts. Negotiating contracts in business differs from the problem solving that occurs in families, neighborhood groups, or organizational staff meetings. Negotiation differs as people and context change. This book explores the challenges provided by each of the contexts and explains how negotiation can best meet these challenges.

CHAPTER 1

FOUNDATIONS OF NEGOTIATION

Ours is an age of negotiation. The fixed positions and solid values of the past seem to be giving way and new rules, roles, and relations have to be worked out. . . . Negotiation becomes not a transition but a way of life.

— Zartman (1976, pp. 2-3)

Tom serves as vice president of sales and marketing for TriCorp, a major supplier of components in the computer industry. His department consistently exceeds sales quotas. Recently, his staff complained to the CEO about Tom's outdated management practices, poorly targeted sales goals, and lack of responsiveness to staff suggestions about improving department processes. Tom says, "I've done things this way for 20 years. It's working. Why change it?" Staff members threaten to quit unless Tom changes the way he works with staff. Coldness and antagonism dominate the staff meetings. Tom's lack of willingness to negotiate with his staff fuels a breakdown of his staff's morale and commitment to goals.

Ten years ago, Bob and Alice, an older couple, moved into a home in a quiet neighborhood where they chose to spend their retirement years. The lack of fences between back yards symbolized the kind of community spirit they wanted. Bob landscaped his back yard, complete with a hedge that bordered his property. As the years went by, the neighborhood began to change. About a year ago, a young couple, Sean and Tonya, moved in next door. Bob looked forward to the energy the couple would bring to the neighborhood. But during the spring, relations deteriorated between the neighbors. Sean measured the property line. He found that Bob had planted his hedge, now 3 feet high, 6 inches onto Sean and Tonya's property. Because Sean planned to build a 6-foot fence between the homes, he wanted the hedge pulled out or moved back 6 inches. Bob wanted neither a fence between the properties nor his hedge touched in any way. He wanted a $1,000 reimbursement if anything was done to his hedge. Sean offered to pay for the fence he wanted, but he had no intention of paying for removal of the hedge. Bob steadfastly refused the offer. The relationship deteriorated to the point of going to court. Fortunately, they were able to negotiate a settlement with a court-appointed mediator, but the relationship remained broken.

Disputes were a common occurrence for Sue, a single parent. When her children were young, she could command obedience through threats of punishment, but now that her children are teenagers, she finds demands and threats ineffective. Although she threatens, they still come home after curfew. When they cut classes or get bad grades, she grounds them. But they sneak out at night. She refuses to give them money, so they steal it from her purse. Coercing, pushing, and threatening worked for many years, but now Sue possesses few tools to influence her children. The problems in this home began many years ago. Each day's conflict looks new but actually has roots in unresolved, underlying issues that date back many years.

Although each of these incidents differs in content, they share a great deal in common. Each situation involves two or more parties whose interests are in conflict, who view others as the problem, and who are willing to endure great personal cost rather than give in. In addition, each engages in a set of moves he or she believes will force others into compliance. Unfortunately, in each of the cases, even if one party achieves its goal through forcing, the winners lose other things they also value. The vice president loses the loyalty of his employees, the neighbors lose a relationship, and the single mother loses the love and friendship of her children.

The cost of unresolved disputes can be high. In one large marketing firm, the CEO estimated a loss of $1 million a year due to lost contracts because his four vice presidents couldn't get along. The dispute got so bad that three of the vice presidents would schedule board meetings while the other was away or, if he was in town, would occasionally forget to tell him when meetings were held. They'd just explain, "Oh, we just forgot to tell you." In another company, five of six regional directors quit over a dispute with their manager. The CEO explained, "I can't replace the manager because she's been here for 30 years, and she's not open to discussing her management style." In an era where it takes 40% longer than in past years to replace employees, the cost of unresolved conflict and the turnover that results can be high.

Inherent in interpersonal, family, work, and community relationships is a growing need to manage relationships more effectively. The cost of broken relationships, employee disputes, and community violence continues to grow, and new ways for resolving differences are needed. Negotiation is one option to transform conflict into problem solving or compromise. It offers an opportunity for people to reduce tensions caused by their differing views of the world. Negotiation provides an opportunity to create change and overcome resistance to change without having to use threats, make demands, or attempt to coerce.

Because our modern work is filled with many complex challenges, knowing how and when to negotiate has become a fundamental skill for success. A single all-purpose success formula about how to negotiate is an illusion. To become effective, we must develop depth of knowledge about contextual factors and the ability to adapt our strategy accordingly.

COMMUNICATION AND NEGOTIATION •

Historically, negotiation was based on self-interest, and tactics involved strategic influence. Parties selectively shared information to achieve an advantage, treating others as adversaries. Claims about knowledge, reports of truth, and bottom-line needs permeated each side's approach. Achievement of short-term goals held priority over the impact of long-term outcomes. Thus, a sale might be closed at the expense of a long-term business relationship, or an argument between neighbors might be settled at the expense of any further contact. The emphasis was on selective sharing of information to create an agreement with little regard for the underlying social processes. Although parties were unaware of it, their interactions influenced the level of trust they held in each other, the way power was experienced, the extent to which each would be open with information, or the kind of relationship that developed.

In a society with complex layers of values, interests, and needs, negotiation has needed to become more than strategic influence or manipulation disguised as negotiation. Deetz (2001) argues that the information-transfer orientation of industrial society is shifting to a society in which negotiation produces a codetermination of understandings about perceptions, knowledge, interests, and outcomes. Negotiation serves as a special type of communication in which parties (a) engage in reasoned discussion and problem-solving processes and (b) develop shared understandings that serve as the basis for agreements. Negotiation becomes a means to facilitate relationships based on dialogue and agreements based on understandings.

Communication serves a valuable role in this process. When differences of opinion or conflicts occur, negotiation serves as a tool for enabling or constraining parties as they consider courses of action. The choice of words can accentuate differences, which further polarizes parties, or emphasize similarities, which closes the psychological distance. Negotiators can accentuate their points or manage the intensity of emotion by slowing their rate of speech or lowering their volume (Neu, 1988).

Negotiation can serve as a tool for managing the dialectical dimensions of conflict displayed in tensions about autonomy or connectedness, openness or closedness, independence or dependence, and control or yielding. Negotiation provides a method for guiding parties through a process that focuses discussion more on understanding and meaning and less on blaming, control, or who gets authority over what. Putnam (2001) explains,

> Negotiators work out their interdependence, not only through exchanging proposals, but also in the way the parties enact and manage dialectical tension. Interdependence, then, is not simply a dimension of all conflict situations; rather it is a dynamic feature of conflict worked out through the bargaining process. (p. 6)

The goals with which one begins a negotiation may be different from the goals achieved. For example, two neighbors negotiating a problem dealing with trees hanging over the fence may not agree about what to do with the trees but may establish enough trust to discuss other issues. A manager negotiating an issue with an employee may not reach agreement but may establish a dialogue about role, authority, and cooperation. Putnam and Roloff (1992b) point out that negotiators "uncover systems of meaning" that influence subsequent messages and communication patterns over time (p. 7). Each negotiation is about more than a single outcome.

The case of the U.S. Forest Service attempting to resolve a 15-year negotiation with the friars of the Atonement in Garrison, New York, provides an example of parties who began with strategic influence and later turned to negotiated understandings to resolve their differences (Box 1.1). The friars held a weak position in their attempts to prevent the Forest Service from creating a land buffer for the Appalachian Trail, but the Forest Service had problems of its own. The public relations fallout for closing down a shelter for the homeless and ill could have serious political implications. Both parties needed to maintain good relations while achieving outcomes they could live with. It was not until both parties agreed that land needed to be protected from development and that they could trust each other that interest-based tradeoffs occurred.

Communication's role in negotiation is captured in various definitions of negotiation provided by scholars:

- "A form of interaction through which (parties) . . . try to arrange . . . a new combination of some of their common and conflicting interests" (Ilke, 1968, p. 117).
- "A process in which at least two partners with different needs and viewpoints try to reach agreement on matters of mutual interest" (Adler, Graham, & Gehrke, 1987, p. 413).
- "An interactive process by which two or more people seek jointly and cooperatively to do better than they could otherwise" (Lax and Sebenius, 1991a, p. 97).

Box 1.1

CONFLICT OVER SACRED LAND

In 1898, Franciscan friars purchased a 400-acre forest site along the Hudson River that bordered the Appalachian trail in Garrison, New York. There, 130 priests, brothers, and sisters built a retreat center to provide free shelter for the homeless, hikers, and people with health problems. The friars described the land as a holy mountain, sacred, and a place of solitude.

In 1985, the National Forest Service feared encroachment of the Appalachian Trail and asked the friars to provide a 57-acre, 50-foot-wide easement (right of way) through the land. Based on a handshake and a payment of $116,500 for a temporary right of way, the friars agreed. Parties regarded the temporary agreement as satisfactory until early in 2000 when the Forest Service became concerned about a pump and a sewage pipe installed by the friars on the easement land. Additionally, some people in the Forest Service feared that the friars would sell the land which might then be used for a housing development, which could further damage the land along the trail. In May 2000, because the parties had reached no settlement in 15 years, the Forest Service began proceedings to take the land plus an additional 18 acres by power of eminent domain. The friars argued that the government had no right to take the land based on fears that the land would be sold. And if it took an additional 18 acres now, how much more later? They fought the eminent domain procedures through members of the U.S. Congress, the Secretary of the Interior, and a Senate subcommittee. They did not want to go to court to determine rights.

In August 2000, representatives of the Forest Service and the friars met once again. They determined that they had common interests: protect the pristine conditions of the land, reduce escalation of the conflict between the two sides, and reach an agreement without going to court. Both parties acknowledged each other's rights. The representatives walked the property together and each reached an understanding about what the other valued. They reached an agreement to construct a different easement through a swapping of land. The friars agreed to include a provision not to sell the land to developers, and the Forest Service agreed on ways the friars could make changes to the land to fit their needs within the boundaries of the site.

- "The exchange of information through language that coordinates and manages meaning" (Gibbons, Bradac, & Busch, 1992, p. 156).
- "The interaction of two or more complex social units that are attempting to define or refine the terms of their interdependence" (Walton & McKersie, 1965, p. 35).
- "Two or more interdependent parties who perceive incompatible goals and engage in social interaction to reach a mutually satisfying outcome" (Putnam & Roloff, 1992, p. 3).

This set of definitions emphasizes the intentionality of the negotiation process, the management of conflicting interests, the importance of communication for resolving differences, and, to a small degree, the importance of creativity in problem solving for overcoming conflicting interests. Negotiation is a transactional form of communication in which parties send and receive messages that trigger mutual cycles of influence that affect future interaction.

Of special interest is the ability of negotiation to overcome resistance that may not be surmounted by other methods of social influence. When friendship, authority, reciprocity, or requests fail to influence others to give us what we want, negotiation becomes a more prominent choice. Watkins (2001, p. 120) identifies some of the sources of resistance that may block the more usual sources of influence:

- *Loss of comfortable status quo.* Parents, managers, and community leaders may be resistant to many forms of influence if concessions could result in their loss of power or authority.
- *Challenge to one's sense of competence.* If granting concessions could be interpreted as a sign of weakness or error in judgment, someone may be more likely to be resistant to influence.
- *Threats to self-defining values.* In some situations, the position someone takes may be linked to his or her identity or to many years of learned behavior for which change would mean a great deal of cognitive dissonance.
- *Potential loss of security due to uncertainty about the future.* People will resist the influence of others if they perceive risks associated with changes to current behavior.
- *Negative consequences to allies.* People value their friendships and alliances and will resist granting what others need if damage to these relationships could occur.

Identifying the sources of resistance—the reasons why someone feels a need to stand in our way, preventing us from accomplishing our objectives—provides a valuable source of information about what needs to be addressed in a negotiation. Patton (1984) explains that when people experience fear, they will probably have to be persuaded that (a) the benefits of change are greater or more certain than they think or (b) the risks of not changing are greater than they think. A negotiated agreement can include provisions that provide a feeling of safety about status quo, statements of support to bolster confidence, or protection against risk. Negotiation can achieve desired outcomes while addressing the social needs of meaning and understanding, which serve as the basis for dialogue and relationship.

ECONOMIC AND SOCIAL-PSYCHOLOGICAL • DIMENSIONS OF NEGOTIATION

Reminiscent of Blake and Mouton's (1985) managerial grid, which looks at task and relational dimensions of leadership, Thompson (1990b) argues that every negotiation possesses outcomes that may be measured along two dimensions: economic and social-psychological. The economic dimension refers to the tangible outcomes of negotiation—that is, the substantive interests and goals achieved. These goals are easily identified in consumer or business negotiations as savings or profits.

The social-psychological dimension involves relational factors such as quality of relationship, satisfaction with communication, perceptions about fairness of procedures, impressions of the other party, or judgments about personal performance. Some people may be satisfied with a negotiation even if they do not fully achieve their economic interests, and some may not be satisfied with outcomes even if they achieve their economic goals (see Figure 1.1).

Box 1.2 describes a conflict between a man and his daughter-in-law. It begins with a statement of concern, a question about health insurance (economic interest), but moves very quickly to an issue about autonomy (social-psychological interest). The example illustrates how interpersonal relationships frequently involve negotiations about boundaries, levels of intimacy, independence, and salience of issues.

The context dictates whether the substantive interests or the social-psychological needs are more important to parties involved in negotiation. For example, in family and community settings, the social-psychological dimension may be stronger. In organizational and consumer settings, the economic dimension may be stronger. But in both settings, both dimensions play a role in achieving a satisfactory settlement. Failing to address both of the dimensions often leads to failure in achieving our goals.

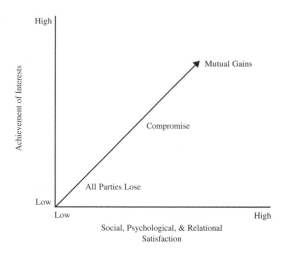

Figure 1.1   Measures of Negotiation

● THE CONTENT OF NEGOTIATION

The importance of maximizing both the economic and social-psychological dimensions of negotiation points out the importance of developing awareness about what you are negotiating. Superficially, it may appear that trading interests may be the focus of discussions. But as discussion of the interests bogs down, it might become apparent that other issues are affecting the ability to trade. The actual content of negotiation may involve many factors:

- *Perceptions.* The attributions, assumptions, and bias with which we view problems
- *Information.* The relevance, meaning, and importance we assign to facts or data
- *Issues.* What we believe the problem to be
- *Interests.* The wants or needs we seek to achieve
- *Relationship.* The respect, communication, or power we want from another
- *Process.* The way we resolve differences
- *Outcomes.* The solutions we're willing to accept

We may be negotiating one or more of these factors at any point in a negotiation. For example, an angry husband points at the checkbook and complains to his wife about how much money was spent this month. The wife, unhappy with how she's being talked to, complains about how he's speaking to her. Both are engaging in negotiations, but about different issues. He wants to talk about his interest: money. She wants to talk about relationship. Unless they align themselves to one issue, the conflict will

Box 1.2

WHEN CARING MAY BE PERCEIVED AS MEDDLING

Friends describe Phil as a father who manages his family's finances with careful planning. Phil rarely uses a credit card to make purchases, paid for his home with a 15-year loan, taught his children the art of frugal buying, and helped his two sons complete college without the need for a school loan.

Phil's eldest son, Jim, married Sarah at the end of his junior year of college. Sarah held a position as a second-grade teacher, a job that she didn't really like. Her plan was to pursue another career in the city they moved to after Jim graduated from college. Late in Jim's senior year, Sarah told her principal that she would not renew her contract because she expected Jim to graduate. As the end of the year approached, Jim found that he couldn't complete all of the courses he needed to graduate. Maybe during the summer he'd finish. It didn't happen. In the fall, Sarah began a job in a preschool as an interim source of income. Late in the fall semester, Jim told Sarah that it might not actually be until May before he completed his work.

Following a Thanksgiving meal, Phil asked Sarah, "By the way, what are you two doing about health insurance? You realize that when Jim gets his job, any illnesses not covered by insurance now will be regarded as preexisting conditions and may not be covered. That would be catastrophic." Sarah replied, "We didn't get insurance because we're both healthy, and we expected Jim to be working by now." Phil said, "You maybe ought to be thinking about insurance if this is going to take until May." Sarah replied, "I've asked Jim to take care of it, but he hasn't done anything." Then Sarah burst out crying, went to her room, and sobbed in Jim's arms for the next 2 hours.

Phil said later, "I know that this isn't about insurance. I'm asking a question out of concern, and she's saying by her action, 'Stay out of our business.' It's a negotiation about boundaries and influence over Jim. I'm involved in a negotiation that I hadn't planned on being involved in." Sarah said, "Things aren't going the way I had hoped, and I'm held responsible. It makes me look like a bad wife."

Although Phil is engaged in a boundary negotiation with his daughter-in-law, perceptions about why he chose to say anything and the hidden meaning behind his words (which Sarah thinks is "I'm a bad wife") are influenced by the greater context of Sarah and Jim's relationship. Superficially, an economic interest fueled the discussion, but by the end, a social-psychological interest became more important.

Is the answer to this boundary dispute that Phil refrain from meddling? What part would you say Jim has in this tension between Sarah and her father-in-law?

escalate and negotiations fail. An effective negotiator needs to probe for underlying issues—the real subject of negotiations—and not get caught up in superficial issues where agreements often prove elusive. Box 1.3 provides an example of a conflict where the *what* (that is, the substance of the argument) varies with which of the disputing parties you ask, making agreements especially challenging.

Sorting out the facts within the information is a challenge in many negotiations. In the trailer park dispute, which information do we regard as evidence that the park owner is trying to force out low-income renters? After a recent comparison analysis of homes, a real estate agent lamented, "This is more of an art than a science. Determining how much a house is worth involves comparisons of homes by different builders, locations, construction, conditions, time of year sold, and quirks in the business climate." In an environmental negotiation, what level of contamination is dangerous and how much is acceptable? In many highly complex disputes, we end up with dueling experts who focus on different aspects of the same information.

Mary Parker Follett, a pioneer in the field of conflict management, negotiation, and mediation, lists many of the difficulties in determining the facts of a situation:

■ Facts do not remain stationary.
■ Pictures can lie.
■ The interpretation of facts depends on needs.
■ A fact out of relation is not a fact.
■ Facts have an intimate connection with the whole question of power.
■ Many facts defy measurement. (Davis, 1991, pp. 133-136)

Facts must be ferreted out of information, negotiated, and agreed upon. Often, in complex negotiations, parties jointly select third parties, regarded as neutrals, to provide research and analysis of the information that serves as the foundation for discussion. Determining facts and relevant information requires dialogue about all aspects of a situation. As Box 1.4 illustrates, even when we know the facts, negotiations can be difficult.

Lax and Sebenius (1991b) describe interests—that is, what we need to be satisfied—as the content of negotiation. Interests vary a great deal among parties, and interests may change over the life of a conflict. Interests may involve economic factors such as money or resources, or they may involve social-psychological factors such as a need to be listened to, to be valued, or to feel included. At times, interests focus on values such as freedom, autonomy, or identity. They may involve philosophical principles such as justice or fairness. The more objective the interest, the easier it will be to engage in tradeoffs that may satisfy all parties in a dispute.

Interests may be clustered into *positions*, represented by statements such as "Here's where I stand on this problem" or "I'm totally against that

Box 1.3

FEUD AT THE TRAILER PARK

The 7-acre Fantasy Island trailer park provides spaces for 126 modular trailer homes, just a few hundred feet from a California beach and a few blocks from the Yacht Club. Historically, the 70-year-old park provided affordable housing for senior citizens and low- to middle-income families. Rent currently averages $304 per month. The homes average $120,000 in value compared to $700,000 in the neighboring beach community.

This past year, Steve Jenson bought the park because he believed it was a good investment. The area has changed greatly in the 70 years the park has been in this location. Many of the modular homes have been significantly renovated, becoming two-story and permanent. The city covenant states that the owner possesses the right to make "moderate, appropriate rent increases." Jenson asked for a 36% increase in rent, based on similar values in the community. The city council turned him down, explaining that the increase would place an undue burden on low-income families. Jenson then asked for a graduated increase, based on level of income. The council turned him down but granted a 7.8% rate. Jenson countered with a request for a court order to raise the rents. He explained that many of the residents are actually subleasers who make substantial incomes. They pay as much as $60,000 for lot rental rights as well as high monthly rent to the original renters. The city attorney countered that only the initial renters needed to qualify as low income when they originally applied for the space. After they qualify, they have the rights to the space.

The residents claim that Jenson is trying to drive them out to make the park into a luxury resort home park. Some believe they have the right to sublease to whomever they choose. Jenson states that he has no intention of closing the park but deserves fair return on his investment. A nonprofit housing development corporation offered Jenson $6.4 million for the park, but Jenson turned down the offer, saying that it's worth at least $8 million.

How do we weigh the interests of the various parties in negotiating a settlement? How important is information about community development or subleasing of spaces? Who determines fair rental rates? What is the most important issue to be resolved here? Each of the parties perceives different outcomes for the park. Which outcome do you think is most important: affordable housing, return on investment, community development, protection of tenants' rights, or protection of owner's rights?

Box 1.4

MUDFEST TURNS DIRTY

Throughout the week, disc jockeys from a popular radio station spoke of an off-road vehicle expedition to the mountains for a mudfest, including cash prizes for anyone who could drive through a bog. No mention was made about where the event would take place, but the disc jockeys spoke of meeting at a freeway exit before proceeding into a "well-known Jeeping area."

About 200 off-road vehicles, including two National Guard Humvees, showed up for the event. About 400 people in 200 vehicles four-wheeled for 6 hours on a 25-acre bog near an old gold mine, despite the fact that a man standing outside the mine was yelling for the group to stop and go home. He couldn't be heard above the roar of the engines. The SUVs left tire tracks, oil slicks, and debris across the land. Later, the damage estimates approached several thousand dollars an acre.

The trouble is that the man who was yelling owned the property. The owner claimed that No Trespassing signs and large boulders stood at the entrance of a road to the property. He wanted all of those responsible punished to the full extent of the law. Later, the signs were found off to the side in a ditch, and the boulders had been pushed to the side as well. Many who drove off-road vehicles claimed they saw no signs and weren't aware that it was private property. In addition, the land was an EPA-protected alpine wetland site that provided one of the few habitats for a nearly extinct species of toad. Penalties for killing the toads can be as high as $100,000 and a year in prison. An additional complication was that officials of the National Guard said that they had not given guardsmen permission to take vehicles to the event.

How do you regard the information as presented? In a multiparty negotiation, who should be responsible for the damages? Should anyone be fined or sent to jail, as the law allowed? What potential settlements do you envision?

proposal." When negotiators hear positions, they frequently begin probing for underlying interests on which the position is built. Stalemates occur more often in situations where both parties hold rigidly to inflexible positions. Positions are rarely negotiable; interests are frequently negotiable. The case

Box 1.5

THE CASE OF THE BLOTCHED BLOUSES

For several years, Kathy, the owner of a small dress shop, has taken blouses that have been sold and are in need of alteration to Martha's Seamstress Shop. Sally, an employee of Martha's for several years, does wonderful work with fast turnaround time. During a 3-week period when Sally was on vacation, Martha, a longtime seamstress in her own right, worked on five blouses for Kathy.

Martha had promised that she would return the blouses in 2 days, but instead her alterations took 2 weeks. In addition, after Kathy gave the blouses to the buyers, the buyers returned them because of Martha's poor work. In fact, the buyers cancelled their sales. Kathy returned to Martha's shop. She requested a refund of $30 for the alterations and $200 for the lost sales (Kathy's economic interests). Martha refused. She didn't have that kind of money to refund (Martha's economic interests). The conversation turned nasty. Martha said, "I don't want to ever see you in my store again." Kathy countered with, "If I see you in my dress shop, I'll snatch your heart out." Two issues emerged from the lack of responsiveness to interests: one involving the deteriorating relationship between the two business owners and the other dealing with processes for resolving problems associated with poor-quality work.

The case went to small-claims court. Even if both parties achieved their economic interests, the issue of the poor relationship would be unresolved between the two women. If Kathy wanted to continue bringing her blouses to Martha's shop, the issue of guaranteeing quality work would also have to be resolved.

of the botched blouse in Box 1.5 illustrates once again that social-psychological and economic interests may be intertwined. It's difficult to resolve the problem without addressing both sets of concerns.

DISTRIBUTIVE AND INTEGRATIVE APPROACHES ●

Negotiation in which strategic influence and guarding information have priority over dialogue and relationship is frequently described as a *distributive* negotiation approach. In this perspective, parties perceive that their goals and interests are mutually exclusive or may be in competition with one another. One party wants to gain as much as possible at the expense of another (win-lose)—that is, every dollar won by one party is lost by another. Keltner (1994) argues that distributive negotiation occurs when "parties are clearly adversaries, victory is the goal, the parties demand concessions of each other as a condition of the relationship, they are hard on people, distrust others, dig in their position, make threats [and] hide or mislead about the bottom line" (p. 72).

Bazerman and Neale (1992) describe this approach as an attempt to divide a mythical fixed pie. Both sides want more than half of the pie and become competitive and contentious in efforts to get their share. Unfortunately, the downside of competitive win-lose approaches is that losers have long memories, so if the parties have to do business again, discussions will be much more difficult. Bazerman (1991) points out that American culture supports this perspective:

> The win-lose orientation is manufactured in our society in athletic competition, admission to academic programs, industrial promotion systems, and so on. Individuals tend to generalize from their objective win-lose situations and apply these experiences to situations that are not objectively fixed-pies. (p. 201)

Behaviors commonly associated with this orientation include argument and debate, extreme demands and grudging concessions, unwillingness to listen, positional statements, and contentious tactics. Historically, parties have approached international negotiations, labor bargaining, divorce settlements, and sports negotiations as distributive negotiations.

Negotiation based on cocreation of understandings about the problem and an integration of parties' needs is known as an *integrative* approach. Parties perceive that goals are compatible and that problem solving will produce a mutually beneficial settlement for all parties (win-win). Behaviors associated with the integrative approach include open sharing of information, willingness to trust others, tradeoffs of valued interests, and interest-based discussion. In effect, parties enlarge the fixed pie through creation of additional benefits for all parties. Table 1.1 summarizes the distributive and integrative approaches to negotiation.

For many problems, integrative negotiation may be seen "as a process by which people collaborate on the basics of their disagreements, which helps them identify what is not working in their relationship, come up with solutions, create deeper understandings, and open possibilities for resolution and transformation" (Cloke & Goldsmith, 2000, p. 212). Box 1.6 provides an example of a firm in which parties, though encouraged to find integrative solutions, remained firmly committed to a distributive solution.

Walton and McKersie (1965) point out that in actual practice, a wide range of potential outcomes exists between the win-win and win-lose extremes. Through tradeoffs, parties may win on some issues and lose on

Table 1.1   Approaches to Negotiation

Integrative Negotiation	*Distributive Negotiation*
Open sharing of information	Hidden information
Trade of valued interests	Demand of interests
Interest-based discussion	Positional discussion
Mutual goals	Self goals
Problem solving	Forcing
Explanation	Argument
Relationship building	Relationship sacrificing
Hard on problem	Hard on people

others. According to Watkins (1999), "The mix of shared, conflicting and complementary interests means negotiators must simultaneously cooperate to create joint value and compete to claim their share of the value" (p. 249). Joint value may involve tradeoffs of economic interests for social-psychological interests. For example, parties may gain greater voice in a decision process in exchange for giving up access to valued resources. On the other hand, a negotiator may give up power to gain economic advantage. Joint gain will depend on the priority each party places on each interest.

Deutsch (1971) points out that the level of gain for disputing parties greatly influences the parties' willingness to cooperate. Deutsch explains, "When a relatively low payoff is associated with competitive behavior, it is less likely to be selected. . . . [Relatively high payoffs] stimulate competitive behavior and attack which verifies and supports further competitive behavior" (p. 50). This explains, in part, why, despite participants' best intentions to cooperate, car buying, house buying, labor relations, sports negotiations, and divorce negotiations become so contentious. There's a great deal at stake.

THE IMPORTANCE OF UNDERSTANDING CONTEXT ●

Successful negotiators possess awareness about the contextual factors that influence the progress of a negotiation. They understand that trust, cooperation, sharing of information, and achievement of objectives can be influenced by the communication norms or values of negotiating parties, the history of the relationship, the structure of the negotiation, or the perceived power of each of the parties. Inherent in contexts are unspoken expectations, formal or informal roles, and psychological boundaries, all of which influence how parties interpret information, understand options, or pursue agreements. Chapter 2 looks at six categories of contextual factors that influence most negotiations. Awareness of these factors enables negotiators to adapt their communication to better meet the needs of the situation.

Box 1.6

DISTRIBUTIVE NEGOTIATION IN WHICH EVERYONE LOSES

Bill and Ann work as research scientists in a small biotech firm. For the past year and a half, they've worked in relative, though shaky, harmony. About 6 months ago, their research project began to move toward a successful completion. Tensions began to escalate. Ann expressed her belief to colleagues that Bill secretly planned to put his name first on a published article. In addition, she believed that Bill wanted to make her look bad. She accused Bill of trying to sabotage her work by contaminating her test tubes or leaving her experiments out overnight.

Then the distributive tactics began. Bill accused Ann of being selfish and unprofessional in her staff relations and of manufacturing evidence against him. It did not set well with Bill when Ann yelled down a hall, "Bill is a liar and an incompetent professional." Ann refused to come to work until Bill was fired. She went to one of the executive officers, Ron, and said, "It's time to look at why he left his past jobs." Ron agreed and began to make phone calls. Bill went to one of the other executive officers, Brian, and asked that Ann be demoted to the grade of a technician and told to stop complaining about him to the rest of the staff. Brian said that he wouldn't do that, but he would think about reprimanding her.

Bill and Ann met with the CEO and the CFO to negotiate a working relationship. The group discussed moving one of them out of their shared office, dividing the lab into two areas (with Bill promising not to cross the line into Ann's half), having them work flex hours so that the two wouldn't have to see each other, and creating a locked area so that no one could tamper with Ann's equipment. Ann responded, "No. I'll not return to work until Bill leaves." Bill was invited to change the way he treats Ann. He responded, "No. She initiated all of this. She can change the way she treats me and talks about me."

After multiple discussions with neither party giving in, Brian and Ron demanded that Bill work harder to change the way he interacted with Ann. Bill quit. Despite the fact that Ann had said she would return to work if Bill left, Ann now claimed that her feelings were sufficiently hurt and that she had no intention of coming back to work.

What would you have done to move this from a distributive discussion to an integrative one? How could the situation have been saved?

SUMMARY ●

Negotiation is a form of communication that channels messages through a constructive process whose goals involve both economic and social-psychological interests. The social-psychological dimension involves issues such as identity, interdependence, power, control, boundaries, and relationship. The economic dimension involves the substantive interests achieved, such as items of value, financial gain, or favorable courses of action. Each of the two dimensions—economic and social-psychological—can influence the other. Overly demanding requests for resources can influence levels of trust in a relationship, and low trust can influence the willingness to grant resource requests.

Negotiation serves as a communication tool for facilitating understanding, consideration of options, and discussion that leads to mutually satisfying outcomes. Rarely are any of the factors of a negotiation purely objective. Parties must negotiate perceptions about issues, understandings about problems, the value of information, and an acceptable way to talk about common concerns.

Distributive negotiation, familiar to many in sales settings, involves moves and countermoves, bluffs, selective sharing of information, and demands. Distributive negotiators will pursue a desired outcome at the cost of a positive relationship or conditions favorable to future negotiations. Integrative negotiation involves a commitment to mutual gains of all parties, the open sharing of information, a commitment to understanding, and protection of the long-term relationship. Competitive parties understand that by cooperating, they can achieve more through integrative tactics than through distributive tactics. Listening, understanding, and sharing reasons characterize integrative processes, while telling, positioning, and manipulating describe distributive processes.

CHAPTER 2

CONTEXTUAL NATURE OF NEGOTIATION

You are always negotiating in some way. When you drive from one place to another through traffic, getting in front of some people and letting others get in front of you . . . you negotiate all the elements of your work life and everything you do or don't do . . . a thousand details all day long. The process is never ending.

— Tracy, 2000, p. 230

How we approach a dispute is closely related to the context in which the dispute is grounded. Hall (1983) states, "No communication is totally independent of context and all meaning has an important contextual component" (p. 60). Each context possesses its own set of expectations and acceptable norms. Each norm serves as a point of reference for ordering, structuring, and interpreting behavior. These serve as powerful prisms for behavioral choices. Cloke and Goldsmith (2000) write,

Every workplace and organization, school and neighborhood, family and relationship generates spoken and unspoken rules about what we should say or not say or do when we are in conflict. Each of these entities produces a separate and distinct culture, which exerts enormous pressure on us to respond to conflict in expected ways. (p. 20)

The manner in which we speak to family members at home during a dispute may not be acceptable or advisable in work settings. The way we talk to a neighbor about tree limbs hanging over the fence will be substantively and stylistically different from negotiating salary for a new job. Some contexts place a premium on conflict avoidance, while others value aggressive, frank discussion. How we approach conflict is mediated by context. This explains why some people are effective at solving problems with colleagues at work but have great difficulties with family members at home.

International negotiators have long understood the importance of context in problem solving. In Japan and China, the relationship between negotiators is as important as the terms of the contract. Process is as important as product. In addition, Japanese negotiators avoid early commitment to the stated objectives, while Americans place high priority on clear statements of position and objectives (Janosik, 1991). European negotiators engage in small talk to size up their competition; in contrast, Americans tend to get right down to business (LePoole, 1989). In a study involving negotiators from seven nations, Brett, Pinkley, and Jackofsky (1996) found that Russians, Japanese, and Hong Kong Chinese negotiators were more oriented toward power and hierarchy than those in more egalitarian and low-status-concern cultures such as Brazil, France, and the United States. Context influences information sharing, goals, strategy, and choice of tactics.

Competitive, highly distributive negotiation occurs in many contexts in the United States. High-stakes poker-style negotiations characterize the history of American management and labor relations. Traditionally, representatives make high initial demands, release information grudgingly, and engage in tactics to keep opponents off balance. These dynamics are different from negotiations in interpersonal relationships or families, where more emotional displays occur. Venting emotions may be appropriate in some homes, but most professionals would regard the tactic as unprofessional in a work setting. The kind of negotiating that goes on in car buying would probably break down a relationship if used on a neighbor. Kramer and Messick (1995) summarize, "In order to understand bargaining phenomena, one needs to take into account the impact of societal and organizational environments within which such phenomena are not occasionally, but inevitably embedded" (p. viii). Box 2.1 provides an example of how culture supports the choice of approach in the press box of a professional baseball team. In addition, the inability of athletes to shift their problem-solving style when moving to contexts other than sports often creates problems for them in the community.

A communication-contextual approach to negotiation focuses on the microprocesses and patterns of negotiation interactions as well as the situational factors that shape the process. Although contextual variables are numerous, we narrowed the group to six categories—structure, norms, relationship, communication, interdependence, and power (see Figure 2.1)—that we believe cut across the five negotiation contexts covered in Chapters 7 through 11.

Box 2.1

SPORTS IS NOT LIMITED TO THE PLAYING FIELD

Two sports journalists at competing newspapers, Tracy and Mike, engaged in a competitive match of their own. The dispute began after Tracy, in a sports column, criticized a sports column written by Mike. Whereas Mike considered his work a scoop, Tracy labeled it coincidence. Tracy said, "He's not capable of a scoop." Mike took offense at the comment, and the two quit speaking to one another.

A short time later, prior to an evening ball game, Mike headed up to his designated chair in the stadium press box. Tracy's greeting was anything but cordial. Lacing his speech with expletives, he told Mike that he had work to do, that he wasn't interested in anything Mike had to say, and that Mike would be better off if he left. The next thing Tracy realized, Mike had punched Tracy in the back, and a fight ensued. The police subsequently escorted Mike from the ballpark, although he insisted he was leaving anyway.

Although Tracy could have pressed charges, he chose not to. Mike boasted that his ex-wives hit him harder than Tracy had. Tracy apologized for letting his emotions govern his critique of Mike but said he had no interest in patching up the relationship. Other journalists explained that competition in the newspaper business can fuel attacks both in print and in person. This highly competitive context influences the writer's choice of tactics with which to manage conflict.

Perhaps it was a coincidence, but later, during the game, one of the pitchers threw a pitch at the head of one of the batters in retaliation for an incident from the day before. After the game, the pitcher said, "It's part of the game. He got the message." No disciplinary action followed the event. Reports of the attack in the press box and the behavior on the field appeared in the next morning's newspaper.

If these kinds of events had occurred at a community event or in a family, would you view the behaviors any differently? What influences the choice of norms for managing conflict in any given context?

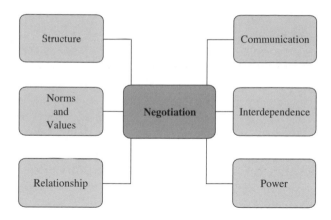

Figure 2.1   Contextual Factors

STRUCTURE ●

The structural components of a negotiation set the parameters within which communication can take place. Negotiation that is hurried will be different from communication over many months. Negotiation that uses voting to choose courses of action will be different from negotiation favoring consensus decision making. Structural components involve factors such as the number of parties negotiating, the amount of time available for negotiation, location, the type of decision-making process, and topics that are allowed on the agenda. For example, negotiating a business deal in your client's office may promote more guarded communication than in your office. Negotiation between parents shifts considerably in agenda and communication style when children are added to the discussion. Structure has a subtle but significant impact on what is spoken and how it is spoken. In one problem-solving session, a teacher was offered the opportunity to negotiate a solution to a problem in the school's conference room. She turned down the request, largely because the conference room was next door to the principal's office.

The number of parties involved in a dispute can add to the complexity of achieving a settlement. More parties can mean more perspectives, a broader range of interests, more goals, and more potential barriers to agreements. One-on-one negotiations may involve positional statements and competing interests, but they lack group dynamics and coalitions, which add dimensions to discussions. Diekmann (1997) found that people took a larger percentage of a valued resource for their group when negotiating against competing groups than they did when negotiating one-on-one. Greed-motivated behaviors seem justified if the motivation is the welfare of fellow group members. In addition, people justified higher demands by explaining that their group performed better than other groups. Group loyalty supports more self-serving behaviors. The attitude is "We did better and we deserve more." Episodes of the *Survivor* television programs would seem to support this view.

Time influences both the processes and the outcomes of negotiation. For example, a job transfer for a seller will often make him or her more flexible about price for the home. A request for a raise during a tight labor market will be better received than during other times. Many labor-management disputes, after months of stalemate and verbal combat, reach agreement moments before the deadline of a contract's expiration. Time pressures influence flexibility, affect judgments of negotiating parties, increase the likelihood of concessions, and frequently contribute to quicker agreements (Edlund & Svenson, 1993; Frye & Stritch, 1964; Lewicki & Litterer, 1985).

Perhaps time pressure's greatest impact occurs in the choice of tactics and strategy during negotiation. When time is perceived as short, negotiators frequently moderate their expectations and begin with more reasonable offers (Stuhlmacher, Gillespie, and Champagne, 1998). Carnevale, O'Conner, and McCuster (1993) report that on single-issue disputes, as negotiators speed up the process to meet a deadline, they will soften demands and demonstrate more openness and concessions. The evidence is mixed for disputes involving complex issues. Dawson (1999) estimates that 80% of concessions occur in the last 20% of time available. Deadlines justify changes in thinking about tactics.

When there is an issue of urgency, incentives serve as a highly motivating factor for both cooperative and competitive negotiators. Parties relax their individualistic, positional orientations when they believe they will miss out on potential benefits (Lim & Murninghan, 1994; Stuhlmacher et al., 1998). If parties feel there is no sense of urgency about an issue, they may be less willing to negotiate or less flexible during negotiations. If there is a sense of urgency or a sense that potential benefits may be lost by delay, they may be more motivated to engage in constructive conversation. A challenging situation occurs when one party feels time pressured while the other does not. Often the time-pressured negotiator has to make concessions to motivate the less-pressured party.

Negotiation can be affected by the decision-making processes used. If agreements must be approved by representatives of parties who are not present at the negotiating table, the representatives may be less clear about what is important or less open to creative options. In addition, commitment to timely solutions may not occur.

A related issue is the agenda that is acceptable for discussion during negotiation. Topics that may not be allowed may have a bearing on the solution of other issues. For example, resolving an organizational conflict may be challenging if management's role in the problem is not open to discussion.

NORMS AND VALUES •

Negotiation in any setting involves both informal understandings and/or formal ground rules that serve as norms for the way issues are viewed and talked about. These norms involve beliefs about fairness, power, goals, and status. For example, in one oil corporation, the human resource manager complained of low morale, low productivity, and high turnover. A facilitator attended a 2-hour staff meeting in which he observed constant sniping and highly charged verbal exchanges among the members. Later, he asked about the practice. Staff members shrugged at his observation, saying, "That's the way we talk around here. It's our normal meeting." In a telephone company, the same facilitator observed that issues were brought up in the staff meetings, but no one spoke about them seriously. After the meetings, a great deal of serious conversation about the issues took place out in the hallway or down in the break room. Kriesberg (1998) explains,

> Contexts vary in the degree to which direct confrontations are regarded as acceptable and in the rules for their expression and management. Among peoples or among particular segments of the society, expression or even acknowledgement of particular kinds of conflict may be improper." (p. 39)

In some settings, maxims embody principles that regulate the way parties engage in problem solving or negotiation. "Don't say something you'll regret later" inhibits the level of self-disclosure. "You've got to give something if you want to get something" sends a message that all parties are expected to make concessions. "Don't let the sun go down on your anger" attempts to limit the duration of emotions. "Don't shoot the messenger" asks for moderation of aggressive or attacking statements. Whether formulated in maxims such as these or not, most contexts will possess behavioral norms that influence the path of negotiation. For example, during 2001, Intel and Hewlett-Packard (H-P) collaborated in a $1 billion to $2 billion venture to develop a more advanced computer chip for Intel's new microprocessor. As teams from the two companies met to discuss the project, the communication norms immediately clashed. H-P management, accustomed to consensus-driven decision making, did not value the interruptions and argumentativeness they encountered in the constructive-confrontation style of Intel executives. H-P found the discussions exhausting. To balance the norms of the joint project teams, the companies developed a 75-page document, fondly called "The Owner's Manual," which provided guidelines for interpersonal communication, conflict management, and decision making.

The stronger the solidarity or cohesiveness of a group, the more influential group norms will be on group members. In addition, Rubin, Pruitt, and Kim (1994) explain that "norms of all types tend to be self-perpetuating, including those that encourage competitive goals and aggressive behavior

Box 2.2

WHEN NORMS COLLIDE: SURF RAGE

Road rage is common in many cities, but now it's surf rage that is plaguing California and Australia beaches. For 30 years, surfers paddled and kicked onto waves with a simple conflict norm that was understood by the surfing brotherhood: The surfer closest to the curl (the breaking part of the wave) gets priority. No one drops in. If anyone had doubts about who entered the curl first, there was a rigid pecking order based on seniority and skill.

Recently, the norms for managing surfer conduct on the waves have broken down. Surfers who come from different areas compete with local surfers for the same waves. Locals tend to follow norms established along the beach—norms that gave first choice of waves to the most senior surfers. In California, surf brawls between the two groups have led to arrests and lawsuits. In Australia, local surfers have severely beaten up visiting surfers. Even world champion surfer Ned Young found that he didn't have priority for the big waves. In a fight with fellow surfers, he suffered two broken eye sockets, two broken cheekbones, and smashed sinuses. In another altercation, a local policeman who was surfing received a beating from a fellow surfer who was described as frothing at the mouth with rage.

In response to this crisis over ineffective norms, 40 elders of the Australian surf community met to create a set of protocols for right of way that they hoped would become new norms for surfers. Young put up $3,000 for a posting of the norms on plaques on surf beaches.

Much as crowded freeways create conditions for enraged drivers, competing claims to waves set up the conditions for surf rage. Norms are difficult to teach or enforce without the presence of community. In many contexts, the negotiation of norms for acceptable behavior may contribute to both the development of relationships and ways to talk about issues that divide people.

toward the out group" (p. 108). Box 2.2 describes events that depict competing norms in the ocean-surfing community.

Tacit rules function as norms in negotiation. These guidelines are scripted behaviors that serve as enabling or constraining forces in a negotiation, and they may be called upon as rationale for preferred actions (Putnam,

2001). Tacit rules involve protocol, setting agendas, selection of participants, decision-making processes, the ways options will be generated, and how tradeoffs will occur.

Shared values (what is expected) guide the actions and thinking in most groups. They serve as the foundation for normative behavior and ethical choices. Pohlman and Gardiner (2000) state, "The success of so-called vision-ary companies is no accident: These are firms that consistently take multiple values into account when they make decisions, plan strategies, or develop new products" (p. vi). Hershey, Blanchard, and Johnson (1996) point out that people in organizations go through a process called *institutionalization* in which "an organization is infused with a system of values that reflects its history" (p. 173).

In many corporate settings, financial interests serve as the value that drives many decisions. However, not all corporations are exclusively based on bottom-line values. For example, Southwest Airlines built a culture based on humor and hospitality, which the company celebrated in impromptu events (Gruner, 1998). Nordstrom trains employees to approach every situation from a customer-satisfaction perspective. Honeywell emphasizes partnership as a defining corporate value in its motto: "Together we find the answers." Innovation characterizes Toshiba's corporate values in its slogan, "In touch with tomorrow." Each of these values is only one of many that define the corporate culture, but they serve as directional pointers for employee behaviors.

Changing values can serve as a source of problems. A telecommunications firm wanted greater diversity among employees and the ideas they brought to the company. This diversity created changes in work habits and communication styles, and longtime employees found it difficult to adjust. In another setting, a senior project engineer for a major appliance-manufacturing firm complained that values shifted depending on which vice president was in power. When the vice president of marketing held the most power, cheap and on-time guided production were the most important values. When the vice president of engineering held the most power, the emphasis was on quality. Staff members were continually negotiating standards for projects based on the changing expectations.

To choose negotiation tactics, effective negotiators need to be sensitive to the values of a given context. For example, negotiation in a Nebraska farm community will weight values differently than negotiation in a Chicago corporate office. Families from different cultures will have different values regarding conflict, authority, power, and communication style.

RELATIONSHIP •

In many settings, relationship is an important context-defining factor for parties in dispute. Greenhalgh and Chapman (1997) provide a useful definition of *relationship:* "the meaning assigned by two or more individuals to their connectedness or coexistence" (p. 211). The way people connect in relationship involves many factors, including trust, approachability, respect, commitment to outcomes, the willingness to disclose information, the willingness to listen, and the manner in which people talk about the issues. Where relationship is strong, people demonstrate more willingness to collaborate and more willingness to find solutions. Carpenter and Kennedy (1988) explain,

> Parties who have a history of unsatisfactory relationships are less likely to trust each other when a conflict arises. Someone who has observed the adversarial tactics of another party in the past will be highly suspicious of any offers to "sit down and be reasonable on this one." (p. 20)

Trust is a significant component of relationship during negotiations. Lewicki and Wiethoff (2000) state that "a party who trusts another is likely to believe the other's words and assume that the other will act out of good intentions, and probably will look for productive ways to resolve a conflict" (p. 101). Relationships that are perceived as positive enhance openness to new ideas, creativity, sharing of information, and commitment to a mutually beneficial settlement. Negotiation and conflict management become more difficult in the absence of factors such as trust and openness.

Goals for parties in dispute may differ based on the kind of relationship they have. Lowenstein, Thompson, and Bazerman (1989) found that in business negotiations or negatively perceived interpersonal relationships, parties' aspirations for personal gain were high compared with goals in neutral or positive interpersonal-relationship situations. Thus, potential mutual-gain settlements may be dependent, in part, on deeper issues of relationship.

Over the past three decades, a great number of studies have provided insight about the impacts of relationships during problem solving and negotiations:

- People will reinforce their prior perceptions. If they come to a situation with a negative attitude, they will see more negative elements in others. If they approach the situation from a friendly perspective, they will tend to see the positive elements in others (Grzelak, 1982; Hastorf and Cantril, 1954; Zadney and Gerard, 1974).
- People who believe they share common interests, attitudes, or values employ fewer divisive tactics and have fewer differences of opinion over decisions that affect both parties (Greenhalgh and Chapman, 1997).
- Strong social-bonded relationships encourage more yielding and problem solving and discourage contentious behaviors (Rubin et al., 1994).
- In relationships perceived as having a future, the fear of escalation and spiraling consequences tends to tone down contentious tactics (Gottman, 1979; Richardson, 1967; Sillars, 1981).

Few problems are problems of the moment. Generally, they have roots in the history of the relationship. In families, every confrontation becomes the background for the next. Some family dynamics date back several generations. In work settings, managers often must deal with employees whose problems began in a previous job. Tidwell (1998) goes so far as to suggest, "Without a good sense of history, no conflict can be understood in a meaningful way for resolution. The importance of history cannot be over-emphasized" (p. 119). Past relationships and problems become the ghosts for current realities and frequently affect negotiations within families, between environmental groups and industries, and between management and employees. Blake and Mouton (1984) assert that past events often limit "a group's view of future alternatives and possibilities. . . . Recommendations that are contrary to history may have been summarily dismissed" because of history's "power over thoughts, feelings, and action" (p. 4).

For example, a U.S. Forest Service public hearing in a mountain community began with protesters shouting at timber workers and off-road enthusiasts, "You clowns, get out of here! No more exploitation!" Opponents responded with shouts and fists in the air. Historically poor relationships between the two sides initially impeded constructive discussion. Disputes such as those that have occurred in Northern Ireland, Israel, South Africa, and Bosnia cannot be understood apart from their histories of misunderstanding, coercion, and unresolved problems. Box 2.3 describes a problem with a history of relationship that fuels cycles of conflict and inability of parties to negotiate solutions.

Psychological boundaries can be especially important as sources of resistance or as aspects of identity in interpersonal or organizational negotiations. For example, a stepfather may find it difficult to negotiate his role for parental discipline if the biological mother says, "I'm their mother, and I'll tell you what and when It's okay to discipline the children." A clear parental boundary is being established. Her identity and role are linked to the issue of discipline, but at the same time he is trying to determine his role. In Chapter 1, Box 1.2, Phil's unintended tension with his daughter-in-law was a negotiation about the boundary of Phil's involvement in the couple's decision-making processes.

Boundaries can be both structural and relationship factors in organizations when managers must make difficult decisions about who should be involved in decision-making processes and the kinds of decisions for which he or she should seek employee input. Failure to get input on decisions affecting employee success can damage the manager's relationship with staff.

COMMUNICATION ●

Although communication has a wealth of meanings, the sending and receiving of information is common to most descriptions. Interpretation of the meaning of the message revolves around two factors: relationship and content.

Box 2.3

CONFLICT OVER HISTORIC RESTORATION OF A ROAD

The Hickmans own a Victorian home in Palisades, a small Western town. Town officials claim that town maps dated 1910 show Iowa Avenue, a 150-foot-long road, running through the Hickmans' property. The town council wants the road reconstructed to preserve its historic value.

If the plan is carried out, the road would go through the Hickmans' white picket fence, their lilac hedge, a 45-foot cedar tree, an 80-year-old oak tree, and a bed of daisies. The road would run only a few yards from the side of the Hickmans' 97-year-old home and end right in front of the Hickmans' barn. The Hickmans ask the council whether historic preservation should have some purpose in mind, and they appeal to the court for help. Soon after a construction crew begins cutting down the Hickmans' fence, the court grants an emergency restraining order against the town.

This is not the first time the Hickmans have had a run-in with the town council. Several years ago, the council wanted to put in a modern sidewalk on Palisades' historic main street. The Hickmans complained that the sidewalk would destroy the pristine look of Main Street. The delay eventually cost the town the $64,000 grant the State Transportation Department was willing to contribute. Some say that the town council is retaliating against the Hickmans because of this loss.

The conflict cycle does not end here. A developer would like to build a housing subdivision in a peach orchard behind the Hickman home. The Hickmans will attempt to block any plans by the town council to do the project, especially if the project has anything to do with reconstructing the historic road proposed by the town council. The town council is ready to condemn the Hickmans' land so that it can proceed with the plans to build the road.

How do we interrupt this cycle of conflict between these parties? On what issues might the parties find common ground?

For some people, information about content will not be fully appreciated until specific relational factors are addressed, such as respect and valuing. For others, unless highly valued information is shared, the commitments to relationship will be limited. For example, in labor negotiations, full disclosure of information may not occur until representatives develop trust in one another. In environmental negotiations, agreement must be reached about factual information, such as toxic levels or damage, before parties will engage in significant relationship building. Interpretation of messages varies based on how messages are communicated and interpreted.

One of the most important context-defining factors is the degree to which parties listen to each other. Contexts involving poor listeners often become adversarial when listeners make inaccurate assumptions or fail to understand the other parties. Fisher, Ury, and Patton (1993) explain the power of active listening during problem solving: "Once you understand the others' feelings and concerns, you can begin to address them, to explore areas of agreement and disagreement, and to develop useful ways to proceed in the future" (p. 7). Effective listening behaviors or actions that characterize communication in constructive contexts include the following:

- Probing to uncover underlying issues
- Paraphrasing to establish understanding
- Clarifying to demonstrate that others are heard
- Exploring to identify areas of agreement and common ground

A second factor that greatly influences constructive processes is the degree to which parties engage in perspective taking. Perspective taking involves seeing the issues from the other party's point of view. Perspective taking encourages openness, sharing of information, and trust. Opotow (2000) explains,

> Individuals capable of taking others' perspectives are likely to think flexibly rather than rigidly; acknowledge rather than deny problems; and take a constructive conflict orientation that includes problem solving, openness, lack of defensiveness, flexibility and full use of available resources. (pp. 420-421)

Negotiators who exchange information and who are aware of the priorities of the other parties are more apt to achieve integrative agreements (Kemp & Smith, 1994; Thompson, 1991). In addition, in many contexts, parties who share information in a truthful fashion about priorities and preferences tend to reach higher joint outcomes (Pruitt, Carnevale, Ben-Yoan, Nochajski, & Van Slyck, 1983; Pruitt & Lewis, 1975). Shapiro and Jankowski (1998) go so far as to define negotiation as "the commerce of information for ultimate gain" (p. 19). Listening facilitates this commerce of information. Contexts low in active listening and perspective taking could be expected to be more adversarial and less able to resolve differences than contexts high in these two factors. Contexts high in active listening and perspective taking tend to encourage problem solving and involve retaliation less frequently (Allred, 2000).

Table 2.1 Negotiation: Frames of Reference

Frame	Description
Substantive	Defines what the issue is about
Outcome	Represents the disputants' preferred solution
Loss-gain	Interprets the issues based primarily on the risks and benefits associated with various outcomes
Aspiration	Views the issues based on needs and interests
Characterization	Applies labels to other parties, the self, or the relationship
Process	Depicts the negotiator's expectations about how a negotiation will or should proceed

In many contexts, the concept of *immediacy* describes the nonverbal cues that indicate a negotiator's willingness to engage in constructive conversation. Immediacy cues such as forward lean, smiles, eye contact, or direct body orientation communicate warmth and liking (Andersen, 1985; Weiner & Mehrabian, 1968). Virtually all body positions that reduce distance or improve visibility suggest a more positive and open attitude (Melandro & Barker, 1983). Immediacy encourages parties to become involved and invested in the discussion. Many scholars point out that immediacy cues are culturally dependent. For example, eye gaze for Arab negotiators signals something different than for Western negotiators. So negotiators involved in cross-cultural negotiation should learn the immediacy cues of other cultures.

Framing serves as an important communication skill in negotiation. As issues are presented, the way a negotiator makes sense of the issue—that is, the words used to frame understanding—influence the dynamics that follow. Bell (1995) suggests that parties derive their interpretation of events and meaning of words in the way they frame issues. He identifies six frames from which negotiators view issues (Table 2.1). Effective negotiators adjust the frame statements made by parties in ways that highlight common ground, common goals, or shared understandings in order to promote agreement about important issues.

Putnam and Holmes (1992) describe *reframing* as employing new metaphors or analogies to transform the way another party views an issue. The shift may be changing how an issue is understood or presenting a novel way to view the issue. For example, a negotiator may reframe a problem from "mine" or "yours" to "ours," an option that was "unacceptable" to one that "requires further thought," a solution that was "not worthy of our consideration" to one that "needs to be further explored." Instead of framing an issue in terms of specific outcomes, a negotiator may talk more about the process by which parties should proceed or goals that negotiators hope to achieve.

The source (that is, the *who*) of messages often influences interpretation of messages. Issues such as source credibility, believability, trustworthiness, status, and relationship influence how much and what kind of information is valued. In a study of confrontational and coercive messages that occur in conflict, Roloff, Paulson, and Volbrecht (1998) found the following:

> Authority figures are perceived to have greater coercive intent than peers do. The discourse of an authority figure is more likely to be looked at as a threat and produces greater feelings of being threatened and warned than does the discourse of peers. (p. 157)

Message source credibility highly affects multiparty conflict or negotiation contexts in which sharing of information and integration of interests in a broad-based agreement are important.

The tendency to personalize issues can create negative involvement in negotiations. Negative involvement frustrates and inhibits constructive discussion. Hample and Dallinger (1995) describe the person who personalizes issues as someone who feels "threatened, anxious, damaged, devalued, and insulted" (p. 306). Parties who personalize conflict view the situation as unsafe and see themselves as locked in a win-lose battle. Face-saving and self-defense lead to either withdrawal or contending behaviors because the person feels pressured. Negative involvement creates greater argumentativeness and contentious tactics. When parties begin personalizing the problem, negotiators must reframe the dispute to focus primarily on interests or take time out to cool down. Personalizing issues damages both the problem-solving process and relationships.

When issues become personalized, parties frequently resort to face-saving in an effort to defend their reputation, self-esteem, or identity. Face-saving may involve a refusal to continue discussions, warnings about the current course of action, or threats about where discussions will lead. The danger of face-saving is that it undermines trust and cooperation while the other party is investing energy in defensive moves. In efforts to minimize the need for face saving, negotiators provide protective face work, such as helping the other party make concessions without loss of reputation, attributing problems to other causes, allowing the other party to moderate demands, or framing the words of others in a positive manner (Fisher, Ury, & Patton, 1981; Pruitt & Johnson, 1970). Depersonalizing an issue allows another party to move away from an untenable position to one that is flexible.

Jones and Bodtker (2001) state that emotions influence a person's orientation toward conflict. This applies to negotiation as well. When emotions are intense, there is a greater tendency for parties to make positional statements or to demonstrate rigidity. Emotion may reflect needs, such as a need for recognition, approval, or a chance to be heard. Emotional displays may be attempts to equalize power—that is, "If I yell loud enough, you'll listen to me or give me more of what I want." Emotion makes a moral statement about what a party believes to be right or wrong, just or unjust, fair or unfair. The importance of recognizing and dealing with emotion in negotiation is reflected in Jones and Bodtker's assessment: "The experience of a negative emotion heightens the propensity to focus on negative information and form negative evaluations of another" (p. 234). This assessment points to the importance of maintaining a safe climate for negotiations to take place and for negotiators to develop understanding about what the feelings say about needs in the current negotiation.

Adler, Rosen, & Silverstein, (1998) propose that fear and anger are the two most dominant emotions in negotiation. Triggers for fear include belief that interests or goals may not be met or that one party may be taking advantage of another. Fear causes distrust, doubts, and defensiveness, which derail productive discussions.

Anger occurs when someone violates norms for expected behavior; examples of such behavior are rudeness, coercion, or devaluing communication. Daly (1991) explains that during negotiations, some of the behaviors that trigger anger are misrepresenting information, making excessively high demands, overstepping the bounds of authority, insulting the other party, failing to honor agreements, seeking to undermine a representative's authority, and making false accusations (p. 34). Adler et al. (1998) argue that anger "clouds our objectivity because we lose trust in the other side; it narrows our focus from broader topics to the anger-producing behavior and it misdirects our goals from reaching agreement to retaliating against the offender" (p. 169). A comment made by a member of a human resources department expresses the kind of emotion that could influence behavior: "I came with high hopes, only to have them dampened by political, egotistical, and immature manipulation from people not even associated with our unit. Just doesn't make sense. Makes you wonder who you can trust."

Summarizing a decade of research, Saavedra and Kwun (2000) report that during conflict, mood affects memory, information processing, problem solving, and social behavior. In addition, individuals in negative emotional states view situations as unsafe, problematic, and threatening; these people also tend to focus on a narrower range of specifics within a situation. Highly charged contexts misdirect energies from problem solving to more face-saving behaviors, attack-counterattack cycles, and attempts to resolve the negative emotions. Box 2.4 illustrates how emotion can overrule reason.

● INTERDEPENDENCE

Negotiation involves interdependent parties who voluntarily enter discussions to create an understanding, form agreements, or resolve problems. The fabric that binds together negotiating parties may be factors such as commitment to an organization, family loyalty, contractual obligations, or business relationships. Negotiators need each other and possess the power

---

Box 2.4

WHEN ADULTS ACT LIKE CHILDREN

In Reading, Massachusetts, a town of 23,000, two men, described by neighbors as fiercely devoted to their children, engaged in a war of words that escalated to a fistfight and eventually to a death.

Grade-school youth at an ice hockey rink engaged in a noncontact hockey skate-around. Michael Costin served as the adult who monitored behavior on the ice. A parent in the stands, 275-pound Thomas Junta, believed that the youths were roughhousing more than should be permitted. In speech laced with obscenities, he yelled at the 150-pound Costin to do more to prevent the contact. Costin yelled back.

After the workout, words between the two men continued. Words turned into shoving and then a fight. Junta began pounding on Costin until Costin was unconscious. Later, Costin died. Junta was charged and later convicted of manslaughter. Similar events with less violent outcomes occur at youth events in many U.S. communities.

How can intense emotion suppress reason to such a degree that adults lose their normal problem-solving skills? How can we manage emotion during times of conflict so that we don't sabotage our efforts to solve problems?

---

to withdraw from the relationship, although the costs may be high. At least three factors affect the level of interdependence in negotiation:

- *Individualistic versus cooperative orientation.* The degree to which each party cares about the outcomes of the other.
- *Distribution of power in the relationship.* The way power is balanced between parties.
- *Sensitivity to the interpersonal aspects of the relationship.* The extent to which parties share interpersonal information, foster trust, and support others during negotiation.

Strong interdependence, which leads to more-integrative agreements, is generally built on high cooperation, equal distribution of power, and high sensitivity to the interpersonal aspects of the relationship. A high individualistic orientation coupled with high power and low interpersonal sensitivity creates a weak interdependence and establishes greater potential for unbalanced agreements. Variations of the three factors can create a great deal of confusion or cognitive dissonance for negotiators. For example, a highly individualistic negotiator who possesses high interpersonal sensitivity can create distrust of motives and suspicion about messages communicated. High power and high individualistic orientation linked to high sensitivity to others can create similar distrust and low responsiveness.

The level of involvement demonstrated by negotiators often reflects the level of commitment to negotiated settlements. It's difficult to negotiate, problem solve, or manage conflict if other people are detached and distant. Involvement demonstrates the extent to which parties care about a situation and want to maintain a future relationship. Involvement may be expressed in terms of commitment to a relationship, the amount of verbal contributions, or the kind of attitude displayed.

Levels of involvement become an especially difficult issue in relationship or family negotiations. Disengagement coupled with strong emotion create positional orientations very difficult to overcome. Devine, Sedikides, & Fuhrman (1989) found that highly involved parties tend to remember more that is shared by others or ask more probing questions. On the other hand, Thompson, Peterson, & Kray, (1995) point out that highly involved parties may develop greater bias as they become passionate about a subject or may make more inaccurate judgments if they focus on information too narrowly.

● POWER

Power is a highly visible component of negotiation in many contexts. It goes by many names, including influence, leverage, and control. Even nonpartici-pation or resistance can be viewed as expressions of power. In many settings, power is often described as the ability to influence others in intended direc-tions. Bell (1999) describes power as a relational or communal phenomenon, "an exchange of influence" (p. 101). She distinguishes between "power over," demonstrated by leverage or control (distributive negotiation), and "power to," demonstrated as empowerment (integrative negotiation). Power can be regenerative as negotiators redefine relationship, roles, or the way they talk about the issues. Power, real or perceived, comes from many sources, including:

- *Political.* The ability to form alliances.
- *Structural.* The use of authority based on formal position or status.
- *Resource.* Control over allocation of rewards or sanctions.
- *Procedural.* Control over a decision-making process.
- *Informational.* Access to privileged information sources.
- *Legal.* Rights and choices defined by law.
- *Ethical.* Influence based on values such as fairness or justice.
- *Personal.* Influenced based on charisma, accomplishments, or reputation.

Although the nature of the outcome mediates negotiator behavior, studies suggest that people with the most power in a situation will use that power to gain advantage or behave exploitatively, and people with low power will tend to compromise more and behave submissively. In organizational or community settings, less-powerful parties will form alliances to offset disadvantages of power.

Rubin and Zartman (1995) reviewed nine international negotiations from the 1980s and 1990s involving both Eastern and Western nations. The study looked at asymmetry of power during negotiations. Contrary to what we might expect in situations, they found the following:

■ Stronger parties typically attempted to dominate the communication exchanges with their less powerful counterparts.

■ Weaker parties typically responded not by acting submissive but by adopting counterstrategies of their own.

■ Negotiating parties were effective to the extent that they adjusted their behavior to the relative power of the other side.

■ Equal power does not necessarily lead to more effective negotiation.

International negotiation is similar to negotiation in other settings in that (a) power can become an exploitive tool in the wrong hands and (b) parties can be more effective by adjusting their power to address the needs of the context. The fourth of Rubin and Zartman's (1995) insights might appear counterintuitive. They explain, "Symmetry produces deadlock because the behaviors associated with the particular power status produce impasse rather than an effective process to satisfying results" (p. 359).

Because power has many sources, negotiators who possess less power can increase perceptions about their strength in many ways. For example, alliances with others who hold power or expertise can be regarded as favorable. Entering a negotiation with a great deal of information can create a greater perception of strength. In business settings, creating "value added" (such as quality, service, or loyalty) can improve a less-powerful negotiator's standing. In addition, there is power in building relationship, talking constructively about options, demonstrating understanding, and working together toward mutually beneficial goals. A strong relationship can offset the inadequacies of other forms of power.

Although power can be exercised in forms of persuasion or reward, people often choose coercion in attempts to resolve disputes. Emotion may play a central role in that choice. At the biotech firm discussed in Chapter 1 in Box 1.6, Ann relied on the CEO's sanction power in attempts to make Bill act in a way that she wanted. Her efforts failed, as efforts based solely on structural power frequently do. Unfortunately, even if the use of structural power is successful, it embodies a great deal of risk for residual damage.

Many negotiators ask, "How important is leverage as a source of power?" Leverage is a factor more often associated with distributive negotiation (hard bargaining) than it is with integrative negotiation. Leverage refers to tilting the playing field so that one party has advantages or power over the other. In theory, negotiation involves a level playing field where parties trade interests of value, achieving mutual gain for both parties.

However, most playing fields are not level, and leverage does appear to be a subtle factor, even if the leverage involves only a good BATNA (Best Alternative to a Negotiated Agreement) to which a negotiator can retreat. Leverage may be *real* or *apparent*, with a BATNA regarded as real. Many sources of apparent leverage can be created by negotiators to have much of the power of real leverage, including:

- *Relationship.* Negotiate in a way that makes others want to do business with you rather than someone else. People don't like change, and you can be a consistent, predictable factor in their lives.
- *Value added.* You can provide something for the other party that will be difficult to achieve with others, such as additional contracts, higher-quality products, or better services.
- *Integrity or reputation.* Develop a proven track record that can be trusted and on which others can count. Reliability may be worth more than other more tangible factors in a negotiation.
- *Desire.* Give the other party a reason for them to want what you have to offer. Impulsive buying sells clothes, cars, stereos, and groceries, to name a few. If you can create a reason for people to want what you have to offer, desire can be compelling.
- *Reasonableness.* People can be motivated by discussions based on factors such as fairness, logic, justice, equality, conventional practice, objective standards, or reasonableness.
- *Timing.* Timing can be used as leverage if you can meet the timing needs of others, if you can reduce the energy, tension, and time they're investing in finding a solution elsewhere, or if you can protect them against price increases or product changes. Time can be used to advance decision-making processes.

Although we espouse negotiation based on trading of valued interests and mutual gain, leverage, apparent or real, can be a subtle factor for creating a need to negotiate. In many negotiations, several unspoken alternatives—arbitration, litigation, or lawsuits—serve as leverage when parties want to avoid them as options. But use strong statements of leverage cautiously. When used, they frequently create greater resistance in opponents. A typical response is, "Are you threatening me?" When all else fails, discussing the cost of no settlement may be the remedy for stalemate.

● SUMMARY

Problem solving, negotiation, and conflict management approaches will be most effective when individuals are able to shift their tactical choices to meet the needs of particular contexts. For example, negotiations in labor relations involve a great deal of shuttle diplomacy, negotiation of tacit rules, and respect for values, whereas negotiations in families demand a deep understanding of the relationship history and interdependence.

Misunderstanding and mistaken assumptions can be reduced through more explanation about the cultural and contextual expectations behind the attitudes of parties. University of Minnesota professors David and Roger Johnson describe this priority as engaging in constructive controversy:

> We are challenged to clearly represent our values and the cultural assumptions underlying them. Instead of polemicizing on the truths or virtue of a fixed position, as we might when speaking exclusively from our own mindset, we must examine our positions in the context of the larger ecologies in which they are embedded. (Kimmel, 2000, p. 469)

Ideally, we will be most effective when we are able to understand the history that frames a dispute, respect the values that parties bring to a discussion, facilitate common ground through careful communication, and create an environment in which balanced concern for self and others promotes mutual gain for all parties. Although we emphasize the importance of adapting problem-solving and negotiation strategies to fit the needs of the context, we approach the task with caution. We should not stereotype all members of a given context. Although similar contexts tend to generate similar norms, individual differences occur within the contexts. In fact, in some contexts—such as auto buying, labor relations, environmental disputes, and families—where positional orientations are common, we must look for collaborative elements within the contexts on which to build cooperative problem solving.

CHAPTER 3

THEORETICAL PERSPECTIVES

There is nothing so practical as a good theory.

— Kurt Lewin (quoted in Marrow, 1969, p. ix)

Many view theory as the least interesting aspect of study in fields such as business, conflict management, or negotiation. They hunger for action: "Let's just do it." They're more comfortable with trial and error than exploring underlying assumptions—that is, those assumptions that explain why we choose to say some things and not others. Without planning based on reliable theory, negotiation can become an exercise akin to Wiley Coyote attempting to trap that elusive roadrunner. Understanding why we make the choices we do and why others respond the way they do increases the potential for greater understanding and more positive outcomes.

Each approach to negotiation reflects a set of assumptions about what people need and how they will respond to what we need. We can improve our negotiations by exploring the physics of our negotiation processes to understand the statements we make or the actions we do that cocreate the situations in which we find ourselves (Follett, 1995). For example, a car buyer demands that a car salesperson accept an offer, expecting resistance and counteroffers. Communication will be firm, aggressive, and perhaps even argumentative. A union representative presents a set of requests to the management representative, expecting some to be accepted and others to be rejected. Communication will probably reflect "us" and "them" perspectives on issues. On the other hand, two friends may negotiate an issue in a different manner. Each expects give-and-take responses, mutual concern for the welfare of the other, and messages that communicate active listening. Each move in negotiation is based on assumptions about human behavior and about which tactics will achieve desired goals. Because human behavior in family differs from business or community, our theories shift between contexts. Applying the wrong theory to a context tends to foster greater resistance and distributive responses.

Tidwell (1998) explains that a theory serves as a road map, "a tentative explanation which serves as a guide to action; it steers that actor toward some objective . . . toward some behaviors and away from others" (p. 61). Often, our theories are based on our experiences with similar situations. When we lack prior experience with a type of situation, we may rely on theories learned in other settings, although they may be less effective. For example, a complaint we've heard in community groups and church groups, composed largely of volunteers, is that members approach negotiation the way they would at work, which creates problems for group members. The volunteer groups have different expectations and norms (or lack of them), creating resistance for people who negotiate as they would at work. Many volunteer participants lack knowledge and skill about how to achieve integrative solutions in groups that communicate many perspectives, agendas, and priorities.

Our choice of words and tactics during negotiation reflects our underlying theories about what we expect of others. An understanding of a few of the theoretical perspectives may provide us with insight about why we say what we do and why others respond in the way they do. Unfortunately, after nearly two decades of negotiation research, no single grand theory of negotiation yet exists. Menkel-Meadow (2001) explains, "Negotiations are conducted in contexts, with different subject matters, parties, bargaining endowments, relationships, goals, purposes and histories . . . The home context of the negotiation writer often sets the 'baseline' from which theories and approaches are developed" (p. 259).

Thus, legal studies, economics, communications, business, and sociology will each favor particular theories to support their perspective of negotiation processes. However, we believe that some theoretical principles apply to many of the settings in which negotiation occurs. For example, concerns about identity and reputation can be found in every context. Personal needs and interests occur in home as well as in business. Pressures from groups to which we belong influence our words and actions in both community groups and international relations. With the understanding that we may be leaving out theoretical perspectives valuable in some subject areas, we've chosen seven sets of principles that we believe cut across all contexts: identity, social interaction, field, human need, rational choice, transformation, and mutual gains. As depicted in Table 3.1, each perspective provides a lens with which to view the needs within the context in which we negotiate.

Table 3.1   Summary of Theoretical Perspectives

Theory	Perspective
Identity	Issues such as reputation, authority, dignity, and self-image play a significant role in negotiation.
Social Interaction	The way we talk about an issue influences our perceptions, attitudes, expectations, and relationships.
Field	Groups to which we belong or whose opinions we respect influence how we talk about an issue and what we value.
Human Need	Factors such as safety, harmony, security, power, social approval, control, and status motivate us.
Rational Choice	We engage in moves and countermoves based on self-interest.
Transformation	We attempt to change the way we relate to another, the way we talk about a problem, or what we determine to be important.
Mutual Gains	We engage in a problem-solving process with a goal of satisfying one another's interests in a way that is fair for both of us.

● IDENTITY THEORY

With intellectual roots in symbolic interaction (see Mead, 1934), identity theory attempts to explain how society shapes social behavior. Individuals form their personal identities based on the self-categorizations and identifications they make with roles they perform (e.g., parent, spouse, male or female, employee), competencies they develop, groups to which they belong, or knowledge they've acquired through life experience (McCall & Simmons, 1978; Stryker, 1980). People make judgments about situations in ways that make their identity relevant, enabling them to affirm or enact that identity (Burke & Franzoi, 1988). Loyalty to these identifications can be stronger than many other factors in people's lives. Identity interests in negotiation may be expressed as needs for recognition, safety, control, or purpose. A negotiator who possesses strong identity needs may approach an issue from the perspective of the following characterization frame: "How will I look to others if I agree to what you suggest?"

Many negotiations, although they appear to be about conflicting interests, may in actuality be negotiations about meaning, expectations, and behaviors associated with the identities a negotiator has formed. For example, an employee asks to negotiate work responsibilities with his or her manager. The manager interprets the request as a threat to his or her authority about work assignments, an identity issue. The employee's intent, a revised job description, cannot be addressed adequately until the employee reduces the perception that the manager's authority is being questioned. Identity issues have long been an issue in international settings. Ethnic groups in settings such as Sri Lanka, Palestine, the Balkans, Afghanistan, and Northern Ireland have reacted militarily to achieve identity needs associated with respect, autonomy, and independence. Additional examples of identity-based issues include (Hicks, 2001, p. 41):

- A boardroom dispute over corporate strategic planning may be more about the parties' needs to assert themselves, to be perceived as forceful and certain, or to have experience, than about the issues themselves.
- A workplace equal opportunity complaint, filed in response to a dispute about an employee's alleged misuse of the organization's credit card, may be difficult to resolve without addressing the issue of the employee's integrity being called into question and the impact on that party's self-image.
- An environmental dispute between business interests and environmental organizations may be as much about worldviews and identity issues of recognition and legitimacy as it is about the specific details of development, policy decisions, or the protection and restoration of riparian habitats.

Identity salience describes the probability that someone will see an identity as appropriate across a variety of situations. For example, a father who is a Marine officer may believe that his family should be supervised in much the same way as his troops are and that his family should provide him equal respect. If his wife does not accept him in this role, negotiations about family issues will be difficult. The higher the importance of the identity, the greater the expectations for self and others that will be associated with it.

Salience extends to issues of cultural background or group affiliation. A negotiator may approach an issue with the expectation that other parties will understand and respect the cultural perspective he or she brings to the negotiation. This type of expectation can play an important role in cross-cultural or international negotiations.

Comments that reflect identity-based issues include the following:

- "Are you questioning my judgment?"
- "I've been involved in this work for 20 years; I know a lot about this subject."
- "Who do you think you're talking to?"

Defusing comments such as these involves active listening and a display of respect for the aspects of identity valued by the speaker. Persons linking an issue to their identity need to maintain a sense of dignity and self-respect. The negotiator must affirm these identities and then return to the substantive issue in the dispute.

● SOCIAL INTERACTION THEORY

Although Morton Deutsch is best known for his contributions to the study of conflict management, his insights apply equally well to negotiation. He explains that people approach problem solving with a set of perceptions, expectations, and skills that are related to social contexts. People must first alter their symbolic environment if their goal is to alter the physical one. Deutsch (1991) proposes the following set of assumptions for understanding the interactions we encounter in problem-solving settings:

1. Social interaction takes place in a social environment that normally has a shared set of symbols, rules, and values that influences the social interaction.

2. Each party in an interaction is influenced by his or her expectations concerning the other's behavior.

3. Each party responds to the other based on his or her perceptions of the other, which may or may not correspond to what the other actually thinks.

4. Social interaction is initiated by motives, generates new motives, and alters old ones.

Deutsch's principles suggest several insights for improving negotiation processes. For example, negotiation may be more effective when perceptions about an issue are clarified: "Impoverished communication, hostile attitudes, and over-sensitivity to differences—typical effects of competition—lead to distorted views that intensify and perpetuate conflict" (Deutsch, 1991, p. 43). In addition, clarifying expectations, rules for interaction, and values associated with an issue can influence the kind of messages communicated during a negotiation.

Second, negotiation's success can be improved by "reframing the conflict as a mutual problem to be resolved (or solved) through joint cooperative efforts" (Deutsch, 2000, p. 31). Parties use language associated with "our problem" and "our solution" in a pursuit of common interests. Although parties may not achieve all of their desired outcomes, they may create a dialogue useful for future resolution of issues or greater understanding about the needs of both parties.

Developing communication that promotes understanding includes creating norms that will support a cooperative relationship. Among the norms proposed by Deutsch (2000) are the following:

- When there is a disagreement, seek to understand the other's views from his or her perspective.
- Acknowledge the full value of the ideas of the other.
- Emphasize the positive in the other and limit the expression of negative feelings.
- Be responsive to the other's legitimate needs.
- Empower the other to communicate cooperatively by soliciting the other's views, listening responsively, and sharing information.
- Demonstrate honesty and morality as a caring and just person. (pp. 32-33)

Summarizing Deutsch's perspective, Tidwell (1998) states that communication and language "serve a central role of coordinating action, of serving as a conduit through which individuals are linked to ideas and as a method for wielding power" (p. 105). People fight over words, so we can reframe the words to be less threatening, less polarizing, and more cooperative.

FIELD THEORY ●

In physics, we learn that the behavior of atoms is influenced by subatomic particles known as protons and electrons. These protons and electrons are affected by smaller forces known as quarks, mesons, leptons, and haryons. Although we cannot see these underlying forces, they affect all movement in life. Just as subatomic forces operate in the physical world, social forces operate in the world of human interaction. Couples may be influenced by in-laws, company decision making is influenced by market forces, and community groups are influenced by subcultures. Many of the forces are visible, but some are invisible, operating much like subatomic particles.

Lewin (1997) argues that individual behaviors do not exist apart from social context. Each organizational or social context possesses systemic forces that create a psychological climate influencing how people think and behave. Three assumptions guide this perspective:

1. A psychological or social explanation for behavior exists.

2. Contending social or political forces work for or against satisfying of human need.

3. A system of forces causes and maintains a level of tension or conflict.

Lewin (1951) identifies some of the properties of these forces in his assessment:

To characterize properly the psychological field, one has to take into account such specific items as particular goals, stimuli, needs, social relations as well as . . . the atmosphere (for instance, the friendly, tense, or hostile atmosphere) or the amount of friction. (p. 241)

Climate describes the overall quality of the context. Fields are frequently characterized in terms such as warm and safe or cold and tense. In terms of a negotiation, the climate may be collaborative or competitive. Climate may also account for the way groups deal with authority and power, degree of supportiveness of group members, sense of identity, and interdependence (Bales & Cohen, 1979; Foa, 1961; Wish & Kaplan, 1977).

The psychological climate serves as the context that supports or inhibits factors such as trusting attitudes, openness of communication, and how people discuss and manage differences. Folger, Poole, and Stutman (1993) conclude, "The prevailing climate of a conflict situation colors members' interpretations of one another, thereby encouraging certain types of behavior and reinforcing the situational climate" (p. 165).

For example, recently a facilitator led a 2-day course in negotiation for a large financial firm. During the program, several of the participants shared with him, "This culture lacks leadership. Few employees trust managers." This assessment of climate was borne out in class discussions. The participants were competitive, distrusted one another and resisted sharing information in class exercises and discussions. Folger et al. (1993) explain, "These perceptions constitute an overarching climate, a sense of the situation that shapes how parties calculate their moves and perceive each other" (p. 20). Significantly, the nature of the psychological climate influences both the development and the resolution of disputes. Lewin (1997) explains, "Whether or not a particular event will lead to a conflict depends largely on the tension level or on the social atmosphere of the group" (p. 71).

The force-field perspective explains many of the underlying forces that influence word choices, emotional responses, pressures, and selection of tactics in negotiation. Our language and communication during negotiation is influenced by the cultural groups to which we belong. For example, the way a union representative interprets the words spoken by a management counterpart and the tactical choices used during the negotiation may be influenced by the expectations of the union to which the representative belongs. In a neighborhood negotiation with white neighbors, a person of color may be influenced by pressures exerted by his or her neighbors to communicate in a particular manner. A negotiator needs to be sensitive to these underlying forces and to adapt negotiation tactics to account for those forces.

Negotiators from this perspective will frame interpretation of words and events based on a substantive frame ("Here's what this problem is really about") or an outcome frame ("How will our agreement affect my other agreements?").

HUMAN NEED THEORY ●

The human need perspective of negotiation builds on the assumption that all people possess knowable biological and social needs that are driven by emotions and values that must be satisfied. These needs cannot be understood outside of a social context. People will use power and coercion to satisfy their needs. This creates a paradox. By forcing others to respond to their needs, they create conflict that frustrates attainment of needs. A human need perspective supports either a loss-gain or aspirations frame for interpreting words and events. Expectations and outcomes are viewed from a perspective of "How does an agreement improve our situation?" or "Does this agreement satisfy our needs?"

Maslow (1954) presents seven basic needs that often guide the thinking of those grounded in the human need perspective:

1. Physiological needs

2. Safety and security

3. Love and belonging

4. Esteem (self and social approval)

5. Self-actualization

6. Knowing and understanding

7. Aesthetic needs (order and balance)

This approach assumes that people motivated by these core needs will engage in a variety of behaviors to satisfy the needs. Cantrill (1967) adds to Maslow's list the freedom to exercise choice and a sense of confidence that one's hopes will be fulfilled, two significant needs during negotiation processes. Burton (1979) includes in his needs list consistency in response, distributive justice, the appearance of rationality, and the ability to defend one's role. Occasionally, because the needs involve both material and non-material satisfiers, priorities may become confused. Negotiation provides an opportunity for people to assess and prioritize their needs. Based on a human need perspective, Sites (1990) explains,

> Family conflicts are, at base, power struggles over which party is to realize his/her respective values and thereby gratify needs. If a property owner highly values holding property as a basis for needs gratification, she/he will fight with a neighbor over placement of a fence. (p. 28)

In an analysis of ethnic and religious conflict in 25 countries, Podestra (1987) found that group identity exists as a basic human need in most countries. Fisher (1990) links group identity to the need for positive self-esteem: "Group identity is seen as supportive of self-esteem in that when the group is threatened, the members are threatened in a personal sense" (p. 104). This explains, in part, the strong cohesion occurring in groups (such as labor unions or community groups) in face-offs with competing groups.

The human need perspective explains why demonstrating respect, establishing relationship, supporting someone's reputation or prestige, or contributing to confidence about safety may be as important as money and resources as tradeoffs in negotiation. For example, in some families, teaching members to listen and respect each other reduces the tension so that they can engage in constructive discussion. In some organizations, workers have taken pay cuts to gain greater job security.

Negotiators who operate from a human need perspective begin by uncovering underlying values and needs that drive issues. Information exchange addresses the need to know and understand. Sharing the reasoning behind needs provides further depth of understanding. The need for choice will occur as alternatives are presented and evaluated and tradeoffs occur. Ideally, the final package will incorporate both the material and non-material needs necessary for a satisfactory agreement.

● RATIONAL CHOICE THEORY

The rational choice perspective describes behavior during conflict as a series of choices supported by moves and countermoves whose goal is to maximize gain and minimize loss. This approach argues that self-interest drives people and that they make choices based on relatively stable preferences. Negotiators from this perspective will interpret words and events from a loss-gain or outcome perspective—that is, "What's in this for me?"

This approach points out the importance of cognitive anchors, which serve as perceptual reference points below which deals are not worth the cost and above which deals are desirable. Although these anchors may be subjective, they greatly influence what makes sense and risk/loss calculations in negotiations. Kahneman (1992) points out that people are averse to loss. Avoiding loss will influence negotiations as much as or more than achieving gain.

An example of rational choice is game theory, in which experimenters use simulations to understand the moves, countermoves, and choices people make in efforts to maximize their interests and achieve their goals. Axelrod (1984) used Prisoner's Dilemma, a game designed to test competitive and cooperative behavior. In this setup, 62 game theorists from 8 academic disciplines and 12 nations engaged in a contest to determine the formula for the greatest payoffs in mixed-motive settings (which are present in most negotiations). Through multiple rounds, a strategy called Tit for Tat created by Anatol Rapport from the University of Toronto was the winning strategy. Axelrod (1984) summarizes four principles central to the Tit for Tat strategy:

1. Be nice; don't be the first to defect (attempt to win at the expense of others).

2. If another defects, punish the action.

3. Be forgiving after punishing defection; resist becoming locked in further escalation.

4. Don't be too clever; clever tactics create inaccurate inferences by others. (p. 110)

An example of the Tit for Tat strategy occurred in the motion picture *War Games* (Badham, 1983). The movie used game theory to answer the following question: What's the best strategy for winning a thermonuclear war? Final segments of the movie depicted a computer testing all combinations of rational choices, moves, and countermoves, and concluding that *not to play the game* was the best strategy.

Tidwell (1998) argues that one of the most important insights in game theory is the role of perception: "Parties may be more than willing to end a conflict, yet may not do so because they perceive the other party as engaging in conflict" (p. 72). This factor points to the importance of negotiators monitoring behaviors; these behaviors contribute to perceptions that are perceived as escalating conflict or preventing settlement.

Resolving conflict through negotiation is the process of facilitating solutions in which people no longer feel the need to indulge in conflict-escalating activity or no longer believe that the distribution of benefits in the social system is unacceptable. Processes deemed fair or appropriate by disputing parties raise the possibility for acceptable solutions. As long as the rules of the game appear fair and parties believe that tradeoffs will be in their best interests, they will participate.

TRANSFORMATION THEORY ●

Kriesberg (1999) defines conflict transformation as the process in which protracted struggles are transformed through conflict management or negotiation into fundamental and enduring changes. The parties may recognize the value of each other's claims, which they previously resisted. They may begin to see goals as compatible rather than conflicting. They may view their relationship in a way that is different than before, or they may talk about the issues in new ways. Their view of the conflict may shift from one that is about themselves to one that is actually part of a larger context. As parties change their behaviors toward each other, the feelings, attitudes, and perspectives about each other and the problems change as well. Negotiation transforms conflict by changing the way people view and talk about problems.

Scholars describe the kinds of factors that situations require for transformation of conflict to occur. Kriesberg (1998), Kriesberg, Northrup, and

Thorson (1989), and Vayrynen (1991) identify the factors that must be present for transformation to occur:

1. Transformation requires parties to recognize the legitimacy of each other's needs.

2. Parties begin to believe that accommodation can alter the course of conflict.

3. Parties perceive that goals may be compatible.

4. The parties cease behaviors that resist or block settlements.

Kriesberg (1999) identifies four stages through which transformation occurs. The first stage is exploratory. Parties discover that the cost of protracted struggle is too high, so they make overtures that promote accommodation to reduce tensions—that is, "peace feelers are tentatively put forward to test whether the other side might accept what is offered as part of the conflict resolution" (Kriesberg, 1999, p. 418). The second stage involves public gestures or actions that demonstrate commitment to a cooperative solution. During negotiations, this may involve concessions, public statements of support, or suspension of hostility. Achieving agreements about specific issues signals the presence of the third stage. Momentum builds commitment to understanding and progress. The final stage involves implementation and monitoring of the agreement. Memorandums of agreement, contracts, or treaties summarize the components of the agreement.

The transformational perspective may link advocacy to negotiation. This approach proposes that in some settings, facilitating changes in the balance of power, social justice, the nature of relationships, or protection of the weak may serve as goals in negotiations. For example, in negotiations between nations, discussions on the definitions of borders may include negotiations about the treatment of refugees as well. For families, negotiations about decision making may include new ways of viewing the roles of family members. Bush and Folger (1994) argue that "the goal of transformation—that is, engendering moral growth toward both strength and compassion—should take precedence over the other goals . . . even though these goals are themselves important" (p. 29). Coser (1957) believes that discussions to resolve differences or to manage conflict can actually generate new norms or new institutions. Thus, settlements may be only a by-product of deeper, more long-lasting changes that either build or inhibit relationship.

● MUTUAL GAINS THEORY

Perhaps the best-known model for integrative negotiation, mutual gains, draws primarily from the rational choice and human need perspectives. Parties engage in a process in which an agreement with each other is perceived as better than no agreement at all. Negotiators frame goals as integrative. Bazerman and Neale (1992) argue that mutual gains holds significant benefits over distributive approaches, including producing higher-quality agreements, creating greater opportunities for agreements when the problems are complex, and strengthening the relationships between negotiating parties (p. 75). Negotiators from a mutual gains perspective will interpret words and events from a substantive or loss-gain frame of reference—that is, "If we cooperate, we can create an agreement that is better than if we don't cooperate."

The mutual gains perspective assumes that parties will engage in rational discussion within a fair process if they believe their interests can be sufficiently met. The move-countermove interactions of distributive negotiation are discouraged in favor of merit-based requests measured against mutually acceptable standards. Parties minimize counterproductive attributions by keeping the focus on resolution of problems or meeting of interests.

Fisher, Ury, and Patton (1991), Susskind and Cruikshank (1987), and Bazerman and Neale (1992) provide elaborate discussions about the elements of mutual gains negotiation, many of which find their grounding in integrative-negotiation principles. The following list summarizes some of the most prominent principles of this approach:

- Assess the impact and determine alternatives if an agreement cannot be reached.
- Focus on interests, needs, and issues, not positions.
- Share information and reasoning behind interests and issues to expand understanding.
- Engage in problem solving that includes opportunity for trading interests of value and inventing options for mutual gain.
- Use mutually acceptable standards for evaluation of interests and an agreeable package.
- Create a process for revisiting the agreement in the event options fail or conditions change.

In negotiation, *pareto optimality* is the term used for the limit or boundary for creative options or achievement of joint gains (Lax and Sebenius, 1986). In some situations (such as in some small-business transactions), this limit may be achieved quickly, but in others (such as labor or international negotiations), this limit may take months or years to fully achieve.

SUMMARY ●

At first glance, theoretical perspective might seem to be more than we need to know about negotiations. After all, a five-step formula might seem sufficient for negotiating a sales contract. But deeper understanding about why we make the strategic choices we make raises the odds of resolving a conflict or achieving our best interests in a negotiation. The friars and government representatives described in Box 1.1 in Chapter 1 were successful because they used principles contained in mutual gains theory. The father-in-law described in Box 1.2 may have been more effective had he been more sensitive to his daughter-in-law's identity needs or the language he chose to express his concern. Understanding the principle of transformation theory may be significant in many interpersonal settings. Changing the way people talk to each other or relate to one another may be the most important achievement of a negotiation.

Many of the theoretical principles provide reasons that negotiations might be successful or break down, including the following:

- Respect and understanding of the identity and role needs that might be blocking a negotiator's ability to focus on substantive issues
- Awareness that social, systemic forces influence how people behave
- Identifying the psychological, social, and substantive needs which give rise to the need for negotiation
- Understanding the link between behavioral choices, driving and restraining forces and outcomes
- The changes that occur in relationship, role, or awareness as we negotiate

PROFESSIONAL PROFILE

WILLIAM URY, ●
COAUTHOR OF *GETTING TO YES* AND
NATIONAL AND INTERNATIONAL ADR CONSULTANT

Building the Theory and Practice of Negotiation

If readers are familiar with any group active in the field of negotiation and alternative dispute resolution (ADR), it is most likely to be The Program on Negotiation at Harvard University. At the time of its founding in 1978, there were few if any courses on negotiation offered at universities. A group of scholars and practitioners from different fields (such as law, diplomacy, environmental sciences, and community planning) came together to share their interests in negotiation. The group met monthly and discovered that even though they came from vastly different disciplines, they had a common set of interests around negotiation. They conceived the idea of a multidiscipline, multiuniversity research consortium that would advance the theory and practice of negotiation.

The Program on Negotiation works on negotiation problems and develops improved methods of negotiation and mediation. Its faculty is based at Harvard, MIT, Simmons, and Tufts universities. Its mission is to improve the theory and practice of conflict resolution. Activities of The Program on Negotiation include theory building, education and training, publications, and action research. William Ury was one of the institution's founders and continues his association there currently as the director of the Project on Preventing War.

Introduction to the Practitioner

Similarly, if readers are familiar with any individual who has built the field of negotiation, it is likely to be William Ury. With Roger Fisher, Ury coauthored *Getting to Yes,* the best-known book in the field of negotiation and alternative dispute resolution. First published in 1981, and with a second

51

edition published in 1991 (in which the first edition's editor, Bruce Patton, became a coauthor), *Getting to Yes* has sold, at the time of this writing, more than five million copies and has been translated into 23 languages. The theory of principled negotiation that it presents has been fundamental to the growth and development of theory and practice.

Since the publication of *Getting to Yes*, Bill Ury has written other books that also contribute to the theory and practice of negotiation: *Getting Past No* and *Getting to Peace* are the best known. He consults both nationally and internationally, serving as an advisor to the International Negotiation Network at the Carter Center of Emory University. Corporate executives, labor leaders, and government officials have received training in negotiation skills from Bill Ury. Through his writing, consulting and teaching, Bill continues to develop the understanding and application of principled negotiation.

Bill's interest in negotiation evolved through his graduate work in anthropology at Harvard. Bill recalls, "Wanting to apply anthropology to the problem of preventing war, I originally proposed to do my research as an observer at a peace negotiation on the Middle East. I wanted to understand the conflicts from a cultural point of view. How would an anthropologist describe the process of conflict resolution among the Arabs and the Israelis?"

Although Bill's focus on the anthropological aspects of international conflict continued, his actual thesis focused on a dispute closer to home. He explains, "I ultimately ended up writing about a bitter dispute in a coal mine, where I was one of the third-party neutrals. [Readers may find an account of this work in the 1988 book *Getting Disputes Resolved: Designing Systems to Cut the Costs of Conflict,* which Bill wrote with Jeanne M. Brett and Stephen B. Goldberg.] A third of the miners had been fired, there were constant strikes, there were bomb threats, people were packing guns to work, and the national union was concerned that this situation might trigger a national strike. That was my baptism by fire into negotiation." That coal mine dispute led Bill Ury to his life's work of reducing violent conflict through the application of ADR tools.

Bill identifies certain skills that negotiators need to master. He muses, "If I had to pick a single skill, it would be the ability to put yourself in the other side's shoes and see the situation the way they see it. That skill was highlighted for me when I was in graduate school and my uncle came to Harvard for his reunion at the law school. He took me aside, saying, 'It's taken me 25 years to unlearn what I learned at the law school. That is, I was taught that all that counts in life is who is right. Now, after 25 years in law and business, I've discovered that people's perceptions of those facts are just as important as the facts. Unless you can put yourself in the other party's shoes, you're never going to be effective at making a deal or settling a dispute.' Actually, this is a very hard thing to do. In negotiation, we're so focused on what we want, and the way we see the problem, it's often very difficult to project ourselves and understand the other person's reality." Negotiation is an exercise in influence, and in order to influence another person, we must first understand them.

Another skill Bill emphasizes is patience. He notes, "It's particularly trying for Americans, who are probably the most impatient culture on earth. For us, time is money. For most people in the world, time is relationships. Negotiation takes time; it takes more time than you'd think to build the relationships that are essential to a negotiation based on the kind of trust that allows you to explore a problem in depth. Time is required to understand the other side's interests, to have them trust you enough to share information about their interests, to do the necessary joint problem solving, and to involve all the relevant stakeholders."

Bill continues, "One of the critical mistakes we make is to try to rush negotiations. We hurry and make mistakes, such as leaving out key stakeholders. In that case, we discover that even if we reach agreement, the agreement is not sustainable because people who were not involved in the negotiation take exception to it and sabotage the agreement. Here's a quote from [former president Lyndon Baines] Johnson: 'If I wasn't in on the take-off, don't count on me to be in on the landing.' Human minds don't change on a dime, so to me, a useful motto for negotiation is, 'If you want to go fast, go slow.'" Patience and the willingness to allow time necessary for productive negotiations are critical skills.

Insights About Negotiation

Bill also advises negotiators to allow adequate preparation time. In his mind, the preparation time should be at least as long as the anticipated negotiation time. He specifies, "If you have only an hour to settle an issue, both parties would be better off to take 30 minutes by themselves to prepare and then use the second 30 minutes to actually negotiate. They are more likely to arrive at a better agreement than if they take the full hour to talk. There's no substitute for good preparation."

Bill specifies questions that a negotiator should ask himself or herself to prepare for negotiation. He explains, "In my lingo, preparation is 'time on the balcony.' Get some perspective, keep your eyes on the prize—and that prize is an agreement that meets your interests and meets the other side's interests. Think through the interests behind your positions. What are the intangible motivations, such as resources or security, that drive your positions? Rank your interests. What are the interests of the other side? Brainstorm by yourself or with a colleague about where some potential areas of joint gain may be and about what some creative options might be. Think through independent standards that you might bring to bear on the issues you'll be negotiating. Think through your Best Alternative to a Negotiated Agreement (BATNA). If you are not able to reach agreement with the other side, what is your best course of action? Think through their BATNA as well." Although these questions are not the only ones a negotiator might use to prepare, they are a very helpful starter list. In a way, preparation questions map out the most likely course of the negotiation ahead.

Preparation for an important negotiation might also involve rehearsal. You might offer your opening statement to a friend or colleague and ask for feedback. You could even ask the friend to try out your strategy on you so that you could see what it was like to be on the receiving end. Rehearsal can be a very useful method of preparation.

For Bill, a typical negotiation starts with attending to the people involved. People have individual perceptions, they have emotions, and they have different ways of communicating. Given these differences, he sees the first challenge as building a favorable atmosphere in which you can later address the problem. He offers, "I was mediating between an automotive union and one of the large automobile companies. They were about to enter some difficult negotiations. There was a great deal of tension. Asked to name the hottest issue, the union responded that it was outsourcing jobs to nonunion personnel. We were talking about interests and options and proceeding well when I overheard one of the union leaders whispering to a colleague, 'What are we doing here! We're giving them all this secret information!' He was in a state of high anxiety. So, I stopped the process and told the union leaders that we had a problem with trust. I asked the man I'd overheard to address the issue of trust. He recounted the long history of distrust on the factory floor." Before Bill could deal with the substantive issue of outsourcing, he had to deal with the people issues—in this case, distrust.

Bill asked the union representatives to think of four or five things that management could do that would signal to them that management could begin to be trusted. He asked management to do the same thing, to list things the union could do that would create a basis for trust in the perception of management. After exchanging the lists, discussing and agreeing to them, the two sides were ready to talk about outsourcing. This example underscores how important it is to examine trust issues and what might be done to address them in the beginning of a negotiation. Bill concludes, "To me, It's an essential prerequisite to build trust, rapport, and relationships before you dive into the problems, looking at interests and options."

The second phase of negotiation is about problem solving. This is an open, exploratory time. Bill advises, "In this phase, it's often useful to adopt the rule of no criticism from brainstorming. The last phase is what I call 'converging.' I call the three phases 'the three Ps': the people, the problem, and the proposal. Negotiation isn't really that neat, but if you want to converge on a good proposal, it requires backing up and doing some effective problem solving. This process requires as a prerequisite having done some very good work with the people. Of course, all three of these strands are to some extent simultaneous." The people, the problem solving, and the proposal phases may be mixed into a concurrent time period. However, the typical negotiation has a basic three-part sequence.

It is very difficult to specify elements that promote successful negotiations. Bill recalls, "I've been in many negotiations where you haven't had any helpful elements. Even in these circumstances, you still can sometimes reach an agreement, so I hate to think that there is a [hard-and-fast] list of preconditions for success. Some people say, 'There has to be the will to reach agreement,' but I've always found that opinion rather tautological, because to me the operative question is, How do you develop the will?" Specifying success elements carries the danger of imagining that negotiation shouldn't be attempted unless a checklist of favorable factors is satisfied.

Bill offers another example of how predetermined success factors may not be operative. He notes, "There are situations in which there are high levels of distrust, such as between the Soviet Union and the United States during the Cold War. Yet the two major powers were often able to reach arms controls accords because they tried to make their agreements independent of trust. They relied on satellites to ensure compliance. At a personal level, these negotiations did require building some trust among the arms control negotiators." There may be a need for a modicum of trust for negotiators to reach agreement, but a high level of distrust does not preclude agreement.

One predictor of negotiation success is the presence of some solutions that are better for each side than what they perceive their alternatives to be. Bill gives the example, "In Indonesia, there were representatives from the government and the independence movement at the negotiation table. The independence movement wanted independence from the central government and would rather go to war than accept something less than independence. The government would rather go to war than grant independence. So, there wasn't any room for agreement. The only way we could move forward was to ask them to reconsider whether there was a process that for each of them would be better than going to war." There had to be some potential solutions that would be more attractive to both of them than pursuing that alternative.

To some extent, one gets to success in negotiation by eliminating barriers. In Bill's opinion, the biggest barrier is ourselves. Our human tendency to react and to act without thinking must be overcome. He quotes Ambrose Bierce: "When angry, you'll make the best speech you'll ever regret." Bill also offers this anecdote: "In one instance, an attorney representing state government negotiated with a large computer company. The state had contracted with the company to design a computer system that would enable the state to issue its welfare payments. One quarter of the way through the fiscal year, the system had effectively spent half of the state's available budget. State officials became quite anxious and decided to take the contract back into their own hands. The state was interested in buying the database with all the information, which was valued at $50 million. To the company, if the state didn't continue in the contract, the database was worthless. To the state, it was worth at least $50 million, because to try to re-create such listings might cost them even more. But, because of the negative emotions generated by the failure of the system, the result of that negotiation was that both sides lost. The $50 million database lay idle, and 10 years later the two were still in court suing each other, spending hundreds of thousands of dollars. That to me is an example of the tendency of human beings to be reactive and to fail to pursue their interests." Success depends on getting around the barrier of reactivity by stepping back from the negotiation and staying focused on your interests in the negotiation. It is all too easy to become caught up in point scoring and revenge against the other side.

One of the toughest challenges for Bill was facilitating the peace talks between the government of Russia and the leaders of Chechnya. Bill recounts, "It was a situation where Chechens took off from their capital of Grozny to come to the talks in The Hague. Some Russian MIGs surrounded their plane and forced it to land, saying that the Chechens didn't have the authority to fly over their airspace. Then, the Chechens insisted that they would travel on their own passports instead of their Russian passports. Since no country in the world, including Holland, recognized Chechnya, we had to have a negotiation with the Dutch Foreign Ministry at the last moment to see if there was some way the Chechens could enter the country without showing their Russian passports. We asked, 'What would happen if they arrived having 'lost' their passports? Would you really send them back?' The Dutch ministers were flexible enough, and our conversation was creative enough, that we found a way for them to land at a different airport, where they were asked to show their visas but not their passports." Even getting to the table was extremely challenging in this situation.

"Once at The Hague, the Chechens insisted on inspecting the hotel rooms to ascertain that the rooms assigned to the Russians were not larger than those they had been assigned. The first opening statement by the vice president was quite vituperative, saying that the Russians should stay in the room where the Yugoslav war crimes tribunal was being held, because they were wanted for war crimes. Then the vice president attacked the United States. I went 'to the balcony,' and when it was my turn to speak, I said that I took his remarks to mean that we can talk candidly to one another, so we must be among friends. I reminded him that we had come to see whether there was a way we could reduce the violence and suffering in his country. By the end of that session, both sides were at least able to negotiate an agreed-upon press statement, which called for an ongoing peace process." It is not difficult to see why Bill thought of this experience as very challenging; despite the best efforts of the facilitators, they were unable to prevent the devastating war that continues to rage there.

One of Bill's frustrations in such conflicts is that they might have been resolved with the help of others from the international community. He notes that these conflicts don't arise suddenly; there are usually stages of escalation and the possibility that early intervention may contain the violence. In his view, "We need to spend a lot more time figuring out how to use negotiation to prevent wars rather than using negotiation just to end wars."

There were alternatives to the breakdown of this negotiation. For instance, in Chechnya, there is a Council of Elders. Bill explains, "The international community or the neighbors of Chechnya might have convened the Chechen Council of Elders to look at what could be done to address the root causes of this conflict. For instance, Chechnya was shattered economically. There were no jobs, so it was very easy to recruit youth into a path of violence. The Council might have considered ways of giving Chechens control over their own lives that would be consistent with the Russian concerns of avoiding the breakup of the Soviet Union. There could have been dialogue to deal with some of the triggers to violence and to agree on a transitional period moving toward independence. The world community might have supported a democratically elected moderate leader when he came to power." However, none of these steps was taken. Without improvement in the economic conditions or assistance from the World Bank or other independent institutions, the situation deteriorated. Raids across the border and kidnappings led back to war.

Negotiations broke down because of a failure to mobilize what Bill calls the Third Side. He cites the African proverb, "When spider webs unite, they can halt a lion." Bill advises, "When each of us takes a role in the conflict, such as provider, or witness, or mediator, or bridge builder, we can serve as a container that gradually transforms serious conflict from violence to a more constructive form of negotiation. The key is to mobilize the Third Side. When negotiations break down, what about all the surrounding players? Where is that container within which you can strengthen that negotiation and support the negotiators in arriving at a reasonable settlement?" When negotiations threaten to break down, the community around the parties needs to address conflict.

Contextual Differences

International negotiations differ in many ways from those in other contexts. For instance, the negotiators represent large constituencies and cannot make independent decisions. There is a level of complexity that is not usually present in interpersonal negotiations and cross-cultural differences that may not be present in other contexts. However, Bill is more struck by the similarities than the differences. He notes, "I've worked in labor management, in interpersonal, in interethnic, and in international situations. I've worked in schools, in neighborhood centers, and in corporations. I've worked in the Kalahari Desert, in the New Guinea highlands, and in the White House. Human nature is constant; in every negotiation there are needs for trust building, for problem solving, and for resolution. The use of third parties may be very helpful, regardless of context."

Changes and Conflicts

Bill identifies several new and emerging trends in negotiation. He calls attention to the increased interest in multiparty negotiation: "For example, in an environmental negotiation, there is coalition building among many parties. It's not always clear that the negotiator has a clear mandate from all the parties. Another trend is that there is more interest in cross-cultural negotiations. The contextual subtleties and hidden assumptions that characterize cross-cultural negotiations have been the focus of recent research. Within our own society, we are increasingly multicultural."

Bill continues, "There is emerging interest in the effect of the Internet on negotiations. How does the Internet change negotiations?" This is one of the areas of disagreement among practitioners. Bill believes, "There is an aspect of face-to-face interaction which is not yet captured by technology. Many people still feel they need to be in personal contact to build some elements of trust. There's a lot of richness that will be lost on the Internet, even when it goes to video."

To Bill, the most interesting question in the Internet debate is not whether or not to employ it in negotiation but, rather, "What negotiation functions can be usefully conducted over the Internet? The Internet is exceedingly useful to keep people informed, to exchange drafts, to get a lot of people involved without having to bring them together physically. It has enormous potential for learning, for sharing lessons, during or after a negotiation, so that the process can be improved. Since a large aspect of negotiation is joint learning, I think the Internet lends itself to that."

Bill continues, "There are also generational differences. The older generation may not choose to negotiate electronically. But, there's an emerging generation who's used to living life on the Internet, so maybe they'll be better able to use it in negotiation. Finally, there's an expectation around speed connected with the Internet. How do we line this up with the time that's required for successful negotiation?" There are many fascinating questions to be asked and answered on this topic.

There is also a divide among practitioners on the importance of culture in negotiation. Bill says, "Some hold that culture is not that important a variable. Others believe that it's absolutely critical—that without understanding culture, you can't understand negotiation." Some people recommend adopting the negotiation protocols of the host culture, whereas others claim the evolution of a global, transnational culture.

Finally, it should be noted that the field of negotiation is still very much in its infancy. Bill maintains, "There is room for innovation, for new techniques and methodologies. We're in the beginning of the challenge that faces all of humanity: How do we learn to collectively make decisions together when we have all these differences? Take the problem of global climate change, which affects us all. How do we make decisions comprising 6 or 7 million actors? How do you engage us all in a negotiation that could save the planet? The potential of this field is enormous. As our world becomes smaller and more interconnected, how do we use negotiation to its fullest potential?"

Bill asks why the field of negotiation is attracting so much interest just now. In his opinion, there is a silent revolution in the way humans make decisions. It accompanies the knowledge revolution but is subtler. Traditionally, in homes and workplaces, decisions were made in hierarchical ways. Increasingly, as those hierarchies flatten into networks, the form of decision making shifts from vertical to horizontal. Bill asserts, "Another name for horizontal decision making is negotiation. In order to get what we want, in order to get our jobs done nowadays, we're compelled to negotiate. When I ask people around the world, 'How much time do you spend negotiating?'

the majority of them will answer that it's more than half of their time. If I ask, 'Over the last 10 years, is the amount of time you spend negotiating going up or down?' universally they say it is going up." Bill concludes that negotiation is an art and that we can all learn by reflecting on how to do it better. Given the increasing amount of time we're spending on it, it makes sense to give the process every chance to succeed.

Bill Ury believes that the United States has a great history of inventing and perfecting new hardware. He would like to see us take that same ingenuity and apply it to new software for peacemaking. For example, we might enhance our chances for success through thorough preparation and the patience to build trusting relationships with the other side. We might address personal issues before tackling the substantive ones. We might resist reactive tendencies by "going to the balcony" and staying focused on interests. We might invent better ways to reach agreements across cultures. We might convert our concerns about violent conflicts into becoming containers for them. Although his past achievements have developed the theory and practice of negotiation, Bill Ury's perspective is firmly fixed on its potential for the future.

PROFESSIONAL PROFILE

● **JAMES FREUND, ESQ.,**
AUTHOR, ATTORNEY, AND MEDIATOR

The Neutral Negotiator:
Negotiating Between Parties in Business Mediation

Does a business context require a different approach to negotiation? Can principled negotiation be applied to business deals, without editing or amplifying it for the rough-and-tumble of corporate practice? Do any of the same skills and approaches apply, albeit in different guises? In the following interview, a skilled negotiator describes how his experience in business law and negotiation is different from the traditional practice of principled negotiation. This practitioner focuses on how effective mediators negotiate with the parties to the mediation.

Introduction to the Practitioner

Jim Freund is an experienced negotiator, helping businesspeople make deals that enhance their interests and keep them out of court. Educated at Princeton University and Harvard Law School, Jim has been a partner at the New York law firm Skadden, Arps, Slate, Meagher & Flom. The primary focus of his career has been representing clients in mergers and acquisitions. Some clients with familiar names are Federated Department Stores, Richardson-Vicks, and National Can. He has helped clients resolve business disputes through negotiation and has served as both a mediator and an arbitrator.

Jim has been teaching business law as well as practicing. He teaches in classrooms at Fordham University School of Law but has informed the greatest number of students through his writing, most notably as author of *Smart Negotiating: How to Make Good Deals in the Real World* (1993). In addition, business students often study his book *Advise and Invent: The Lawyer as Counselor-Strategist* (1990). Many of his articles, such as "Anatomy of a Split-Up: Mediating a Business Divorce" (1997) and "The Neutral Negotiator: Why and How Mediation Can Work to Resolve Dollar Disputes" (1994), have been published in law journals. The latter was awarded First Prize for Professional Articles by the CPR (Center for Public Resources) Institute for Dispute Resolution in 1994. These titles reflect the perspective Jim brings to negotiation and its use in mediation. In his experience, the context of business disputes drives a mediator's role toward negotiating with each party rather than toward facilitating their dialogue.

In the mid-1980s, after having practiced business law for many years, Jim was asked by litigators at his firm for help to resolve some litigation through negotiation. He did so and began to write about how dispute resolution was different from deal making, as well as how deal-making techniques could be used to help resolve disputes. That led to involvement with mediation and his attempts to bring mediation to the attention of corporate lawyers. One of the mediation services selected him for its panel, for which he now does most of his mediations. Reflecting on his involvement with alternative dispute resolution (ADR), Jim says, "Mediation fascinated me. I came in the back door, because most attorneys come to ADR from the litigation side, where they're used to dealing with disputes. I come from the deal-making side, where I'm not so concerned about future disputes. I recently retired as a lawyer, but I've stayed active in mediation and writing about ADR."

Jim believes that the most critical skill for mediators, as well as for the parties, is negotiation. He explains, "This is not always recognized. What I brought to mediation is, this is the toughest of all negotiations, because the people who come to mediation aren't able to resolve it on their own—if they could, they wouldn't be here. Therefore, the mediator has to function as a negotiator. My approach is to separate the parties so the parties are not negotiating with each other directly. They are negotiating through me. So, it's just as important that they be effective negotiators, only instead of talking directly to the other party, they're talking to the mediator."

Jim advises parties to mediation that although the manner of negotiation changes, they must realize they're still involved in a negotiation. He cautions, "The parties must not treat the mediator as a judge, someone who's high and mighty; they must communicate with the mediator as someone who has to be moved and has to help them. To me, it's all about negotiating." Because the skill of negotiation is primary for a mediator, the business lawyer has the advantage of practice. A judge has the probity of an effective neutral and may be able to predict how a court might rule in a given dispute. However, because judges have little occasional to practice deal making or to use negotiating skills, they may not be the best candidates for mediating business disputes.

Other skills essential to effective business mediation are those needed for mediations generally. For instance, Jim reminds readers of the importance of being fair-minded: "You can't let your predilections enter into it. One side may be very appealing in its presentation and the other side may be boorish, but you can't let that affect your judgment. Second, you not only have to be fair-minded, you have to appear fair-minded. These two things are not always the same and are not always so simple." He explains that the perception of neutrality suffers most when something which one side may think reflects mediator bias is said in front of both parties. This is one of the reasons Jim finds advantage in separating the parties. When he does make a statement demonstrating he sees more merit for the other party on a particular issue, at least the other party is not present.

Elaborating on this approach, Jim says, "If you really want to be frank as a mediator, you're better off doing so privately. Even when you do this privately, you run the risk that one party may question your neutrality. He may say, 'Hey, are you really neutral? You sound like you're working for the other side!' It's the most damning thing that can be said to a mediator, so parties should not bring this charge lightly because it gets a mediator's dander up."

A business mediator needs several other skills as well. Listening is critical and so is establishing trust. Jim explains, "Even though one party will say more to the mediator than he will to the adversary, there are some topics the party will be reluctant to cover. In order to make progress, there must be a certain level of candor present. The party will only be candid when he trusts the mediator. You don't get that trust automatically; you have to build it up gradually over time." The party must believe the mediator who says he or she will not disclose confidential information and also believe that the information will not be used in some inimical way.

In addition, a business mediator must be a problem solver. In Jim's experience, "Your job is to move beyond the simplistic way the parties are presenting the situation. If you looked at that, you'd never solve anything. Their points of view are so opposed that you have to be able to see other avenues of reconciliation. The *Getting to Yes* philosophy is that parties will sit down and share ideas, brainstorm options. This *never* happens in business mediation. They hate each other and there's always litigation in the offing. Litigation may even be going on at the same time as the negotiation, and the lawyers are very loath to share anything that might be considered weakness with the other side. So, it behooves the mediator to generate the options, see the avenues for creativity, and create value." The option-generation function remains, but in the business dispute, the mediator, not the parties, perform this function.

Finally, in Jim's experience, the mediator needs a sense of how a dispute might fare in court, because every dispute is mediated against the backdrop of possible litigation. In his words, "It's very hard for me to conceive how a nonlawyer mediator might anticipate how a court or an arbitrator might come down on a given dispute. The sense of alternatives is very important." In Jim's experience, an attorney's ability to forecast legal outcomes is necessary in mediating business disputes.

Insights of the Practitioner

Preparation for a business mediation involves several steps. First, Jim is clear with potential parties to mediation about his approach—that is, that the parties will be negotiating through him and that he will be actively constructing plans to reconcile interests. He does not want to serve parties who are simply looking for a facilitator. In essence, what he tells them is, "If you want someone to serve coffee, I ain't the guy! If you're looking for a judgmental, opinionated mediator to help you, I'm it."

If parties to a dispute are seeking an activist mediator and choose to proceed, Jim usually asks them to prepare documents that set forth their positions in the dispute. After reading the position papers, if Jim finds he needs further interpretation, he will ask for that to read in advance. In his words, "Not too much. I don't overprepare. I'll be really educated once the mediation begins."

The period necessary to conclude a business mediation varies considerably. Resolution of the dispute may require from 2 days to several months. Primarily, this is because both parties are actively pursuing their business interests simultaneously. Unlike a court case, where parties come together day after day until a case is concluded, the mediation will typically be conducted for a few days, and then a longer period of time will pass when the parties return to their places of business. Coordinating schedules is typically difficult to do, but eventually another mediation session will be scheduled. Jim feels, "If you could get everybody to stay in one place for a week or so, you'd have it resolved, but that doesn't happen. These people have many other responsibilities to be juggled along with the negotiations around this dispute. This can present difficulties in that sometimes people revert to their original positions and I have to knock heads to get them back to where they were."

Jim contrasts disputes and deals, saying, "In a dispute, there is seldom the kind of time pressure that forces people to the table for marathon sessions because the focus is on past events, whereas in deal making, there is always time pressure, such as, 'We have to get this done before it leaks to the press, we have to get this done before year end so that we can get it into the financials.'" Typically, six or more all-day sessions, over the course of several months, will be needed for dispute resolution. Jim says he doesn't believe in "making a big deal" out of location. Usually, sessions alternate between offices of the parties but occasionally they may be held in law offices.

The typical content of a business dispute is either (a) a transaction that occurred in the past, but now one party feels disadvantaged, often charging that they were misled or, (b) there's a current dispute over the interpretation of a contract. Whatever the content, Jim says the tone of the first session is that "the parties feel very strongly, sometimes to the extent of not being able to talk to the other side. They're keyed up for this, they're going to war if they don't settle it here. The lawyers are frustrated because they want to get to court and do their thing. They're not crazy about the idea of settling."

Jim has an approach to deal with this volatile first session. He recounts, "I bring the parties together and let them vent, an hour or so for each side. I ask very few questions, just for clarification. I don't take issue with anybody. I give them the ground rules of the mediation. I make sure that businesspersons who are authorized to settle are present—that's very important. I also ask, 'How did you get here?' I want to know if they've had some settlement talks that broke down and, if so, how far they got. Sometimes they've had settlement talks that have produced some progress from their initial positions and now that they're in mediation, they've reverted to their original further out positions. Once I know they've moved that far, I know they're at least prepared to go that far again. Then, I say, 'Okay, you go in this room, you go in that one,' and I never bring them back together. I'm aware not everyone conducts business mediation this way, but I find I achieve much more negotiating with parties one on one."

Separate negotiations with each side work well because the typical business negotiation is about money. Jim sums up the typical business dispute: "It may masquerade in many different ways, and it may look as if there are many different issues, but most disputes come down to money. If you can figure out the right amount of money that should pass from one individual to another, it will come into line. The driving force is figuring out how much. That's more straightforward—not necessarily easier, but more straightforward. The problem with negotiating here is that $1 up for side A is $1 down for side B." Principled negotiators would refer to these as distributive negotiations.

Parties in these business disputes are typically not interested in preserving or establishing relationships. Jim sees them as interested in "racking up a disputed amount of money. That makes for difficult negotiations, but they're finite. You either reach your goal or you don't."

Jim's approach begins with the premise that both parties have come to this dispute far apart in the positions they're taking. One example is: "He owes me $50 million." versus "I don't owe him a cent." However, Jim also understands that underneath those initial positions they have responsible positions at which they'd be willing to do a deal. In his words, "If those more responsible positions overlap—for instance, in the scenario above, there might be overlap in the $20 to 30 million range—then it might be possible to conduct mediation as so many writers advise, as a facilitator. That is, make the parties comfortable, clarify the issues, carry proposals back and forth, and help the parties into that zone of agreement. *No* dispute that I've ever mediated was like that."

Fisher and Ury (1981) write about the advisability of getting behind the parties' original positions to more basic interests. In contrast, Jim notes, "In the disputes I see, when you get underneath those original positions and find out what the parties really want, interests are just other sums of money—more reasonable perhaps, but still just money. In our example, party A may have moved from $50 to $35 million, while B moves from 0 to $15 million. They have no intention of moving further. Interests don't range as widely in a business context as *Getting to Yes* would like. What I find is when I probe positions with each party separately, there is still a wide gap. So, you could facilitate 'til the cows come home and you wouldn't reach a deal. Both parties are still far apart, and they're willing to take their chances in the courts."

Jim concludes, "Therefore, in my view, the neutral has to be very activist and very judgmental. If the mediator isn't able to convince party A that he's not going to get $35 million and should be looking for a sale in the $20 million range, nothing's going to happen. And if the mediator isn't able to convince party B that paying $15 million isn't going to produce a deal, nothing's going to happen. The only way I know to convince them is for the mediator to pass judgment on the positions the parties have taken. And not only the positions they've taken publicly, but the positions they've taken privately with the mediator. The mediator becomes 'an agent of reality.' What you say is, 'Hey, you guys are in a dream world. Here's what a judge is going to do.' And you have to say this to both sides, because almost never are you going to get one side to move all the way to the other side's position."

The activist mediator challenging each side is bound to meet with resistance. Jim advises, "The more you play the agent of reality, the more each party looks at you as the enemy. So, you have to balance what you do that way with things that are appealing. To the party who's asking for $35 million, you say, 'Look, I think your argument on point No. 1 is flawed, and here's why. I'm not convinced myself, so how could I convince the other party? However, I think you've got a strong case on point No. 2, and if I understood that better, I'd be able to present that to the other party to get him to come up.' In effect, you're offering to become his agent on point No. 2. Then, at least the party who's asking $35 million understands your style—that you are balanced and that you will call them as you see them." The activist mediator judges the merits of each issue and communicates his judgments to each side privately, balancing his positive and negative opinions for each side.

Some ADR practitioners worry that the activist approach forces a settlement on parties. In Jim's view, "You're not imposing anything on the parties. You're not trying to persuade them to adopt some number that you think is the right or a fair one. I'm far away from fairness. I admire people who can find fairness. Who knows what is fair? It's like religion. Each party has a different concept, and it's very hard to relate something to fairness. I've never done a deal where each side didn't feel something was unfair against them."

Jim replaces the elusive standard of fairness with the more practical one of satisfaction. In his approach, "I'm striving always for *satisfaction*. When the parties are satisfied enough to do the deal and don't feel they've left too much on the table, I'm happy. That's enough for me. At least you can say the deal is not unfair. My goal is to help them figure out what is *feasible*. Where might these people find a zone of agreement? You must figure that out, because that's going to be your lodestar. You might revise your number as the mediation progresses, but that's the point you're trying to move people toward." The effective mediator judges where a feasible deal may be made; this will not necessarily be the deal he thinks is either right or fair, but where both parties can be sufficiently satisfied.

In the activist approach, both parties are negotiating with Jim. Because of the level of distrust between parties, it's very difficult for them to make offers to one another with any hope of success. It's too easy for them to take positions that they don't really believe in but that they think will counter the other side. He explains, "They know they can't fool me, and they don't have to. I try to move them in the direction of that feasible outcome." Therefore, Jim is not carrying offers back and forth between parties. He is actively negotiating with one to produce an offer more likely to be accepted by the other. Jim continues, "When it works, the two parties don't really know where the other party is until we finally say we have a deal. I'll tell them, 'We're getting close,' but I don't put numbers on the table. I don't speak in tangible terms; I keep it to myself. This method works for me, it might not work for everyone." At the end of each session, Jim schedules the next one and gives the parties "homework," which is typically background information on different issues.

Jim finds the toughest challenge in mediating business divorce, a term given to the dissolution of partnership. He explains, "It involves emotions stronger than those in a typical business dispute. The bitterness of a failed partnership is like the bitterness that follows a failed marriage. It's only when the partners are at each other's throats that they think of splitting up. Each side wants the mediator to hate the other. On top of the emotional tension, there are both deal issues and dispute issues, so you can't just resolve past disputes—you have to help them make a plan for going forward. I find mediating the business divorce very strenuous." Keeping the perception of neutrality is especially difficult for mediators in this setting. Occasionally, it's a family business and the partners are related; then, the emotional troubles are compounded. Lawyers on each side reflect the animosity of their client. Despite the challenges, Jim believes that these cases are resolved better in mediation than in the courts.

What happens when negotiation breaks down? The simple answer is that if it was about a future deal, the parties walk away to look for other opportunities; if it was about a dispute, the parties are probably going to arbitration or court. The more complex view of breakdown is that, in a difficult mediation, it happens every day. According to Jim, "Part of what the mediator has to do is a delicate balancing act to prevent breakdowns. On the one hand, you have to challenge, 'You guys are too far apart. You'll both have to move before we can get anything done.' You've got to tell them that—otherwise, no one's going to move. On the other hand, the mediator needs to reassure, 'You're not so far apart that you should give up.' I try to strike a balance between the positives and negatives to keep the parties engaged and moving."

Even with all the mediator's encouragement, Jim says there may come a time when "the arteries harden." Both parties are ready to walk out. Jim recalls one incident: "This happened to me recently. Although we'd made a lot of progress, there was still a gap. Both of them seemed to have gone as far as they were willing to go. The breakdown would have meant arbitration. The arbitration was scheduled, the arbitrators had been selected, the depositions were scheduled to start within a month. At this point, there's typically a lot of macho. Each side tries to convince the mediator that they're tougher than the other, saying, 'We don't need this deal anyway.' That's when you earn your wages as a mediator."

When negotiations are at the point of breakdown, there may still be approaches the mediator can use. Jim shares the one he used in the case described above: "When I had pushed each party as far as I could see pushing them, I took a step I don't always do, saying, 'You guys are a little apart here. You really should make a deal when you're this close, given how hard you've worked. The arbitration is just going to be a war and, if you each request, I would be prepared to suggest a compromise. If you both buy it, great. If not, the negotiation is over.' They each agreed, and I worked out a compromise somewhere between the two positions with reasons attached to it. Both sides accepted the compromise." Jim acknowledges that this approach isn't foolproof either, and that when one or both sides are determined to go to court, litigation will follow.

Contextual Differences

Jim contrasts negotiation in business mediations with the practice in other contexts. In the business context, the mediator is trying to appeal to people's rational self-interest, whereas in more personal situations, this may not always be possible. Jim offers an example: "Let's say I have the leverage in a certain negotiation with you. What I want is to get across my arguments on this point in a way that you will see your rational self-interest satisfied by my proposal. So, I have to explain, I have to offer rationale. If I am overbearing, that's a terrible approach, because you would get your back up and would lose sight of your own self-interest." This is related to the *Getting to Yes* pointer of separating the people from the problem. Jim agrees with Fisher and Ury (1981) on this point, assessing business disputes as follows: "While they generate a lot of heat, in the end, parties usually see their rational self-interest. You have to make it so clear that they would be crazy to resist. And you can't always tell them that directly. You put it to them in the end, saying, 'If the deal is good enough to do at $XXX, the question you have to answer is whether it's good enough to do at $XXX,500.' You ask the question straight, but the answer suggests itself."

Another feature of the business context is the lack of continuing relationships. Typically, these parties will not meet again. This aspect puts a premium on letting go of who did what and said what in the negotiations. Jim advises, "'Forget how you got here [to the deal]; just take what's on the table.' Another piece of advice is, 'If you don't close on this deal, how will you feel in the morning?' Both of those formulations usually lead parties to see their own self-interest." Another approach is to remind parties of the alternatives to successful mediation. This is similar to what Fisher and Ury (1981) call the BATNA (Best Alternative to a Negotiated Agreement), against which agreements should be measured.

Jim also reflects on how negotiation in the context of mediation differs from straight negotiation. In his view, "Parties negotiating through intermediaries such as mediators mustn't forget that they are still negotiating with the mediator. When you are one of the parties, you have to do two things.

First, you try to convince the mediator that you are right and the other side is wrong, using the merits of your arguments. Second, you must convince the mediator that unless he or she communicates to the other party that he or she sees the merits of your case, this will have no effect. You must give the mediator the factual evidence to show your adversary why he or she is persuaded by your argument. That's when the mediator acts as an agent of reality. The argument coming from the mediator is much more forceful in moving the other side than if it were made directly by you." Finally, Jim believes that if you have a proposal for the other side, the best chance of it being adopted is for the mediator to suggest it as the mediator's idea. If your mediator doesn't suggest changing the ownership of the proposal, Jim recommends that you ask him or her to do so.

Changes and Conflicts

Jim does not have a view of the field that is sufficiently broad to speculate about how business negotiations are changing. However, he notes that in their 2000 book, *Beyond Winning: Negotiating to Create Value in Deals and Disputes*, Bob Mnookin, Scott Peppet, and Andrew Tulumello bridge the Freund deal-making perspective with the Fisher and Ury (1981) model. Jim describes the *Getting to Yes* perspective as presupposing a world in which everything can be resolved by being creative, generating options, and getting behind positions to interests. In Jim's opinion, "In the business world, that is simply not the case. There are too many places where that doesn't work. Even if you went about negotiation that way, you don't find lots of creative options because the driving question is 'Who's going to return with the majority of the money?' Mnookin recognizes this tension. He looks for opportunities to create value. But he also recognizes that it's not only about how to enlarge the pie, but how to carve up the pie. This approach is more in tune with the real world."

Jim hopes that one trend in negotiating business matters is and will continue to be the inclusion of mediation clauses in agreements. Jim notes that you can't always get people to mediate when a dispute arises. Some people even feel that to suggest mediation is to admit weaknesses, which is not his view. With a clause in the agreement, people are obligated to attempt mediation before going on to more adversarial processes. In Jim's view, "That way, even though no one is obligated to agree, the mere process will cause parties to realize how cost effective it is relative to litigation. This should lead to more use of mediation in business disputes. Without such a clause, parties may never experience mediation."

The largest disagreement in the field of business disputes concerns the proper role of mediator. Jim reports, "A lot of people are appalled at the activist approach. Those who espouse the facilitative approach would never make a judgment about the merits of a dispute, much less generate proposals. I find this approach typical of academics. I respect them, but I don't handle cases where a facilitative approach would succeed. And I don't see the facilitative approach being practiced by guys in the trenches. When businesspeople come to mediation, they want that help [the activist approach]."

Another major disagreement is that many mediators follow the principled negotiation model. In Jim's opinion, "They are trying to create value and to enlarge the pie, which is terrific. I don't eschew that; if I see opportunities to create value by meshing interests, I'll pursue that. However, I think more focus has to be given to leverage, to where it's feasible to see an agreement, and how to move people there." In Jim's view, principled negotiation doesn't seem to be much involved in these three topics, which are vital to business negotiations. His disagreement is not with what's included in principled negotiation, but with what's missing from it.

Jim Freund's experience in business negotiation has shaped his understanding of what processes are successful. In the business context, money is both the position and the interest. Relationships between disputants are not likely to be continued. Parties are not able to deal directly with one another, nor do their attorneys care to share information. Out of his experience in this context, he has evolved an activist role for the business mediator, who separates the parties after the first session and negotiates with them, offering his opinion on the merits of each case. Eventually, he discovers the area where a deal can be made, constructs it, and sells them on it. Although this deal making is not consistent with processes of principled negotiation, he makes a strong case for its effectiveness in the business setting. Through his negotiations, mediations, writing, and teaching, Jim Freund informs and challenges those who would argue otherwise.

CHAPTER 4

NEGOTIATION PROCESSES

In addition to diagnosing these structural, strategic, psychological, and cultural processes, they [good negotiators] are able to craft strategies to overcome them by, for example, reframing the issues, building productive working relationships, setting up confidence building mechanisms, and achieving greater cultural understanding.

— Watkins, 1999, p. 253

For some people, negotiation involves opening with statements asking for more than they think they can get, providing as little information as possible, making concessions grudgingly, and eventually settling for the best deal that they can get. The process will include statements such as "I just have to have this much or I don't think I can make a deal," "This is my position and I don't have any intention of changing it," or "If you don't give me this, I'll make it rough on you." Unfortunately, as statements become demanding, resistance and distrust grow, and integrative solutions become harder to achieve. A great deal of negotiation research provides insight into the phases of negotiation and the kind of language that promotes the highest potential for success. This chapter looks at negotiation from the perspective of five phases (Figure 4.1).

Prenegotiation

Opening

Information
Sharing

Problem
Solving

Agreement

Figure 4.1   Negotiation Processes

PRENEGOTIATION •

The more complex the situation, the greater the number of parties, and the more contentious the negotiations, the more important prenegotiation becomes. Fisher and Ertel (1995) argue, "Lack of preparation is our most serious handicap . . . on average, we think that you should spend as much time preparing as you expect to spend in face-to-face negotiation" (p. 34). Investing time in preparation saves a great deal of time in later discussion.

Before negotiations begin, negotiators need to consider the consequences of failing to reach an agreement. Bazerman and Neale (1992) argue, "Remember the goal of negotiating is not to reach just any agreement, but to reach an agreement that is better for you than what you would get without one" (p. 68). The first step in negotiation is scanning alternatives, a task that normally involves research.

In addition, the first stage of negotiation involves an evaluation of the alternatives if the other side does not want to negotiate or suggests agreements that are worse than what you currently have. Examining your options is described as determining your BATNA (Best Alternative to a Negotiated Agreement). Fisher, Ury, and Patton (1993) explain that your BATNA is "the standard against which any proposed agreement should be measured" (p. 100) and that knowing your BATNA "enables you to determine what is a minimally acceptable agreement" (p. 106). For example, the buyer of a car will be in a stronger position during negotiation if he or she knows what the cost of the car would be at other dealers.

Roloff and Dailey (1987) found that negotiators who possessed BATNAs achieved higher outcomes. But Pinkley, Neale, and Bennett (1994) point out that not just any BATNA will do. The BATNA must be a high-quality, realistic alternative. In their studies, low-quality alternatives fared no better than having no alternatives in negotiation. In a follow-up study, Brett, Pinkley, and

Jacofsky (1996) found that BATNAs can be enhanced through two additional factors: clear goals and confidence about expectations and performance. These factors have additive properties that enhance negotiators' BATNAs and eventual outcomes. These studies all point to the importance for negotiators of creating high-quality alternatives if they want to improve their negotiated outcomes. BATNAs provide negotiators with a source of power because they enable negotiators to walk away from a negotiation if goals are not achieved.

A related task for negotiators involves assessment of alternatives of other parties if they do not reach agreement with you. If others can get a better deal elsewhere, your leverage significantly diminishes. Understanding the negotiating zone of all parties provides more informed discussion about potential options. In high-stakes negotiation, Nierenberg (1968) extends this principle even further: "It is essential to examine the opponent's past history, inquire into previous transactions he was connected with, and look into every business venture or deal he has consummated" (p. 49). Most of us lack the time or resources to do this much research, but the principle is still sound: Know as much as you can about the person with whom you are negotiating.

The well-prepared negotiator assesses and prioritizes interests prior to negotiation (see Figure 4.2). This will enable better evaluation of options as they are presented during negotiation. Bazerman and Neale (1992) explain, "Assessing this information before entering any important negotiation prepares you to analyze the two primary tasks of negotiation: integration, or the enlargement of the pie of available resources, and distribution, the claiming of the pie" (p. 71).

Prenegotiation is an especially important priority in multiparty negotiations. Let's look at the example of a negotiation concerning cleanup of a hazardous waste site; negotiations involved representatives from the U.S. Army, an environmental group, state and local governments, community leaders, and local neighbors. In dispute were issues of financing the cleanup, the level of cleanup, monitoring the cleanup, and the time expected for the cleanup. Negotiating the agenda publicly might have taken years because of different priorities for each of the issues. Prenegotiation involved assessing and prioritizing the issues. This list became the working agenda for the first meetings.

Prior to negotiations, determining common interests or common goals contributes to collaborative processes. Focusing on commonalties before differences significantly raises the potential for successful resolution of many conflicts. Cloke and Goldsmith (2000) explain,

> In recognizing that we have similar wants and desires, a bond begins to develop between us. We become more aware of the need to talk about our problems with one another, and we are able to collaborate on finding solutions. (p. 151)

Zartman (1989) suggests that prenegotiation should include several additional tasks: assessment of the level of commitment to negotiation;

My BATNA:

Their BATNA:

My Interests: What do I need?	My Options: What are my choices?
•	•
•	•
•	•

Their Interests: What do they need?	Their Options: What are their choices?
•	•
•	•
•	•

Common Interests:

Common Goals:

Figure 4.2   Prenegotiation Tasks: Assessment Phase

creation of expectations for reciprocity; transition in the nature of the relationship; agreement on definition of problem; and weighing the benefits, costs, and risks of negotiation. Prenegotiation provides an opportunity to determine how willing the other parties are to negotiate. We may ask questions such as the following:

- "How negotiable are you on this issue?"
- "Is there room for further discussion about the price?"
- "Are you open to considering alternatives for resolving this issue?"

Answers to these questions frame the context for discussions. If parties do not consider negotiation as a policy option, education may be a first step. If parties appear committed to distributive negotiation, the initial goal may be to transform elements of the context to be more collaborative.

In highly conflictual negotiations, prenegotiation can serve as a phase of discussion where negotiators might suggest norms of reciprocity. A negotiator might include in opening discussions, "I would hope that we both realize we'll need to give a little, make a few concessions along the way, if we're going to reach a settlement that benefits both of us." Beginning negotiations with an expectation that concessions will be repaid supports the commitment to negotiate. Zartman (1989) states, "A belief in reciprocity is the second most important element in beginning negotiations. . . . Prenegotiation is the time to convince the other party that concessions will be required, not buried and run away with" (p. 245). In family, neighborhood, or international negotiations, this principle might serve as a first step for overcoming initially rigid positions.

Prenegotiation can serve as a phase of transition from adversarial relationships to partnerships. This is when it may be important to create a temporary cease-fire and suspension of conflict activities. "Cease-fires and moratoriums are down payments on confidence; temporary, vulnerably provisional concessions" (Zartman, 1989, p. 249).

For example, two department chairs at a university had a history of noncooperation. Potential agreements rested on developing greater cooperation. Before any discussions began, the Director of Faculty, one of the chairs, and a faculty member from that chair's department paid a visit to the chair of the other department. The discussion began with the second chair listing past wrongs. The three just listened and validated feelings. After the chair completed the list, the Director offered, "I know that the ways things were done in the past was not satisfactory to you and your faculty. These new faculty would like to do things differently. Are you willing to give them a chance?" The four discussed only a small amount of business at this first meeting. The goal was to alter the nature of the relationship for future discussions. In the interview with Linda Putnam presented in Chapter 5, Putnam points out that negotiation provides parties with the opportunity to build a new understanding of their relationship and reframe issues where there may have been problems.

For complex negotiations, agreement on a definition of the problem and assessment of alternatives may be important tasks in prenegotiation. For some problems, open discussion may not be able to address the issue sufficiently. For example, in meetings in one organization, one employee brought up problems that consumed a great deal of the department manager's and staff's time. After months of group negotiations that resolved few of the problems, it became apparent that the problems all centered on behaviors of the employee raising the issues. The manager constructed a memo detailing changes in behavior that he wanted from the employee. The conflict ceased immediately. The staff had been dealing with the wrong problem. Zartman (1989) summarizes,

> Any conflict can be defined in several ways, some of them more susceptible to resolution than others. . . . There are some which imply greater difficulties, complex ramifications, and more cost than others, and successful prenegotiation works to eliminate these, leaving only a few

definitions and alternatives in place to deal with in depth in the formal negotiation. (p. 247)

Negotiators in this early phase may look at the problem from many perspectives and invent frames of understanding so that parties can see benefits of discussion more clearly. How problems are framed influences risk-taking behavior, choices of preferences, and negotiating behavior (Quattrone & Tversky, 1988; Tversky & Kahneman, 1981). The framing effect suggests that negotiators, tactically, will produce more concessions and raise the potential for successful settlement through exploration and testing of different ways to describe the challenges and barriers that confront parties. Framing the issues in a positive tone, as an opportunity, will produce more beneficial results. Rackham (1985) reported in his study that skilled negotiators emphasized common ground (framing similarities as opposed to differences) in about 38% of their communication compared with only 11% used by average negotiators.

Assessing prior to negotiation the benefits of an agreement as well as the risks, costs of concessions, and costs of failure is an important task of prenegotiation. A clear evaluation of costs improves assessment of alternatives and may influence flexibility during discussions. For example, in the Israeli-Palestinian negotiation, which culminated in the 1993 Oslo agreement, Israelis wanted recognition as a sovereign nation and security for their borders. In an agreement for peace, Israel needed to weigh the cost of conceding land to the Palestinians, the location of the land, and the cost of the concession. Each side needed to evaluate both the short-term and long-term costs of concessions.

In international contexts where a great deal is at stake, prenegotiation provides a valuable opportunity for reducing uncertainty about the negotiation process or about outcomes. Stein (1989) explains that prenegotiation enables leaders to determine "who will come, what their roles will be, how the table will be structured, and what will be on and off the agenda" (p. 429). Some of these same issues exist in business and community negotiations as well. Reducing uncertainties may lower perceptions of risk and promote greater sharing of information. Determining the agenda prior to negotiation provides the opportunity for parties to assess the value of discussions and potential outcomes.

OPENING ●

Negotiation begins with an introduction of parties and an explanation of the role they will play in the negotiations. The more formal, complex, or large the negotiations, the more important these initial introductions are. When parties use representatives to negotiate for them, representatives often need to establish their authority to make agreements for their clients. Straus (1993) recommends that in negotiations we include "stakeholders who have the power to make decisions, are responsible for implementing them, are affected by them, and have the power to block them" (p. 35). If authority is not established, a negotiation may be sabotaged later by clients who reject an agreement forged by their representatives. A great deal of time and effort is wasted.

After introductions, one of the parties, using neutral terms, reviews the purpose for the negotiations. This is followed by ground rules—that is, norms for behaviors that will guide the discussions. The greater the number of parties involved or the more volatile the issue, the greater the importance of ground rules. Carpenter and Kennedy (1988) explain,

> People in a conflict need explicit guidelines when they are embarking on something as unfamiliar as problem solving with others with whom they are unfamiliar or whom they consider to be adversaries. . . . Ground rules explicitly spell out behavior and procedures that people normally consider to be fair but sometimes abandon in carrying on a fight. (p. 118)

A few of the ground rules common to negotiations are as follows:

- Listen to understand before judging.
- Listen without interrupting.
- Demonstrate respect for others.
- Focus on one problem at a time.
- Only one person speaks at a time.

Multiparty disputes involve additional factors, such as group dynamics, coalitions and their power, scheduling problems, hidden agendas, and multiple priorities, interests, and goals. Carpenter and Kennedy (1988) propose ground rules for people involved in these more complex, multiparty negotiations:

- Personal attacks will not be tolerated.
- The motivations and intentions of participants will not be impugned.
- Commitments will not be made lightly and will be kept.
- Delay will not be employed as a tactic.
- Disagreements will be regarded as problems to be solved rather than to be won.
- Before a decision is requested on any matter, sufficient time will be provided for participants to seek advice from constituents, counsel, or experts.
- Participants will provide pertinent information. (p. 123)

In the case of labor union-management contract negotiations, discussions involve both intragroup and intergroup dynamics and both contract and relational interests. In this context, teams of people negotiate with each other. Cairns (1996) suggests the following ground rules:

- The union is given equal status with management at the negotiating meeting.
- The place and time of the meetings are mutually agreeable.
- The frequency of meetings suits the purposes of both parties.
- The length of meetings is known beforehand and is mutually acceptable.
- There are facilities for the union side to meet separately.
- The size and composition of negotiating teams are known and acceptable. (p. 61)

Whether the ground rules are written or oral, formal or informal, parties should be reminded when they violate them. In multiparty negotiations, a representative may be asked to leave if violations occur repeatedly. Ground rules protect the processes and attempt to prevent manipulation or sabotage of constructive discussions.

Following discussion of ground rules, parties will establish an agenda for the discussion. Parties will agree to an order for discussion, such as:

1. Identify problems.

2. Propose options for resolving problems.

3. Evaluate the options.

4. Select the best one.

5. Agree on how to implement the solution.

The agenda may be as simple as a few statements about how to proceed or be as complex as a printed list of issues and procedures. Figure 4.3 summarizes the requirements for an opening.

Information sharing and problem solving are the very essence of constructive negotiation. The willingness of parties to reveal relevant information and engage in discussion about creative options has a direct bearing on the quality and duration of agreements. Willingness to listen to the perspectives of others, to temporarily suspend personal bias to achieve greater understanding, and to negotiate the interpretation of information will be fundamental in these processes. Shell (1999) points out that the initial sharing of information tests "our counterpart's commitment to the norms of reciprocity" (p. 133) for establishing a working relationship and openness to joint gains.

INFORMATION SHARING ●

Following agreement about ground rules and a statement about the purpose of the negotiation, parties begin the first stage of formal negotiations. In this

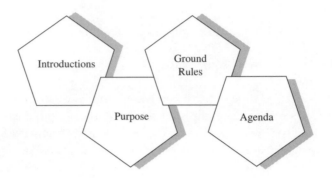

Figure 4.3   Requirements of Opening

phase, participants explain their perception of the problem, identify specific issues that need to be addressed, and list interests that need to be satisfied for a satisfactory agreement. The more open negotiators can be in the sharing of information, the greater the possibilities for solving underlying issues and creatively addressing needs.

Rackham (1985) compared the behaviors of successful negotiators with average negotiators. He found that the skilled negotiators asked more questions, tested for understanding more often, and summarized more of what they heard than average negotiators (see Table 4.1).

During these early statements, there is a tendency for parties to state positions before identifying interests and issues. For example, in a staff dispute, one of the managers said, "This company doesn't care about people. I really oppose the way they're doing things." One of the vice presidents responded, "All our managers do is whine. I really don't like the way they make us the problem for their ineffectiveness." The two sides polarized fast. Craver (1993) recommends that negotiators look behind the opening statements to the deeper interests if the other party begins with a position:

> Many negotiators make the mistake of focusing entirely on the opponent's stated position. They assume that such statements accurately reflect the desires of the other side. . . . It helps to go behind stated positions to try to ascertain the underlying needs and interests. (p. 298)

Both the manager and vice president might have prevented the polarization by asking for specific issues or unmet needs. During opening statements, negotiators need to share information that identifies specific interests, concerns, and needs; they should not use the opportunity to create further escalation of differences.

A second tendency is for parties to move too quickly to proposing and evaluating options before sufficient information has been shared to understand the problem. Craver (1993) explains that some negotiators "are anxiety-prone, risk-averse advocates who want to diminish the tension associated

Table 4.1   Frequency of Behaviors (as Percentage of All Behavior)

Behavior	Skilled Negotiators	Average Negotiators
Asked questions	21.3%	9.6%
Tested understanding	9.7%	4.1%
Summarized	7.5%	4.2%
Shared feelings	12.1%	7.8%
Totals	50.6%	25.7%

Based on information from Rackham (1985).

with the uncertainty inherent in the negotiation process" (p. 297). A clue that option generation is occurring too quickly is when one of the parties responds, "Yes, but . . ." to each of the suggestions and provides reasons why proposed solutions cannot be carried out. Devoting more time to problem definition and information gathering provides higher-quality solutions.

Evaluating interests and issues during negotiation can be difficult. For example, a manager negotiating a special interest flex time with one employee might find that the solution creates a need to negotiate special interests with other employees. A wife who wants to further her career, an important interest for her, may create a power issue with her husband when she finds that a promotion means a move to another state. Lax and Sebenius (1991b) point out that interests can go beyond the obvious and tangible, be difficult to evaluate, and may change during the life of a negotiation: "In short, interests include anything that the negotiator cares about, any concerns that are evoked by the issues discussed" (p. 164). Negotiation involves sharing information that may change in importance during negotiations and defy categorization. The wife's need for autonomy and success will be difficult to balance against financial, home, and marriage factors.

In business negotiations, although we focus on price, price is rarely the only element that matters. If you make price the dominant factor, the negotiation quickly becomes distributive as parties attempt to divide the fixed pie. As negotiators expand discussions to include other factors, packages become easier to create that will satisfy the breadth of mutual interests. In addition, Harinck, Carsten, DeDreu, and Van Vianen (2000) argue that "negotiators reach higher joint outcomes when they make offers that concern multiple items simultaneously than when they make offers that consider items one by one" (p. 342).

Isenhart used multiple items to reduce fixed-pie orientations in a university negotiation. The discussion involved large-scale curriculum revisions that involved all of the school's departments. The discussion began with opening statements in which each department explained why its work was the most central to the mission of the university, the most likely to recruit qualified students, and the most attractive for alumni donors. Lively debate among the faculty raged on for many months without making any appreciable progress toward the curriculum revisions. The breakthrough came when the groups began talking about programs that cut across all departments. Dealing with multiple issues and resources, faculty could see more opportunities for tradeoffs and ways that the departments could complement each other.

The goal of the information-sharing phase is to learn as much as possible about preferences and goals. This goal might be sidetracked when parties overstate their interests in initial statements. Many negotiators use overstatement as a tactic that they hope will make later requests, although still strong, sound reasonable. Dawson (1999) recommends this as a useful negotiating tactic: "You might just get it. It gives you negotiating room. It raises the perceived value of what you're offering" (p. 17). In international negotiation, overstatement of interest or extreme initial demands regularly occurs in negotiations involving representatives from countries such as China, Korea, Japan, Israel, or Russia. Copeland and Griggs (1993) explain that overstatement occurs because negotiators expect to back down as the negotiations proceed. Because much of negotiation involves reciprocal moves of collaboration or competitiveness, overstatements and extreme demands may promote destructive cycles of negative escalation of the conflict.

Understanding that overstatement of need might be a negotiating gambit, we might counter the tactic with requests for more explanation and support for the statements. We might go further by asking for examples of interests to deepen understanding. Freund (1993) argues that negotiators who begin with inflexible, overstated initial positions are unlikely to be believed: "They're stuck with the baggage of the trade—the perception, reinforced in countless other deals, that some movement will occur" (p. 113). Unrealistic initial statements need not create despair. They only mean more work to create collaborative problem solving.

Frequently, negotiations involve many interests of varying levels of importance. Clear priorities and weighting of the interests provide the building blocks for a focused agenda or for later tradeoffs. For example, Spangle led a multiparty negotiation involving 50 teachers. The group presented 30 concerns and interests, which he listed on a large chalkboard that stood before the group. With the teachers' help, he separated the list into five categories based on similar themes. Next, he asked the teachers to prioritize the five categories in order of importance. About 80% of the group favored one of the categories. With the group's agreement, he took this favored category and asked the teachers to prioritize the six issues within that topic area. This time, about 90% of the group favored two of the factors. The group agreed to begin discussion on these two items. After they completed these discussions, they finished the category and moved on to the category that was second in priority. Interests of value were traded as participants moved from one category to the next.

An example of trading issues of value occurred between Bid4Vacations.com and Trip.com, separate online travel companies. Bid 4Vacations, with 2 million customers a year, specializes in vacation packages; Trip.com, with 5 million customers a year, caters to business travelers.

Because of high competition in the travel industry, both firms lacked referrals and resources. They negotiated an agreement that supports each other's work. For referral fees, Bid4Vacations will refer any callers who ask about business trips to Trip.com, and Trip.com will refer any inquiries about vacations to Bid4Vacations. In addition, Bid4Vacations will share its relationships with leisure suppliers, and Trip.com will share its relationships with airline and hotel companies. For both companies, the deal lowers the costs associated with attracting new customers and provides support services that both companies need.

Remaining interest-focused can be a challenge when other negotiators choose forcing, demanding, and competitiveness as negotiation strategies. In a study of 25 negotiators that looked at the choice of negotiation approaches, Lytle, Brett, and Shapiro (1999) found that negotiators engage in a great deal of reciprocation—that is, they respond in like manner to the approach initiated by their opponent. Specifically, Lytle et al. found that negotiators reciprocated communication to the following degrees:

- Interests: 42%
- Proposals for settlement: 43%
- General facts about the situation: 55%
- Rights: 22%
- Power: 27%

The evidence suggests that negotiators may frequently trigger integrative or distributive responses in their opponents. Negotiators will match their messages to the kind they are receiving. When negotiators make statements involving rights or power, they significantly raise the probability that their opponents will respond in kind, creating a negative conflict spiral. Focusing on interests creates a positive spiral in which you demonstrate commitment to identifying what the other party needs and to helping the other party understand what you need.

Of equal concern is how to respond when others begin with communication involving demands, rights, or power. Lytle et al. (1999) recommend staying interest-focused and resisting reciprocation with rights or power messages. They found that 77% of the time, when negotiators did not reciprocate in kind, creators of the forcing and rights messages refocused their messages in more collaborative directions. When confronted with forcing messages, negotiators need to re-emphasize their commitment to focusing on interests and problem solving. Figure 4.4 lists the requirements of the information-sharing phase.

PROBLEM SOLVING •

After interests, concerns, and needs have been presented and prioritized, the parties move to a problem-solving phase. In this phase, negotiators generate

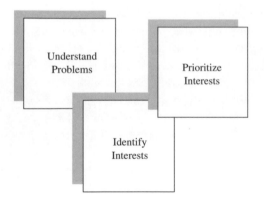

Figure 4.4   Requirements of Information Sharing

ideas, suggestions, options, or courses of action that might resolve the problems presented. Resistance occurs because negotiators find it difficult to break out of old patterns of thinking. Face saving, investment in previous courses of action, and fear of change add additional barriers. Context will significantly influence parties' willingness to engage in problem solving. Strutton, Pelton, and Lumpkin (1993) found that people will choose problem solving over distributive approaches when parties perceive the psychological climate to be fair and open to innovation and where success will be recognized.

Agreeing on a no-criticism rule during idea generation reduces some of the resistance to thinking in new and different ways. Asking questions that enable parties to think outside the box sometimes helps, such as "Is there anything we haven't considered that might help us here?" or "In an ideal world, what could we do about this?" Some negotiators use *supposals*: "Suppose we tried this . . . .". Because supposals lack commitment to courses of action, parties feel more willing to consider new ideas.

Much of the task of problem solving involves reducing the need for parties to rigidly defend positions or engage in attack-your-solutions and defend-mine communication cycles. A free exchange of ideas, where inventing is separating from deciding, provides a forum for looking at options that would not have otherwise been considered. Listening to ideas does not mean agreement. Evaluation of the ideas will occur later, after negotiators have brought all possibilities to the surface. In some cases, such as in multiparty disputes, to reduce potential conflict, option-generating sessions might be most effective if done apart from the formal negotiations. In a noncommittal setting, parties can propose ideas and options without the need to defend the merits of what they suggest.

Generation and use of options to resolve problems can take one of two forms. In the first, negotiators generate options for *each* of the problems (one issue: many options). Parties evaluate each of the possible solutions based on its ability to resolve the dispute or satisfy interests. This is the most familiar method for looking at options as solutions to problems. The second form involves creation of a comprehensive package in which parties use their differences in expectations to create tradeoffs (many issues: many options). Some issues are resolved to greater satisfaction than others, but overall the agreement is satisfactory. Social-psychological research on negotiation processes consistently demonstrates that negotiators produce higher-quality agreements when they negotiate multiple issues as a package rather than sequentially (Froman & Cohen, 1970; Mannix, Thompson, & Bazerman, 1989). According to Rubin, Pruitt, and Kim (1994), "Such holistic negotiating allows the principals to explore all types of concession exchange and come up with wiser solutions" (p. 209).

Many integrative techniques exist for getting the most potential from options and tradeoffs. When priorities differ on issues, negotiators may engage in *logrolling*. This practice involves parties making concessions on issues of lower priority to themselves but of higher priority to others. Each party gets what it values most. For example, employees may forgo a pay raise in exchange for increases in health-coverage benefits. Employees may agree to management needs for workers on Saturdays in exchange for less evening and overtime work during the week. Box 4.1 provides an example of developers and conservationists making concessions of lower-valued interests for interests of higher value.

The integrative technique called *linkage* occurs when parties expand the scope of negotiation by linking agreements of the current discussions to other negotiations between the parties. Linkage occurred in 1980 when the United States' representatives linked discussions about the release of American hostages to negotiations about unfreezing Iranian assets in the United States. Former U.S. Secretary of State James Baker (1995) identifies this potential in his assessment of past international negotiations:

> How you worked the other side in developing the solution to the first problem had ramifications far beyond the single issue. Indeed its resolution could set not just the logical precedents for subsequent issues, but the very tone of the relationship between negotiators. (p. 134)

Spangle facilitated negotiations for middle-school teachers and administrators that involved linkage. Teachers coupled negotiations about pay raises and days off to negotiations about attendance at mandatory faculty retreats during the summer and release time for implementing state-mandated curriculum revisions. On the other hand, during the summer and fall of 2000, United Airlines fought linkage in the separate negotiations it had with airline pilots, flight attendants, airline mechanics, and baggage-system workers. It was to United's advantage to negotiate separate contracts.

Negotiators engage in *bridging* when both parties back off on their original demands in favor of new options that satisfy their underlying interests. Neale and Bazerman (1991) explain that bridging encourages parties to escape their existing definitions of a conflict and engage in new integrative

Box 4.1

TRADING RESOURCES FOR COOPERATION

In the late 1980s, the Killington and Pico Ski Resorts in central Vermont ran into financial difficulties. To solve the problem, the two resorts agreed to merge operations. The merger required the building of new ski lifts and trails between the two resorts. Because the development involved Appalachian Trail land, the developers needed to get a permit from the National Park Service (NPS).

If the developers adopted an unfriendly stance toward environmental concerns, they stood little hope of getting the NPS permit. If conservation groups adopted an antidevelopment position, the ski resorts would close down. To best serve regional interests, the two groups needed to look beneath their respective positions to underlying interests.

The anti-development groups expressed concern about the potential impacts on the Appalachian Trail, water use, and protection of black bears. The developers wanted permit approval so that they could begin construction by July 1991, or they would end merger discussions.

For the first meeting, 33 people representing many constituencies came together. According to NPS policy, if any party objected to granting a permit, the process would be delayed well beyond the July approval required by developers. Low trust characterized the meetings but, in the end, the parties achieved a settlement. The developers would donate nearby land known as Parker's Gore in exchange for cooperation in the permit process. A subcommittee composed of community members and planning officials would work on a design for the new trails and for an alternate route for portions of the Appalachian Trail through this region. To the land donation, environmentalists attached the provision that the land would be set aside to be forever wild.

The July deadline significantly pressured the representatives to negotiate a settlement. Do you think the deadline creates an unfair burden on making decisions? What impact might the deadline have had on their behaviors during discussions?

formulations that open the door to solutions. For example, a young couple was looking for a new home. The wife wanted to live downtown, where she could have activity and close neighbors. The husband wanted to live in the suburbs, which he viewed as an oasis from his demanding job. They agreed on a townhouse in a complex with a recreation center, pool, and golf course, located 20 minutes from downtown. Neither party achieved the solution he or she had envisioned, but both achieved satisfaction of their underlying interests.

Negotiators use a *cost-cutting* technique when one party achieves its interests, but at reduced cost to the other. High joint benefits occur not because one side or the other wins, but because both sides feel good about the settlement. For example, a consumer pays $150 for a car tune-up at a repair shop. Later, the consumer returns to complain, "The tune-up did nothing for my car's performance. I want my money back." It is not the policy of this shop owner to refund money. The owner may engage in cost cutting if he suggests something like, "It's not our policy to grant refunds, but I will give you five free oil changes during the next 3 years to compensate you for your dissatisfaction." The joint gains of continuing relationship and business outweigh the minimal concession of inexpensive oil changes.

Because parties approach negotiation with different expectations for time and risk, expectations can serve as a basis for tradeoffs. The ski resort case study discussed earlier illustrates the importance of time as an interest in negotiations. The principle of trading higher returns for time and risk occurs every time people buy new homes. Buyers must decide whether to purchase using a 3-, 5-, 15-, or 30-year loan. The bank is more than willing to negotiate longer terms of repayment, but for the higher risk, they trade higher interest rates. With a longer-term loan, the bank protects itself against the risk of higher interest rates 10 years from now, and the buyer lowers the risk of not being able to make a payment.

An example of the principle of settlements built on differing expectations can be seen in the Law of the Sea Negotiations. Northern nations, which possessed the technology to mine the ocean, were deadlocked with southern nations, which wanted a significant share of the profits from mining the ocean's resources. The North argued that the high initial investment limited the amount of profit for many years. The South believed that the profits would more than pay for investments. In the settlement, the representatives agreed that the South would receive a large percentage of the profits in excess of an agreed-upon level of production and costs in exchange for receiving a smaller percentage if production and costs fell below specified levels.

When trust is an issue, negotiators may create options that use time to sequence segments of the agreement to protect all parties. For example, let's say we agree to option 1 for the next year. If both parties meet their obligations, we agree that at that point, option 2 will begin. At the end of an additional segment of time, if obligations continue to be met on the first two options, option 3 will begin. Sequencing options can protect parties who have low trust that their opponents will fulfill their responsibilities. Figure 4.5 summarizes the phases of problem solving.

Concessions may serve as low-cost tradeoffs, motivators, or stalemate breakers during negotiation. Some form of concession, even a small one, demonstrates commitment to settlement. A concession communicates, "I'm

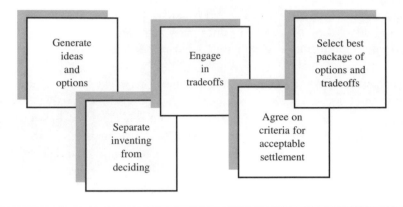

Figure 4.5   Phases of Problem Solving

willing to give a little; now, how about you?" For example, a manager sent a written warning to an employee. The employee, angered by the move, resisted cooperation until an intervention by a human resource professional. The human resources director said to the manager, "The employee is willing to abide by all of the provisions of the memo and agrees largely to the charges; but she doesn't want to be described as a non-team player. Would you be willing to make a concession and delete that phrase from the memo?" The manager agreed to delete the phrase in an effort to resolve the problem.

Concessions can create value where none had existed. People who have been in conflict for many years may find a great deal of appeal in the offer, "I'm willing to cease hostility as a first step." In one family, two brothers had feuded for more than two decades. When one of the brothers offered, "I'm willing to stop my belligerent comments to get us past our block," an opportunity opened for new possibilities. The concession was not an apology, nor did it admit wrong, but it served as an important commodity to be traded for relationship.

In many contexts, concessions possess high symbolic value. For example, during the 1960s, Leonid Brezhnev accepted limitations on the Soviet Union's nuclear arsenal in exchange for recognition by the United States as a coequal superpower. During the 1970s, Israel returned oil-rich land in the Sinai Peninsula to Egypt as a concession toward a peace treaty. Concessions should be accompanied by a statement of the concession's purpose and value in the negotiations, such as, "I'm giving in on this point because I want to move this deal along. Is there some way you can give a little on this as well?" Lebow (1996) explains,

> One way to foster accommodation is to find a concession that is highly valued by one side but relatively cost free for the other side to make. . . . The cost of making these depends on the bargainer's understanding of the substantive and symbolic value of what is at stake. (p. 69)

Concessions made without explanation or expectation of reciprocity may become risky, high-cost gambits.

Based on an analysis of the events of the brief 1982 Falklands/Malvinas War between Argentina and Great Britain, Mitchell (1998) reached the following insights about the use of conciliatory gestures or concessions in highly conflictual negotiations:

- The greater the change from established patterns of behavior represented by an action, the more likely the action will be perceived as a genuine concession.
- The fewer the benefits conferred on the initiator and greater the benefits for the target, the more the concessions are likely to be perceived as genuine.
- The less an action appears to result from one party's demands or coercion, the more likely the action will be perceived as conciliatory.
- Conscious, voluntary and deliberate actions that take the form of refraining from harmful behavior are more highly regarded as conciliatory gestures.
- An action that is precedent breaking and that clearly confers benefits on its target has higher probability of being perceived as genuine. (pp. 418-424)

In summary, effective, well-regarded concessions will be those conciliatory gestures that appear to be voluntary, demonstrate a shift in direction, and involve benefits valued by the target of the concessions.

Selection of the best option or synthesis of options must be based on criteria that are relevant and agreed upon by negotiators. Criteria involve many factors, such as industry or community standards, precedent, market value, price, ease or cost of implementation, or value to relationship. The criteria will very much depend on context and need. In some negotiations—such as those involving families, neighbors, and unions—objective standards become difficult to assess because either no standards exist or they're in a constant state of change. In any case, negotiations involve clearer choices when standards are available. Fisher, Ury, and Patton (1991) make the following recommendations about the use of criteria for evaluating options:

- Reason and be open to reason as to which standards are most appropriate and how they should be applied.
- Focus on objective criteria firmly but flexibly.
- Never yield to pressures, only to principle. (p. 88)

At some point during the problem-solving phase, the parties will invariably begin making offers. Unrealistic offers will damage progress. On quantifiable issues, Freund (1993) recommends that negotiators make "an opening offer that's not less that 10 percent nor more than one third away from the client's realistic expectation" (p. 119). He expresses a preference for 15% to 25% above expectations. Dawson (1999) agrees, supported by his assessment that "another reason for asking for more than you expect to get will be obvious if you're a positive thinker. You might just get it" (p. 15). An initial offer should be accompanied by rationale for the offer and an explanation of how the offer solves the problem equitably for all parties. Where possible, the offer should be based on mutually acceptable standards and include tradeoffs of both tangible and intangible benefits. The more an offer can maximize joint gains for all parties, the higher quality the agreement.

Assigning value to interests so that they can be used in tradeoffs is rarely done with quantitative precision. It may be easy to assign a number to the cost of a car loan or to health benefits in a job offer, but intangibles such as quality, job security, reputation, continuing relationship, or anxiety level are difficult to measure. In some negotiations, the intangibles may be worth more than price or profit. Box 4.2 illustrates a case where intangibles held greater value than money and where the party made a major concession to achieve a goal.

● AGREEMENT

As is the case with the other phases, the manner in which parties move to agreement will be context dependent. Some parties move slowly and grudgingly, based on a history of distrust and changing relationships. Other parties move methodically through agreed-upon processes. Here are a few of the strategies that we see from parties as they move to agreement:

1. *Incremental convergence.* Parties make gradual concessions and engage in tradeoffs until they reach an acceptable agreement (Walton and McKersie, 1965). Based on an acceptable process, parties engage in problem solving, addressing of issues, and mutual gain.

2. *Leap to agreement.* Parties move slowly, offering few concessions and, as a deadline approaches, leap to a packaged settlement (Zartman and Berman, 1982). We defend our interests as much as possible while conceding as little as possible to the interests of others. Car buying, sports contracts, and labor negotiations frequently demonstrate this kind of strategy.

3. *Development of agreements in principle.* Parties engage in discussion, eventually reaching a conceptual agreement in principle and then, based on this agreement, look for specific incremental agreements (Zartman and Berman, 1982). We agree first that something needs to be done, and then we work on specifics. Agreements in principle are usually the first stage of child-custody discussions, family disputes, and departmental staff negotiations.

Box 4.2

THE COST OF AN INHERITANCE

John died at the age of 96 in a small Midwest town. He named his granddaughter Sara as the sole beneficiary in his will, because she was his closest living relative. Sara lived 500 miles away in a large city. She would visit him for a few days once a year during her vacations.

During the last 5 years, two of Sara's cousins, who lived in the small town and whom Sara didn't like, cared for John. They visited his home, cleaned it occasionally, took him on outings downtown or to the doctor, and remembered him during holidays.

After lawyer's fees, the will left about $200,000 to Sara. She was delighted until it was contested by the two cousins. They believed that the fact that they cared for her grandfather warranted about $50,000 each from the will. Sara said, "No. You cared for him only because of his money." They responded, "We did more than you did. You rarely visited him and were never there when he needed someone."

The case was filed with the district court. Sara had a choice: She could take the $100,000 and not have to face any further proceedings, or she could fight her cousins in court. Because she disliked them and believed they cared for John only because of his money, the principle of beating them held great appeal. But going to court meant years of anxiety and travel back to the small town, which held less appeal. Even if she won, a significant share of the $200,000 would be lost in lawyer and travel costs. How much is being right worth? She decided that a life free of the anxiety was more important to her than the gain she could achieve by fighting.

Sara gave in. Was there another negotiation she could have engaged in to better her gain in this situation? What factors are more important to you than money?

4. *Procedural agreement.* Parties who have difficulty agreeing on resolution of specific substantive issues may first pursue agreement in decision-making processes (that is, they agree on how to handle this type of dispute) before they turn to discussions about substantive issues (Fisher & Ury, 1978). International negotiations and human resource issues frequently begin with this level of agreement.

Shell (1999) recommends, "Don't be satisfied with an agreement, get a commitment" (p. 195). A manager may get an agreement from a staff member to perform at a certain level, but the agreement won't be worth much unless the employee demonstrates commitment to the agreement. A father may reach agreement with his teenager to be home by midnight, but if the teen fails to demonstrate commitment to the agreement, the problems will continue. Many agreements, such as those contained in contracts, environmental and labor agreements, and court-related negotiations, include provisions for penalties in the event that commitment does not follow agreement. Some agreements include stipulations that an outside party will monitor compliance to performance standards. Others include performance bonds (money set aside that is forfeited by parties that fail to comply with the agreement).

Formal negotiations frequently end with an agreement drafted by the parties who participated in the discussions. Parties construct drafts of agreements in one of three ways:

1. *Single text procedures.* One of the sides or a small group of participants with representatives from all parties prepares a written document that will be presented to the full group (Fisher & Ury, 1978; Raiffa, 1982). Participants are asked to edit and revise the working draft until all parties express satisfaction with its content.

2. *Two text procedures.* Each of the two parties constructs its own version of the agreement. The two versions are brought together and integrated. This format would become extremely complicated in multiparty negotiations.

3. *Neutral write-up.* A draft of agreement is prepared by a third-party neutral who will circulate a document among the parties for revisions.

Whether agreements are informal or formal, verbal or written, they should include a summary of understandings that include the following elements:

- Expectations of each party (what and who)
- Implementation of agreement (how)
- Timing of implementation (when)
- Consequences for failing to abide by agreement
- Provisions for further discussions if agreement needs revisions

Over the length of a negotiation, negotiators go through a great deal of change, especially if the negotiation occurs over several months. Parties undergo changes in expectations, reassessment of interests, and shifting of goals. They may even forget provisions that they agreed to earlier. The first step of the agreement phase involves summarizing with precision each point of the proposed agreement. The danger, of course, is that someone will say, "I didn't agree to that." But better to find out now than during implementation.

Bingham (1986) identifies four factors that affect the likelihood of success in reaching agreement in multiparty disputes. Many of these factors apply equally well to two-party negotiations:

1. Initial assessment determines if negotiation is the best course of action for the dispute and if parties are committed to a mutual gains solution, are aware of expectations, and are willing to abide by ground rules for discussions.

2. Parties must have an incentive to negotiate. The gains for working together must outweigh other courses of action (recall Lax and Sebenius's (1991a) definition of negotiation in Chapter 1).

3. The way parties conduct negotiations influences the likelihood of success. Interest-based negotiations stand a better chance of satisfactory settlements than positional or distributive negotiations.

4. Involving in the negotiation the parties with decision-making authority to implement the agreement raises the likelihood of settlement.

Success—which results from perceptions about negotiations, some spoken and some unspoken, some relational and some substantive—may be elusive. Often, success means that both sides achieve their interests and improve their relationship. When the issue is conflict, success may involve learning how to channel conflict constructively and the ability to discuss what is needed or not working in order to prevent the development of future conflict. In some cases, no settlement may be the best course of action. This option occurs when costs outweigh benefits, if a BATNA is better than a negotiated settlement, if total victory is the goal and could be better achieved in court, or if blocking settlement serves a longer-term strategic plan. Figure 4.6 lists the phases of agreement.

SUMMARY ●

Negotiation is more than a set of techniques that someone uses in communication to another to achieve personal gain. It is more than stating an initial offer, grudgingly making concessions, and then turning to compromise to settle differences. Negotiation is a way of life, an attitude, and a perspective about handling problems in a principled manner.

Negotiations begin with careful planning. The more you can know about context, the interests and constraints of others, your own BATNA, and the negotiating style of your opponent, the greater your potential for success. Know *what* you are negotiating. Is the need to fix a dysfunctional process? Is the need to change the way someone wants to relate to you? Or does

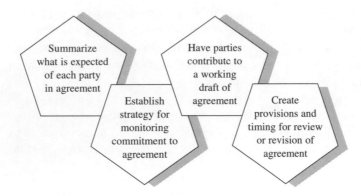

Figure 4.6   Phases of Agreement

someone need the resources that you have to give? Addressing the right problem saves a great deal of frustration. In addition, because norms and expectations differ, an understanding of the negotiating style that is effective in a given context will be necessary preparation.

Successful negotiation begins with effective prenegotiation. Information about the value of interests, the needs of opponents, and alternatives if discussions fail strengthens a negotiator's power. To negotiate for a home or car without knowing the market value of each is a high-risk strategy. When it looks as if opponents are engaging in distributive tactics, talk about the norms expected for the discussions or the risks if negotiations break down.

Prenegotiation serves many purposes, including assessing the willingness of others to engage in problem-solving discussions, establishing common interests or shared goals, agreeing about potential agenda and ground rules, planning the timing of discussions, and determining the kinds of information each party needs to bring to the table. All phases of negotiation are important, but these initial phases set the tone that will influence the nature of the working relationship and the kinds of problem solving that occur.

Generally, the goal of negotiation is to achieve interpersonal or economic interests through tactics that lack the high costs of demanding, forcing, or coercing. Integrative negotiation seeks to achieve this goal through discussion that develops greater understanding about interests and problems. Formal negotiations begin with information sharing, summarizing of interests, and clarifying of issues.

Negotiators in the problem-solving phase use a variety of tactics, including nonevaluative brainstorming of potential solutions; the trading of valued interests; the leveraging of factors such as timing, risk, and financing; the bridging and linking of agreements; and the use of concessions to break stalemates. Problem solving requires a significant commitment and openness to collaborative discussion. If one party resists collaboration, discussion about expectations for settlement and the costs of no settlement may need to be revisited. Incentives may need to be built into the process to promote greater cooperation.

Parties move toward closure in many different ways. Some will move slowly and grudgingly. Some will move methodically through agreed-upon processes. Some will look for agreements in principle before they are ready to problem-solve individual issues. And some will be content just to establish dialogue with an expectation that more intensive discussion of specific issues will occur after a relationship is established. Whatever path negotiators choose, they need to generate a list of expectations for the parties that identifies the next steps of the process. Remember that getting an agreement does not equate to getting a commitment. Include provisions that protect you and promote accountability.

PROFESSIONAL PROFILE

● **LAWRENCE SUSSKIND,
FOUNDING DIRECTOR OF THE
CONSENSUS BUILDING INSTITUTE, MIT
PROFESSOR, FACILITATOR, MEDIATOR, AUTHOR**

Workable Peace

Newspapers, TV, radio, magazines, and online news services remind us daily that the world abounds with complex problems. Northern Ireland, Jerusalem, the Balkan states, and the Horn of Africa are among the areas where conflict is historic, violent, and seemingly intractable. Some of the elements that present difficulties are the history of the disputes, the numbers of stakeholders, and the difficulty of leading and maintaining stable coalitions of stakeholders. In addition, differences in language, culture, and values often play a role. The media sometimes profile individuals and institutions that work toward managing conflict and crafting settlements. One of those who facilitate these difficult, dangerous, and complex negotiations is Lawrence Susskind.

Introduction to the Practitioner

Although he now works internationally, Larry began his work in negotiation in U.S. communities. He was originally trained as a city planner, and in the course of assisting communities, he found that "The more successful I was at involving community members in the process of thinking ahead, the more difficult it was to make decisions. It became clear to me that the process of community participation needed a kind of multiparty negotiation that would lead to informed consensus. After a while, I realized that when participants have strong feelings about what they want and need, the process of getting agreement requires somebody to tend to the process. I viewed my job as assistant to the parties who were negotiating. I looked at how mediators play that helping role. I found there are many problems about how a neutral helps people in a multiparty negotiation. For 20 years, I have worked in public disputes as a mediator, helping people solve complex problems. Later, I trained others to do this work. I built the Consensus Building Institute, a nonprofit organization that provides assisted negotiation to people around the world."

The Consensus Building Institute is based at the Massachusetts Institute of Technology, where Larry is a professor of urban studies and planning. Larry was a founder of and the first director of The Program on Negotiation at Harvard Law School. This institute works on negotiation problems and develops improved methods of negotiation and mediation. Its faculty is based at Harvard, MIT, Simmons, and Tufts Universities. Its mission is to improve the theory and practice of conflict resolution. Activities of The Program on Negotiation include theory building, education and training, publications, and action research.

Susskind's publications on negotiation are numerous and highly regarded. Students of environmental, community, and international negotiations read his articles and books. Practitioners use them as references and guides for the most difficult negotiations. Larry's writing is grounded in his record of building theory that results in practical solutions to complex problems. Some of his best-known books include *Breaking the Impasse: Consensual Approaches to Resolving Public Disputes,* written with Jeffrey Cruikshank in 1987; *Negotiating on Behalf of Others,* edited with Bob Mnookin in 1999; and the 1999 winner of the Center for Public Resources Book Prize for Excellence in Alternative Dispute Resolution, *The Consensus Building Handbook,* edited with Sarah McKearnan and Jennifer Thomas-Larmer.

Larry explains that someone who facilitates complex negotiations needs two bundles of skills. First, a facilitator needs knowledge of the substantive issues in the dispute. In his experience, "In a complex negotiation, you can't help by just assisting with the talk. You have to know about the substance. So, I have to bring skills of a planner, someone who knows environmental questions. I have to bring skills of an organizational development specialist, because many of the issues involve how to build institutional capacity."

Second, the facilitator needs a bundle of skills that relate to process management. There are mediation and facilitation skills, such as how to facilitate a meaningful conversation in a large group and how to clarify when parties are not talking to each other effectively. There are skills for dealing with the media, such as how to explain the negotiation to the world at large, while it's going on, in a way that supports the negotiation. There are documenting skills, such as how to report and make sense of what the parties are discussing.

Work of the Practitioner

In Larry's view, "The prenegotiation phase is probably the most important phase of any in a negotiation. There is a menu of activities which we help people do. We help them clarify and order their interests, we help them think about the interests of others with whom they will be interacting, we help them be hardheaded about what will happen if there's no agreement (that is, developing their BATNA). Then, we help them analyze the BATNAs of the other party as best they can before the negotiation begins."

The next phase of prenegotiation focuses on the generation of options that might be suitable for a settlement. Larry helps parties develop packages of proposals that meet their interests well and meet the interests of the others. Next, Larry assists clients in framing the arguments in favor of the packages that they favor, so that others have a basis for agreeing with what's being proposed. These arguments should evidence the reasoning behind the packages that are favored.

In addition, Larry helps people deal internally with their own side or within their organizational group. Larry advises, "Parties must understand what their latitude is. What is their mandate? What is the scope of their authority? We help people prepare for negotiation by getting everyone in the group to enter into this prenegotiation assessment that will guide the one who will represent them. It's too late for the representative to come back later and tell everyone what assessment was underlying his or her approach." Involving all the stakeholders in the prenegotiation assessment helps to consolidate agreement in the group as the negotiation proceeds.

Finally, Larry helps parties understand the most probable scenarios of the negotiation they are about to undertake. He believes it is important that parties anticipate what the steps will be as the negotiation proceeds. He observes, "It's no good to be thinking ahead only one step at a time. All this is essential to adequate prenegotiation. Parties who omit careful preparation are like kids who don't do their homework." Prenegotiation demands that all interested parties consider what no agreement would mean, that they analyze the interests of their own and other parties, that they generate options to meet those interests, deputize their representative with a clear mandate, and develop some sense of the probable steps of the negotiation.

In an actual negotiation, there are four basic phases: prenegotiation, creating value, distributing value, and anticipating the problems of follow-through. Larry explains, "Parties add value through cooperative moves. They listen to each others' needs and interests, they generate options, they keep trying to add to the package and embellish it." Larry notes these sessions are marked by the exchange of ideas and careful listening.

Eventually, parties reach the limit of value that they can create to serve their joint interests. At that point, the third phase, distributing value, begins. There will be gains for some, losses for others. Larry notes, "This phase must be handled in a way that doesn't undermine relationships, because this phase will be followed by implementation of the agreement. These are the most difficult sessions, especially where there are very high stakes. People are nervous; they don't want to go back home and face their constituents with too little. [As mediators assisting the negotiation,] we find ourselves throwing ourselves between the parties, caucusing with them, dealing with whatever psychological dimensions there might be." The success of implementation will depend on the positive relationship between the parties.

Larry offers a list of essential success factors in multiparty, multi-issue negotiations. First, all relevant stakeholders must be represented by someone they chose. Second, there must be a list of ground rules that everyone helped to shape. Third, there needs to be a facilitator who agrees to manage the negotiation according to those ground rules. Larry cautions, "You must have sufficient resources if information needs to be collected jointly so that the parties can gather information together. Basically, the key stakeholders must believe that they are better off exploring the issues jointly than staying away. Usually it takes somebody other than the parties involved to make the case that they have more to gain by negotiating than by pursuing other alternatives."

Larry identifies cross-cultural and international settings as the most challenging. He elaborates, "I work in a lot of settings which are very high stakes. I work in settings in which there is a long history of hostility and mistrust. In such settings, you have enormous problems with communication, with understanding what's being said, what's involved. You have pessimism and hostility. Situations such as these are the most difficult to assist negotiations. For instance, we are part of the only Israeli-Palestinian nongovernmental organization still operating in Jerusalem (as of June 2001). The Consensus Building Institute (CBI) works with a partner on the ground called The Israeli-Palestinian Center for Research and Information (IPCRI). We work jointly through a collaboration called the Joint Environmental Mediation Service (JEMS). We have teams of experts trained to mediate resource disputes in contested areas. CBI manages the training activity and supports the implementation of this work. This is a tough spot right now. We are also working in the Philippines, trying to help a partner group there launch a public dispute resolution program. We are trying to work between First Nations (aboriginal groups in Canada) and pipeline owners and other economic interests." Larry and his associates at CBI work in highly contested, cross-cultural settings where there are large reservoirs of hate.

On the preventive side, CBI runs a program called Workable Peace, which teaches high school kids about interethnic relations and racial conflict. Larry reports, "We teach in three Israeli and three Palestinian high schools. It's not easy, and it's amazing that the kids and the teachers are still trying to work together, given all the pressure on them from each of their sides. Many institutions are sending negative messages, but we're continuing to try to counter that, working through these individuals."

Larry describes the breakdown of international negotiations he has witnessed: "People were not prepared in the sense they were not clear about their interests. Sometime parties came with unrealistic expectations so that they held out for concessions that couldn't happen. They had failed to assess their BATNAs. In other cases, parties made promises they couldn't deliver on." There have been failures when international groups were unable to garner internal support from their own constituents.

Negotiations may fail when parties are too worried about perceptions, particularly about looking too cooperative. Larry explains, "In the value creation phase, they don't engage in the kind of information sharing that will lead to settlement. Or, they reach the point of distributing value, and they have no concern for the future of the relationship. Politicians can trash the relationship in the process of dividing up the value. When they do that, you can't expect implementation to work out."

Contextual Differences

Larry discusses international negotiations by first making the distinction between dual and multiparty negotiations. Next, he points out, "When multiparty negotiations concern the kinds of things that get decided in the public arena, you don't have the privacy that most two-party negotiations afford. Everything is required to happen in a transparent way. Also, enormous public pressures may be exerted on the negotiators, who cannot be shielded. In addition, cross-cultural negotiations involve problems in communication. Mediators have to go very slowly and make sure that everyone understands everything that is said, because it can easily be wrongly interpreted. When you take something that is bigger and more complex than a two-party negotiation and you overlay communication problems, you have compounding difficulties."

Multiparty, complex issue negotiations are also complicated by the presence of a professional neutral. Although the mediator may be helpful in moving the parties toward settlement, the mediator's goals are not always consistent with those of each party. It is common in large negotiations for parties to have attorney representation. Such agents have their own sets of goals that presumably complement those of the stakeholders. However, the presence of these agents adds further obstacles to achieving resolution. The level of sophistication that people must have to operate in these large-scale negotiations is awesome.

Value differences are common in international negotiations. Larry notes, "You're not just talking about having different interests and discovering shared values. You have both different interests and different values."

Changes and Challenges

Larry notes that the most important new trend in negotiation since 1985 is the ascendance of the mutual gains model, which is replacing the win-lose approach that was common before that time. During the recent past, there is also more focus on the need to tend to the added complexity of multiparty negotiation. Larry asserts, "It's not a difference in degree, it's a difference in kind. There were earlier efforts to deal with complex multiparty disputes but, recently, serious continuous efforts by professional mediators have resulted in significant progress. They have codified the role and responsibilities of mediators. Legislation has been enacted to regularize the conduct of large public disputes. Rosters of qualified mediators have been published. There has been the emergence of professional associations." Multiparty dispute resolution in the public arena is itself a relatively new thing.

There has also been recent growth in online negotiation services. There are online services advertised to save people time and money. Larry says, "They are going to fail. We know that when people are not face to face, they ask for more, resist more, and are less oriented toward effective problem solving. So, while we might think we are gaining in efficiency by not spending money and time in face-to-face communication, we are in fact going to produce inferior results. This happens because of the dynamics of what happens when people do not have to confront the other's expressions and reactions in real time." The growth of online negotiation services has been stimulated by the insurance business, which sees the Internet as a cost-effective way of managing many claims in which the money involved is not large. Larry believes, "People have been conned into believing that the negotiation done by a machine is more fair. The fact is, you can insert any bias you want into a computer program. There are huge numbers of cases being resolved in this way."

Larry highlights two disagreements among practitioners. The first is the extent to which people assisting negotiations should be knowledgeable about the content of the dispute. There are some who say that content knowledge isn't important, but Larry's response to that is, "I don't buy it. The more you understand context, the better you can assist people. Disputants don't want your help if you don't know what they're talking about. Most practitioners now agree with this assessment, but there is still debate about how much knowledge is necessary, what expertise is adequate."

The second debate concerns the purpose of assisted negotiations. Larry notes a large disagreement. In his opinion, "The goal should be reaching an agreement relative to the parties' interests and their best options away from the table. On the other hand, Bush and Folger [1994] say that, in theory, the goal ought to be to transform people to get them to appreciate the other. They describe what I do as 'mere problem solving.' I find that problematic. I have no intention of transforming people. The notion that I'm going to make them into better people is manipulative and self-serving. It makes me very uneasy that people might define the work we do as somehow surreptitiously seeking to change parties without their knowledge." There is a stark difference between those who see the goal of mediation as transformative and those who see the goal as problem solving.

In conclusion, Larry Susskind is one of the most experienced and highly regarded practitioners in the area of multiparty, public policy debates. From his perspective, there are four phases of negotiation: prenegotiation, creating value, distributing value, and anticipating the problems of follow-through. The prenegotiation phase is especially important; successful negotiators need to spend substantial time reflecting on their BATNAs, their needs and interests, and constructing cogent arguments in support of those interests. They also need to anticipate how others will perceive their interests and BATNAs and then make some assumptions about where common ground may be. Through the Consensus Building Institute, students and managers learn to maneuver successfully through these phases. Through his many articles and books, Larry has educated and helped to change the concept and practice of negotiation from a win-lose model to a mutual gains model. In his own practice, he models the theory and the skills about which he writes.

PROFESSIONAL PROFILE

MARVIN JOHNSON, JD, ●
MEDIATOR OF FEDERAL EMPLOYMENT DISPUTES

EEO Disputes: Finding the Gaps and Standing Back

In the following interview, the practitioner explains how the generic processes play out in an EEOC negotiation. He acts as a third-party neutral, assisting the employee and the employer's representative to come to agreement. In the information-sharing phase, he sees his job as asking questions where there are gaps in their perspectives. These gaps define the dispute and signal where each party may be willing to make a concession. He next attempts to motivate both parties to engage in the problem-solving phase, as opposed to asking an outside party to decide the dispute. He uses his reputation and reasonableness as leverage in persuading them. If they negotiate, his facilitative approach involves allowing them to craft their own settlement.

Introduction to the Practitioner

Marvin Johnson has negotiated and assisted negotiations in many different contexts. He has worked for the United States Department of Labor, the Federal Mediation and Conciliation Service, the National Treasury Employees' Union, and the National Football League Players' Association, among others. His experiences also cross functional lines, for in addition to an active alternative dispute resolution (ADR) practice, he has taught in higher education, has provided ADR training in settings as diverse as Russia and Africa, has written training materials, and hosts a biweekly cable TV program that addresses current dispute resolution issues. Marvin participates in a number of panels and commissions, such as the Federal Service Impasses Panel, to which he received a presidential appointment. For purposes of this profile, he elected to focus on federal employment disputes. Whether or not we are federal employees, as citizens and taxpayers, we all benefit from effective settlement of such disputes.

Marvin notes that he has considerable background in federal employment issues. His undergraduate degree is in industrial and labor relations, with a concentration on the employment arena. He reminds us, "The Equal Employment Opportunity Commission (EEOC) was one of several entities that initially experimented with assisted negotiation as an alternative to litigation. An agency that utilized an ADR mechanism in their EEO-complaint process was given additional time to complete an investigation of a complaint. Because of my experience in the federal arena, a number of agencies asked me to mediate in their pilot projects. Then, having had that experience in the federal sector, I was asked to participate in EEOC's work in the private sector as well." Marvin was also involved in dispute resolution programs administered by the National Academy of Conciliators.

Marvin mentions several skills that are critical to disputes involving charges of discrimination. In his opinion, "The basic skills are really listening and the ability to communicate. Your goal is for the parties to reach a resolution on their own; your job is to help them and to guide them through that process. Secondarily, it's important to have an understanding of the Equal Employment laws. Not that you have to be an expert, but you need to have a basic understanding of the law. You do not have to be a lawyer to do this work. In Maryland a few years ago, a court rule was proposed that would have given attorneys the exclusive right to mediate court-referred cases. I went to Annapolis with other mediators, mostly nonattorneys, to testify before the Maryland Court of Appeals, and we were able to persuade the court not to adopt the proposed rule."

Insights About Negotiation

There are two schools of thought about how to prepare to mediate a discrimination case. One is that you need to get all the information about the complaint, gathering all the documents that have been filed. The other school of thought is that you should know the identities of the parties to the complaint and what the issues are. Marvin says, "I subscribe to the second school of thought, where I want to know who the parties are and what the issues are. Because I'm not going to decide the case, I don't want to be influenced one way or another by a party's perspective. I take a more facilitative than evaluative approach. A person who is skillful can come in and work with the parties and help them come to agreement without knowing every detail in the case." Marvin prefers to assist negotiations so that the parties are the ones who take responsibility for settlement decisions.

In a typical EEO dispute, Marvin says, "The complainant may be represented by an attorney or union representative about 50% of the time. The other half of cases finds the complainant without representation. Management tends to mirror the employee in numbers, so that in this latter half, one representative from management will negotiate with the complainant. Sometimes the direct supervisor attends, sometimes it's the second-level supervisor."

The most common reasons federal employees file EEO complaints are failure to achieve a promotion or to receive the performance appraisal they expected. After registering their disappointment and being denied a remedy, the employee files a complaint and at some point in the process has the option of electing mediation as a means of resolving the dispute.

In the EEO negotiation, it is up to the complainant to demonstrate that he or she was discriminated against because of gender, age, race, or religion. The complainant must provide data supporting their claim. Marvin explains, "They would say, "I've performed my job functions, I've handled my work assignments, and other individuals who did less or nothing at all received a higher evaluation."

Then, management gives their reasons for making the original evaluation. Marvin explains, "Management might say that the other person's evaluation was based on specific performance standards. Then I ask questions of each side. For instance, I might say to management, "In applying the performance standards, did you take into account the special assignments performed by this employee?""

The process of assisted negotiation in EEO disputes is standard mediation. Marvin's first step in the first mediation session is to determine whether parties understand the process of mediated negotiation. If one party is unfamiliar with the process, he explains what mediation is and how it works. He stresses the confidentiality of the process. One party will begin to describe how the dispute arose and proceeded to mediation, and then the other gives his or her view. Marvin then facilitates the discussion.

Marvin reasons, "My job is to ask questions where there are gaps in their viewpoints. I look for gaps in the story so they can explain them. Typically, there are gaps on both sides of the story, which is why there is a dispute. I want them both to recognize that they each have a chink in their armor and wonder whether it makes sense for them to settle or move the dispute forward to a more formal process. They might be able to resolve the dispute in mediation, if there has been something overlooked."

Marvin sees his job as raising the queries that motivate both sides to negotiate a settlement. Sometimes he uses these questions in a joint session; at other times, the embarrassment factor is such that he raises them in caucus (a separate meeting with one of the parties). Marvin says, "When the parties accept the fact that their stories have gaps, they move to the next phase of negotiation, asking, 'What is it that you want?'" At that point, the sides may go into caucus and figure out what it is that they want to offer. Then, they come back together and explore what's acceptable to one another."

Once the parties move into the settlement mode and start talking to each other, Marvin sits back and listens. Sometimes at the end of an negotiation, parties will say, "What do we need you for?" Marvin replies, "Well, you weren't able to do it before I got here, so I must have done something right!" Marvin believes that "they have to be the ones to make the suggestion, they've got to be the ones to decide. I believe the parties are smart enough to know what's best for them. Of course, you don't want them to decide on something that's illegal, but that can be remedied by having the agreement reviewed by an EEO attorney if they are not present during the mediation. In any event, when the parties are making progress during the discussion, I keep my mouth shut. When there's something I think is important, I will jot it down and follow them along to make sure that it and all their issues have been raised and discussed. It's their dispute, and in order for it to be resolved, they've got to resolve it through negotiations. More likely than not, they walk away with some type of agreement."

Agreements may take one of several forms. Marvin offers a typical example: "This might be in the form of an adjusted evaluation, where a phrase in the evaluation that is objected to by the employee is removed. The solution might be that a different manager performs a subsequent evaluation. Another scenario is that another manager trusted by both parties will review the evaluation and determine the outcome. Occasionally, an employee is offered a monetary adjustment."

In EEO negotiations, it typically takes 4 hours for parties to reach an agreement. But, Marvin recalls, "I've had negotiations that lasted all day, and we still had to reconvene one or two additional times before reaching a resolution."

The parties who enter mediation with an open mind and who are willing to engage in the give and take of meaningful, good-faith negotiations are more successful. In addition, Marvin notes that the organization in which the dispute occurs can encourage negotiation through proper intake procedures—that is, clarifying for employees just how mediation works in EEO disputes. Marvin achieves success by looking for oversights. He explains, "Oftentimes in employment situations, if you can get one party to understand why the other party sees things as they do, you can begin to get them to move toward resolution. If they can say, 'I can see why you had that view or now I see why you did that,' it's the beginning of success."

Challenges arise when parties do not bring an open mind, when Marvin hears phrases such as, "It's the principle of the thing." He notes, "When they don't try to see the other person's point of view, when they're not willing to consider that they may have overlooked something, it's very tough."

Significant challenges also arise when it's not really an EEO dispute. Marvin elaborates, "Someone is hurt because something has happened and the other party doesn't recognize that what they've done has harmed the party. They haven't done the harm based on race, sex, or other EEO factors, so they can't see that someone has been hurt. Coming to agreement may not necessarily be an EEO agreement, and it may not necessarily be a monetary agreement. The hurt person needs to have recognition and respect in order to move on with their work, in order to have a better relationship with the supervisor, and become a more productive employee. This can be challenging, especially when the hurt person is stuck on their position."

Marvin reports that disputes grounded in lack of respect and recognition usually take longer than the true EEO complaints. He compares them to "peeling an onion, where the hurt has been going on for a long time. The hurt person never said anything, then finally came the straw which broke the camel's back, and the complaint was registered. The mediator has to engage the parties in deep discussion to bring all the concerns up and out. It can take all day. It's about how people are being treated. Often, there's no money involved." In these cases, charges are brought because people want to be heard, and no other channels seem to be available. Some of the EEO people are allowing these types of complaints to be heard because assisted negotiation can be a learning tool to change situations and relationships for the better.

If Marvin sees negotiation start to break down, he calls a caucus with each side. He says, "I separate the parties and go to them separately to see what's going on with them. I may ask one party, "We've made some progress; is there anything that can be done that will continue to move this negotiation forward?" And then I might ask the same question of the other party. And it may be that the other party has a proposal to make. I will ask that the proposal be made when we get back together in a joint session. I can't say that I never go back and forth between the parties carrying information, because that's not true, but it's always best when the information comes directly from the parties." Many times, useful ideas emerge from these caucuses so that the breakdown of negotiation is avoided.

Occasionally, the exchange of proposals does not work. In those cases, Marvin raises questions about other possible outcomes. If that still doesn't work, he asks if either of the parties has anything else that might possibly work. If the answer is no, Marvin reminds them that the complainant has the opportunity to go forward in the EEO process. If the complaint was informal, they may register a formal one that involves an investigation. If it's already been investigated, the next step may be an agency determination. A negative ruling may be appealed to the EEOC for a decision, or the complainant can go to court. Later in the EEO complaint process, after consulting their agency representative, either party may be able to get the dispute back into the mediation process.

Contextual Differences

Negotiation in employment disputes differs from that in other contexts. Most often, there are ongoing relationships involved in employment cases. Marvin elaborates, "If the person wants to stay in their job, the relationship with the supervisor will continue. If the person has been terminated and wants to be reinstated, there will be a continuing relationship. The mediator wants to build on that relationship and use that as an incentive for a successful resolution. If the person has been terminated and doesn't want to be reinstated, it does make the negotiation somewhat more difficult." The ongoing relationship provides a vehicle to advance communication in the negotiation.

Another key element in EEO disputes is the heightened emotion around feelings of discrimination. Marvin believes words hurt, and he tries to minimize the impact by avoiding the word "discrimination." According to him, "When someone alleges that a manager has discriminated, the manager feels bad about it. I focus the discussion on what happened and not whether those happenings constitute discrimination. In that way, people see how decisions were made and focus on that rather than discrimination. You'd be surprised how amenable people are when you approach the dispute this way."

Employment disputes also evoke strong emotions because our jobs are often a significant part of our personal identities. Marvin says, "You've got to get those emotions out, because there's usually a lot of emotional history involved in these disputes. How did the dispute get started, and how is it affecting the parties? Once you get the feelings out, you can move on. If you get an agreement, and the emotional aspects haven't surfaced, the parties may become entangled in conflict again." Negotiation in this context has a heavier layer of emotional freight than it does in most business disputes, and the solution must take the conflict history into account to assure a lasting resolution.

The final point about the employment discrimination context is that negotiation of individual cases may not respond to the underlying problem. Marvin points to system flaws that may be driving cases: "Mediation isn't a panacea. You have to go back to the sources of the conflict. Where are the cases coming from? What are the issues? You may need to make organizational changes, it might be a policy, it might be a rule, it might be training for managers. You can't just put an assisted negotiation program in place and expect all the problems to go away. The problem may not be with the particular manager with the EEO complaint as much as it is with organizational practices." A distinguishing feature of EEO negotiations is the possibility that the complaint may not be fully addressed in an interpersonal setting but requires organizational change for resolution of discrimination.

Changes and Conflicts

The trends that Marvin identifies relate to the growing use of ADR in federal employment disputes. There is an average 1-year complaint processing time at the agency level before electing an option for a hearing before an EEOC administrative judge or final agency decision. He relates, "Agencies are recognizing that mediation is a valuable tool for resolving complaints before they reach the formal complaint process. There are pilot mediation programs throughout the federal government."

There are differences of opinion among practitioners on several issues. First, there is the range of styles—from facilitative to evaluative—that was discussed above. There is the difference of opinion about whether a mediator in this context should be a lawyer. There are questions about how deeply immersed or specialized mediators should be in a particular subject matter.

In addition, practitioners disagree about whether a complainant should be represented.

Whatever differences there may be about approaches to EEO disputes, we may be sure that Marvin Johnson will continue to advance the practice of negotiation in this context not only in his practice, but also in his teaching, writing, and broadcasting. His methods of listening for the gaps in stories, encouraging parties to craft their own settlements, and eliciting conflict history to achieve lasting resolution work particularly well in employment disputes, where long-term relationships and heavy emotional investment are typical. However, these methods are also transferable to other negotiations where recognition and respect are key elements in the conflict.

PROFESSIONAL PROFILE

● **EDWARD I. SELIG, JD,**
ENVIRONMENTAL ATTORNEY AND MEDIATOR

The Horrors of Litigation

No matter where we live, we are likely to be aware of environmental matters that affect our homes, the organizations we work for, or our communities. For example, contaminants may have migrated from one property to another, involving previous owners, insurance carriers, and government regulators. A property owner may have a dispute with a government agency over regulatory requirements for clean air or water. A landowner may admit liability but disagree with the government agency over proposed penalties. Property owners and insurance carriers often dispute coverage issues related to environmental damage. Communities may engage in conflict with organizations or government agencies because of risks to health.

In the following interview, a practitioner who helped to build the field of environmental negotiation reflects on the negotiation processes that build effective agreements. He offers insights about how a third-party neutral works with clients whose emotional need to punish is balanced by the neutral's goal of staying away from litigation. His experience is congruent with advice about information gathering given in the preceding chapter; he notes that the factual research process is supplemented by an experienced practitioner's intuition. He also includes understanding the psychology of the other negotiator and discerning the relationship between the other negotiator and his or her client. In the problem-solving phase, environmental negotiators consult frequently with scientific and technical advisors. In terms of generating options, the ability of the environmental negotiator to imagine new approaches is particularly valuable. In his arena, negotiating tactics such as overstatement are usual—just part of the game.

Introduction to the Practitioner

Ed Selig is an environmental negotiator who works toward out-of-court settlements. A graduate of Yale University and Harvard Law School, Ed was one of the pioneers in developing environmental negotiation. After several years at the Justice Department in Washington, D.C., he was awarded a Russell Sage Research Fellowship in Law and Social Science at Harvard.

While in Massachusetts, Ed joined the Council on Law-Related Studies, funded by the Ford Foundation. The environmental area attracted Ed and, abetted by the passage of the National Environmental Policy Act in 1970, proved to be the starting point of his subsequent legal focus. Ed recalls, "I concentrated on the problems of Massachusetts in meeting the new federal standards for water pollution control. After I'd studied them for a while, I ended up with a contract to consult to that state, which called upon me to draft the Massachusetts Clean Water Act. I'm happy to say that the basic framework and the basic provisions of the Act have survived intact to this day."

The next step was for Ed to start a legal consulting practice, building on the Massachusetts law that he had drafted. Ed summarizes, "So the beginning of it was not litigation, but consulting. I helped states to draft legislation and interpret the reach of regulations. I started to participate in negotiations then and there, because there were inter- and intra-agency conflicts as to how regulations should be interpreted. The legislature wanted it this way, the agency wanted it that way, there were citizen groups screaming that it go their way. From the outset, I found myself negotiating with different interest groups over the shape of legislative and regulatory provisions."

Eventually, government agencies were no longer mystified about what they had to do. Ed explains, "But, gradually, commercial and industrial clients also retained us for advice and representation. We negotiated permit conditions, penalties, settlement, and contractual agreements on environmental matters. You see, almost everything is negotiable in the law. There is always wiggle room. Even with a government agency that is hellbent on enforcing the law and claims not to have much discretion, the fact is that they do have discretion—about wording, about permit conditions, about timing and other matters. We litigated only as a last resort."

Ed alludes to his growing self-awareness: "I've participated in enough litigation to know that out–of-court settlement is a much better option. The great majority of these cases settle anyway, so you may as well do it early as late. My most satisfying moments have been those where I've worked with the attorneys on the other side and we would hammer out a settlement. There are plenty of members of the bar who have good negotiating skills, who are good to have on the other side of the table. There are a few who don't value negotiation, and they're crazy. Eventually, they will end up in litigation, but even there, sense will prevail after the client has spent thousands of dollars to be represented in court."

Ed describes the skills requisite to environment negotiation where there are serious questions of law. The first skill is knowing the law, knowing the client's case, and being very articulate. At the same time, the attorney must possess advanced listening skills to hear the essence of the other person's case. The client cannot be expected to do this because, by definition, the client is usually outraged, hurt, and/or insulted. Ed reports, "The client's charge to me is 'Go and wipe the floor up with those guys!' Clients tend to be somewhat unreasonable, and the problems are only compounded if the lawyer gets sucked into that. The attorney must walk a fine line between being zealous in advocacy for the client's cause and maintaining objectivity."

The effective advocate is also skilled in assessing risk. Ed notes, "There are all sorts of books about risk assessment. Sure, you can put numbers on things, but it's really more of an intuitive judgment, knowing where the case is strong and where there may be trouble. The effective negotiator will plant doubt in the client's mind about how watertight the case is so that the client is softened up a bit for making concessions in the future. Client relationships are critical to success in this area."

Ed subscribes to Roger Fisher, Bill Ury, and Bruce Patton's (*Getting to Yes,* 1991) principle of being tough on the problem but easy on the people. Ed's philosophy is as follows: "I like to maintain friendly relations even with the most deadly adversary. I think it really helps. There are lawyers who practice the reverse. They are as obnoxious as they can be toward one another. But I see no profit in that."

Imagination is a quality that Ed values in negotiators. In his experience, it's often the negotiator who can think beyond the box. For example, he was the one who broke the logjam in a recent case, saying, "Do you really have to rip this dam out? What would be entailed in repairing it? Is this the only way to go, or can we think of other approaches?" He had a case where his client owned a piece of land through which the other party wanted an easement. This had nothing whatsoever to do with the environmental dispute. Ed suggested giving the easement to "sweeten the package." The easement was a very small concession for the landowner but highly prized by the other party. This simple side transaction facilitated the settlement of a rather complex dispute.

Finally, the best negotiators are those who also present the most credible threat of litigation if the negotiation were to break down. Ed is frank: "You can't be a pussycat. On the other hand, if all you do is pound your fist and do the testosterone bit, nothing happens. So, it's a high-wire act. And there's a lot of gamesmanship involved: 'No, we couldn't possibly accept that offer. That's just nonsense. We're not even in the same ballpark.' And then they'll come back and offer this and that, so you're all sweetness and light again. It's like a poker game. You have to be able to bluster and bluff in order to smoke them out." Ed concludes that these negotiation skills are not immoral, but amoral.

Insights About Negotiation

Ed relies on his legal training to guide preparation for environmental negotiation. He believes that "the key to preparation is knowing what the case is about and where you think it's likely to go, what route might be fruitful to follow. And, of course, the more you know about the psychology of the other negotiator, the better you are. If this is a guy who is excitable, I calm him down. Or, if you can't trust the other negotiator, you must follow up every decision with a paper trail. It definitely helps to know who's on the other side."

Ed elaborates, "It's also important to know who calls the shots between the other negotiator and the client. There are principals who will do whatever the lawyer says, and, on the other hand, there are lawyers who are very constrained agents. And when the principal is a corporation or a board, it becomes very difficult. Sometimes the client of the other negotiator is a hydra-headed monster, such as the subdivision control board I had to deal with recently." Clearly, identifying and assessing who on the opposing side can make decisions is a critical step in preparation.

The typical environmental negotiation proceeds in stages, Ed explains. It opens with a sequence of letters in which the attorney writes, "My client is prepared to offer you X dollars. We think your case is totally without merit, but we're busy and are willing to offer this money to make it go away. Sincerely, The Opponent." To which the other attorney replies, "How insulting! However, we do want this and that." Each side is very careful to not appear weak.

These offers and counteroffers continue until it appears that the two sides are moving into the same ballpark and that it might be possible to negotiate between their offers. At that point, there should be a meeting where the attorneys sit across the table from one another with their scientific and technical consultants. Questions such as (a) "What went on there in the ground water?" (b) "Was this project improperly engineered?" (c) "Did you model it correctly?" and (d) "What is the chemistry of this air quality control region?" are likely to surface. Each side will reiterate its case.

At this point, the negotiation will function very similarly to a mediation. Ed explains, "There will be private sessions between the client and the attorney, there will be joint sessions where the two sides will try to bargain over the table, and when both sides are really searching for a settlement, you can make progress. Both sides need to be willing to hang in there and keep exploring. You'll hear phrases such as 'We can either do this for you or we can do that, but not both.' 'We're taking that off the table.' 'Okay, we can agree to a $5 million payment up front provisionally, provided that it's part of an overall settlement. Of course, you're not getting anything unless we can agree to an overall settlement.'" Such language typifies environmental negotiation during settlement talks.

During this bargaining, it is not unusual for the lawyers to mediate between their own clients and the other side. Ed explains that the lawyer suggests to his or her client, "Hey Joe, I know this isn't what you wanted, but if we take this thing into litigation, you're looking at a legal fee of half a million dollars. Of course, I'd be happy to earn it, but here's your opportunity to settle for a fraction of that." Often the clients are not present at environmental negotiations, but they make themselves available by phone as negotiation moves toward settlement.

The length of environmental negotiation varies according to the complexity of the dispute and what deadlines are pertinent. Ed recalls, "I negotiated a settlement for a dam that was threatening to burst. That was a sword of Damocles, and the negotiations moved at record speed. Both parties knew they could be swept away if they didn't come to a prompt settlement." There may be judicial deadlines that affect the time taken to resolve environmental matters, either stretching them out or compressing them to meet an upcoming trial date. Overall, without judicial pressure, the typical environmental negotiation takes many months to complete.

Ed believes that the primary factor determining whether a negotiation is successful is a shared fear of the outcome of litigation. Experienced lawyers estimate greater or lesser possibilities of success in different cases but appreciate the risk of losing in court. He explains, "It's winner take all. It's like a poker game: Do I bid this guy up, see what's in his hand, or fold?" No litigator can promise his or her client success. Moreover, the process may bleed corporate litigation budgets. These are strong reasons why, in the alternative, negotiation should be attempted and often succeeds.

Second, success depends on client motivation to reach a reasonable settlement. Most negotiators realize they cannot be successful for a client whose motives are vindictive. Ed relates, "When you have a client who needs to establish that he is right, to protect his injured ego, to teach the other guy a lesson, it won't work. You've got to have dispassionate concentration on the problem." Successful negotiators exercise objectivity and make every effort to encourage it in their clients.

Similarly, Ed says challenges arise when negotiators "turn deaf ears to factual presentations." Ed recalls a case when his environmental consultants did an exquisitely thorough job preparing factual background for their arguments, including a three-dimensional model. "It was a masterful piece of work, demonstrating how their client's effluent had polluted our client's property," says Ed. The response was, "This is an inadequate presentation, we don't agree with it, it isn't worth paying attention to." When opponents claim they want to negotiate, but are actually just going through the motions, it is not only challenging but extremely frustrating. Ed's interpretation of this behavior is that "often they pretend to be negotiating in order to discover your case, to smoke you out, but when push comes to shove, they are not interested in working out a settlement."

This false negotiation posture is increasingly in evidence, as more laws requiring negotiation or mediation are passed. In addition, frequently the court demands that the two sides sit down together and try to settle. The judge calls the parties into chambers and says, "Look, I don't want to decide this case. You guys go out there and settle it so that we can clear it off the docket." But either or both sides may then simply go through the motions of negotiation, without any intention of arriving at a settlement. Negotiators must be competent in assessing the motives of their opponents, discerning which ones are serious about settling and which ones are not. When negotiators are open to settlement, just sitting down together in the same room is a major step toward agreement.

Other challenges typical of environmental negotiations arise from contested or unknown information. One side will assert, "We can't do anything until we know more. We really don't know what went on out there 10 years ago. We need more information about risk factors, about the nature of the soils." The difficulty comes when there is no agreement between the parties about how that information will be obtained, by whom, or at whose expense. There are unknown facts critical to the case, and it's harder to settle in the face of ignorance. When facts are developed, experts hired by the two sides may not agree. In one case, where the experts were far apart, Ed proposed that the two experts name a third consultant whose interpretation of fact would be final. The other side replied, "Look, we know enough through our own consultant; we don't need anyone else." At that point, negotiations stalled and litigation ensued.

That was a typical jump from the frying pan into the fire. Ed explains, "What drives negotiation of environmental disputes is not some notion of social transformation but the horrors of litigation as the alternative course of action. Except for resolving major issues of public policy or constitutional dimension, litigation is a dreadful alternative to settling disputes. When you see it up close, you see wildly inflated claims, suppression of facts, endless discovery, and the party with the most money can wear down the party with the least. The aggravation for those involved and the ruin of any future relationships are not worth it."

For a privileged few, a political alternative may be available. Ed explains, "When negotiations stall, one side says, 'The governor's chief of staff is a friend of mine. I'm going to the State House on this one. Senator Bombast is going to introduce a bill in the legislature at our urging." Particularly when there are sensitive land use issues, the conflict may be "booted" to the political arena." Ed offers another example: "You've got a company that is financially insecure, and you're asking them to spend a lot of money to improve their environmental performance. They have contacts in the Department of Natural Resources and go there for a waiver. Material branded as hazardous may be delisted by a state agency. The manufacturer is then absolved of liability." In this way, the conflict is solved by political action rather than by negotiation.

Contextual Differences

There are dramatic contrasts between environmental conflicts and conflicts in other contexts. Ed lists some of the challenges: "You have highly uncertain outcomes in litigation; environmental regulations are horrendously complicated, even internally contradictory at some points; there is uncertainty about which agency is in charge; the rules of liability keep changing. There's new information coming out all the time from local, state, and federal levels. Legal principles are still in a state of evolution, so every environmental lawyer has to operate in a thicket."

In addition to the legal complications, there is the challenge of establishing ownership and actions that took place long ago. Ed explains, "Some of these cases involve actions that took place 50 years ago, so there's a lot of historical uncertainty. Who owned the property then? There may have been 12 changes of ownership. Some of the companies have gone out of business. Other companies may have set up subsidiaries to hide their tracks. So, you have all sorts of historical complications."

Third, there are many scientific uncertainties in environmental conflicts. Ed's examples are: "What are those contaminants doing under the ground? How much exposure to the toxic material did the plaintiffs have? How did it get into their system in the first place?" These are all questions typical of environmental negotiations.

Fourth, there are economic uncertainties. "What's the magnitude of the damages? How badly has the natural resource been degraded? How do you put a dollar figure on the loss of winter flounder?" Because of legal, scientific, and economic uncertainties, the transaction costs of environmental disputes are high.

Finally, the involvement of government agencies adds to the difficulty of environmental negotiation. The settlement must be agreeable not only to the parties, but to the agency or agencies which must sign off on it. The mindset of the agencies is enforcement. Ed's experience with regulators is that they have the following attitude: "By God, we've got a mission to perform. We've got to enforce the regulations, and you're telling us that you want to do this or that? We've got to make an example of these people!"

In Ed's opinion, "They're not particularly imaginative, and they're some-times self-righteous. I remind myself that their client is a far worse polluter than mine. In spite of the difficulties of negotiating with regulators, the effective negotiator can usually find some wiggle room—you just have to find where it is." For these reasons, negotiating environmental issues with government agencies is a dramatically different context than dealing in the private sector.

Changes and Conflicts

Ed notes many new trends in assisted negotiation or mediation of environmental disputes. "Court after court is now setting up multidoor models, where cases come in and a case coordinator looks them over and determines which ones might be mediated. States are setting up offices of dispute resolution, and there are United States district court panels that can be called upon to assist settlement of environmental conflicts." Many courts are encouraging the facilitated negotiation of environmental conflicts.

Education and training also suggest more use of assisted negotiation of environmental matters. Ed notes, "There's a lot of training of environmental mediators, and more and more law schools are providing training in the basic negotiation skills, including application to environmental issues. When you look at the publications and conferences of The American Bar Association Natural Resource Section, you see more and more articles and speeches on this subject. Law firms are sponsoring presentations." There is increa-sed focus on negotiation as a learned art and skill among environmental attorneys.

Disagreement among practitioners is most obvious to Ed in the area of styles. He often sees the hard-nosed negotiator, whose motto is "Grab as much as you can get!" This confrontational approach aims to wear down the other side, maintaining an inflexible posture up until the nego-tiator believes he or she has squeezed as much as possible from the other side. In Ed's experience, confrontational negotiators use pretexts and threats to accomplish their goals. He labels this the "huffing and puffing style."

A contrasting style involves accommodation. Accommodating negotia-tors tend to be more open and to level with the other side about their inter-ests. In Ed's experience, they typically say, "Now, let's see how we could find a way out of this thing." Most negotiators have an inclination toward either confrontation or accommodation.

Ed Selig has settled many environmental disputes working between the two extremes of negotiating styles. His thorough grounding in the law, his opportunity to participate in the beginning of environmental regulations, and his inventive approach to resolving issues have resulted in a successful career. His articles and presentations have instructed other attorneys in the art of negotiation. Through his efforts, many clients and government agencies have avoided the horrors of litigation.

CHAPTER 5

QUALITIES AND SKILLS OF EFFECTIVE NEGOTIATORS

The complete negotiator, according to 17th to 18th century manuals on diplomacy, should have a quick mind but unlimited patience, know how to dissemble without being a liar, inspire trust without trusting others, be modest but assertive, charm others without succumbing to their charm, and possess plenty of money and a beautiful wife while remaining indifferent to all temptation and riches and women.

— Griffin & Daggett, 1990, p. 116

In *The Wizard of Oz* (originally titled *The Wonderful World of Oz;* Baum, 1900), Dorothy needs help from a tin man (brain), a scarecrow (heart) and a lion (courage) to reach the Wizard and eventually to return to her home in Kansas. Input from all three of these characters helps Dorothy achieve her goal.

We can use this analogy to address similar needs in effective negotiation. Using a specific technique (brain) can be effective in some contexts but can fail in many others. Having a concern for the interests and welfare of others (heart) cannot replace the need for achieving self-interests or negotiating strategically. Courage to share information, engage in open communication, or pursue creative solutions must fit the context. All three factors must work in concert:

- *Brain.* Persuasion, problem solving, concern for self-interest, strategic planning
- *Heart.* Relationship building, concern for interests of others, fair process
- *Courage.* Creativity, sharing information, mutual gains

Negotiation is a state of mind for managing relationships, dealing with disputes, or working through contractual agreements. It defines the quality of a relationship. It involves problem solving rather than forcing. Negotiation is a process of doing things in ways that are engaging and inclusive; it is not a set of techniques that one does to another. It values both planning and intuition. Negotiation is contextual in that it adapts and flexes in style as the situation changes rather than being a rigid formula that can be used everywhere in the same way. A lack of flexibility explains why some people can negotiate with clients but can't get along with their staff or why some can be successful at work but fail in relationships at home. Rutheford (1998) points out the importance of negotiation for our age in his assessment: "The world works by agreements that are invisible, visible, understood, not understood, implicit, written, unwritten. All of these are open to negotiation and we all function in a negotiated world" (p. 20).

Constructing a list of qualities that describe effective negotiators is a little like trying to determine what a successful negotiation looks like. These descriptions are context-dependent. The skills required for negotiating with a neighbor may be a little different from those necessary for negotiating a business contract and will be significantly different from those valuable in negotiating via the Internet. Fisher and Davis (1987) point out that negotiators must possess a broad range of skills so that they can "change pace and approach," "demonstrate independence while being cooperative," "look for pragmatic solutions while being imaginative," and "maintain control while being expressive" (p. 117).

Box 5.1 illustrates how a manager's lack of negotiation skills began affecting his job performance. As you read the scenario, identify skills that you think he needs to work on. Afterward, we'll describe the skills about which he was coached.

Roger's situation is more common in many settings than we'd like to see. Fisher, Ury, and Patton (1991) summarize problems such as Roger's: "Everyone wants to participate in decisions that affect them; fewer and fewer people will accept decisions dictated by someone else. . . . Whether in business, government, or the family, people reach most decisions through negotiation" (p. xvii). In private sessions, Roger worked on his interpersonal skills,

Box 5.1

THE MANIACAL MANAGER

For the past five years, Roger has been the vice president of marketing for a major national firm, Mega Products. Previously, he served as director of marketing for two similar firms. He came to Mega Products with lofty accomplishments in his former positions.

Roger's achievements at Mega Products have been phenomenal. He exceeds all sales quotas and market predictions. But he's been having some difficulty. His 10-member staff complains about his inflexibility. When he talks to agents in the field, he's firm, rigid, and often insensitive. The agents do what he says but take their anger out on Roger's staff. His staff fares no better. They regularly go to Human Resources complaining about his unwillingness to put down his clipboard and listen to them. They would like to revise marketing meetings. He still wants balloons, group singing, and skits performed by the staff. The staff would like to improve many of their department procedures, but he says, "I've been successful with these procedures for 20 years. There's no need to change them." His staff says that he is unbending on department goals and goes as far as to yell at them "till the veins pop out on his neck" if they try to revise them. Roger monitors his staff's work until some members of his staff get frustrated and quit.

Roger's response to the criticism is to point to his department's accomplishments. His managerial style has achieved all corporate goals. He says, "The employees of today are lazy and fail to work as hard as they need to. They're too sensitive. They need firmer managing, not less."

The feud escalates; morale disintegrates; and employee turnover increases. The Human Resources director and the CEO intercede. They tell Roger that if he doesn't learn to negotiate with his staff and clients, he'll be replaced, in spite of all of his accomplishments.

What do you see as the central problems here? What skills does Roger need to improve to be able to negotiate expectations and goals with this staff? Roger is unaware he has a problem with staff or is resistant to information that his style might be ineffective, in spite of the statements of Human Resources and the CEO. What do we do with this factor?

and in parallel sessions, his staff discussed the kind of responses they needed from management to function most effectively. Roger learned to put down his clipboard and focus his attention on staff when they spoke to him. He learned how to break projects into smaller pieces so that he could hold high expectations on some issues and give his staff more flexibility on others. He learned that creative solutions could be trusted and promoted greater commitment by staff. And, finally, he learned to manage his temper, which had escalated his problems unnecessarily. Negotiation is more than just creating contracts; it also involves how we work with others, make decisions, and manage expectations.

Although a single set of qualities that describe effective negotiators changes with contexts, a few factors appear to cross contexts. To identify the characteristics of effective negotiators valued most often, we reviewed the work of 21 scholars or practitioners who represent many different groups, including business professionals, union and management representatives, contract negotiators, bankers, lawyers, real estate agents, and international negotiators (Dawson, 1999; Fisher & Davis, 1987; Fisher & Ertel, 1995; Fisher, Ury, & Patton, 1991; Griffin & Daggett, 1990; Karras, 1970; Keltner, 1994; Koh, 1996; McCrae, 1998; Mnookin, Peppet, & Tulumello, 2000; Pouliot, 1999; Rackham, 1985; Schaffzin, 1997; Shell, 1999; Skopec & Kiely, 1994; Williams, 1992). Our review identified eight factors that occurred with the most frequency.

Figure 5.1 lists each of the eight factors in one of the three *Wizard of Oz* categories identified earlier. Although we could debate whether listening is an activity of the head or heart, whether building relationships is an act of courage, or whether integrity is a product of our mind or heart, we think the categories generally capture the need for all three domains to be effective in negotiation.

The lists of these most important factors describes skills that cross a great number of contexts and may be necessary regardless of subject matter. Other factors may be important but may not apply to some contexts. Of equal interest are the factors missing from the lists. Although the media stereotype negotiators as assertive, strong, even ruthless, the picture that emerges in these lists is different. The scholars and studies reviewed describe an effective negotiator as someone who seeks understanding through dialogue followed by persistent, creative problem solving.

● QUALITIES OF THE MIND

Preparation

The more important and complex the negotiation, the greater the need to understand the contextual variables of a negotiation. Buying a house may

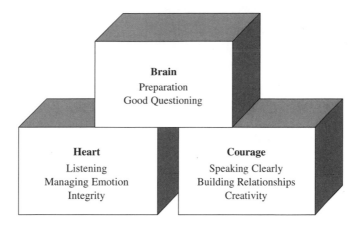

Figure 5.1   Characteristics of Effective Negotiation

require only a survey of sales of comparative models, knowledge about interest rates, and choice of a good real estate agent. But purchasing a business expands preparation to include knowledge about community economic conditions, previous history of the business, reputation of current owners, and impact of neighboring businesses. A study conducted by Shell (1999) supports the importance of preparation. Student negotiators who used a formal preparation system "reached better agreements in both the face-to-face and the computer network conditions—not just for themselves but for both sides" (p. 16). Preparation involves factors such as the following:

- Choosing optimum timing and location for the negotiation
- Making sure the decision makers necessary for an agreement are at the table
- Assessment of the options, expectations, and BATNAs of negotiating parties
- Awareness of ground rules or norms for behavior important for the context
- An understanding of the negotiating style that other negotiators might display

For some negotiations, a quick outline about expectations, interests (ours and theirs), and BATNA may be sufficient for preparation. For negotiations where outcome may have long-lasting implications, a systematic approach that looks at all essential elements that might affect outcomes may be necessary. Some negotiators spend as much as 50% of their time preparing for negotiations. How do we know how much preparation is necessary for a negotiation? Fisher and Ertel (1995) provide valuable questions (which we have reframed) to assess the amount of preparation necessary for a negotiation:

- Are we likely to be quarreling about the nature of the problem or interests?
- Am I clear about what the other party believes about these issues?
- Is the situation by nature one that promotes winners and losers?
- Do the outcomes have short-term or long-term consequences?
- How important is it for each of us to reach agreement?
- Will the level of power or leverage greatly affect how well we collaborate?
- How difficult will the other parties be to work with?
- How much will be expected of me in the final agreement?

MIT professor and negotiator Larry Susskind leads 50- to 60-member multiparty negotiations. He regards preparation as a critical phase in which parties agree on meeting times and agenda, and assess the resources required for potential options (Isenhart & Spangle, 2000). Preparation reduces the unknowns and provides greater confidence in the process. It is equally vital in organizational staff negotiations, community negotiations, and business negotiations. For example, in negotiations with a 10-member department staff, Spangle used anonymous assessment surveys and interviews with managers to identify problems. Based on the initial assessment, he mailed to all participants a proposed agenda requesting additions or revisions. When the 6-hour negotiation took place, the staff expressed confidence that they were discussing the most important issues in a process about which they had some input.

Negotiation often has less to do with issues than it does with unsureness about potential outcomes, emotions underlying the issues, or participants' fear that they will be taken advantage of in the settlement. Preparation can reduce these potential barriers by promoting greater confidence in the process and by soliciting participants' input regarding outcomes. People will engage in a greater level of open participation if they believe they have some measure of control over the process.

Good Questioning

Skilled negotiators ask more than twice the number of questions (about 21% of all behaviors; refer to Chapter 4, Table 4.1) than average negotiators do during a negotiation (Rackham, 1985). But this skill refers to more than just asking questions, or negotiation could fast become interrogation. The questions are of a particular type and serve different purposes than questions in other settings.

Questions used in negotiation tend to be open-ended, probing for information that will provide clues for creative solutions. *What* is asked more often than *why*. *What* questions promote descriptive responses that uncover hidden information. *Why* questions tend to be confrontational, promoting judgment, evaluation, and defensive responses. Although the purpose of questioning in some settings is to prove a point, the purpose of questioning in negotiation is to promote dialogue about an issue, test for understanding, or probe for underlying issues and interests.

Marsick and Sauquet (2000) propose that, in addition to uncovering valuable information, questions serve as an important tool for critical reflection about an issue:

- What else is going on in that environment that I might not have considered but that has an impact on how I understand the solution?
- In what ways could I be wrong about my hunches?
- In what way might I be using inapplicable lessons from my past to frame problems or solutions, and is this framing accurate?
- Are there other ways to interpret the feelings I have in this situation? (p. 389)

Questions widen our understanding so that we can better assess the problem and alternatives that are available.

After more than a decade of teaching negotiation in both university and corporate settings, we have found that less-skilled negotiators have a great deal of difficulty asking the "right" question—the one that unlocks the mystery behind the problem. This skill is difficult to teach. It involves listening as much to what isn't being said as to what is being said. It's sensing that something is being left out of the story or that some information is being stretched to the edge of truth. Becoming an effective questioner requires practice, patience, and tenacity to get at the hidden information.

The questions we choose will depend on both the phase and context of the negotiation. A few of the questions that might be useful during the different phases are listed next:

Information sharing:

1. What is important to you?

2. To help me understand, prioritize your needs for me.

3. What would you like to know about us in this deal?

4. What's not working that we need to fix?

5. Can I ask you a few questions to see if my facts are correct?

6. What is the problem as you see it?

Problem solving:

1. Are you willing to do some problem solving on areas where we appear to have differences?

2. Can we break the problem into smaller parts?

3. What are we trying to achieve by . . . ?

4. If we thought outside the box, what's a different way we could handle this problem?

5. Is there a better way we can do this?

Option generating:

1. In an ideal world, what would you like to see happen?

2. Can you reframe your proposal in a different way?

3. Would you consider . . . ?

4. Suppose we tried . . . ?

5. What if . . . ?

6. Can you explain the drawbacks you see in this option?

7. What do we need to do to make this work for you?

Settlement:

1. Are you willing to give a little on this one issue so that we can finalize this agreement today?

2. Do you see any problems later if we choose this course of action?

3. What will you need from me in order to sell this agreement to your group?

An intuition about appropriate timing is an important facet of questioning. Asking a question at the wrong time may elicit feelings that present new barriers for discussion. When unsure about timing, ask permission to ask a question, such as, "Is it okay if I ask you about . . . ?" Asking permission provides feedback about your timing.

In meeting with a new client for the first time, Isenhart begins by asking herself: What isn't being discussed by this team? What topic is consistently avoided by this manager? Some consultants call the hidden topic "the elephant in the room." Everyone knows it's there, but no one dares to mention it. The consultant's goal is to identify the elephant and make it possible for the group to openly discuss it.

● QUALITIES OF THE HEART

Listening

To be able to listen effectively, we need to be able to manage our own self-talk (the things we think while others are speaking). If we are creating counterarguments while others speak, we reduce our ability to understand. Rackham (1985) found that average negotiators create twice as many counterarguments compared to skilled negotiators. Effective negotiators observe longer, attempting to get a broader picture of what's going on before engaging in argument. Dawson (1999) states, "You get more by finding out what the other person wants than you do by clever arguments supporting what you need" (p. 17). In one corporate intervention, Spangle conducted staff negotiations about how to handle department problems. For an hour, members argued their points with little progress. Eventually, Spangle pointed out that it would be difficult to resolve differences until members took more time to listen to each other. If everyone's talking, who's doing the listening? After this point, the tone of the discussion changed along with the constructiveness of problem solving.

To listen to another, we must temporarily suspend judgment and focus attention on potential shared interests or goals. The challenge is to quiet our internal judges who would like to impose a way of thinking or behaving on others. Negotiation challenges us to get beyond the narrow limits of rigid thinking to see a wider spectrum of possibilities. Negotiation challenges us to make choices among:

- One right answer or many answers
- One path to outcomes or many paths to outcomes
- A single understanding of events or several understandings
- Linear thinking or systemic thinking
- Selling, telling, and demanding or learning through inquiry

If the outcome is primary in importance for us, then suspending judgment means we are willing to allow for several answers to problems and many paths to outcomes. But by trying to impose our preconceived outcomes, we may actually sabotage our goals.

Keltner (1994) explains that the effective negotiator must be able to "control the imposition of his or her own thoughts onto what he or she hears others saying; and to avoid hearing what he or she wants to hear. The ability to separate out issues, attitudes and opinions is vital" (p. 78).

Perspective taking is a listening skill often associated with success in negotiation. This skill involves seeing the issue from different viewpoints. Communication that demonstrates awareness of another's point of view facilitates better understanding of assumptions and barriers associated with problem solving. Krauss and Morsella (2000) identify the principles associated with perspective taking:

- When listening, try to understand the intended meaning of what your counterpart is saying.
- When formulating a message, consider what the listener will take your words to mean. (pp. 135-137)

One of the goals for listening is to create *dialogue*. Dialogue, which involves inquiry and learning, differs from advocating positions, which involves telling and restricting information. Constructive listening probes for underlying assumptions, judgments based on inaccurate information, early prejudices, and inaccurate attributions, all of which can get in the way of discussion. If information is power, dialogue promotes greater shared power, which promotes better solutions and easier implementation. In the example in Box 5.1, Roger restricted information, unaware of his actual potential with his staff.

Additionally, listening involves two important qualities of relationship: respect and confirmation. In every setting where we have conducted surveys, *respect* consistently emerges as an important factor for working productively with others. Whether in families, community groups, or corporate settings, people resist working with others who they believe fail to demonstrate respect. For Roger, respect began by putting down his clipboard and focusing his attention on employees. Respect means allowing for appropriate expressions of differences of opinion. The attitude "my way or the highway" has high costs in terms of relationship and accomplishing goals. Respect communicates openness to feedback and a desire for deeper understanding about the context of a given problem, the hows and whys. This is contrasted against advocacy, which promotes self at the expense of others. Constructive listening balances respect for both self and others.

Closely related to respect is a factor called *confirmation*. Confirmation involves statements that are supportive, display agreement about some aspects of content, express positive feelings, and affirm the contributions of others. It is one of the best predictors that a relationship or a negotiation will be successful. Wilmot (1987) explains, "Confirmation involves more than just noticing the other; it entails responsiveness, 'tuning in' to them, and enacting appropriate conversational and relational skills. As such, confirmation is one of the most effective ways to receive positive responses from another person" (p. 230). *Disconfirmation* involves devaluing behaviors, demonstrated in interrupting responses, irrelevant or tangential statements, or remarks that discount the contributions of others. It is not surprising to find that ineffective negotiators make five times more statements regarded as irritating than effective negotiators do (Rackham, 1985).

Disagreement in a way that impugns the competence or contributions of others causes others to increase their commitment to their own ideas and reject the information and reasoning we bring to the problem (Johnson, Johnson, & Tjosvold, 2000). Roger displayed disconfirmation toward his staff when he looked more at his clipboard than his employees. Even in the presence of disagreement, affirming the competence of others tends to create conditions in which others are less critical of our ideas, more interested in what we have to say, and more willing to incorporate our ideas and reasoning into their analysis (Johnson, Johnson, & Tjosvold, 2000). People who feel confirmed will be more willing to disclose information and engage in give-and-take because they believe that their contributions will be valued.

Ellinor and Gerard (1998) identify a practice called *defensive listening*, which occurs when someone listens from a perspective of competition, an attitude of "it's me or you," or from a perspective of fear. Ellinor and Gerard (1998) state, "We build walls and peer over them. Listening becomes defensive, information gathering about the adversary" (p. 103). Overcoming defensive listening involves suspension of our internal conversations and quieting of our internal judges, which see only one way to handle the issues. Instead, we refocus our attention on specifics of the issue before us rather than outcomes. To deal with our internal judges, we might even volunteer, "Help me with my fears about . . ." or "I'm feeling a little anxiety about . . . ". We might reduce anxiety by checking out our assumptions about the issues.

To reduce defensive listening, we might demonstrate more willingness to be persuaded by others. Small concessions about aspects of a problem or principles that are less important to us can serve as bridges to greater achievement of outcomes. The willingness to be persuaded may even be reciprocated by those approaching the issue as stubbornly as we are. Ellinor and Gerard (1998) advise, "This requires temporary letting go of attachments both for and against your own and others' positions. This provides space where thoughts themselves can be examined and creatively influence one another" (p. 105).

At a personal level, we can reduce our resistance to emotion-laden messages by *depersonalizing* the issues. Separate personal worth from criticism of ideas. The more we attach self-esteem to acceptance of an idea, the more we will be triggered into highly positional and emotional responses.

Managing Emotion

Probably no one factor sabotages principled negotiation more than the inability to manage emotions. Statements during difficult negotiations trigger emotional reactions, which cause people to make defensive or attacking statements. Sometimes, negotiators will purposely attempt to trigger emotions to manipulate others into making concessions they might otherwise not make. In this sense, it becomes a manipulative tool. Even in the best negotiations, emotion emerges because parties care deeply about an issue. Allowing the emotion to influence responses seriously harms a negotiator's ability to get the best deal. Family and marriage negotiations quickly disintegrate when emotion suppresses reasonableness. Box 5.2 describes how emotion severely harmed a mediated family negotiation.

Many issues in negotiations will trigger hot emotional reactions such as those described between Mark and his stepdaughter. The challenge will be to manage impulsive responses that sabotage progress in discussions. Failure to control responses will escalate emotional spirals, which undermine our achievement of interests. Mischel and DeSmet (2000) offer a number of self-regulation techniques designed to interrupt the cycle of provocation and reduce the influence of emotion on discussions:

Box 5.2

FATHER AND DAUGHTER SQUARE OFF

Mark and Teri are parents of two daughters—Jenny, who is 15, and Kara, who is 7. Mark is Jenny's stepfather and Kara's biological father. For the past few months, boys have begun calling Jenny at home or stopping by for visits. With Teri's approval, Mark felt forced to establish a family rule: No boys in the house after school or in the evening and no phone calls to boys unless parents are home. Following multiple infractions of this rule, reported by Kara, Mark engaged in a series of threats with potential violence toward Jenny. The family called a mediator to help resolve the problems before the situation escalated further.

At the negotiation, Mark presented his side first. He ended with a statement deploring the lack of respect for rules or authority by modern teens. "Teens don't listen anymore." Jenny began her story but was soon interrupted by Mark, who said, "See, there she goes. Lack of respect for authority and won't listen to us." The mediator cautioned Mark about such interruptions. Jenny began two more times, and each time Mark interrupted with admonitions.

Although Mark was aware of negotiation ground rules, he could not control his emotions about the situation and continued his interruptions. His background in law enforcement taught him that rules are meant to be followed and enforced. Jenny responded with anger and frustration. The stronger her requests for some give by Mark on the rule, the stronger and louder he got. Emotion began to suppress any possibility of reasonableness. Jenny began crying and eventually quit talking. Mark complained of Jenny's attempts to manipulate the family. Discussions ended in a cease-fire and a commitment to talk about the issues in a couple of days.

The next morning, Mark and Teri found a note on Jenny's pillow that read, "I've gone looking for someone who will listen." It was many years before Jenny resurfaced, and even then it was only in a private meeting with her mother to let her know she was okay.

The negotiation failed even with the presence of a mediator. How could this negotiation have been conducted so that emotion would have less power over discussions? What could have been done to create common ground or shared interests?

- Take time out to step away from the emotional triggers.
- Where appropriate, try communicating in writing instead of face to face.
- Manage stress through exercise, rest, and diet prior to a potentially stressful situation.
- Allow more flexibility in your goals for a negotiation.
- Look for small achievements in the movement toward larger goals.
- Reduce the intensity of situations through appropriate humor.
- Talk over the problem with a third party. (pp. 268-271)

The important thing is to do something to de-escalate potentially damaging emotional displays.

If the issue is the other party's emotional display, the first rule is to resist a similar emotional response. This will only make matters worse. Stop and refocus. Clarify the deeper message that you are hearing. Reframe the problem in more approachable, less stressful terms. Occasionally, reassurance that you want to improve the situation coupled with expressions of a concern for undersatnding can momentarily reduce anxieties. If it appears that the emotion may be spiraling out of control, it is time to either set some ground rules or break off discussion until tensions subside. Fisher and Davis (1987) recommend the following actions when others display strong emotion in negotiation:

- Acknowledge their feelings.
- Withdraw from discussion long enough to recompose.
- Step aside; let them vent.
- Separate the causes of the feelings from the substantive problem and deal with them in parallel.
- Return to the purpose for the negotiation. (p. 119)

Because emotion plays a significant role in the negotiations that matter the most to us, managing our own emotional triggers and the dynamics that trigger intense emotions in others becomes a critical skill in achieving our goals. Box 5.3 describes a small town's council meeting during which emotion escalated to stalemate. Although the incident is unusual, the situation depicts emotional dynamics that occur when there is a lot at stake for negotiators.

Integrity

The willingness of others to share information with us, engage in constructive problem solving, make concessions, or refrain from distributive tactics is related to the integrity with which we conduct negotiations. Although some people engage in distributive tactics regardless of whom they negotiate with, most people respond favorably to a negotiator who demonstrates high integrity. Genuine honesty, supported by a good reputation, may be the most important asset a negotiator possesses. A history of being fair and

Box 5.3

WHAT'S A TOWN TO DO?

The rural town of Plainsville, incorporated in 1928, is home to 924 residents. Because of the town's small size, there hasn't been the need for a police force, lawyers, or municipal town ordinances. The town council and fire department members donate their time. Stretching the town's $50,000 budget for maintenance of the water and sewer systems consumes most of the council's discussion time.

A crisis now faces the town. Rueben Smalley operates a business out of his home. He gets paid by auto shops in nearby communities to haul away tractor-trailer tires, which he stores in his back yard until he is able to sell them to a tire recycler in Preston. Unfortunately, Preston's need for the tires is sporadic. Currently, Rueben has more than 2,000 tires in his back yard waiting to be sold to the recycler.

The neighbors have been angry about this town eyesore. The town council members say that there is no ordinance against storing the tires and, if they did have one, they couldn't enforce it. There's no money for legal fees. So the town council asks Rueben to attend a meeting to negotiate an agreement about the tires.

The meeting begins cordially enough. Rueben speaks of his right to have a business. The town council speaks of its need to care for the upkeep and appearance of the community. Then it begins. One of the council members says, "If a bolt of lightening hit those tires, the whole town would become a hazardous gas cloud. We'd all be just a memory." Rueben responds, "You have a gift for exaggeration. That is nearly impossible." Another council member adds, "Our children are at risk from all the mosquitoes breeding in your back yard. Your yard is a public nuisance." Rueben counters, "I have a right to use my property in any way I want. I don't say anything about the junk cars in other people's yards or the lawns that aren't watered." Another member points at Rueben. "We can make you do it. We'll pass a hazardous materials ordinance." Rueben responds, "You can't enforce it. I'm a law-abiding citizen, and you're harassing me." The meeting dissolves into threats and counterthreats, and discussion breaks off without progress.

What might have prevented escalation of emotions? If you were a negotiator for the town council, what process or tactics do you think might have been more effective?

honest with people translates into higher-quality relationships and fewer barriers to overcome. A lesson that too many negotiators learn the hard way is that once you leave the high road of honesty and trustworthiness, it's very difficult to get back on it.

Shell (1999) points out that once negotiators sacrifice their integrity in questionable moves, they lose the right to protest other people's conduct: "Once you join them in the gutter, you forfeit your moral and legal advantage" (p. 228). Nyerges (1991) goes further; he claims that without honesty and integrity, both intellectual and moral, the negotiator is doomed to fail. Integrity is expressed through the following:

- Faithfulness to one's word
- Resisting destructive tactics even when they might produce greater gain
- Demonstrating concern for the interests of the other

A negotiator who acquires a reputation for genuineness, reliability, and trustworthiness will find that others are more willing to establish relationships and exchange information.

Demonstrating a lack of integrity involves behaviors such as misrepresenting information, engaging in deceptive tactics, or agreeing to a settlement that may be unfair for the other party. People will choose to do repeat business with those who they believe treated them fairly. A family member may win in a negotiation with another family member through deceptive tactics, but the residual effects may last for years. People talk. Your reputation for integrity or the lack of it may influence others with whom you'd like to negotiate in the future.

QUALITIES OF COURAGE ●

Speaking Clearly

The goals for communication influence outcomes. If our goal is to persuade or defeat our opponent, we're likely to encounter a great deal of resistance. Rackham (1985) found that average negotiators use three times as many attacking, confronting, and defending statements compared to effective negotiators. Attack-and-defend statements trigger defensiveness and reluctance to cooperate in opponents.

Speaking clearly involves framing issues so that the issues can be understood. Statements should include values, interests, or aspects of a situation valued by our listener. Fisher and Ertel (1995) suggest that we try to put ourselves in the other party's shoes and "imagine what he might think or say—not about the whole issue but about each of the points important to us" (p. 84). Boldly saying something is not enough; what we say must be spoken in such a way that others may have greater openness.

In addition to our spoken words, our body language communicates a great deal during negotiations. The way we sit, stand, react, and respond sometimes communicates the wrong messages to the other party. For example, in simulated negotiations between Japanese and U.S. businessmen, Graham (1981) found that favorable negotiation outcomes were associated with facial expressions that most closely matched or mirrored the other party's and negative outcomes were associated with brow wrinkles. Nierenberg and Calero (1971) identify closed body posture, signified by crossed legs, as a sign of resistance in sales negotiations. Many behaviors characterized as nonverbal may influence discussion in unintended directions. This supports the conclusion of a DePaulo (1992) laboratory study that found that restricting nonverbal communication by phone, fax, or computer may actually improve the potential for integrative, win-win solutions.

The following lists identify many of the behaviors regarded as positive or negative in negotiations:

- Negative: flinching, sighing, wincing, frowning, squirming, looking away, piercing eye contact, backing up, arms folded, higher volume of voice, rolling of eyes, pointing at others, no longer speaking much, avoiding eye contact
- Positive: leaning forward, taking notes, smiling, returning to a topic a second time, pleasant eye contact, turning toward others, open body posture (arms or legs uncrossed), relaxed face, open palms, head nods

Highly effective negotiators are skilled at reading nonverbal cues, which communicate a great deal about another's level of cooperativeness or interest in resolving differences. However, Stark (1994) advises caution when reading nonverbal cues: "A single gesture is like a word standing alone" (p. 47). Gestures must be read in clusters, such as fidgeting while avoiding eye contact or turning away while frowning. Clusters of behavior will often reveal more accurate and truthful representations about the way others feel than the words they use at the moment.

Building Relationships

In some contexts—such as house buying, car buying, or legal transactions—relationship may not play a significant role in influencing negotiated outcomes. In other contexts, relationship plays a background role that influences many of the variables of the negotiation. The high priority placed on this factor by so many of the scholars reflects relationship's importance in many contexts. But even Fisher (1991a) cautions,

Most negotiators would be well advised to consider whether their interest in a short-term substantive outcome is in fact greater than their interest in good long-term relations. Sometimes a one-time sale to a stranger for a high price will be more valuable than an ongoing relationship. (p. 123)

Many scholars and studies support relationship's impact on negotiation, including the following:

■ Negotiators with high aspirations and high trust produce more cooperative behavior and information exchange than do negotiators with low trust. (Kimmel, Pruitt, Magenau, Konar-Goldband, & Carnevale, 1980)

■ Familiarity with the other party's position on the issues and preferred tactics for handling differences correlates with disputants spending less time on competitively oriented conflict. (Papa and Pood, 1988)

■ "Good working relationships based on some combination of respect, admiration, perceived need, obligation, and friendship are a critical source of power in helping to get things done." (Kotter, 1985, p. 40)

■ "A poor, hostile, or competitive relationship makes it harder to talk about what really matters to you, increases the amount of posturing and misdirection by both sides, and leads to less attractive outcomes." (Skopec & Kiely, 1994, p. 140)

Developing the qualities of relationship necessary to promote sharing of information, trust, and cooperation requires negotiators to engage in several kinds of behavior:

1. Create an environment in which people feel safe to share what's important to them. People do not want to appear vulnerable, so they'll begin with positional statements to protect themselves. As we listen and value their input, they'll have a greater tendency to lower their guard and their need to maintain their position. Feeling safe promotes a greater sharing of information and trust.

2. Break the nonproductive communication patterns people expect when they negotiate. Because of past experience, many people expect their opponents to begin with unrealistic demands, to make confrontative statements, and to demand rather than to ask. By demonstrating our interest in the perspective, goals, and interests of others, we reclaim a middle ground of partnership and problem solving.

3. Demonstrate a willingness to learn and understand. By demonstrating an attitude that you're willing to learn from others, they begin to trust you and share more of themselves. Ellinor and Gerard (1998) explain that "your willingness to be vulnerable becomes a strength that helps others share responsibility with you and build their own confidence and self-reliance" (p. 181).

Fisher (1991b) defines a good negotiation relationship as one built on trust and effective communication and believes relationship so important that he concludes, "A good working relationship is so helpful to the negotiation of satisfactory outcomes that it is often more important than any particular outcome itself" (p. 132). This conclusion certainly supports the goals we might expect for negotiation in marriage and family, communities, or ongoing business dealings. Box 5.4 describes a negotiation in which many factors, including good relationship, saved a buyer money.

Creativity

Peace educator Betty Reardon once said, "The failure to achieve peace is in essence a failure of imagination" (Coleman and Deutsch, 2000, p. 365). Negotiation has greater potential when negotiators invest imagination and creativity in their problem-solving processes. Creativity involves seeing problems from new perspectives, arranging familiar elements in new, innovative ways, or arriving at answers born of insight into situations. Wycoff (1986) states, "Creativity is seeing things everyone around us sees while making connections that no one else has made" (p. 21).

DeBono (1973) distinguishes between *vertical thinking*, in which "one selects the most promising approach to a problem, the best way of looking at a situation," and *lateral thinking*, in which "one generates as many alternatives as one can . . . even after one has found a promising one" (p. 39). Lateral thinking involves the willingness to explore new pathways and expand the boundaries of the current situation. DeBono (1973) proposes that lateral thinking in problem solving occurs in several ways:

- Looking again at things that are taken for granted (re-examining assumptions)
- Reducing division and polarization on issues, which are natural tendencies of the mind
- Engaging in deliberate generation of ideas
- Repackaging information in different ways

Negotiators engage in lateral thinking when they engage in brainstorming to identify innovative ideas or when they invite others to look at a problem from a different perspective.

Creativity lies behind Lax and Sebenius's (1986) principle of *creating value*, a process that they say is innovative, creative, and uses ingenuity to put "familiar pieces of the problem together in ways that people had not previously seen, as well as by wholesale reformulation of the problem" (p. 31). Negotiators take the elements of a situation and ask, "What's missing that all parties need?" Hargrove (1998) points out that "creative people do not merely focus on what already exists . . . they're too busy exploring white

Box 5.4

KIM'S GOOD BUY

Kim went to a computer store where she had shopped many times before. Because Kim had already researched computers and prices, she approached her purchase with a great deal of confidence.

When Kim arrived at the computer department, she asked for Sal, a salesperson she'd made purchases from in the past. She discussed attributes of the model she wanted, joked with him about difficult clients he'd worked with that day, and reviewed prices. She asked about the price for adding more computer memory. He told her the cost for the extra memory would be $75 and that it would take only 15 minutes to install. Kim said, "I've checked elsewhere for this computer, and I may be able to do a little better, but if you can give me the computer and the extra memory for that price, I'll buy the computer *today*."

After 10 minutes, Sal returned from the service department. Apologetically, he said, "I've got some bad news. We don't have the memory you asked for, but we can put a *larger* amount in for only $125 plus installation." Kim responded, "I'm not prepared to spend more money. If you can do the additional memory at *no* cost, go ahead and put it in." Sal said, "I don't know if we can do that. We'll need to speak with the manager. Let's go together."

Kim and Sal went back to the service department to speak with the manager. The manager said, "I'm not sure what to do because we can't sell the memory to you for the same cost as the lower memory." Kim, politely and respectfully, asked, "What options do you have? What can you do to save this deal?" The manager said, "You've done a lot of business with Sal in the past. Let me do some checking."

Five minutes later, the manager returned. He said, "I'll give you the additional memory at cost. However, I will not charge you for installation, and we will apply a $20 rebate from the company, which is not advertised." Kim mentally calculated that the cost would be very close to the original, but the deal allowed her to gain substantial computer memory. Kim added, "I've also wanted this computer book. But I notice that its publishing date is 1997, several years old. What can you do for me there?" The manager responded, "We'll give it to you at half price."

Kim received a very good deal from the company. She attributed the deal to many factors, including possessing a good BATNA, maintaining a cordial atmosphere with humor and respect, asking questions instead of demanding or threatening, and the factor she believed to be the most important: nurturing a good relationship with the sales staff.

spaces between what already exists and inventing 'what's missing' that never existed before" (pp. 188-189).

Coleman and Deutsch (2000) propose several guidelines for fostering creativity during problem-solving discussions:

- Develop a serious but playful atmosphere.
- Foster confidence to take the risk of being outlandish.
- Provide the right environment (few distractions) and sufficient time.
- Allow for alternating phases of closed or rigid thinking and open or novel thinking. (pp. 361-363)

Creativity is an important, often overlooked element of negotiation. It requires a setting where innovation is valued, parties feel safe suggesting novel ideas, and someone takes the risk of inviting others to expand the boundaries of thinking about solutions.

● COMMUNICATION COMPETENCE

Some scholars describe the communication skills associated with problem solving, conflict management, and negotiation as falling within three domains of communication competence: communication's effectiveness, relational appropriateness, and situational appropriateness (Papa and Canary, 1995). Communication is effective when it is helpful, useful, and successful in achieving objectives. It is relationally appropriate when it is pro-social and constructive. Communication is situationally appropriate when the communicator possesses the ability to adapt communication to the needs of the situation. From this perspective, negotiation competence would measure a negotiator's ability to deliver effective communication in terms of listening, speaking clearly, and engaging in good questioning. Relational appropriateness involves the ability to build relationship in a constructive manner and sensitivity to the norms and values of context. Situational appropriateness means the ability to prepare properly for the needs of a situation and to engage in creative problem solving.

Gross and Guerrero (2000) conducted research to investigate the relationship between communication competence and conflict style. They wanted to know how the choice of conflict style (integrating, dominating, obliging, compromising, avoiding) was perceived as situationally appropriate by 100 participants involved in decision making. They found that the integrating style was perceived as the most appropriate and effective of the styles, whereas the avoiding style was perceived as both ineffective and inappropriate. The compromising style received mixed support, regarded as moderately effective and appropriate. Participants judged the dominating style as effective in some situations, although it was also generally regarded as ineffective. Table 5.1 summarizes their results.

Table 5.1   Communication Competence Related to Conflict Style

Conflict Style	Appropriate	Effective
Integrating	High	High
Dominating	Moderate to high	Low
Obliging	Moderate	Low
Compromising	Moderate	Moderate
Avoiding	Low	Low

DOES PERSONALITY STYLE MAKE A ● DIFFERENCE IN NEGOTIATION?

The answer is *yes* and *no*. It may be *no* in the sense that the qualities and skills described in this chapter may exist in many different styles of personality, from introvert to extrovert, from analytical to expressive. Each style of personality can involve effective or ineffective listening, effective or ineffective questioning, or the ability or inability to prepare for negotiations. Negotiators who have personality traits such as stubbornness, quick temper, self-centeredness, or aggressiveness may find it difficult to engage in perspective taking or working in a collaborative manner with others. Particular personality traits may create predispositions to specific kinds of behavior in negotiation. Gilkey and Greenhalgh (1991) explain, "Situations simply trigger what comes naturally to each individual" (p. 280).

In a study that looked at the correlation between personality and approaches to conflict, Antonioni (1998) found that personalities described as extroverted, conscientious, and open tended to choose integrative approaches and did less avoiding. In addition, agreeableness as a personality trait was positively correlated with avoiding and negatively correlated with dominating. The ability to achieve integrative outcomes appears to be related more to clusters of personality traits than to global descriptions such as extrovert or introvert, expressive or analytical.

Shapiro and Jankowski (1998) argue that personality influences tactical choices in negotiation. They distinguish between four personality types: extrovert, pragmatist, analytic, and amiable. They explain these types as follows:

- Extroverts like to tell stories and won't focus on details.
- Pragmatists play hardball negotiation, like to take charge, and will be impatient.
- Analytics are well prepared, logical, methodical, slow, and lack sensitivity to others.
- Amiables will listen, value win-win solutions, empathize, but may be difficult to pin down on issues.

The weakness of personality approaches is that the stereotypes depicted fail to account for context, goals, subject matter, and individual variations. People will use different styles and goals as contexts and opponents change.

The real issue of personality and its relationship to negotiation may be the negative traits that create barriers to collaborative processes. Some behaviors need to be unlearned. Negotiators with an expressive personality may need to develop a highly tuned awareness to contexts, situations, and word choices that trigger something within them that undermines their ability to manage emotion. Similarly, some personality types may lack creativity, a highly valued attribute of effective negotiators. These people may have to rely on structured processes to facilitate discussion about creative options rather than rely on their ability to be creative.

● DOES EXPERIENCE INFLUENCE EFFECTIVENESS IN NEGOTIATION?

Experience appears to improve effectiveness in predictable ways. For example, Thompson (1990a) found that experienced negotiators are better able to judge the priorities and preferences of others and make better strategic use of compatible issues. Experienced negotiators are better able to identify and strategically use information. Murninghan, Babcock, Thompson, and Pillutla (1999) found that experience correlated with better personal and joint outcomes. They found that getting and exchanging information about preferences was central in the experienced negotiator's success. Even naive, uninformed, experienced negotiators performed as well as informed, experienced negotiators because they were adept at getting the information they needed to put a deal together.

● DOES GENDER INFLUENCE EFFECTIVENESS IN NEGOTIATION?

Although it is difficult to assess the influence of context, purpose, and goals from the conclusions reached in many of the studies that looked at the impact of gender on negotiation outcomes, some generalizations are beginning to emerge. Women apparently experience negotiation differently from men (Deaux, 1987; Eagly, 1987). Kolb (1993) suggests that because women often view situations in terms of relationships, they will treat negotiations more contextually in terms of ongoing relationships. Tannen (1994) describes the difference as one of goals: Men pursue instrumental goals (fix or change the situation), and women pursue tangible goals (get through the situation).

Kolb (1993) proposes that women engage in problem solving through dialogue more than men. Men tend to be more preoccupied with agreements, use more persuasive tactics, and prefer more structured processes. Calhoun and Smith (1999) support this conclusion. They found that women used laughter twice as often as men (9.3% to 3.9%), made more statements and asked more questions about feelings (3.8% to 2.5%), rated both their own and others' tactics as more friendly, and when concern for the other was high, made more concessions.

Because of concerns for others and a greater need to preserve harmony, women may settle for lower joint outcomes than men. However, when women have high self-concern to go along with high other concern, they achieve joint outcomes equal to their male counterparts' (Calhoun and Smith, 1999). Both males and females engage in problem solving when incentives are sufficiently motivating.

Kolb (1993) observes that negotiation communication styles differ between men and women. Women tend to use more qualifiers, show more flexibility, talk less and be more easily interrupted, and be less likely to advocate their opinions openly. Men tend to engage in more linear thinking, use more self-enhancing statements, and use more confrontational techniques. Women will use tactics that are less contentious, engage in fewer extraneous arguments, use fewer put-down statements, and make fewer threats than men (Kimmel et al., 1980; Pruitt, Carnevale, Forcey, & Van Slyck, 1986). Halpern and Parks (1996) found that women delay discussions of money longer and talk about it for less time than men. Women tend to begin with interpersonal concerns before turning to issues involving money.

Fiske and Taylor (1984) propose that a great deal of the differences in style between men and women center on the environmental cues each focuses on. Whereas men may focus on legal issues, money, or power, women tend to focus on the broader situation with all its connections. Kolb and Williams (2000) arrive at similar insights. They argue that men favor negotiations that are rational exercises in problem solving. Women use "skills of connection" to read "shadow" factors of the situation such as the nonverbal messages, the underlying assumptions, the level of flexibility, terms of the relationship, or how strong a party feels about an issue (pp. 20-21). Women may use a different negotiating style, in part because they see different factors as important.

SUMMARY •

Although the kind of qualities or skills necessary for effective negotiation changes with the context, some skills appear to be important in many contexts. The top four skills, which the scholars approach consensus about, are preparation, listening, speaking clearly, and questioning skillfully. The factor that differentiates experienced from inexperienced negotiators is the ability to get information and to use it effectively.

The common theme among the most valuable qualities is communication. Negotiators demonstrate many of the same kinds of qualities we might expect of counselors, physicians, or researchers. Good negotiators must articulate their ideas clearly, listen to hear underlying messages, be sensitive to nonverbal cues, summarize information, and draw information out of people who may be reluctant to share it.

Effective negotiators manage themselves. They do this by managing their emotions during discussions. They demonstrate patience and, with the tenacity of cartoon character Wiley E. Coyote, are persistent in finding mutual-gain solutions. Qualities such as integrity and reputation speak to the importance of character in negotiation. *Who we are* communicates as much as the *words we speak*. Success with others begins with management of self.

PROFESSIONAL PROFILE

LINDA PUTNAM, ●
PROFESSOR OF COMMUNICATION,
TEXAS A & M AND DIRECTOR, PROGRAM
ON CONFLICT AND DISPUTE RESOLUTION

Negotiating Skills Required by Organizational Managers

Whether an organization is for profit or nonprofit, its managers use ncgo tiation skills to fulfill their responsibilities. They must negotiate with colleagues, executives, and subordinates to achieve results in a timely and consistent manner. Organizational goals depend on managers who, in addition to obtaining authorization from the executive level, collaborate with their colleagues in the hiring or reassignment of necessary personnel and in the allocation of resources among departments and projects. The practice of negotiation within organizations has been the focus of study for Dr. Linda Putnam.

The following interview highlights many skills that were covered in this chapter. The practitioner agrees that listening, questioning well, and speaking clearly are essential to effective negotiation in organizations. She emphasizes the importance of the skills of persuasive speech—specifically audience analysis—to the achievement of organizational goals. In this setting, preparation should involve consultation with the other parties to the negotiation in order to discern their interests as well as what authority they have over issues in negotiation. Because organizational members are by definition interdependent, successful negotiation depends on building and maintaining collegial relationships. This practitioner looks at managing emotion in a more nuanced way than does the literature cited in this chapter, pointing to the useful information emotions supply.

Introduction to the Practitioner

Linda Putnam became involved with the topic of negotiation through experience and her graduate study in human communication. She received her master's degree from the University of Wisconsin and taught at a community college; she was named department head and assigned to the first faculty bargaining team. Linda reports, "This was a somewhat traumatizing experience. I had no idea this was so involved and there was so much difficulty in reaching agreement. I became intrigued with the process and how to make it better. I studied game theory and interpersonal conflict; I decided negotiation would be an area I wanted to focus on."

In 1977, Linda completed her doctorate and joined the faculty at Purdue University in the area of organizational communication. She served there for 16 years, at which time Texas A & M named her chairperson of the communication department. Currently, she is the director of the Program on Conflict and Dispute Resolution at Texas A & M. She explains, "This is an interdisciplinary faculty that concerns itself with research, outreach, delivery of training, and colloquia. The program stretches me because it covers many arenas of conflict management: organizational, environment, health, and others. It's been interesting to work with such a wide array of disciplines."

In addition to her duties at the university, Linda trains corporate leaders in negotiation skills. She has worked with companies such as Proctor & Gamble providing skills training for labor-management negotiators. Some of this training has been provided to hospitals and hospital associations. One of Linda's interests is women managers and specific patterns they need to develop as negotiators.

Linda is well known in the field of organizational communication through her writing. She has published many articles and books. The best known of her contributions are editing (with Michael Roloff) a 1992 book called *Communication and Negotiation* (1992a), coauthoring an article in *Human Communication Research* on the role of communication in negotiation (1982), and writing an article on challenging traditional views of negotiation in *Negotiation Journal* (1994).

Linda identifies negotiation skills that apply across contexts. She asserts, "The most essential skill is a set of reframing skills—how to begin to think creatively inside a negotiation process. I spend a lot of time with students teaching them how to move among levels of abstraction in defining issues and situations." Linda contrasts this approach with negotiation that deals with issues from either an offensive or a defensive basis.

Other negotiation skills include the ability to ask open-ended questions. Linda elaborates, "Circular questioning is useful, as is how to move outside the problem arena. Active listening is important, so you're listening for what's not being said, along with statements about what you think this means, so that parties can operate from meaning and interpretation levels, not just levels of language."

Linda continues, "Persuasive skills are critical, because the negotiator needs to be able to articulate a position and support it and to understand the other person's values and orientation. What do you need? What are the values of the larger organization? Then, the negotiator must be able to translate needs and goals into bottom lines. For instance, a middle manager may be thinking about the broad arena of the organization, such as where it should be in the marketplace or where the cutting edge is, whereas you may be thinking in terms of your department needs and anticipating allocation of additional resources for a particular project. Even though the project may be serving the larger needs of the organization, you must translate the department's project into the mission for the cutting-edge market. More than likely, the project does relate to the cutting-edge mission; it may not be directly connected, but it does have a relationship that can be established. This skill is analyzing where the organization is going and how the particular project you're dealing with fits into that mission. The skilled negotiator makes that inferential leap, understanding how the connection operates, and articulates how this project contributes to the marketing mission."

Insights About Negotiation

Linda suggests a generic preparation for internal organizational negotiations. In going into a negotiation, the party needs to understand what the issues are and what are multiple ways to define those issues. The research shows that when there are multiple interpretations of what the situation is, success is more likely. The next step is to prioritize the concerns and needs of each side. Linda recommends, "When you're in an organization, consult with others before the negotiation begins. You are more likely to understand the issues better through the process of interaction. This is a critical stage in planning. Using the example above, where a department head goes to his or her manager requesting resources, it's critical to understand the needs and priorities of the people who are in the design phase or who will implement the project. A manager can't do this without a lot of consultation."

Linda cautions, "Some of these needs will conflict, so you need to understand them before you get into the negotiation. Then, there's the stage of analyzing the other party, who could be a higher-level manager or a manager from another unit. You should understand their needs and interests; you should define the problem from their point of view."

Another very important prenegotiation step is to understand the other party's authority. Linda asks, "Can they make a decision then and there? Sometimes parties don't like to admit that they don't have authority. But they delay the process when they don't have the ultimate say. So, it's critical to understand where they fit in a larger hierarchy, and what are the sets of relationships around decision processes."

Understanding the other party's style of bargaining also helps negotiators inside the organization. What strategies and tactics do they use? In an organization, there is usually someone who has dealt with this person before and can help you anticipate negotiation behaviors.

Linda adds to the mental preparation list: "Then, you set goals for yourself called 'target and resistance points.' Targets are what you can live with reasonably. It's extremely important to understand resistance points. These are your essential economic or resource needs; you must clearly understand what you can't relinquish and still accomplish your goals. Parties must know these limits before they negotiate, or they may end up with convoluted packages. Without these points, people don't know what is going to happen to them. Options aren't always understood prior to the negotiation."

An example of these steps is seen in a negotiation for new hires in an organizational unit. Linda offers, "In this scenario, a manager could reasonably get by with two (target) new hires and still meet their goals. However, they would like three (goal). And, they absolutely can't get the job done with only one (resistance point). You must know the connections to the organization and hold firm on that. Firmness on ends and flexibility on means are the keys."

Also, Linda advises thinking through what sorts of tradeoffs might be possible and how to package them. She advises negotiators to develop supporting arguments for each of the main issues. One planning step is to understand your Best Alternative to a Negotiated Agreement (BATNA). You need to know what this is and what its consequences are. There are times when you're willing to use your BATNA, when it is so costly to get agreement that you're willing to look at more alternatives for dealing with a situation.

Finally, all these parts of preparation rest on having an attitude that avoids the fixed-pie, win-lose mentality. Linda believes, "The negotiators should try to establish a collegial process whereby all parties gain. If they encounter something different when they're in a negotiation, they can switch strategies. However, I think they need to figure out how to set up the negotiation to find options and alternatives for a collegial process." Linda cautions against overconfidence and bias; don't be cocky about what you might be able to achieve. For example, in negotiating with upper management, managers may feel a sense of entitlement to certain resources. They go into the negotiation overconfident, and it hurts their bargaining. Managers should prepare with an orientation to make a negotiation work and with the sense that they are not necessarily privileged in this situation; the other parties have needs as well.

The typical organizational communication scenario that Linda names concerns the collective allocation of resources among managers. She recalls a group of managers all seated around a table: " There were only a certain number of dollars available to support laboratories for various units. The question was how to divide the resources. It had been very difficult in the past to go outside the organization for resources." The question of resource allocation was bogged down by perceptions of past unfairness. The result was competitive, often resentful feelings among managers.

One of the managers recognized how divisive this process had become over the years. Linda believes the breakthrough came when "he initiated a way that parties could compensate those who didn't have labs versus those who did. The parties could also be involved in expanding the pie; in this case, that meant a creative arrangement for charging lab fees. After studying how similar departments handled this situation, they were able to adopt new thinking and new options. Then, the middle managers had to convince their boss that the plan was viable. This executive opposed the new plan, and it took considerable persuasiveness on the part of the managers to bring him around." Eventually they convinced him to experiment, and the plan was successfully implemented.

Resource allocation among managers may also involve sharing staff. Linda offers an example: "The accounting department needs a new financial computer system, so its representative sits down to negotiate with a manager from the management information systems (MIS) department. The accounting department has worked with an MIS manager before and requests his help with installing the computer system. However, MIS is unwilling to release the employee because they have him assigned to one of their priority projects. So, the negotiation revolves around who from MIS should be assigned to the accounting department, when should the project be completed, and who should pay for the staff member's time." This situation can create friction and bad feelings between managers. There are several options that skilled negotiators use to avoid such outcomes, such as postponing the computer installation until the desired employee is free. Managers need to see the bigger organizational picture and be willing to package tradeoffs where both departments' needs are addressed.

Linda names several elements of successful negotiation. Most important to her is the following: "If there's a high level of conflict when negotiation is happening, parties should shift the way they *name*, *blame,* and *claim* what's happening in the conflict. What typically happens in negotiation is that the parties label the conflict differently—that is, they have different definitions for what the conflict is about. They blame the other party for the conflict and they have no ownership of it. If they are to reach a satisfactory agreement, they must act in ways that preserve their relationship. In order for negotiation to be successful, naming, blaming, and claiming have to shift. In successful negotiation, parties jointly feel ownership and responsibility for the problem. They quit blaming everyone but themselves or they jointly switch and blame the system at large. They begin to define the problem in ways that reflect the other party's perspective as well as their own."

Linda's definition of success is grounded in these shifts of negotiator thinking about the conflict. Her perspective is not "All parties get something"; of course, they must come to satisfactory agreements. However, those agreements are based on shifts in naming, blaming, and claiming. Success occurs when parties have reframed some issues, allowing them to build their understanding of the conflict as well as their relationship. Linda finds that the most satisfying and lasting agreements result from negotiations where parties have shifted their basic frames of reference.

Linda identifies hidden agendas as significant challenges in negotiating. In her experience, "When behaviors aren't consistent, or there isn't a standard of trust, you get a sense that the bargaining is about something else, not the issues on the table. I've had experiences where the hidden agenda was about saving face, or it involved rectifying past practices, or even political attacks. Somehow, those hidden agendas have to be unearthed, and parties have to sort through whether they're relevant or not to what's going on. Otherwise, they'll keep raising their ugly heads in some form or another!" Hidden agendas are challenging for managers who are involved in negotiations.

Another problem that many people face is dealing with latent and recurring conflict. The residue from past conflicts may color present negotiations. Linda offers an example: "Take two departments that have a history of conflict. When they try to agree on a joint policy, the residue of past conflicts enters in. They are quickly caught up in a repeated conflict cycle. What's needed here is an organizational development process: a new form of team building and a new form of understanding how to build cooperative relations from deep roots. When you get into such negotiations, you realize that the issue on the table is not really what you're here for. Somehow, the parties have to agree to disagree and put their history aside, or they must enter into a large-scale intervention." If the conflict history prevails, negotiations have little chance of success.

Another challenge is multiple parties in a negotiation. In Linda's view, "It's more difficult to find the good for the whole when there are many stakeholders. More and more negotiations involve multiple parties—joint ventures aren't just between two stakeholders; project teams involve multiple parties, and there are multiple units within those teams. What's happening in organizations is extremely fluid, and that fluidity means the dyadic nature of negotiation is breaking down. We're not to the point of contending that our old models don't work in large group settings, but we need to alter those models to fit more complex negotiations."

When negotiations break down, a cooling-off period is very important. If parties want to try negotiating again at a later time, there should be certain techniques used. Linda advises, "Try to redefine the issues, talk about who should be at the table and who should not, analyze where this issue should be placed in the organization. In other words, address why the negotiation broke down. The difficulty may not be simply the dynamics of the parties involved. There may be larger organizational issues they need to wrestle with. They need to find a new angle from which to address the issues."

If the cooling-off period and the broader organizational perspective don't work, third-party intervention may be employed. However, in Linda's opinion, "This should be a last resort. I think third-party intervention is used too often in organizations. People run to the next level of management too quickly, and managers at that level are really busy. Often, in order to save time, the manager will arbitrate rather than helping the parties to work through a conflict. The manager doesn't have a full understanding of the issue and is not very good at arbitrating. Unless there's a full-fledged alternative dispute resolution (ADR) program with ombudsmen, going to the next higher level to resolve a problem is not always effective."

Another thing the manager does is to throw the conflict back to the disputants, demanding that the parties work it out within a (usually brief) time frame. Linda believes, "If they can, that's great. But, if they're totally stuck, they need to move outside themselves. Going right back into the same frame of reference is usually not successful. Parties may find help from someone in the human resources department. This department is broadening its role to mediation, conflict management, and other constructive ways of resolving problems between employees." When negotiations break down, human resources departments in many organizations provide assisted negotiation.

Contextual Differences

In organizational negotiations, the systemic factors of organizations create major differences from negotiation in other contexts. Linda elaborates, "In organizations, no one is operating on an island; no group, no sets of individuals, are independent. There are lots of systemic factors impinging on negotiations. This doesn't contrast with all contexts, but it is critical to bring systemic factors into the process of organizational negotiation."

There are also differences related to the organizational bureaucracy. There are policies and regulations that both cause conflict and impinge on conflict management generally, and negotiation specifically. Linda says, "For instance, there are policies about hiring practices that impact relations across units. Dual career hiring is always difficult, because it runs right into those policies, involving the autonomy of one unit relative to another unit. Grievances and appeals must work within and around these policies." Organizational regulations may limit the options that negotiators have to reach settlement.

Another difference in the organizational context is the need to separate negotiation from other kinds of decision making. Linda explains, "Negotiation is not simply joint problem solving. A lot of issues are better handled by putting a group together to decide how to address the problem. In joint problem solving, people seldom come to the table with predisposed positions. Managers need to know when to convert a negotiation to a joint problem solving, when to convert it to litigation, and try to move among the ADR processes with more fluidity." The organizational context differs because of the systemic nature of organizations, their bureaucratic nature, and the range of decision-making models available to managers.

Changes and Conflicts

Significant changes influence the dynamics of negotiation in the organizational context. In Linda's view, "The nature of organizations is rapidly changing. Re-engineering and rapidly changing marketplaces are quickly reshaping arenas in organizations where negotiation is practiced. One trend is that negotiation has never had as much prominence as it enjoys today. It's not just around contracts—it's around everyday life." The rapidity of change forces a reliance on negotiation to conduct organizational business that was formally the domain of hierarchy and procedures.

Linda also notes the trend toward intercultural prominence in negotiation. She finds that many managers are involved in cross-cultural negotiations.

The understandings of conflict and negotiation differ across cultures. Linda observes, "Managers must struggle with what to do when they are highly familiar, medium familiar, and less familiar with a culture. In these cases, we now see a hybrid of the traditional Western negotiation model. Often, it's an adaptive hybrid, particularly at high levels of familiarity. There has to be much more fluidity for both the procedures and the process of negotiation, because those cultural interpretations are important and need to be 'on the stage.' The Japanese have a stronger relational model of negotiation, where they want to spend a lot of time becoming acquainted before they negotiate. Prescriptions do not work, nor always do essential beliefs about cultures. We're finding that while the study of high- and low-context cultures may help, negotiations depend on the dynamics of a particular duo or group."

Those who study international joint ventures discover various hybrids of negotiation models. Often what happens is that the French people come to negotiation expecting to bargain U.S. style, whereas the U.S. negotiator adapts her style to the French model. Where each side knows the other's culture, negotiators tend to accommodate each other's negotiation model. Where there is less familiarity, negotiators who are off site conform to the negotiation model of the host country, or they rely on interpreters and assisted negotiations. Intercultural negotiation is the cutting-edge arena for the study of negotiation.

Another trend is the study of women in negotiation. Linda thinks that "there are challenges coming in the academy and in industry, in that women do not fit the scripted models very well. They negotiate somewhat differently, and often there are variations. Feminist scholars suggest we rethink our negotiation model based on the different approaches women take. Deborah Kolb and I have written a chapter [called "Rethinking negotiation: Feminist views of communication and exchange"] where we examine a negotiation between a company and a consultant who are writing a contract. We show how that negotiation differs when you add a more feminist twist to integrative bargaining. This chapter is in a book called *Rethinking Organizational and Managerial Communication from Feminist Perspectives* [2000]." New and emerging trends include the rapid reshaping of organizations, the increase in intercultural negotiations, and the different ways women approach negotiation.

Another new area is the transformative model of negotiation. Linda notes that there's a lot of effort in ADR devoted to thinking about the relational outcomes of negotiation. And there is more effort than ever before at looking at the process. In the past, studies focused on cognitive bias, procedures, or stages in negotiation. Now scholars and practitioners are questioning whether there are techniques that transform the process or change the way disputants understand the conflict and their relationship.

Linda cites three differences among negotiation scholars and practitioners. First, she notes differences with regard to ethical behavior in negotiation. Negotiation is one of the arenas where there is some degree of ambiguity and deception in the beginning of the process. In Linda's experience, "What seems appropriate and ethical varies across organizations. In corporate training, we try to work out what constitutes an ethical contract. How much should the negotiator reveal? What's the difference between ambiguous statements and erroneous facts? The question becomes muddled in the business context." Disagreements about negotiation ethics mean we should pay more attention to this area.

There is disagreement about the role of emotions in negotiation. Linda feels strongly that "the new thinking needs to infuse traditional ways we've viewed negotiations. In the traditional models, emotions were removed from the scene because they infuse high-level conflicts in destructive ways. But rather than treating emotions as illegitimate or quickly removing them from the scene, bargainers should seek to understand them. For instance, in a major grievance case, where a manager feels particularly under attack, it's most helpful for him or her to understand that emotional process. In team bargaining, emotions may signal moves toward different directions. In personal negotiations, emotions are clues as to when you need to get outside help. Emotions may signal when negotiators need to reframe and redefine issues." Linda feels that practitioners need to get past the old thinking that emotions in negotiations are bad or destructive. The role of emotions needs attention in negotiation research.

There is disagreement about the role of relationships in negotiation. In Linda's opinion, "Relationships are very central. Complexities of trust, power, and affiliation are operative in negotiation but have often been left out of the discussions. Models of decision making show that no matter how skilled the negotiators or how perfect the processes they engage in, the outcomes are bombarded by relational problems. The area that has made more inroads on relationship management is hostage negotiation. These negotiations are not about substantive issues as much as they are about developing relationships to protect the lives of the hostages. By looking at how people change social distance in bargaining, you can build better relationships through the process." Disagreements among organizational practitioners center on ethical behavior, the role of emotions, and the centrality of relationships to negotiation.

Linda Putnam's work in organizational communication provides a unique perspective on negotiation. As teacher, scholar, writer, and practitioner, her reflections are broadly based. The generic skills she emphasizes are reframing, questioning, listening, and persuasiveness. She stresses the importance of the mental shifts of parties in naming, blaming, and claiming issues. The organizational context is characterized by its systemic nature, by bureaucratic procedures and regulations, by increasingly intercultural interactions, and by the rapidly changing structures of organizations. Linda offers cutting-edge insights about where the latest work in negotiation is happening: in the role of feminist thinking about negotiations. In her opinion, ethical behavior, the role of emotions, and the centrality of relationships deserve more attention. Her extensive writing, training, and teaching insure that these topics will not be neglected.

PROFESSIONAL PROFILE

● **ROBERT WATERMAN,**
  COAUTHOR OF *IN SEARCH OF EXCELLENCE*

Playing Columbo: The Best
Consultant Is a Skilled Negotiator

The following interview reinforces and expands on the skills outlined in this chapter. In consulting, preparation includes not only factual analysis, but many informal meetings with clients to understand them and their issues. The relationships built with clients result in both more information and more leverage for the consultant. As the number one skill, the practitioner names knowing oneself and one's organization. The consultant/detective must be adept at questioning; part of the Columbo approach involves asking just one more question. In consulting terms, brainstorming multiple options is termed "expanding the solution space."

Negotiation skill is right at the top of Bob Waterman's list of success factors in consulting. Negotiation lands the assignment in the first place; continuing negotiation, as the project progresses, is the outside consultant's only tool for making change happen as the project progresses. According to Waterman, even after a project is technically over, the best consultants check back with the client periodically, identify issues, and negotiate solutions. The care that is shown in both checking back and in offering to help often results in new assignments. Thus, in some important sense, the best consultants are always negotiating.

Introduction to the Practitioner

Most of us know Waterman as the coauthor (with Thomas Peters) of *In Search of Excellence* (1982). What we know less about is his 21 years at McKinsey and Company, Inc., where Bob was a senior director and manager in offices in San Francisco, Melbourne and Sydney, Australia, and Tokyo and Osaka, Japan.

150

Waterman's education began with a degree in geophysical engineering from the Colorado School of Mines; later, he received his MBA at Stanford Business School. Eventually, Bob joined McKinsey and Company where he worked from 1964 to 1985. Now Bob is on the board of several public companies, including AES, Inc., which is the world's largest independent power producer and a company he helped found, and the boards of a variety of non-profit organizations, including the World Wildlife Fund and the Restless Leg Syndrome Foundation. Bob assesses the importance of negotiation in his life: "Negotiation has been crucial to my career as far back as I can remember it."

Bob reflects on the publication of *In Search of Excellence*. "Tough negotiation should have been a stronger part of Tom's and my initial book contract. We were so happy to have a contract at all that it never occurred to us to get an agent. Big mistake. The typical book contract gives too many rights and advantages to the publisher." For readers who may not be familiar with this book, it has sold more copies that any other business book (around 7 million, Waterman estimates). "Needless to say, my buddy Tom Peters and I were better negotiators on subsequent books. But who would have dreamed that sort of success possible for a first book?" Since *In Search of Excellence* was published, Bob has written three other books: *The Renewal Factor: How the Best Get and Keep the Competitive Edge* (1987), *Adhocracy: The Power to Change* (1990), and *What America Does Right: Learning From Companies That Put People First* (1994).

Insights About Negotiation

Bob loves problem solving and views negotiation that way. He offers a visual aid: "Think of it as a Venn diagram—you know, that one where the two circles intersect. Think of one circle encompassing the needs of one party to the negotiation and the other circle surrounding the needs of the other party. At the beginning of the negotiation, there probably is some overlap in their needs; after all, they found each other in the first place. But at the outset the area of overlap—the intersection of those circles—may seem small. The negotiator's job is to bring those circles together, to enlarge that area of overlap."

As a problem solver, Waterman thinks of that area of overlap as the "solution space." The job of the consultant, in his view, is constantly to work at trying to enlarge the solution space, the area of overlap between those two circles. Bob says, "It's a process. You never get total agreement. And as time moves on, the circles tend to move also. So, just as in the rest of life, where some problems are for solving and other problems are for working at, negotiation is one that's for working at. Still, viewed as problem solving, it can be a lot of fun."

Bob has several suggestions for skills that effective negotiators need. He begins, "The number one skill is knowing yourself and your organization well enough so that you don't take on projects that don't fit—no overlap in the circles could ever be wrought. There's often pressure from the other party to do something that isn't really you or doesn't fit the strengths of your organization. The trouble is that at the time of negotiation, you're in a conflict of interest with yourself. On the one hand, you really want the job, and there's pressure on you to do the deal, do it at a low price, and agree to do it the way the client thinks it should be done. But in doing so, you give up too much of your part of the solution space. You give up your independence. Or your objectivity. Or simply the wherewithal to do the job right. A good deal is a good one for both parties. Thus, knowing yourself, what you do well, what your limitations are, is the number one step toward effective negotiations."

The second important skill is to develop a deep understanding of the other party's needs and wants. At that point, the consultant can begin to problem-solve in earnest. Asking questions, listening carefully, building relationships, running the numbers, figuring out what makes sense and what doesn't—all these activities become very important here. They are central to understanding the client's part of the solution space and how to enlarge that part of the overlap.

Another critical skill is to understand where power lies between the parties. Bob asks himself, "What do they need from you? Who are the key decision makers? How strong are your relationships? Who is competing, and what is competition apt to do? The trouble is that, as a consultant, you really don't have much power, at least not much in the traditional sense. But as I became more and more senior at McKinsey, I found that most of my clients were ones of long standing (or ones who knew me well by reputation). Therefore, the solution space was already large going into a new project. I knew them well; they knew me well. That alone is a source of real power. The relationships were strong, another source of power. I probably knew the CEO well, and his key reports, and others fairly deep in the organization. In fact, with some clients, I'd been around longer than most of the senior executives. That was a real source of power."

Bob reflects, "Of course, your ultimate power is to walk away from the deal. It's only a source of power if you're willing to use it. But using it can occasionally work magic. I can recall more than a few situations where the potential client and I just weren't getting anywhere. I'd tell them: 'This isn't right; we're not the consultants for you.' For them, it was so astonishing to have a consultant walk away from something that they'd be back. 'What's wrong with us?' they'd ask. 'How can we adjust so that we can work together?' By walking away, when the situation just doesn't fit, sometimes you can completely switch roles with the other party. Suddenly they are in the role of salesman, trying to convince you. The ability to walk away from the deal, exercising what Fisher and Ury [1981] call a BATNA, is an essential skill."

Another important consideration in consulting negotiations is knowing whom to talk with at what times. Bob cautions, "If you don't involve the chief executive or chief of the division at the outset, you find yourself working for staffers who have a different agenda from the company's top management.

You could do the most splendid project only to have the CEO or another top line officer say, 'We didn't ask for that!' Identifying and talking with the key decision makers, typically including the CEO, can be crucial, especially if you define your end product as real change, not just a good-looking document."

Bob continues, "Later in the project, you should be negotiating with those who will implement the changes. If something's going to really work, people down the line will have to buy in also. I learned this in Japan, where management is very good at getting buy-in from lower levels of the organization. Once I returned to the States, I insisted that we spend as much or more time on the implementation phase as we did on the problem-solving, analytical part. By implementation, I mean working with people down the line who are affected by the changes. The consultants need to show them how the plan can work, what we came up with and why. Listening remains crucial. People down the line are typically closest to the real action. They know the flaws in the consultant's and top management's grand schemes. Once they understand what the top is trying to do, they often have the best ideas for making change. Further, they can easily sabotage the best-laid plans. Take the time. Let down-line people into the problem-solving process. Let them argue. Listen carefully. What you want is for them to eventually feel the plan is theirs." So, negotiation is continuous and it is going on at all levels in the organization.

Bob discusses how an effective consultant prepares for a negotiation. In his view, "Preparation involves a certain amount of background reading that informs a consultant about an organization. However, in my case, the emphasis is on lots of informal talking. For instance, I'd be asked to do a project, but I wouldn't agree until we'd spent days or even weeks of discussion." Ideas were offered in rough draft or slide form. "The rougher, the better," says Bob. "The idea is to encourage discussion. Give them things that beg to be changed rather than polished analysis and presentations. That way, real and efficient information exchange takes place. I presented early-stage proposals that were intended to look rough; they were on yellow paper, they were marked up, the edges were torn, there were notes on the margins. That way, the other side wouldn't treat it as the final document. If they saw something they didn't like, they felt free to scratch it out and write in something else."

Bob continues, "What I'm trying to do is get them in the position where they're selling me on why I should do the project. I'm trying to get myself out of the salesman's role. Everyone in the Western world has built up incredible sales resistance because we're bombarded all the time. So, I say, 'I understand A, I think we might do B, here are some of the reasons we can't do C." Bob's goal is to communicate that he does understand their needs but has some doubts about meeting them exactly as presented. He says, "The goal is to get me out of the role of salesman and into the role of true advisor and collaborator."

At the end of the discussion period, Bob does produce a formal document. But it's typically a memorandum of understanding, not a contract. He explains, "By the time I write something formal, I want to already know they're going to say 'yes.'"

Bob characterizes much of his negotiation and consulting as "the Columbo approach—you know, Peter Falk's detective on TV. My European colleagues called this my 'dirty raincoat' approach. But this metaphor keeps the continuous problem-solving idea alive and well. I walk away from a discussion asking, 'What doesn't make sense?' Then I ask, and keep asking, some seemingly innocent questions. "It's Columbo in the doorway, turning around and saying, 'Sir . . . just one more question.' For me, it often works better to appear to be a little bit harmless and stupid rather than to come on too strong. But the good problem solvers are always asking themselves: 'What doesn't add up? What doesn't make sense?' And that most important word: 'Why?'" For Bob, who views negotiation and problem solving as closely related, the Columbo approach is a natural.

Bob offers several consulting examples that illustrate Columbo in action. For example, there was an Australian mining company that spent a ton of money on minerals exploration but wasn't finding any mines. Many in the company argued that it was just a dry period, like a hitting slump in batting. But, statistically, that made no sense. Their luck had been too bad for too long to be just in a slump.

So Bob and his team started surveying the companies who did find mines. They treated their exploration departments like gold. People on the board who understood exploration, exploration departments reporting to the top, top management trips to the field, steady spending on exploration even in bad years. The detective work was fairly easy. Bob's client was doing none of those things.

Then, the negotiating problem was how to get top management to change its ways. Bob decided that the willingness to walk away was the only answer. He sat down with top management, presented all the findings on what the top managements of the finders do. Then, he observed: "You don't do any of these things. In fact, you act like you really don't need to find mines." At that stage, he made no more recommendations but, rather, turned the meeting over to them, saying, "Either admit that your company is now so well off that it doesn't need exploration (and can save a lot of money by not spending on exploration), or take the next hour and write out your personal programs for the next year. Each of you (the CEO and his top two VPs) should note how you will personally change to elevate the status of exploration. Or you should just admit that you're not interested. I don't care either way."

In another Columbo case, Bob recalls working with a large consumer goods company that wasn't inventing new products at the rate it expected. After some study, Bob discovered that "they were not organized into project teams, so I recommended this approach be adopted. One of my associates delivered this proposal. The product development people were furious at me and outright rude to her."

Bob continues, "Here's the Columbo part. How could they possibly be so mad about a simple recommendation like project teams? Then it dawned on me. Teams would affect their compensation structure. They were being paid for where they sat in the hierarchy, not for results, and certainly not for service on teams. When I pegged this concern, they admitted it readily and with some relief. So the "solution" got adjusted to include the compensation plan. It's a good example not only of Columbo in action, but also of having to broaden the solution space to treat the whole problem."

Bob prefaces his remarks about success by defining how he views it: "You're always negotiating in some sense. In my mind, a good deal is a good deal for both parties, whereas most of what I read about is where someone in business has trumped someone else. That's great for 1 day, but the other party will find a way to get even." It is critical to enter negotiation with the attitude that the deal has to work for both parties.

Bob mentions a number of factors that are essential for success. First, negotiators should take the point of view that interaction with clients is a continuing process. He points out, "Americans seldom make the distinction between problems that are for solving and ones that are for living with. Some organizational problems will never be solved—you just keep working on them. If you can make that distinction, you can sort out longer- and shorter-term problems."

Another success factor involves setting boundaries about when to be hard and when to be soft as negotiators. Bob elaborates, "If there's something that's built into the project that would limit your ability to do your best work, that's a boundary." Some boundaries are determined within a specific business. For instance, in the energy business, a boundary might be where retrofitting to meet emissions standards would take an inordinate amount of investment.

In naming challenges, Bob returns to the conflict of interest experienced by the consultant in contracting negotiations. On the one hand, he or she wants to take on the project. On the other, there will be conditions the client wants that makes the decision to accept the project problematic.

Another challenge is to make sure that the contract is adequate for getting lots of people involved in the implementation phase. As stated earlier, Bob believes that unless the hands-on folks feel they own the proposals, they won't be successful. Bob reflects, "This is a different kind of problem solving. This is trying to herd cats. Some consultants don't treat implementation as noble work, and neither do clients. So, it's hard to negotiate enough time for that phase."

A third challenge comes when many constituent groups are involved. For instance, at AES, rebuilding power plants requires horrendously complex contracts and multiple stakeholders. Bob names many groups: "There are the neighbors, the various levels of government involved, the power companies, as well as a coalition of 10 or 12 banks that have to agree to the deal. The big challenge is to put together complicated deals with just about everyone in the universe looking over your shoulder. These open negotiations require a long time to conclude. We've been working on one in Puerto Rico for 15 years." The complicated nature of the deals, different constituent groups, and public scrutiny make power plant negotiations challenging and lengthy.

Sometimes negotiations do break down; the experienced consultant expects that. In Bob's experience, "If you can pick up on the fact it is breaking down, you have the power to walk away. You'll probably be in a stronger position than if they use that power. The consultant should say, 'Look, this isn't going well. Let's take a break and come back in 2 weeks.' Again, you've transferred the sales role to them, assuming they want to work with you. Basically, you adopt the attitude that if you get the business, that's great, and if you don't, that's okay, too." When the client does want to work with the consultant, taking a breather usually results in a contract that is good for both sides, written at some later date. Occasionally, a contract will be written but negotiations will break down somewhere in the implementation phase. At this point, the consultant tries to find ways of proceeding that are less difficult for the client.

Contextual Differences

How does consultant negotiation differ from negotiation in other contexts? In Bob's opinion, "The consultant has the luxury to stay on one problem and explore it in great depth. A manager must make a lot of decisions in a hurry. The manager tends to be on call all the time." Bob doesn't feel a great need to run things or be in the spotlight. He does feel an attraction for problem solving and synthesis, so the consulting role fits him well.

Changes and Conflicts

Emerging trends in consultant negotiation include more attention being paid to it, as evidenced by the growth of seminars and articles in business journals. However, in Bob's view, the fundamentals of effective negotiation remain the same.

In the business context, some recent developments may influence negotiations negatively. For instance, there is a fixation on strategy that pervades the marketplace. In Bob's view, "There's the pursuit of the 'right answer'; in the software business, this has been the search for the 'killer' application. Staying power has much more to do with organizational arrangements than it does with brilliant strategy."

Another development impacting business generally is the dot.com aberration. In Bob's opinion, "It's one of those bubbles that roll through the economy. It's like a chain letter in that a lot of wealth gets transferred, and little people get pulled in just at the time it's collapsing. It's bad for the economy, and it's bad for long-term relationships. In the fast-moving dot.com world, today you're a good guy, tomorrow a bad one. These companies are ruthless, dishonest, nasty; the industry has a Wild West, unruly nature. It's destroyed the younger generation's belief in the possibility of long-term relationships." The rapid rise of the dot.coms and the instant wealth it created for a few contributed to a business climate that does not support the long-term relationships basic to trusting, collegial negotiation.

There are several significant differences among consultants with regard to negotiation. Some think it's their job to find *the* answer and see themselves as prescribing to clients rather than negotiating. Another difference is the one Bob mentioned earlier: the importance of organization versus strategy. Bob reinforces the point, "My personal belief is that the way one organizes is much more important and strategic than what is commonly called strategy. However, I am in the minority on that point."

There are differences of opinion about the final reports that consultants issue. The general feeling among clients is that once the report is written, the consultant's job is over. Bob's practice is to "avoid treating the report as the end product. The function of the report should be to sum up where you are and where to go next. If too much effort goes into making the report look great, it becomes too long and cumbersome. Some companies, such as Proctor & Gamble, won't tolerate reports longer than a page. Winston Churchill used to demand one-pagers during wartime to force more rigorous thinking." The role of the report is an issue of difference among consultants.

Finally, Bob raises the question, "Why are there so many consultants used by business?" He believes that so many consultants are retained because clients don't know how to run their own task forces. Members are so deeply embedded in the bureaucracy that ad hoc groups can't function well. People get paid for where they sit in the hierarchy rather than for how well they're managing task forces. Most of the problems that come along are those that cut across functional lines, so bureaucracy isn't needed. For instance, Bob estimates that within AES, a typical employee spends half of his or her time on some kind of task force. The emphasis on "adhocracy" means that within a typical plant, there are only three to four levels of employees. The company uses very few consultants. As you might imagine, the necessity for consultants vis-à-vis more effective task forces is a subject for debate.

Bob Waterman's opinion on using fewer consultants differs from current practice. So does his informal approach to negotiating with clients during the contracting phase and his emphasis on the importance of the implementation phase. He is one of a minority who stress the importance of asking for client feedback after proposals are adopted. He writes and speaks of the futility of searching for the perfect strategy when the best strategy is a flexible organization with clear values. His ideas come not from the average company, but from his experience of the way the most successful companies operate. His definition of negotiation is a continuous process in the context of a long-term relationship. Through his consulting, his writing, and his speaking, his views continue to challenge current practice.

CHAPTER 6

WHEN NEGOTIATION BREAKS DOWN

[Conquering negotiation barriers] requires you to suspend your reaction when you feel like striking back, to listen when you feel like talking back, to ask questions when you feel like telling your opponents the answers, to bridge the differences when you feel like pushing for your way, and to educate when you feel like escalating.

— Ury (1991, p. 145)

Life experience would suggest that principled negotiation may be good in theory but difficult to achieve in practice. The divorce rate in the United States is around 50% for first marriages, and it's just as high for second marriages. The shootings in homes and schools seem to be occurring more frequently in the affluent suburbs as well as the inner city. Disputes in places such as Kosovo, Cyprus, Israel, Lebanon, and South Africa may subside for short periods of time, but differences between disputants are rarely resolved. Even people trained in integrative negotiation will occasionally use distributive tactics when important interests are at stake.

Michigan State negotiation professor James White (1984) describes the tension faced by many negotiators: "The negotiator's role is at least passively to mislead his opponent about his settling point while at the same time to engage in ethical behavior" (p. 118). Even the best negotiators have moments when they withhold relevant information or stretch the facts just a little. Although the benefits of integrative negotiation are well documented, the following statements about negotiation tactics demonstrate the mixed messages that influence many negotiators:

■ Friedeman and Shapiro (1995) propose, "The message 'do not ever deceive' does not recognize the fact that, even when integrative bargaining works well, there is still a need to engage in distributive tactics, nor the fact that being completely honest about one's fallback position can diminish one's power" (p. 249).

■ Wokutch and Carson (1993) argue that in business negotiations, it may be in the best interest of a negotiator to lie or deceive, providing that it does not overly harm the other party.

■ Lewicki and Robinson (1998) found that negotiators who use deception may benefit by increasing their power.

■ Swiss scholar Raymond Saner (2000), who works with multinational corporations, proposes, "A good negotiator may occasionally attack the other side if his strategy demands it, but then he knows how to hit right between the eyes, with decisiveness and power, without forewarning. He leaves the other side no time to construct an effective defense" (p. 167).

Schweitzer and Croson (1999) studied 80 dyads engaged in negotiations. Almost all of the participants admitted that if conditions warranted, they would use misleading statements to prospective buyers, and about half actually used deception during the negotiations. In addition, there was no difference in the results for the half of the group who had taken an ethics course during their college studies. Such studies illustrate the conflicting cultural messages that influence negotiator tactics. They demonstrate the importance of skilled negotiators having both the knowledge of the principles of integrative negotiation *and* the ability to detect tactics that may create unfair advantage or lead to impasse. Both skills are important.

BARRIERS THAT CREATE IMPASSE ●

Mayer (2000) states, "Genuine impasse occurs when people feel unable to move forward with a resolution process without sacrificing something important to them" (p. 171). Disputants don't like the feeling of impasse, but they don't believe the proposed solution is any better than their other options. They will lose too much if they agree to the current terms. The loss may be financial, creation of unwanted precedents, lack of access to future resources, lessened authority or power, or loss of control. Cloke and

Goldsmith (2000) explain, "People who resist do so for a reason. Instead of thinking about their refusal as unreasonableness or as difficult behavior, start with the assumption that *all* resistance reflects an unmet need" (p. 228). Some of the sources of impasse include the following:

- Lack of trust that the other party will fully honor agreement
- Getting even for events of the past
- Needs or interests that are insufficiently addressed
- Unrealistic expectations
- Inability to get past negative feelings from prior interactions
- Lack of negotiation or communication skill
- Influence of colleagues, manager, or coalition
- Incompatible values with which negotiators evaluate evidence and options
- Parties believing that winning means others must lose
- Inaccurate perceptions about the problem

Barriers to constructive discussion about issues arise in one or more of three dimensions: emotional, cognitive, and behavioral. The *emotional* dimension involves negative feelings developed prior to or during negotiations. These emotions impede a negotiator's willingness to listen to new information or consider new options. Box 6.1 describes a negotiation impasse based on a great deal of unresolved emotion.

Cognitive impasses occur when negotiators are unable to change their perceptions of the conflict or of each other. Negotiations characterized by psychological anchoring on unrealistic expectations, unreasonable beliefs about value, or belief that the way it was done in the past is good enough for the present can significantly limit the ability to achieve settlements. Sometimes the issue may be that the other party isn't aware of the potential gains that can be achieved through cooperation. How negotiators frame a problem has a significant influence on the ability to solve the problem. A cognitive barrier called *loss aversion* occurs when negotiators place more significance on potential losses than on potential gains. The result is a reluctance to make tradeoffs even though the gain from the trades would outweigh the loss. Overcoming cognitive impasses requires redefinition of the problem or greater clarification of the words used to describe the problem. These can be some of the most difficult conflicts to resolve.

Behavioral impasses occur when negotiators cannot agree on courses of action, such as what, when, or how something should be done. This might involve the procedures for negotiation or the selection of options to resolve differences. Solutions to this kind of impasse may involve an expanded list of options or an integration of the preferences expressed by each of the parties. Frequently, a hidden interest that has yet to surface underlies unbending perceptions, unresolved feelings, or disagreement about courses of action.

Box 6.1

THERE ARE MANY WAYS TO GET EVEN

Phil and Beth had been married for 10 years. Together, they bought their dream home and parented a son. The marriage began to deteriorate when Phil met Barbara. Phil left Beth and filed for divorce. Using a "bridge loan," Phil bought a new home with Barbara before his divorce to Beth was final. He planned on applying his half of the equity in the house to the loan on his new home.

After Beth reluctantly agreed, Phil put their home up for sale. Shortly after the real estate agent put a sign in front of the home, Beth took it down, storing it in the garage. When Beth left for business trips, Phil put the sign back up. When she returned, she took it back down. This cycle continued for 4 months.

During one of Beth's business trips, potential buyers viewed the home and made an offer. Beth returned and said, "The offer is not enough." Phil argued, "It's a fair offer. Let's counter." Beth said, "No." After several weeks, the buyers offered an additional $15,000. Phil said, "Let's take it." Beth said, "No." Phil hired an appraiser. Beth disagreed with the appraisal and said she'd get her own, which she didn't. Eventually, the potential buyers bought another house.

The impasse involved a strong emotional component of revenge. Phil and Beth took their disagreement to court; the court ordered the house to be sold based on a new appraisal. But Beth slowed the process, taking the sign down when she was gone and being unavailable for timely counteroffers. Eventually, the judge ordered that the price of the house be lowered by 5% a month until it was sold.

Getting to a point of deadlock in negotiation actually occurs gradually over a period of time through predictable phases, including the following:

1. One party believes that another is interfering with his or her achievement of interests or goals or is attempting to gain unfair advantage. ("This person is trying to harm me.")

2. Perceiving potential harm, this party assigns blame to another for not being more flexible and for creating the factors that created the deadlock. The search for allies begins. ("He or she is the one causing this impasse.")

3. Positions become hardened, and parties become closed to new information about potential problem-solving options. Hopelessness begins to set in. ("I don't know why I even bother to try.")

4. Parties engage in fixed patterns of response, which involve threats or coercive statements, further entrenching positions. ("If you don't give in on this, I'll make this really rough on you.")

5. Parties withdraw from the negotiation or engage in cycles of attack-counterattack. They lose sight of their interests and frame the problem as the other party.

By the time parties reach the fourth stage, impasse becomes difficult to resolve. Trust disintegrates, and negative emotions begin to accumulate. Resistance tends to reinforce itself. Preventing impasse involves early identification of the negative perceptions or attributions. Parties reaffirm the commitment to a positive, mutually beneficial solution and provide for the safety needs of the other.

Pruitt, Parker, and Mikolic (1997) found that the movement to impasse proceeds through a predictable sequence. People begin with requests, then move to demands, complaints, angry statements, threats, and, under severe conditions, harassment and abuse. Disputants tend to use each of the tactics for full effect before moving on to the next tactic. Preventing negotiation impasse involves early detection of this path and discussion about the needs that are not being met.

Some negotiators strategically use impasse as a negotiation tactic. They will stall negotiations, aware that an impending deadline will force further concessions from their opponent. Contract negotiators demonstrate this tactic when they stall an agreement, aware that the sellers have to meet sales quotas at the end of a financial quarter or fiscal year. At other times, a party may have no intention of reaching an agreement. He or she may be using the current discussions as leverage for other negotiations. For example, management negotiations with airline mechanics or flight attendants may be linked to negotiations with pilots. Employees will interview for a job they have no intention of taking as leverage for a salary raise in their current job.

● OVERCOMING BARRIERS

Our first inclination is to attempt to push or force noncooperating parties toward our goals. But forcing tactics generally promote greater resistance instead of cooperation. The first principle is *not to react or strike back*. Former Soviet leader Mikhail Gorbachev, considered by many as a major leader in the ending of the Cold War between the United States and the Soviet Union, confirmed this point in an April 2001 speech in Denver, Colorado. Gorbachev (2001) said,

The greatest mistake Putin [the new Russian leader] could make would be to heed the advice of those who say it's possible to conduct reform by coercive methods. . . . Some believe a tough approach is what's needed in any situation. Don't believe that. Look what's happened in the end. Force may be necessary to stop a conflict, but resolving a problem is something only political leadership can do.

A second tactic involves attempting to *understand the problem from the other's perspective*. Seek to understand the unmet needs, identify the underlying interests, or demonstrate an attitude of understanding. Few behaviors promote a willingness to cooperate as much as active listening. We will tend to cooperate with someone who acknowledges our feelings. Summarize what you hear the other party saying. Agree in principle to the relevance of the other's point of view without conceding your need to achieve your interests. Ury (1991) recommends creating "an inclusive atmosphere in which differences can coexist peacefully while you try to reconcile them" (p. 31).

How we state a problem makes friends or enemies. Neale and Bazerman (1991) found that negotiators who use *positive framing* ("Here's what you gain") achieve more agreements than negotiators who use negative framing ("Here's what you lose if you don't do this"). Additionally, in their choice of language, negotiators tend to mirror the kind of framing demonstrated by their opponents (Putnam & Holmes, 1992). A negotiator will alter his or her language about an issue to match the opponent. Studies such as these support the importance of framing a problem in a way that motivates parties to work together and minimize blame. Framing a problem in terms of gains influences the willingness of others to take risks and even induces a willingness to make concessions.

Tjosvold, Johnson, and Fabrey (1980) found that attacks on another person's competence increased closed-mindedness and degradation of the source of the attacks. Issues can be discussed as "our problem" instead of "your problem." Reframing attacks on people to attacks on a problem may reduce polarization. If discussions continue to deteriorate, Ury (1991) advises to negotiate about the negotiation: "Take your opponent aside and tell him: 'It seems to me the way we're negotiating isn't going to lead to the kind of outcome we both want. We need to stop arguing about the issue and discuss the rules of the game'" (p. 82).

Occasionally, strong emotion will cause negotiators to become psychologically anchored to positions that create impasse. They will be resistant to reason and will distort thinking to support unreasonable requests. In Box 6.1, Beth's rigid position, which demonstrated unresolved anger, created a psychological anchor that could not be overcome with negotiation. Reducing the psychological anchoring involves finding a way of creating *bridges* from staunch positions to openness about possibilities. How can we help a stubborn negotiator back away from an emotional entrenchment and save face? Tactics might include talking about how conditions have changed, how we've developed a better understanding of need, or how fairness can be better evaluated, or by requesting a third-party evaluation, removing the "my way" or "your way" tug of war.

A fifth principle for overcoming barriers is to "make it hard to say no. . . . Bring them to their senses, not their knees" (Ury, 1991, p. 111). Educate your opponent about the benefits of achieving an agreement now. The impasse can be costly to both of you. Return to a statement about your commitment to problem solving and a desire to resolve the issues that are getting in the way.

If the cost is reasonable, a *conciliatory gesture* may unfreeze an impasse. Research suggests that conciliatory gestures may be effective if negotiators announce what they are offering and why they are offering it before offering the concession. Additionally, the gesture must be presented as noncontingent and irrevocable to be most effective. Although the goal is to promote reciprocal moves, the gesture must be perceived as an act of goodwill, not an attempt at manipulation.

A technique used by many negotiators is to *flip the tables* on difficult people and shift responsibility to the other party. When the other party continually resists discussion of issues or options, say, "I have offered a number of potential options, but you refuse to consider them. What do you suggest we take a look at?" or "We seem to be stuck. What would persuade you to work with me on this?" or "We seem to be moving in different directions. What do you think is going wrong?" The goal is to move the other person out of the attack or criticizing mode and into a contributing mode. Ask the other person for help. If he or she still resists, it may be that the person believes that no agreement is the best option.

● WHEN PEOPLE ARE THE PROBLEM

When people are the problem, negotiation can be both frustrating and energy draining. No matter how strategically you focus on central issues, they focus on tangential issues. Difficult people learned long ago that using high-pressure tactics, quibbling over details, and changing procedures to fit their goals can be effective ways to get others to capitulate. We will give them anything just to complete the deal. We can minimize effects of the tactic by making others aware that we're not giving in so easily, that we have no intention of being manipulated, and that we intend to conduct reasonable discussions based on fair processes.

Spangle and Moorhead (1998) identify a group of people called crazymakers with whom it is very difficult to negotiate. The tactics of this group of difficult people lead others to ask, "Am I crazy? This doesn't seem reasonable. I feel pressured to do something I know isn't right." Crazymakers create anxiety and manipulate situations to achieve their goals. Behaviors identified in crazymakers that contribute to problems in negotiation include the following:

- They surprise you with last-minute requests and changes that seek to alter previous agreements or add incentives in their favor.
- They pressure you to do something about which you are unsure. Without sufficient time or resources to understand all elements of the agreement, you may make unsound judgments.
- They will use relationships for leverage. If you want to get along with them or continue to work with them, you feel obligated to give them what they request.
- They isolate you from support. You are expected to act quickly without additional information or consultation with others.
- They shift expectations or moods. They may move from cheerful to angry, agreeable to disagreeable, without warning, keeping others off balance.

Spangle and Moorhead (1998) explain, "In the presence of crazymakers, our self-confidence takes a beating. Because we have doubts about our ability to cope, we resort to willing compliance rather than create disappointment or anger in the crazymaker" (p. 128).

Managing negotiations with crazymakers can be psychologically and emotionally challenging. A few of the tactics that professionals find effective include the following:

- Don't try to change the crazymaker. Stern words of warning, bursts of anger, and complaints about lack of understanding are often met with a deaf ear by crazymakers.
- Manage your emotional reactions to crazymakers. You decrease their power by limiting nonverbal behaviors that communicate that they're getting to you. Ury (1991) suggests, "Be quick to hear, slow to speak, slow to act" (p. 29).
- Ask a lot of questions. Divide the big issues that require a great deal of trust into smaller issues that require less risk.
- In a broken-record style, communicate your expectations and unwillingness to agree to terms that do not address your needs and interests.
- Communicate understanding. Because crazymakers are aware they create tension in others through their manipulative tactics, they are frequently caught off guard by a demonstration of understanding about their pressures and interests.
- Decrease your own rigid thinking. The shoulds and oughts may create unnecessary tension. Listen constructively.

MEDIATION ●

Dawson (1999) states, "A deadlock is when both sides are so frustrated with the lack of progress that they see no point in talking to each other any more"

(p. 145). Both sides become so entrenched and so polarized that they quit listening to each other. The disputants need a mediator, an impartial third party, who can get the sides to once again engage in constructive problem solving. Moore (1996) defines mediation as "the intervention into a dispute or negotiation by an acceptable, impartial, and neutral third party who has no authoritative decision-making power to assist disputing parties in voluntarily reaching their own mutually acceptable settlement of issues in dispute" (p. 15).

The presence of a mediator alters the structure of interaction between parties by changing the way they talk to each other, the way they approach the issues, and the way they generate and evaluate options. A mediator helps parties systematically explore interests and facilitates openness to new possibilities for agreements. Singer (1994) states that mediators help get negotiators back on track "by soothing ruffled feelings . . . helping disentangle interests from positions . . . serving as an agent of reality . . . occasionally providing an outside opinion on the merits of a dispute . . . keeping negotiations going when the parties are ready to give up . . . [and] acting as a scapegoat when things go wrong" (pp. 19-20). Much of the work of mediators occurs outside the formal processes, including connecting the parties in dispute with substantive experts, gathering data, keeping lawyers or constituents informed about progress, and establishing subcommittee meetings.

Mediation has the highest probability of success when conflict is moderate and when all parties are highly committed to resolution of the issues. The potential success for mediation decreases when disputants are competing for highly scarce resources. Interest-specific negotiations stand a greater chance of resolution than issues involving fundamental principles or values. In some cases, mediation may be more effective if arbitration is expected as the next step. Parties prefer to maintain control of their outcomes. More than two decades of research supports the following conclusions about the benefits of mediation:

- Mediation produces formal agreements 40% to 70% percent of the time across a variety of settings.
- Parties are generally more satisfied (typically about 75%) with decisions produced through mediation than those produced through arbitration or judges.
- Parties are more likely to comply with terms of an agreement and its implementation than with legal settlements.
- Mediation crafts better agreements than can be accomplished through simple compromise or win-lose discussions.
- Mediated agreements can preserve relationships or ease the tensions associated with termination of relationships.
- Compared to arbitration, mediation is often less expensive in terms of both time and money.
- Participants in mediation perceive that agreements are fairer than they believe they would get from court decisions.
- Mediated agreements tend to hold over time.

According to evidence from neighborhood justice centers, mediation has limitations. Kressel (2000) explains, "The most consistent negative evidence about mediation is that it typically has little power to alter long-standing, deeply entrenched negative patterns of relating" (p. 524). In hostile contexts, disputants frequently greet mediators with suspicion. In addition, the goal of mediation is to help parties who've reached impasse to negotiate. If one or both of the parties doesn't want an agreement, mediation may be ineffective.

Bush (1996) argues that the role of a mediator is to lower the barriers to settlement. The mediator accomplishes this goal by reducing the cognitive distortions disputants have created about information, by increasing each party's participation in and control over decisions, and by providing a setting where parties feel that their side will be heard. Looking more specifically at tasks, Ross and Stillinger (1991) explain that mediators do the following:

- Add reason to compromise so that parties can save face and not worry about perceptions of "giving in."
- Propose package deals that can be evaluated more on their merits than by the source of the proposal.
- Speak separately with disputants to determine potential bases for compromise.
- Create implicit or explicit deadlines, which will add pressure to negotiators to compromise instead of prolonging discussions hoping for more favorable terms.
- Help redefine or reframe the parties' perceptions of a proposed settlement in a way that facilitates concession making.

Because impartiality is central to a mediator's role, mediators are usually outsiders to the organization or parties in dispute. The mediator is more interested in facilitating fair processes and achieving agreement than in influencing the terms of an agreement. The mediator may even lack expertise about the subjects under discussion.

Frequently, a mediator will meet both separately and jointly with disputing parties. In the separate meetings, the mediator will identify interests and concerns that parties may be reluctant to share publicly. In addition, the mediator will explore potential options to avoid the emotion frequently attached to discussion of courses of action that occur in joint discussions.

In the joint session, a mediator facilitates a fair hearing of each side of the dispute. Encouraging open and honest communication of interests, the mediator identifies areas of both agreement and disagreement. Positional statements are discouraged, and expression of strong emotion is limited. The initial ground rules should control most of the nonproductive tactics. Figure 6.1 lists common ground rules used by mediators to manage inappropriate displays of emotions and to reduce counterproductive behaviors.

Mediation occurs in a series of stages ranging from initial contact to discussion of formal agreements. The following list summarizes typical stages of mediation:

1. In an initial conversation between the mediator and the disputing parties, the mediator educates each party about processes and seeks commitment. In addition, the mediator discusses with each party specifics of a strategy for resolving problems between the parties.

2. At the first meeting, the mediator seeks to achieve common goals, come to agreement about ground rules, and review the problem-solving process chosen.

3. The mediator helps parties define and understand the issues that cause the conflict.

4. The mediator promotes open sharing of interests, needs, and problems.

5. Parties begin to generate options that will address the interests of all parties.

6. Based on tradeoffs, agreeable criteria, and established standards, parties select a package of options that best achieves mutual gains for all parties involved.

7. Parties produce formal agreement that summarizes expected courses of action.

Only one person talks at a time.
No interruptions are allowed.
All parties will be given equal time to tell their story.
No personal attacks or name calling will be allowed.
Information shared during mediation will be considered confidential
    unless agreed upon by all parties.
Individual caucuses may be requested when deemed necessary
    by the mediator or by either party.
If necessary, a timeout may be called by the mediator.

Figure 6.1   Mediation Ground Rules

In most cases, mediation concludes with a *settlement agreement* or *memorandum of understanding*, which provides a written statement of responsibilities agreed to, a timeline for completion of responsibilities, a penalty for failing to complete responsibilities, and provision for revising the agreement in the event that conditions change. Settlement agreements are frequently voluntary but may include provisions for making them legally binding. Moore (1996) warns, "The success of a substantive agreement frequently depends on the strength of the implementation plan. . . . Insufficient consideration of implementation may result in settlements that create devastating precedent . . . damaged interpersonal relationships and losses in money, time, or resources" (p. 301). Success depends not just on achieving agreement. It also depends on the implementation to achieve the desired goals.

ARBITRATION ●

Arbitration is generally used to resolve business disputes. In 1997, about 60,000 disputants filed with the American Arbitration Association. About 95% of all collective bargaining contracts contain a provision for binding arbitration. Most of the cases focus on insurance claims, labor disputes, construction contracts, securities transactions, claims based on lemon laws, and even civil rights disputes. In arbitration, a third party regarded by disputing parties as an·impartial subject-matter expert listens to evidence provided by both parties and renders a decision. During the preliminary meeting, the arbitrator may explore the possibility of mediation but, if conditions warrant, the case will proceed to arbitration. Dawson (1999) points out that the big difference between mediation and arbitration is that in arbitration, there's a greater chance that one side will be a winner and the other a loser; "parties don't expect to go through arbitration and have the arbitrator suggest that they split the difference and settle" (p. 155). In many cases, the threat of arbitration can make mediation more effective.

Cooley and Lubert (1997) list the conditions in which arbitration may be the best alternative:

- Parties are deadlocked after an attempted negotiation or mediation.
- Parties will not have to maintain a relationship after resolution of the dispute.
- Legal issues predominate over factual issues.
- Parties have dramatically different appraisals of the case's facts and how the law may be applied.
- Parties have a history of acting in bad faith in negotiations.
- An immediate decision by a third party is needed to protect the interests of a disputant. (pp. 35-36)

Crawley (1995) adds,

Arbitration is suitable for disputes where the issues are clear cut or concern an interpretation of an agreement. Good examples of arbitratable issues are disputes over pay or job gradings, dismissals and disciplinary matters, and demarcation of work. Issues of principle or complicated many-sided disputes are regarded as less suitable. (p. 237)

Cost is sometimes a factor for choosing arbitration; arbitration costs between $500 and $1,000 per half day per party.

Arbitration is less formal than court proceedings, and rules of evidence are not strictly applied. Arbitrations are private and rarely allow public access. Compared to court proceedings, most professionals regard arbitration as speedy. Arbitration processes involve the following stages:

1. *Request for arbitration*. Disputing parties file a request for arbitration through an organization such as the American Arbitration Association, the Center for Public Resources, or the Federal Mediation and Conciliation Service. An administrator schedules a conference between the two parties.

2. *Selection of arbitrator*. From a list of qualified arbitrators, parties jointly select one that they believe will provide an impartial decision.

3. *Preliminary meeting*. The arbitrator gathers information from the disputing parties. Lawyers may be present and may speak for parties. Parties make clear the amount or type of claims they are seeking. They agree to the amount of research that should be conducted and the time schedule for exchange of reports and depositions prior to the formal hearing.

4. *Arbitration hearing*. Each party makes an opening statement. Witnesses may be called to speak on behalf of each party. The arbitrator clarifies and evaluates the information presented.

5. *Rendering of award*. Within 30 days of the hearing, the arbitrator issues a decision in writing to both parties. The arbitrator is not required to provide an explanation for the decision. If the arbitration is nonbinding, either of the parties can proceed to litigation. If the arbitration is binding, the decision can be appealed only under specific conditions, such as arbitrator misconduct, excess of authority, or failure to conduct the processes properly. Binding arbitration will be recorded by the court. Failure to comply with decisions reached in binding arbitration constitutes contempt of court.

Because of the growing appeal of mediation, the number of arbitrations has decreased (Singer, 1994). Yet arbitration continues to serve as a valuable option in lieu of going to court for many kinds of disputes. Former Supreme Court Chief Justice Warren Burger (1985) concluded, "My own experience persuades me that in terms of cost, time and human wear and tear, arbitration is vastly better than conventional litigation for many kinds of cases" (p. 6).

● ETHICS

Deceptive tactics can include withholding information about the bottom line or stretching the truth about the value of a resource. A few of the tactics that fall somewhere between truth and deception are exaggerating information, withholding relevant information to create advantage, bluffing, or misrepresenting data in ways that favor one side. Tripp, Sondak, and Bies (1995) found that deception, once detected, can have a lasting negative impact on the relationship between the parties. Yet despite this fact, many negotiators

---

Box 6.2

OUTWITTING THE FOX

Brer Fox chases Brer Rabbit for a long distance before he finally catches him. Brer Fox begins to gather wood with which to make a fire and cook Brer Rabbit. Brer Rabbit begins to negotiate for his life by helping Brer Fox evaluate the options before him. Brer Rabbit says Brer Fox can hang him as high as he'd like, drown him as deep as he'd like, tear out his eyes or his hair by its roots, or even cut off his legs—but he begs Brer Fox not to throw him in the brier patch.

The fox thinks about these options. He has no string with which to hang the rabbit, no water deep enough to drown him, and he wants to do as much harm as he can to the rabbit. So he flings the rabbit into the brier patch. Of course, Brer Rabbit has been born and bred in the brier patch. He escapes the fox, ready for an encounter another day. (Harris, 1896)

Many negotiators see negotiation as a game in which they match wits with adversaries. Unfortunately, as in the tales of Brer Rabbit, winning through deception creates adversaries for future encounters and seriously inhibits the ability to resolve differences.

---

engage in these high-risk tactics. Brer Rabbit's motives or tactics, described in Box 6.2, are similar to those of some negotiators, who may use deception to outwit the competition.

Intentional misrepresentation for the purpose of manipulating another into an unfavorable agreement edges into the realm of unethical practice. The ends don't justify the means. Misrepresentation of information that affects outcomes is rarely acceptable as a negotiation tactic and in fact may be illegal under some circumstances.

Miller and Jentz (1993) establish a line between unharmful misrepresentation and fraud as follows: "A statement is fraudulent when a negotiator knows it is untrue, and the other party relies on it in a reasonable manner and suffers damage as a result" (p. 112). Mnookin, Peppet, and Tulumello (2000) add that knowingly omitting information in partial disclosures can be fraudulent if that misleads the other party.

Lewicki, Hiam, and Olander (1996) attempt to explain *why* someone would engage in unethical negotiation. They argue that at times negotiators use deceptive tactics for *ego gratification*. Businesses reward achievement of sales quotas, and negotiators may base their self-esteem on achieving organizational goals. In other situations, creating a *power advantage* in a relationship or business dealing may motivate negotiators. For example, the World Wrestling Association devotes as much time to wrestlers challenging, insulting, and boasting to each other as it does to the matches. The wrestlers posture themselves for a psychological advantage. This tactic characterizes negotiations in many settings. Many labor and management disputes include challenges and threats in the newspapers on the path to achieving agreements. In some settings, *revenge* may be a motivational factor. Unfortunately, the revenge may have more to do with past agreements and other parties than it does with current negotiations. And finally, an unethical tactic may be used because the tactic is within *expected norms* for the setting: "Everybody does it." In these settings, negotiators must get third-party opinions and develop high sensitivity to missing information and information that sounds too good to be true.

The tradeoff for fraudulent behavior may be the inability to implement an agreement and loss of future business with parties who feel harmed. Additional tactics that fall into the unethical range include the following:

- Disguising information so that it is more acceptable to the other party
- Manipulating the other party through emphasis on false deadlines
- Making false statements about expertise or understanding about issues
- Lying to mislead the other party
- Using information gained through covert methods to create unfair advantage
- Using bribes or kickbacks that may be hidden from some of the negotiating parties
- Manipulating the constituency of the other party to undermine authority
- Insulting or demeaning the other party to inhibit confidence or judgment
- Making promises that can't be fulfilled

Any of these tactics cross the boundary of acceptability in most contexts. When discovered, unethical tactics may inhibit future trust and undermine the ability to conduct constructive discussions, or they may jeopardize reputation. Some practices described in Box 6.3 fall into a shady, unethical realm. What do you think?

Based on analysis of 74 negotiations involving the buying and selling of used computers by business school students, Schweitzer and Croson (1999) found that increasing the number of *direct* questions you ask the other party minimizes deception caused by omitting relevant information. When sellers were not asked directly about information, they did not volunteer the information. When sellers were asked directly, deception through omission

Box 6.3

PERKS THAT GIVE NEGOTIATORS A LIFT

State and federal government officials and their spouses occasionally receive free first-class airline tickets, money for daily expenses, and free accommodations for trips to Europe and Asia. For example, in a single year, a governor's office received $180,000 in free airline tickets for staff (Ethics at issue in trade missions, 2001, p. B1). Several months later, the German airline used for the trip received a $700,000 reduction in its airport landing fees. One large city mayor received a gift of $36,000 for hotels and airfare for an 8-day visit to China. Many government officials receive free upgrades to first class.

The officials argue, "We're saving the government money by using the freebies to establish trade relations or to conduct government business." Members of a citizens watchdog group counter, "If acceptance of gifts results in preferential treatment to anyone, it is unlawful. If the benefactor is looking for something in return, it's of great concern." Some state ethics codes include statements such as, "Government officials shall not receive any compensation, gifts, payment of expenses, or anything that would influence their decision making judgment." Yet the practice is common.

Do you think the freebies given to government officials are ethical aspects of establishing or conducting business negotiations?

declined. Negotiators can limit the effects of this form of deception by generating questions that will illuminate missing information. Additionally, to reduce deception caused by false statements, negotiators "should routinely verify relevant claims and obtain written guarantees" (Schweitzer & Croson, 1999, p. 244).

What should we do when we become aware that the other party is using unethical tactics? Begin by openly identifying the tactic and describing the effect the tactic is having on you. Describe inconsistencies and ask the other party to explain the meaning of the tactic. Fisher, Ury, and Patton (1991) explain, "Discussing the tactic not only makes it less effective, it also may cause the other side to worry about alienating you completely. Simply raising a question about a tactic may be enough to get them to stop using it" (pp. 130-131).

Following identification of a problem behavior, warn the other party that continuing the behavior will jeopardize progress in negotiations. Expect the warning to be met with resistance because of face saving, but don't back down. Be firm and state your principles clearly.

Mnookin, Peppet, and Tulumello (2000) advise, "Structure your negotiation agreement so that you do not rely upon these statements [misleading, unethical] and so that you hedge the risk if it turns out that they have not told the truth" (p. 289). Minimize the potential risk with an escape clause, a guarantee, or a warranty.

If the other party persists with a problematic behavior, it may be necessary to request a different negotiator. Tell the other party, "I want an agreement, but I don't think we're going to make enough progress with the two of us talking about this. Is there someone different I can talk to?" Fisher, Ury, and Patton (1991) advise, "Whatever you do, be prepared to fight dirty bargaining tactics. You can be just as firm as they can, even firmer. It is easier to defend principle than an illegitimate tactic. Don't be a victim" (p. 143). Box 6.4 presents three cases that raise ethical questions.

● SUMMARY

Negotiators who are successful in some settings may be unsuccessful in others. Each setting requires sensitivity to specific emotional, psychological, and behavioral characteristics. People who are successful in business negotiations may prefer cognitive-based negotiations and may dislike the more emotional kinds of negotiations that occur in families. Some people enjoy the group dynamics of multiparty negotiations, whereas others prefer to negotiate with others one-on-one. When we fail to address the needs of a specific context, problems tend to escalate, and negotiations move toward impasse. Barriers may involve the deteriorating trust of relationships, unrealistic perceptions, inaccurate perceptions about problems, or counterproductive behaviors.

Overcoming negotiation barriers involves a great deal of patience. Overreacting to a barrier tends to escalate the problem and further entrench others in their positions. Listening to understand provides a bridge for renewing commitment to integrative processes. The way we frame a problem can either highlight opportunity or further polarize parties. Small concessions may demonstrate commitment to the relationship and to mutually beneficial solutions.

When people are the problem, impasse can be especially difficult. People tend to use tactics that they have found successful in past negotiations and to resist new tactics where there is a perception that they may have less control. Negotiating with difficult people involves protecting yourself from manipulation, educating the other party about how you intend to conduct negotiations, and a great deal of repeating what you expect in negotiation processes.

When negotiation breaks down, negotiators frequently seek the help of respected, impartial third parties. Mediation (assisted negotiation) is the

Box 6.4

WHAT CONSTITUTES UNETHICAL TACTICS?

Case 1: Sara bought a $500 diamond pendant that had been incorrectly marked at $250. She decided that she didn't like the pendant, so she returned to another one of the store's many outlets. She didn't have a receipt, but the store recognized the pendant as one of its products. Sara decided that she wanted a $750 diamond tennis bracelet. She asked for the price of the pendant to be applied toward the purchase. The clerk said, "Okay, then that means that with a $500 credit toward the bracelet, you will owe us $250." What should Sara do? Is this an ethical negotiation?

Case 2: Needing a mortgage for a home he is purchasing, John speaks with Tim, who works for American Mortgage. Tim says, "You check with every mortgage company in town. I'll give you a 1/4% to 1/2% better rate than any of them. After calling the other companies, John returns to speak with Tim. Tim says, "Do the paperwork and then we'll lock in the rate." Looking forward to the low interest rate, John completes the necessary paperwork. Two weeks before closing, Tim says, "Well, Tim, I did everything I could for you, but here's the best rate I could get." The rate is 1/4% higher than those John found at any of the other companies but, because it is too late to get a loan approved at another company, John agrees to the terms. Was Tim's behavior unethical?

Case 3: Bill sold his 3-year-old motor home to Gus, a colleague where he worked. Gus received a great price of $10,000 in the "as-is" sale. When asked about the condition, Bill said "It uses a lot of oil, but all of these motor homes do. I've not had any problems with it." A few days later, the motor home quit on the freeway, and Gus had it towed to a repair shop. The repairman said, "This vehicle has a badly cracked block and needs a new engine. It'll cost about $5,000." Gus returned to Bill, asking him, "What are you going to do for me here? You sold me a defective vehicle." Bill responded, "I didn't know anything about the cracked block. I sold the vehicle as is, and I don't intend to do anything about it." Would you regard the negotiation as unethical?

least formal and least expensive of these options. Through discussion based on ground rules and predictable processes, mediation gives parties the greatest control over outcomes for resolving disputes. Depending on the context, the agreements may be binding or nonbinding (voluntary).

Arbitration involves the next level of formality and cost for third-party intervention. The disputants agree to give an arbitrator the power to resolve the dispute after hearing both parties tell their side of the dispute, hearing witnesses, and weighing evidence that is provided. For contractual, legal, and complex disputes, arbitration provides a more private and cost-effective way to resolve problems than formal litigation does.

When negotiators engage in unethical tactics, it's time to call a halt to the discussions. Tactics such as lying, deception by disclosing partial information, withholding information that would alter decision choices, or manipulating data to create unfair advantage are unethical and may constitute fraud. When confronted with unethical tactics, negotiators have at least four choices: End the negotiations immediately, educate the other party about behaviors that will not be tolerated, create enforceable penalties for future infractions, or request a different party with whom to continue negotiations.

PROFESSIONAL PROFILE

ELAINE TAYLOR FREEMAN, ●
FOUNDER AND EXECUTIVE DIRECTOR OF
THE ETV ENDOWMENT OF SOUTH CAROLINA, INC.

Walking the Tightrope Between
Nonprofits and State Government

Many of us enjoy public television on a daily or weekly basis. We may watch the Jim Lehrer News Hour or tune in to Sesame Street with our children. If we think beyond the content of a given hour, such programs may call to mind the artistic and journalistic talents required to generate them. If we consider the financing of such programs, it is likely to be in terms of the appeals for membership that interrupt the programming on a regular basis or recognition of the local sponsors who bring such programs into our community. In reality, there are lengthy and complex negotiations with a number of agents before such programs reach our screens. Elaine Taylor Freeman has spent her career in such negotiations, interacting with the General Assembly in South Carolina, the press, the talent for individual programs, her board of directors, and a host of other stakeholders.

According to Elaine's experience in public television, negotiating with members of the state General Assembly about funding is challenging but successful. Nonprofit executive directors expect to negotiate with staff, board, and the press. Contract negotiations with performers require much skill and tact, but they usually end in mutual gains. Negotiation breaks down when one party, such as the federal government, refuses to come to the table to negotiate about an unfunded mandate.

Introduction to the Practitioner

Elaine Taylor Freeman's career in education began in the classroom and continued into the boardroom. Directly after graduating from Wellesley College, she taught junior high and high school in Spartanburg, South

Carolina. Elaine went on to Harvard Business School for the Management Course for Non-Profit Executives. She has been chair of the Southern Humanities Media Fund and the South Carolina Humanities Council. In the 1990s, she was appointed by the governor to South Carolina's Commission on Higher Education.

Elaine has received numerous awards and honors for her many civic volunteer activities. She has been named Business and Professional Woman of the Year, Career Woman of the Year, and Citizen of the Year by the state of South Carolina. She has been given several honorary degrees. In 1998, she was the recipient of the Governor's Award in the Humanities.

Elaine has also received awards for her work with the ETV Endowment of South Carolina, for which she is the founder and director. The Endowment is a public charity that exists to support the educational mission of the South Carolina Educational Television Network (SC ETV & Radio) in that state and in the nation. SC ETV was one of the nation's first instructional television networks. It has grown to become one of the foremost instructional state networks in the country, as well as a national producer for PBS. The network operates 10 PBS affiliates and 8 NPR affiliates. The South Carolina state legislature funds the technology and instructional production of SC ETV in-state, but the Endowment has made the critical difference in allowing SC ETV to serve the state and nation as instructional and cultural producer.

The ETV Endowment has managed more than $97 million in project grants. Major foundation and corporation grantors to the ETV Endowment for national program production include the National Endowments for the Humanities and the Arts, National Public Radio, the National Science Foundation, and many others. Individuals and corporations also contribute to the ETV Endowment. Grants, membership money, and state funds have built a public-private sector partnership that requires oversight and leadership provided by Elaine, her staff, and her board.

Insights About Negotiation

Elaine has several ideas about the skills that support her negotiation with agents of the state government. In her view, "The first thing is patience. Don't be hotheaded."

Elaine and her board often negotiate with the General Assembly of South Carolina in her role of steward of funds. For instance, the South Carolina ETV was long overdue for renovations; there had been several fires in its studios, its location was a converted supermarket, and employees were located in 23 separate buildings. Elaine recalls, "The Endowment leaned on the state, being careful of restrictions on lobbying because of their nonprofit status. There was a lot of delicate working with the governor and the House Ways & Means Committee. We were able to buy a building at a modest price. We raised nearly $4 million for capital to put toward a new Telecommunications Center, and the state put money into a building we owned. It is rare to have this kind of trust between nonprofits and state government. Several years later, we gave the building to the state for a dollar."

Currently, there are important negotiations concerning the unfunded federal mandate to digitize all public television. In South Carolina, it will cost $40 million dollars to digitize the network. Elaine explains, "In addition to the cost, our independent-minded legislators do not like federal mandates one bit! (Remember, we had a huge fight just to get the Confederate flag off of the Capitol dome). We did a feasibility study, which proved that the 67 donors to our initial capital campaign do not perceive that digitization (the infrastructure going into schools and colleges) is their responsibility. So, there's that constant tug." In the situation where complex negotiations require years to complete, Elaine's emphasis on the skill of being patient makes perfect sense.

Elaine also names several other skills vital to negotiating with a legislature. In her words, "The ability to analyze what the other side wants is vital. And it's important to be creative in what you are willing to do. Don't tip your hand; keep your own counsel. I never reveal what we're willing to do. This year, we have increased our support to the network by 19%. The legislature is looking for more out of us. To do that, we would have to dip into unrestricted assets unless the corporate outlook improves. So, in the beginning of the negotiation, we'll be looking at what they need and not committing to what we will give them until we're able to reach a compromise. Eventually, we will arrive at what they want to get and what we're willing to give to help them get there." Keeping one's own counsel until the facts are established is a skill that promotes effective negotiation in this context.

In several instances, Elaine has helped to cover unanticipated expenses and shortfalls for ETV. For example, the press was going to make a big deal out of the fact that the network was going to spend state funds for a $50,000 digital projector for high-definition theatre. Elaine notes that "the journalist was criticizing SC ETV for this expenditure. So, it was not in our budget, but I volunteered to use other funds to cover the expense in order to take the burden off the state."

Another time, ETV had ordered some expensive architectural studies for a studio in Charleston. However, all state agencies were mandated to cut back their budgets by 15% because of revenue shortfalls. Elaine specifies, "For ETV, 15% means the loss of 50 people; 85% of the network's budget is personnel. ETV wanted us to pay for this architectural study that we did not authorize. We did have some restricted money given to the studio by a donor. I started out the negotiation by suggesting that I give ETV the $50,000 in its capital fund and they could use that money. ETV wanted the Endowment to pay for the study directly. I couldn't agree, because that would mean I'd have to go back to the donor and tell him that we spent his money on an expensive study that we did not authorize. Since the studio will not come to fruition, I'd have to tell the donor we're using his money to pay for something that will have no benefit. They didn't like that idea. So, I suggested giving them a portion of the bill, to split it. At that point, they admitted they'd already paid the bill. So, even though you work with these people every day, they don't always tell you the truth." In this instance, Elaine's skill is being canny—knowing that everyone you negotiate with will not always be truthful.

Finally, Elaine discusses how effective it is to have the active negotiator reporting to an authority who is not at the table. Elaine recalls, "In another episode, a British producer defaulted on a $1.6 million contract. I had to go to London to the parent company, who argued that the former signatory had no power to bind the company. I went with the director of the SC ETV network. The London company would offer $100,000, and I said, 'I've got to call my trustees.' The trustees I relied on were there at the ready: the former governor of South Carolina and our lawyers in New York. Three times I called them, and three times I said to the head of the network and the head of International Video, 'I'm sorry, my board will not accept that.' Finally, we thought that we had gotten them as far as they would go. I know that I can turn to my board when the going gets tough. They will back me."

In bargaining with others, Elaine can use the spending restrictions of her board to move the other side to her position. The Endowment's policies and practices do not give Elaine authority to spend more than $1,000 unbudgeted. For $5,000 to $10,000 unbudgeted, she goes to the finance committee. For $10,000 and up, she goes to the executive committee. Elaine explains, "The network is always looking for unbudgeted money; that's true of every state agency a foundation supports. And because of that ability to utilize my board as the policy-making power, it gives me an advantage with producers. We have strict policies because producers always want more money. And it even gives us an advantage with the legislators, because they respect that board. When you have a strong board, people won't buck you." Elaine's leverage as a negotiator is enhanced by the policies of the organization she represents and the respect it enjoys from the other side.

Elaine's preparation for negotiation is quite straightforward. She explains, "I sit down with two or three of my key members of my staff, and we try to anticipate what the other side is going to want. Then, we form our strategies. It's about lining up their needs with what you can do and not tipping your hand."

One typical negotiation for the Endowment is budgeting. This involves sitting down with each department and seeing what their needs are. In Elaine's experience, "While they will represent that everything is important, the Endowment must come to some assessment of what the most important needs are. Once the essential needs have been identified, the two sides must agree that they might work together in grantsmanship."

Programming is another typical setting where negotiation is practiced. South Carolina ETV is one of a half dozen affiliates that produce for public television. Elaine estimates, "We usually have about 60 active productions going at any one time. For example, take the piano jazz series for which I am executive producer. This involves Marian McPartland, a noted jazz pianist, in 26 one-hour programs. It is the largest distribution and longest-running program (20 years) in public radio. Keeping such stars requires lengthy and delicate negotiation."

Elaine elaborates, "Stars need to be nurtured and, when they are happy, they tend to be generous. However, there are some things that she wants that we can't do—she wanted to do a program in London for the 20th anniversary of the series. We worked with the BBC to make that happen, and then the BBC management changed, and it was no longer a priority, so we had to negotiate with her for another venue." In public television, there are many entities whose decisions have a bearing on the success and failure of negotiations involving one series.

Elaine reports on a variety of other negotiations that are typically required to air a program. She reports, "We are constantly raising money from foundations, such as the National Endowment for the Arts. We will not sign union contracts, so National Public Radio does that for us. We also persuade the networks to make a contribution that is not an out-of-pocket cost for them. The National Endowment for the Arts likes to see the entity that is producing and presenting a series to assist. We can't get as many grant funds unless we can show that they will bear some of the cost. The network is always trying to get us to pay the salary of the producer as well as all the talent. There are so many elements of finding a compromise to get one series on the air." Elaine considers this to be great fun.

The most critical element of a successful negotiation that Elaine names is emotional control. In her view, "Even when you're furious and feel the other side is being unfair, always be willing to try again. Never lose your patience. Keep smiling, use good humor and, if you have to, call on your board." When it comes to negotiating with state government, it's appropriate to possess the velvet glove, especially when the iron fist of board power is within. Finally, successful negotiations should encompass the concept of moral integrity.

Elaine describes several challenges she has experienced negotiating for the Endowment. First, she is frustrated by the inability to get the federal government to come to the table with regard to getting digital funding—an unfunded federal mandate—from the network in order to own the station. Elaine says, "PBS has a membership dues formula that consists of paying dues for programs for the core schedule that is based on the amount of money that you raise. The problem with this formula is that ETV has a $20 million annual budget from the state for educational infrastructure. When you add ETV's money and our funding that is for PBS and radio programming, little old rural South Carolina, with a population of 3 million, pays in dues second only to WNET in New York (out of 340 affiliate stations). Our state has a lower median income than most, and it has a lower educational level, so this doesn't seem fair."

Elaine continues, "The dues requirement makes our situation very difficult, but PBS has not relented, because there are only a dozen state networks in our position, and all the rest are community affiliates or stand-alone nonprofits. The statewide networks bear the brunt of this dues formula, and we carry the heaviest burden because of our large educational outreach through public television. Naturally, those other affiliates are not going to change the dues structure, because it would then be increasing their dues. This situation is frustrating to me, because it has gone on so long, and no negotiation has been able to change this reality."

Elaine asserts that the toughest challenge she has ever faced is the unfunded federal mandate to digitize the station. She has not been successful in persuading the legislature that the money must be raised or the license will be lost. Elaine compares her state to North Carolina, which 2 years ago allocated $65 million for digitization compared with South Carolina's $10 million. For a time, it appeared that some funds might be available through a bond bill but, because of the economic situation, there may be no bonds issued. Again, her frustrations focus on getting to negotiation and the education of the legislators that it takes to get there.

The lack of moral integrity in a negotiation also creates frustrations for those who must negotiate their way through messy personnel situations. Sometimes, to avoid costly lawsuits or avoid embarrassing someone publicly, the Endowment has made deals that made Elaine very uncomfortable. However, she and her colleagues do what they must to remove problem employees from the organization.

Elaine notes that there have been no breakdowns in negotiations with either the network or with state government: "Don't forget, our biggest problem is with trying to get PBS to negotiate with us." Once both sides come to the table, there are generally ways to discover common ground and meet shared interests. It is the *lack of negotiation* that is the problem in this context.

Contextual Differences

Elaine compares negotiations between the Endowment and state government to that of negotiations that involve other boards on which she sits, such as a bank, the nuclear regulatory oversight commission, or a public utility. In all these instances, she is dealing with government agencies and large bureaucracies. Elaine explains, "When you're dealing with federal agencies, they're the big elephant that can sit on you. And there's very little room for negotiation. I'm the chairman of a corporate audit committee and have been wading through all the new independent audit standards. There's no negotiation there. During the public comment period, before new rules are set, the big firms—Deloitte & Touche and PricewaterhouseCoopers—respond to the proposed rules that are coming out from the SEC [Securities and Exchange Commission] and the Board of Independent Auditors, but once they're out, you comply. We've had to rewrite our committee charter and make other changes." With the federal government, compliance, not negotiation, is the proper response.

Changes and Conflicts

Regulations that restrict the possibility of negotiating room are becoming even more prolific. Again, digitization is a prime example. The federal government wants to balance the budget by requiring PBS to digitize. When this is completed, they can take back the analog signals and auction them off for pagers and cellular phones. In Elaine's opinion, "The system will increase the digital divide between the haves and the have-nots; a digital high-definition television set costs $8,000. However, it will be wonderful educationally. We'll broadcast six channels simultaneously. There will be foreign language and PBS programming, teacher certification courses, and you'll be able to download data right into your home. The question is, Can you afford it?"

Elaine explains a complication: "For digitalization, the federal government won't mandate a 'must-carry' for the cable systems; 60% of this country can receive cable. If there is no mandate for cable systems, in rural areas particularly, and in some suburban areas, we have to spend all this money. At this point, congress has not made the cable companies carry a digital signal and invest in it themselves." The situation with digitization becomes more complex, more financially burdensome, and more restrictive.

At this point, experts in the field debate whether digitization will really fully happen. Are the benefits commensurate with the costs? Elaine reports, "The commercial broadcasters are dragging their feet because they do not want to spend the money." Whenever and however digitization takes place, there can only be negotiation outside of issues the federal government mandates.

Elaine Taylor Freeman has, since its founding, been guiding and growing the Endowment that supports SC ETV as one of the major producers for public television and radio in this country. Her job involves negotiating with many entities, but especially governments. With the state legislature and agencies, the typical task is identifying and maximizing resources. In production, negotiation involves creating agreements with the talent, the producer, the network, and the funders. There is little room for negotiation with the federal government, which basically issues edicts to follow. With this exception, negotiation is critical to the underwriting and success of programs we all enjoy.

PROFESSIONAL PROFILE

● **ROBERT COULSON,**
PAST PRESIDENT, THE
AMERICAN ARBITRATION ASSOCIATION

From Negotiation Impasse to
Private Dispute Resolution

Many readers are aware that failed negotiations often end up in arbitration. This dispute-resolution process may be built into a contract or selected by the negotiating parties. For years, there was one primary source for arbitration: The American Arbitration Association (AAA). Recently, competing organizations have sprung up, but the AAA still dominates the field.

The American Arbitration Association is a not-for-profit organization involved in the development and administration of dispute resolution procedures. These procedures are suitable to a broad array of controversies. Typically, procedures such as mediation and arbitration dispose of disputes in a shorter time and at a more reasonable cost than would litigation. There are more than three dozen AAA regional offices located in major metropolitan areas of the United States.

Robert Coulson served for 30 years at the AAA, first as executive vice president and later as president. Under his leadership, the organization embraced a broader approach to dispute resolution than just the provision of arbitration services. In addition to offering mediation, AAA offers training programs, publications, and library services.

Introduction to the Practitioner

Bob Coulson's background includes 7 years of law practice in New York City; during this period, he specialized in the collective bargaining area of labor law. Bob recalls, "I also became a director and officer of various non-profit agencies, including the Association of the Bar of the City of New York. As I became more interested in those activities, I drifted away from the practice of law. When I first joined AAA as executive vice president, it was already established as an administrator of business and labor arbitration cases. But we soon became interested in other forms of dispute resolution, such as mediation and partnering. Specifically, we became involved in the dispute resolution process *before* arbitration."

Arbitration is usually initiated by a clause in a contract, whereby the parties agree to arbitrate rather than go to court. Bob explains, "As our case-load grew in various areas, and as our interest in pre-arbitration dispute resolution grew, I became more involved in trying to conceptualize how these out-of-court processes could be used. Of course, that led back to negotiating. I was already familiar with collective bargaining. I wanted to see if mediation and arbitration could be used in other fields as well."

Bob's conceptual work resulted in a dozen books published over his career. The first one was seminal to the field of alternative dispute resolution (ADR). He remembers, "In 1968, I wrote *How to Stay Out of Court*. It was the first book written about ADR and featured an introduction by the Honorable Arthur J. Goldberg (Supreme Court Justice). It had wide exposure at that time and was republished several times." Later, Bob wrote other titles, including *Business Arbitration: What You Need to Know* (1980) and *Business Mediation: What You Need to Know* (1987).

Insights About Negotiation

As an experienced administrator and one who has observed negotiations and dispute resolution in a large variety of contexts, Bob's advice is to begin by thinking about the purpose of the negotiation. He warns, "Don't be distracted by emotions or submit to habits of thinking that might stand in the way of successful negotiation. It is hard to generalize beyond that, because there are so many different settings in which negotiations take place, from international to corporate to neighborhood and family." Control of emotions and clear thinking are critical skills regardless of context.

There are also some significant understandings that cut across contexts. Bob continues, "A successful negotiator understands what the facts are, what the power structure is, and what the motives of the various parties are. The successful negotiator has to be able to understand the interests he's representing. He must know what interests are involved, some of whom may not be at the table but share in the dispute. He must have a basic understanding of the law that's applicable to that particular dispute." These are the factual and interpretive considerations a negotiator must master.

Bob makes an interesting point with regard to prenegotiation preparation. He advises the negotiator to investigate issues pertinent to the negotiation, saying, "You have to understand the setting within which the negotiation is embedded." This advice is often given, although experienced practitioners vary in the extent to which they prepare in advance. Bob makes a distinction between what a party wants or expects and what is possible. He explains, "You have to develop insight into the best interests of yourself and the other party. Interests are not always the same as what people want and may be less obvious. For instance, a company or a group may go into a negotiation with an expectation that is unrealistic. As the negotiator, you have to be able to figure out what will be possible and, if feasible, sell back the possible settlement to the group that has an overreaching expectation." An effective negotiator must understand the original positions, identify a possible settlement, and move the other party from an unrealistic beginning to a feasible ending. When you are the negotiator representing a party, the process is the same, but the party you may have to move is your own client.

Bob names several characteristics of a successful negotiation. He says, "The most common aspect may be that the result is practical, that there's inevitability about both sides reaching either a compromise solution or a solution that's in the best interests of both, the so-called win-win. Some negotiations end in settlement because both parties want it. The negotiation may be just about reaching an agreed-upon price. There is a single dimension—price—and both parties want to settle. In addition, negotiations are more likely to be successful when there are no significant emotional or political barriers between negotiators." Simplicity of issue, focus on price, and the absence of political and emotional quarrels are predictors of successful negotiations.

Bob continues, "Solutions may be reached in which the parties at the table are satisfied, but at the sacrifice of some third party. Just about every negotiation involves more interests than those that are directly represented. For instance, in a separation agreement, the husband and wife may reach an agreement that involves a loss to the children or to the taxpayers. Or, in a labor negotiation, the two parties may reach agreement on the basis of a price increase, in which instance the customer loses. In international negotiations, two national interests may reach an agreement that will have a negative impact on its neighbors or on minority populations living within the area being disputed." The search for a win-win solution is often the search for other interests that can contribute to solving a problem for the parties at the table.

Contextual Differences

Bob next comments on how negotiations differ, pointing out, "Some negotiations are very simple. They may be bilateral. The parties are clearly identified. On the other hand, some negotiations involve many interests. In those cases, typically, the issues are complex. Often, there is preliminary work behind the scenes trying to move parties closer to solution so that progress can be made at the table. My experience with collective bargaining and other complicated negotiation settings is that not everything happens at the table. Most of the negotiation happens before people come to the table. There must be internal negotiations on the part of both labor and management so that they arrange themselves before sitting down with the other side. In those cases, the negotiators (for example, a bargaining committee) will have done a great deal of work deciding whose interests will be asserted at the table and whose will be jettisoned." Internal negotiations determine what positions will be taken once the parties come to the table.

A second way in which negotiations differ is in their factual structures. Some negotiations deal with complex technical issues, some are simply about prices, and others involve issues of emotion or "face." In this latter case, the emotional context often leads to more difficult dealings.

A third way in which negotiations differ is the presence or absence of a lawyer. In Bob's view, "This is a delicate subject. An attorney may bring a level of sophistication and knowledge of the legal issues. On the other hand, a potential conflict of interest may arise. A lawyer acquires an interest in the settlement. The lawyer's fee has now been added to the previous problems of reaching agreement. Under the American system, the claimant's lawyer may get a percentage of what is recovered. In some cases, the lawyer's fee will be subtracted from what the represented party will receive. On the other side, a lawyer representing a defendant may be charging a substantial amount for that service." To the extent that attorneys have an interest in the monetary value of the settlement, another complication is added to the negotiations.

In addition to attorney's fees, there may be other effects from involving lawyers. Bob explains, "A conceptual problem may arise when lawyers are involved. This is sometimes encountered in divorce settlements. Sometimes, when lawyers get involved, the dispute hardens, and punitive actions are taken on behalf of the parties, which may make it more difficult to think in terms of resolving the dispute amicably. The involvement of lawyers is not always positive, but in some cases it is necessary." Lawyers make a significant contribution when they bring additional understanding of the problem and its solution, or when there are legal issues. They may create problems when they introduce an adversarial tone to negotiations.

Many failed negotiations end up as arbitration cases at the AAA. In Bob's experience, there are some common causes for failure: "Often, impasse results from unrealistic expectations on the part of one or both parties. It could be on price or value. It could be the value of a claim. It's a miscalculation, a rigidity. When parties are unrealistic, it's more likely that that negotiations will fail."

Unrealistic expectations between client and negotiator may also abort negotiations. Bob offers examples: "It could be a disconnect between a lawyer-negotiator and a client. It could be a disconnect between a corporate executive delegated to negotiate and someone in the power structure of the company who expects more than is possible. Management may be unwilling to make the concessions necessary to reach a settlement. A corporation is a collection of people who have various powers within that organization. An effective negotiator has to break through the balloon of the corporation and see what those personal relationships are in a particular dispute." Because corporations are not monolithic in their interests, negotiations may fail because powerful stakeholders are unable to communicate their concerns to those representing them at the negotiation table.

What does Bob see as ways to avoid impasse? In his experience at AAA, "I'm a great believer in the ability of neutral professionals to help parties close the gap that causes impasse. A professional mediator can be very effective. The growth of mediation in a variety of fields in recent years shows that if mediators are trained and qualified, they can help the parties to better understand their dispute and communicate with each other. Basically, mediators help parties close the gap, and they can very often resolve disputes that otherwise would remain in impasse."

Bob next assesses how arbitration may assist impasse: "Arbitration is a somewhat more mechanical way of getting across those gaps. In general, parties who have attempted negotiation but been unable to resolve their dispute are not in a mood to agree to arbitrate. They will sometimes agree to mediate, subject to last offer arbitration, although it is still true that most arbitration cases administered by AAA result from arbitration clauses in contracts. A smaller percentage of cases result from parties agreeing to arbitrate a failed negotiation. This doesn't seem logical to me; since parties have attempted settlement, they should have some idea of the gap between them. You would think that they would then be willing to submit that dispute to an arbitrator, but it seems very difficult for them to do that. On the other hand, it seems relatively easy to agree to mediate. It's less threatening, because the parties haven't given anything up by agreeing to meet with a mediator." Arbitration triggered by contract clauses has a long history as a dispute resolution tool for failed negotiations. Mediation is more recent, but its growth rate suggests that parties find it more appealing than arbitration because they do not give up control to a third party.

Changes and Conflicts

Having worked for the past 30 years in private dispute negotiations, Bob has not only observed the growth of the field, he has stimulated it. When he first joined the AAA, the organization was focused almost exclusively on arbitration. Along with his predecessor, Donald B. Straus, Bob extended its reach to other forms of dispute resolution, obtaining grants from the Ford Foundation and other funders to branch out. Bob recounts, "We began to develop a better understanding of how to use mediation in family, community, and public sector labor disputes. We were among the founders of the Society of Professionals in Dispute Resolution (SPIDR) and created a broad interest in the emerging field of dispute resolution. We established a National Center for Dispute Resolution with offices in Washington, D.C., that tried to identify disputes that could be resolved through mediation."

Bob comments on the development of professionals: "There has been tremendous growth of interest in negotiations and in new ways of looking at dispute resolution. The creation of SPIDR some years ago and other family and community mediation organizations have contributed to such growth. Increasing numbers of people are participating as mediators and arbitrators. The third-party role has been adopted by people who've been drawn from the practice of law and other professions."

Bob also mentions increased interest in dispute resolution on the part of academics. Graduate courses in dispute resolution and conflict management have multiplied mightily in the '90's. There are ADR programs and courses within the curricula of business, law, liberal arts, social work, and international relations schools. Some universities, such as George Mason, offer undergraduate and graduate degrees in conflict management. Courses offered include the processes and practices of negotiation.

Bob emphasizes the international interest in conflict management. He will be traveling in Vienna, Austria to serve as judge of the international moot court competitions. Law schools from Russia, New Zealand, and many other countries will compete against each other, with students arguing the complainant and defendant sides of a given problem. A panel of three arbitrators will judge each hearing in the tournament. The goal is to stimulate interest in international arbitration so those young attorneys will be more familiar with and more likely to use the process.

Bob Coulson remains an honorary member of the executive committee of the AAA. The legacy of his leadership there includes expanding the original arbitration services to include those that focus on the negotiation of disputes by the parties involved. As one of the SPIDR (recently renamed The Association for Conflict Resolution) founders, he can point with pride to an international organization of thousands of ADR professionals. His books are known for their practical suggestions and accurate information. His insights on negotiation are invaluable to current practice.

PROFESSIONAL PROFILE

● **ANTHONY ROISMAN,**
  COFOUNDER AND FORMER EXECUTIVE
  DIRECTOR OF TRIAL LAWYERS FOR PUBLIC JUSTICE

Hazardous Duty Negotiating Hazardous Waste

A Civil Action (Hall & Zaillian, 1998), *The Insider* (Spinotti & Mann, 1999), and *Erin Brockovich* (Soderbergh, 2000) are recent movies that drew large audiences and high praise. They focus on high-profile legal cases where the public interest in a safe environment conflicts with the corporate interests in maximizing profit. The high drama and (relatively) happy endings of these stories are primarily set in courtrooms. Less well known is the steady growth of public interest law and its representatives, who invest years of work in cases that often are settled through negotiation rather than litigation. Tony Roisman is a practitioner whose work occurs in both arenas; he has defended the public interest against toxic waste in both the high-profile courtroom and in behind-the-scenes negotiations.

The nature of public interest conflicts involves many barriers, the most familiar being an imbalance of power between corporations and citizen groups. In counselor Roisman's experience, barriers also include the challenge of preventing feelings from dominating where issues of injustice are alleged. What is deserved in a settlement is not always what is possible. Other barriers include a lack of expertise on the part of citizen groups in the technical matters involved and the lack of trust between adversaries.

Introduction to the Practitioner

Tony's first legal job gave no hint of his career course; however, a few years of private practice tax law convinced him that his direction lay elsewhere. He identified a lack of legal representation for the larger community and committed himself to the pursuit of public interest law. Tony became convinced that industry was prepared to consider resolving environmental problems rather than fighting over whether anyone had the right to compel them to take action. In 1969, with two other attorneys, Tony conceived the idea of a private, public-interest law firm that could represent consumer and environmental interests in the way that large private firms lobbied and influenced administrative hearings for their corporate clients. This idea later came to fruition in the form of Trial Lawyers for Public Justice.

In the 1970s, Tony became active in representing citizen groups. Later, he was asked to create a new area of environmental enforcement litigation in the Department of Justice under the Carter administration, where he served in the Division of Lands and Natural Resources and specialized in law related to cleaning up hazardous waste sites.

In 1982, Tony was cofounder and first executive director of Trial Lawyers for Public Justice. Trial Lawyers for Public Justice is a nonprofit organization funded primarily by contributions from individual trial lawyers. The organization partners with lawyers and firms in private practice to represent the public interest in trial litigation.

The reputation of the organization and Tony's work brought him national attention. Tony worked collaboratively on the *A Civil Action* case of ground water contamination in Woburn, Massachusetts, for several years with Jan Schlichtmann, central character of the book (Harr, 1995) and movie by that name. Between 1987 and 1998, Tony worked for a Washington, D.C., law firm; all but one of his cases in that period was negotiated to settlement. Currently, he practices law in Vermont.

Insights of the Practitioner

Tony names several skills critical to negotiating in the public interest where toxic waste is concerned. He begins by noting, "One of the reasons why it's difficult for trial lawyers to negotiate is that negotiation requires a smaller size ego. Trial lawyers must have a large ego to withstand the buffeting you get going in front of a jury and being turned down. You have weeks or months invested in the plaintiff's case, but the jury finds for the defense. If you didn't have an unassailable ego, you'd probably have to find other work. Ideally, one group of lawyers should be the negotiators, and another group should litigate. This doesn't happen, so you have to be able to get yourself separated from your ego, as well as the cause for which you're fighting."

Coming from a public interest law background, Tony attracts clients who are interested in justice for themselves, their families, and their communities. However, he must separate his motivation and feeling for a just cause from the reality of what's possible in a negotiated settlement. Tony says that one of the essential skills in these negotiations is to be "cold-hearted enough" to keep focused on what is possible in a given negotiation.

Not only must Tony separate his feeling about the public interest from the realities of settlement, but he must also help his clients to do the same. If the toxic tort plaintiff cannot accept the inevitable compromise in litigation, even litigation which results in a trial, then litigation is not right for them. He has learned to brief his clients by explaining, "Here are all the things a lawsuit is *not* going to do for you. If a family member has died, I can assure you that this lawsuit will not resurrect your family member. This lawsuit will not result in the death of the person you hold responsible for the loss of your family member." Where toxic wastes are concerned, issues of life and death clash head on with the realities of what a defendant can and will do by way of redress as well as the uncertainty of what a jury might decide.

To reinforce the message that a negotiated settlement will probably fall short of what a justice-seeking client wants, often Tony uses the example of *The Sting* (Hill, 1973), wherein Robert Redford asks Paul Newman to help him get revenge. Newman agrees, but he cautions Redford that when the sting is concluded, "Whatever we get, that's all we're getting, and you've got to be willing to accept that." Redford agrees. When the sting has been pulled off, Newman looks at Redford and asks, "Was it enough?" Redford replies, "No. But it was damn close." Tony advises his clients that he will try to come close, but the negotiated settlement or verdict will never be enough to completely satisfy them.

Besides having an unassailable ego and being able to provide a reality check, a negotiator must bring a third skill to the table: an understanding of the position of the other side. Again, this is especially difficult for those who are drawn to issues of justice. Tony describes the skill as follows: "I have to find out what they want. When I do know, I can employ the fourth skill, which is creativity." Tony offered the example of a conflict between two businesspeople who had bargained for a set of papers but became stuck at a gap between the buyer's last offer of $2,500 and the seller's bottom line of $5,000. Both sides were discouraged and unwilling to make further concessions. Tony suggested to his client, the buyer, "What if we frame a deal in which you'll pay $2,500 now and, if the papers generate X amount of business over Y amount of time, you'll pay him a $2,500 bonus." The buyer was delighted because he expected that buying the papers would generate more income, from which he could pay the amount at a later time. The seller was willing to wait for the money because he felt confident about their value. Tony crafted a creative solution to bridge the gap, another way to get to yes.

The last skill Tony notes is building an investment in success for both parties. In his experience, "You have to get far enough into the negotiation that both sides get more committed to the process being resolved favorably. Then, they are more willing to be more accommodating. When you get far enough, people have become invested in the negotiation and are unwilling to give up their investment of time."

Tony gives an example of using the time investment principle from Herbert Cohen's 1980 book, *You Can Negotiate Anything*. "A man walks into Brooks Brothers to buy a suit. He knows that the salesmen work on commission. He is precise about his requirements for the suit in terms of lapel size, color, and style. After 45 minutes, there is a group of six suits to try on.

After an hour and 15 minutes the man has made a decision. While he is being fitted, he turns to the salesman and says, 'What tie are you throwing in with the deal?' The salesman knows what his commission is on a $500 suit, he knows that he can buy the tie for wholesale, and he knows that he has over an hour invested in this sale. He figures that the net to him will still be a substantial plus, so he gives the man the necktie. Even in a fixed-price store like Brooks Brothers, both sides realized that they had invested enough time in the process that they wanted to get to yes."

In Tony's mind, preparation for a negotiation depends on the circumstances of a particular case. Specifically, Tony believes it depends on what the other side has in mind. Tony offers an example of what Jan Schlichtmann did in *A Civil Action:* "You complete your discovery and put your plaintiff's case together just as you would present it to a jury, and then you present it to the corporate defendants, saying, 'Here's what you're going to face in the courtroom.'" Tony explains that if the defendants are open to negotiation, they will then have a more realistic assessment of the public interest case and, hopefully more motivation to settle. As the book demonstrates, the problem with the negotiation prior to trial in that case was that the plaintiff's attorney did not have a realistic assessment of the value of his case.

In a completely different scenario, Tony appeared with attorneys from his firm at a mandated pretrial negotiation for a complex toxic waste case. Tony recounts, "We met, and the chief lawyers from each side went off into a room by themselves, and 30 minutes later they returned, saying, 'Case is settled.' I shook my head in amazement, and we left. Afterward, I asked my partner, 'What did you do?' He told me that he asked the chief lawyer for the other side about himself. He learned that he had been a policeman who had put himself through law school at night, becoming the first lawyer with such a history to join and become partner in a very prestigious firm. My partner had come from a similar bootstrap path, having been an MP [military police] in the Marines. He simply asked, 'How much can you get us?' The answer was given, an increase requested and rejected, and they shook hands on the deal." Detailed knowledge of the case was not a factor in this negotiation; trust based on common background and intuition were. Preparation for different cases can vary enormously.

Tony's career in public interest law has encompassed so many different activities that it is impossible to speak in terms of typical negotiations. However, there is no doubt that his most high-profile case arrived in 1982 by way of a phone call from Senator Ted Kennedy's office. This case later became the basis for the film *A Civil Action*. Tony and Trial Lawyers for Public Justice were asked to represent citizens of Woburn, Massachusetts, whose children were experiencing unusually high rates of childhood leukemia. For several years, Tony and Trial Lawyers for Public Justice partnered with attorney Jan Schlichtmann, who was representing one of the families. Up until that time, Schlichtmann had no experience with hazardous waste law nor did he have contacts at the EPA. Tony supplied these essential ingredients in preparing the cases against W. R. Grace and a division of Beatrice Foods. He and Schlichtmann ably defeated two critical motions of the defense to dismiss the case. In 1984, the attorneys had different ideas about how much the case was worth and how it should be developed. Schlichtmann decided to continue to pursue the case without substantial assistance from the Trial Lawyers for Public Justice, although they were retained as consultants.

According to Tony, the first question in the trial ("Did any contaminants from either company reach wells in Woburn?") was answered in the affirmative for W. R. Grace, in the negative for the division of Beatrice Foods. At that point W. R. Grace negotiated a settlement with the affected families. The amount of that settlement is reputed to be in the neighborhood of $8 million; it remains one of the largest environmental toxic tort settlements in the United States almost 20 years later. Even so, by the time the attorneys took 40% and the rest was divided among many families, individual awards were not nearly as high as Schlichtmann had anticipated.

Tony lists several success elements for toxic waste negotiations: "First, both sides must know the same facts. In this way, they can adequately balance the strengths and weaknesses of the two sides. If there is some secret piece of information that one side knows and the other doesn't, you can't have a successful negotiation. Of course, each side will attempt to keep some secrets from the other side. Some of that is to be expected, but what you need to feel is confidence that you're not being taken." Negotiation success partly depends on both sides having access to relevant information.

Another success factor relates to timing and deadlines. According to Tony, negotiators must recognize that "no case ever settles until you're at the deadline. Prior to the deadline, no one gets serious. The deadline may be an artificially created one. One side says, 'If this case doesn't settle by June 30, our next step will be . . . .' At that point, the public interest lawyer goes to his client and says, 'I know you wanted $500,000, but the best I'm going to get without trial is $425,000. At trial, we might get $2 million, we might get nothing. You want to take the $425,000 *now*.' I know that my client will never tell me that $425,000 is enough, until I tell him that this is his last chance to get it. And the same is true for the defendant. Their lawyers have to go to their clients and say, 'This battle will go to court unless we can add $XXX to the pot.'" For both sides, the last chance to control the case takes place at the last minute. Success in negotiation depends on a solid factual base of what a case is all about and when it will be over.

Tony offers one of his partner's rules as a success factor: Always leave a little money on the table. Tony explains, "In the law business, what goes around comes around. You get a reputation for being a reasonable person. The next time you negotiate, there will be the basis for a good working relationship and some trust between negotiators."

Tony has faced many tough challenges, but the worst is when there is no rapport between negotiators. He says, "Once I had a case where the other lawyer was making false accusations in writing about me to the judge. These were heinous and unsupportable. I had to tell the other lawyer that I would not deal with her. I refused to proceed or accept her phone calls until she sent a letter to the court withdrawing the charges and until she apologized to me. Then we could resume litigating the case. I didn't leave her any way out, any way to save face, because what she did was grossly improper." Tony faced the challenge by issuing one of his own. In the end, the other side used a different lawyer to negotiate the case and the case did settle.

When negotiation breaks down, litigation begins. However, Tony emphasizes, "Cases may be settled any time during trial. Both sides may get cold feet. They didn't believe that the trial was the real deadline. Even after appeal, a case may be settled through negotiation. The only time two sides cannot negotiate is when a judgment is final. Money has to be paid." Just because negotiation has failed once doesn't mean that it might not be successful at some future time.

Contextual Differences

Negotiation in public interest tort cases may differ little from those in other contexts. In Tony's experience, "The details may differ; the principles remain the same. I wouldn't negotiate with my teenager if I didn't have all the facts. Obviously, there's a certain structure, a certain formality to a legal negotiation. For instance, I stay away from negotiating in my community affairs, because I bring to it a certain edge that I believe is counterproductive. Our town is a collegial setting—everyone lives together and knows each other. I'm too much of a stickler about tying down the details. Even though I know that by not doing it, there is a chance that the settlement will fall apart because of an ambiguity that was not dealt with up front, my neighbors are comfortable living with the ambiguities. So, I stay out of it." The attention to detail and formal agreements so essential to success in negotiations with corporate polluters are out of place in neighborhood negotiations. The desire not to damage continuing relationships in the neighborhood dictates a softer approach to negotiation.

Changes and Conflicts

Tony points to the growth of alternative dispute resolution (ADR) as the biggest change in his field. He says, "ADR changes the horizon. I've never been in a situation with an intermediary. It's just been one-on-one. Now, in many state and federal courts, having a mediator is mandatory." Other than that, Tony isn't aware of changes or disagreements among his colleagues about the practice of negotiation.

Tony Roisman has contributed to negotiation in public interest law in several ways. He has a long and distinguished personal record as a negotiator and litigator of issues settled in favor of the public interest. His success in negotiating toxic waste cases has contributed to the health and safety of countless citizens, both today and in the future. As a founder and director of the organization Trial Lawyers for Public Justice, Tony helped to build the involvement of private attorneys in the prosecution of corporate and governmental polluters. The advancement of public justice depends upon the negotiation savvy of Tony and practitioners like him. How fortunate for us all that Tony was bored by tax law.

CHAPTER 7

INTERPERSONAL NEGOTIATION

Every person is a potential adversary, even those whom we love. Only through dialogue are we saved from the enmity toward one another. . . . Dialogue can bring relationship into being, and it can bring into being once again a relationship that has died.

— Howe (1963, p. 3)

When friends or families engage in problem solving, they may not call it negotiation because of the term's connections to business; however, negotiation is occurring just the same. Each of the parties identifies needs, issues of concern, or problems that require discussion. Some issues require decision about substantive outcomes, and many require adjustments to the relationship. Underlying most substantive issues are implicit understandings and tacit rules that influence how parties conduct the relationship. Among the understandings negotiated are:

- Identity (I am respected for who I am or what I can do.)
- Communication (This is how I expect you to talk about this issue.)
- Control (Who manages the family budget?)
- Roles (Who will vacuum or who will drop off the children at soccer practice?)

■ Interdependence (How often do you want me to call you?)
■ Power (Who has the most influence about important decisions?)

Disputes involving work colleagues, neighbors, couples, and families provide special challenges to those interested in negotiated settlements to problems. Business contexts may be influenced by emotional and relationship factors, but not to the extent that interpersonal disputes are. Business negotiations are often limited in substance and time, but social relationships have few boundaries. Goals may be clearly defined in business discussions but, in social relationships, goals are often subjective and elusive, changing as the relationship changes. Many people prefer to negotiate with strangers than with family or friends because of the perceived emotional risks associated with negotiation (Kurtzberg & Medvec, 1999).

Spitzberg, Canary, and Cupach (1994) develop a case for the development of negotiation skill in interpersonal contexts through their discussion of communication competence. They found that people's level of satisfaction with a relationship is related to their judgments about how their partners deal with conflict. People regard a relationship as rewarding if their partners communicate in effective and appropriate ways. "If partners see one another as incompetent in handling conflict, they become much less invested in the relationship and turn to others who support their goals and their vision of appropriate ways of accomplishing those goals" (Donahue and Cai, 1999, p. 264). Negotiation serves as one tool for demonstrating effective communication in an appropriate manner for resolving conflict in social contexts.

● ANTECEDENTS

Negotiation in interpersonal settings generally follows incidents involving a buildup of tension or conflict. Rarely do interpersonal disputes occur suddenly. A pattern of actions or a series of irritating statements creates the conditions out of which a conflict grows. Keltner (1995) describes the events that lead up to an interpersonal dispute as a *struggle* along predictable dimensions of a *spectrum* ranging from mild differences to fights. Keltner (1995) states,

> The origins of conflict are found in the struggle between people as they seek to cope with conditions that resist their direction, goals, or desires. Struggle is the basic experience that underlies all the forms of tension humans experience from mild disagreement to violence. (p. 320)

Based on Keltner's stages, we propose the development of problems that at some point will require negotiation involving differences (see Figure 7.1). These problems occur in stages, as follows:

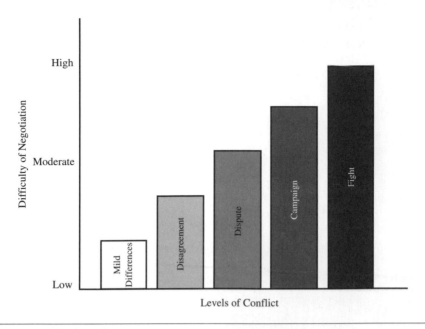

Figure 7.1 Difficulty of Negotiation as a Function of Conflict Level

- *Stage 1: Mild Differences.* This phase involves subtle irritations, differences in expectations, and disappointments that may or may not be talked about but that become antecedents of later conflict.
- *Stage 2: Disagreement.* Parties meet resistance in achieving their interests. Each party begins to form and support a position about the issue.
- *Stage 3: Dispute.* Discussions become arguments. Parties crystallize their positions and argue more forcefully. The charged atmosphere begins to include threats or demands.
- *Stage 4: Campaign.* Each party talks to others to enlist support for its position. Each party speaks positively about itself and negatively about the other, clearly highlighting the differences and polarization of positions.
- *Stage 5: Fight.* Parties strike at each other emotionally, psychologically, or even physically to force the other party toward their position. Retribution and revenge guide tactics.

Negotiation during the early stages, while tension is building, will generally be more successful. As people get more stressed about an issue, they tend to gravitate toward more rigid or extreme behaviors, creating difficult conditions in which to do problem solving. Ideally, if parties can identify antecedents of disputes early, then needs, interests, and problems will be more manageable. To wait and negotiate in later stages involves time dedicated to venting of feelings, concessions that demonstrate commitment to

---

Box 7.1

THE SCREAMER

Happy Acres was a quiet neighborhood until a dispute arose between two neighbors, Joe and Mary, who had adjoining back yards. On a sunny summer afternoon, Mary met Joe at the back yard fence. She asked him, "Could you water your lawn less often? The water runs into my yard." Having great pride in his yard (identity issue), Joe said, "I'm trying to build up my lawn, and it needs a lot of water." Despite Mary's pleas, Joe argued that until his lawn was lush and green, he would water it regularly. Mary asked, "How long will that be?" Joe answered, "Hard telling. We'll just have to wait and see."

A week later, as Joe was out checking the progress of his lawn, Mary shouted, "Shut that damn water off." He laughed and walked back into the house. During Joe's next few times to the back yard, the shouts turned to screams, so that Mary's words could be heard the entire block. One neighbor called the police. Mary said to the policeman, "Get him to shut his water off." The policeman, though sympathetic, said no laws were broken by the watering. Still, Mary continued to scream whenever Joe was in the back yard. Mary told her neighbors what a louse Joe was. Joe told his neighbors what a fruitcake Mary was. Neighbors took sides, and many quit talking to either Joe or Mary, depending on where their allegiance fell.

Eventually, the dispute went to court. Joe explained that he wouldn't try to work things out with Mary because of her screaming. The mediator asked Mary to demonstrate. Her high, shrill scream brought in bailiffs and security personnel from all directions. The mediator asked Joe if he'd like her to stop this behavior. Joe nodded yes. The mediator explained that it would take negotiation on the water issue if he wanted this behavior to stop. Joe nodded yes a second time. Mary explained that when Joe was at work, his automated sprinkler system ran so much water that her flowers and garden were underwater much of the day. Joe responded, "I didn't know that. Why didn't you say so?" He agreed to split the cost for soil to build a small hill along the fence line to prevent water runoff. Both agreed to speak to neighbors about repairing the broken relationships.

What did Joe do or fail to do that escalated the problem?

---

repairing damage, or involvement of neutral third parties to restore balance. Box 7.1 illustrates how failing to deal with antecedent conditions (Stages 1 through 3) allowed a dispute to escalate to the point of screaming (Stage 4), the involvement of neighbors (Stage 5), and eventually to court (Stage 5), where negotiations occurred.

CONTEXTUAL FACTORS FOR ● INTERPERSONAL NEGOTIATIONS

Structure

The structure of interpersonal negotiations differs from negotiation in other contexts. These types of negotiations are private, involve small numbers of people, involve moral obligations established by culture, and are characterized by communication based on norms and tacit rules negotiated in a history of interaction. Enforcement of agreements tends to be informal and, even though agreements may be broken, parties tend to remain committed to the relationship.

The privacy component of interpersonal discussions allows for more uninhibited, frank, and emotional statements that might not be present in other settings. Without the norms associated with other settings, interpersonal disagreements can become loud and even abusive. To control for unacceptable behavior, interpersonal relationships usually negotiate a tacit set of rules by which partners agree to communicate, such as "We will never go to bed without completing an argument," "We will never raise our voices to each other," or "We will listen before we argue." Each time two friends or partners engage in problem solving, they reinforce past norms or consciously or unconsciously negotiate new ones that will guide the next interaction. Because identity, role, and interdependence have links to expectations associated with agreements about norms, changes to the norms can be difficult to make without altering the relationship. In Box 7.2, two sons resist any changes to the structure of their family. Mom's potential friendship could alter the family's current informal agreements about identity, interdependence, and power.

Norms and Values

In interpersonal negotiations, norms serve as expectations about how each party will behave during discussions. They vary according to the kind of interpersonal negotiation being conducted. In friendships or family, tacit agreements may exist about how emotions are expressed, the volume with which we speak, the choice of words, or the kinds of subjects that can be talked about. On the other hand, negotiations with people we wouldn't label as friends, with neighbors, or with business associates may involve few shared rules. In these kinds of settings, people must assume the goodwill of the other parties and sufficient ethical principles to engage in an honest, constructive conversation. The lack of formal rules makes these negotiations dependent on the integrity of the individuals involved.

Box 7.2

A FAMILY THAT PLAYS TOGETHER

Dorothy is a 50-year-old single mother of two sons, Bruno, 25, and Butch, 20. Neither Bruno nor Butch works, so they spend a great deal of time at home. Dorothy has been single for 18 years and has recently expressed an interest in dating. Tom, a neighbor, is interested in her but doesn't care very much for her sons. Both of Dorothy's sons have difficulty imagining their mom with a man. They view themselves as the men in her life. During the day they sit in front of the television set and drink beer. They regularly empty the refrigerator. Pleas by Dorothy for them to get jobs are met with the reply "when the job market is better." Many evenings, Butch and Bruno have friends over who trash the house. Dorothy complains, but then she picks things up before she goes to bed. Neighbors complain about the noise, but she just shrugs her shoulders.

Dorothy's early attempts at resolving this problem included screaming at the boys, changing the locks on the doors, calling the police, and threatening to move to a one-bedroom apartment. Nothing worked. Bruno says, "If you move, we'll just find you and move back in."

Dorothy describes her ambivalence: "I like being needed by the boys. I'm all the family they've had since their father ran out on them. I would like to negotiate a different kind of relationship with them." Butch says, "Mom needs to loosen up. She's way too serious. We don't stop her from dating men. Bring them home; we don't care. We'll go to work just as soon as the job market gets a little better. We're not going to let her down by leaving. She needs us more than she knows."

What does this family need in order to negotiate an agreement? The way the mother eventually solved the problem was to move on a day when the boys were not at home. She left no forwarding address.

In family settings, roles and rules have been modeled over many years and in some cases many generations. A grown child going home for the holidays walks right back into roles that he or she performed as a child. Partners in marriage relationships frequently approach problems the same way their parents approached them. Unlearning behavioral patterns can be more difficult than learning new ones. Evidence that attitudes and expectations may recur through many generations is contained in a quote attributed to Socrates from the fifth century B.C.:

Our youth now love luxury. They have bad manners, contempt for authority; they show disrespect for their elders, and love chatter in places of exercise. They contradict their parents, chatter before company, gobble up their food and tyrannize their teachers.

In friendships and family, relationship can be used as leverage during negotiations, limited only by the desire of parties to remain committed to each other. Companionship, love, and loyalty can serve as rewards for willingness to compromise and problem-solve. Pouting can trigger guilt in both partners and parents who value relationship more than the consequences of giving in. Withholding affection can send strong messages to partners with differences of opinion. Negotiation in interpersonal settings must take into account many verbal and nonverbal strategies designed to balance power or gain advantage that would not be appropriate in other settings.

Relationship

The history of a relationship affects friendships, marriage, and family more than any of the other contextual factors do. History creates emotional entanglements and attributions that might not occur as readily in other contexts. Studies show that past experience is a good predictor of what will occur in interpersonal negotiations. Past success or prior experience with cooperation produces higher levels of cooperation. Gottman and Silver (1999) estimate that 94% of the time, couples who put a positive spin on their history are more likely to have a happy future. Thus, every problem-solving encounter in a relationship serves as an antecedent for either later success or later failure.

Prather and Prather (1990) point out that the large numbers of digressions in arguments are "actually commonplace and illustrate the typical residue of unsettled questions found in most long-term relationships" (p. 349). Words thought but unspoken, the residue from past experiences, become emotional or psychological ghosts for current discussions. Parties often negotiate residue of the past in discussions of current problems. Box 7.3 illustrates a negotiation by a recently married couple that involves more than the money they are discussing.

At times, parties fixate on events of the past and resist efforts to discuss current issues. Discussions are characterized by *history giving*, rehearsing events of the past over and over. This may mean that the harmed party has no intention of forgiving the other. They don't want to get past the problem. Additionally, fixating on events of the past prevents responsibility for changes in current behavior. One of the parties, by remaining focused on the past, avoids having to do its part in making the current situation work. Box 7.4 illustrates how events of the past can inhibit frank discussion about issues in the present. Although the problem didn't surface until the wife's surgery, antecedents of the current tension had affected problem solving for many years.

Box 7.3

DECIDING WHAT "FOR RICHER OR FOR POORER" MEANS

Terry and Rob lived together happily for 5 years. They lived in a home paid for by Rob. Both Rob and Terry liked having their own checking accounts because this supported their individual autonomies while they were developing a life together. Neither has been in favor of a joint checking account, although each allows the other to sign on their personal accounts.

Last month, Terry and Rob married. Terry wants the portions of bill paying to be renegotiated. She explains, "Rob gets paid more. He should contribute more." Rob responds, "Marriage is 50-50. We're both working, so we should just split the bills." Terry counters, "That's not fair. I think we should create a formula for a percentage of bills based on the level of income." Rob answers, "No. I think I should be responsible for car and mortgage payments. You can have the rest." Terry, becoming agitated, responds, "But my car is paid off and we both eat groceries. We both use trash bags. We both drink the water. We should share these expenses." Rob closes the negotiation, "Splitting all costs 50-50 worked before we were married. Why should it change now?"

This negotiation involves internal needs, power, control, and history. Which of these factors do you think has the strongest influence on their discussions? How might these two develop a constructive negotiation process for their marriage? What would you do if you had this problem?

Underlying personal conflicts may be even more difficult to recognize when they involve conflicts between neighbors, who see each other often and may assume they know all about the other's life. For example, Isenhart mediated a dispute between two neighbors who disagreed about the boundary between their two properties. Although the difference between their positions was only a few yards, the dispute became intractable and rancorous. When Isenhart questioned each of the homeowners, she found that one was losing his job and that the other's mother was suffering a fatal illness. Neither man was aware of the other's distress. When the two disputants were able to separate their personal losses from the boundary dispute,

Box 7.4

SHOULD SHE TELL HIM?

For 20 years, Ruth and Jeff have had a comfortable marriage. They parented three children who are now 16, 10, and 6 years old. Until now, Ruth has successfully negotiated most problem areas of her marriage, but, recently, discussions have become tense and argumentative. Simple discussions about time at work, paying of bills, and decisions about the children have become explosive discussions. Ruth wonders, Is the love gone from their marriage? Have they become incompatible like other couples? Is Jeff becoming lazy, rigid, and insensitive like other men she has known? She'd like to negotiate resolution to many issues, but every attempt is met with frustration.

Ruth asks her friend Sally for help. Sally asks, "What's different now than a year ago or 5 years ago?" Ruth answers, "Nothing. We're just the same." Sally asks, "Are there any pressures you're feeling elsewhere in your life?" Ruth says, "Only an impending surgery. I guess that I'm a little concerned about the surgery, but it has nothing to do with Jeff." After an hour of circling the family issues, Ruth returns to the issue of the surgery. She says, "There is one little thing. Should I tell him?" Sally asks, "About what?" Ruth responds, "I guess I am a little worried. If I were to die during the surgery, Jeff will never know that he is not the father of our oldest son. Should I tell him?"

Ruth's internal conflict greatly influences her ability to negotiate solutions to problems with Jeff. Should Ruth tell Jeff her secret? If she doesn't tell him, how can she effectively solve problems with him?"

they were able to negotiate a reasonable settlement to their problem in a short time.

Frequently, a communication dynamic that occurs in relationships is called *triangulation*, in which "a third person serves as a go-between for two other family members, thus sparing these two family members from interacting directly" (Yerby, Buerkel-Rothfuss, & Bochner, 1990, p. 173). One member acts as a mediator for the other two. Unfortunately, the negotiation more closely resembles manipulation than it does problem solving. A child may manipulate Mother into convincing Dad that the child should stay up late. Triangulation is a way family members compensate for the lack of power they feel with other family members. Box 7.5 describes a family whose problem solving involves a great deal of triangulation.

Box 7.5

WHEN NEGOTIATION BECOMES MANIPULATION

Tom and Elaine have been married 20 years. Elaine came from a conservative religious family, whereas Tom's background was much more liberal. They are parents of one daughter, Wendy, a sophomore in high school. Because of her own church background, Elaine preferred that Wendy attend a private church school, but she could not convince Tom that it would be a good decision. Because of the family's poor financial state, Tom didn't want to go farther into debt because of school expenses. After a lot of discussion, Elaine convinced Wendy that she'd be happier in Southwest Academy, a private church high school. To please her mom, Wendy pleaded with her dad to let her go to the Academy. Over Tom's objection, Elaine enrolled Wendy in the school. At the end of the semester, Wendy dropped out of the school, claiming that she missed her friends in the public school.

During the first part of Wendy's senior year, Wendy had difficulty with her courses. Elaine argued that she'd get better grades and better college preparation at Southwest Academy. Once again, to please her mother, Wendy pleaded with her father to let her return to the Academy. He responded, "No. You dropped out of there once before. We can't afford it. You can't be bouncing from high school to high school." Despite Tom's feelings, Elaine enrolled Wendy at Southwest Academy. At the end of the semester, Wendy quit the school, explaining that the students were "too snooty." She returned to the same public high school.

Do you see any triangulation occurring between the three family members? If this family wants to engage in productive problem solving or negotiation, what do they need to do?

Interpersonal negotiation *lacks clear boundaries* of either time or substance. One issue may affect judgments about many others. For example, decisions made now about career have implications in future decisions about parenting children. Decisions made about failures in a relationship involve openness to options and attitude in future negotiations. A negotiation about child rearing may have implications for travel plans during the holidays, work schedules, and commitments. Boundaries may involve people as well as issues. In families, discussions between husband and wife may be influenced by relationships with other family members. Discussions between a son and his mother may be influenced by opinions expressed by the son's father, who

---

Box 7.6

WHEN THREE OUT OF FOUR ISN'T GOOD ENOUGH

Paul and Meg have been married for 3 years. They have one child, a son, who is a year old. Recently, after Paul came home from his evening job, Meg greeted him by saying, "We have some things to talk about, some problems I'd like resolved." She explained that she wanted Paul to do the following:

- Get over his dislike for her brother.
- Get along with her father.
- Help more with their son.
- Have more sex with her.

Paul points out that negotiating with Meg can be difficult because commitment to three out of four issues isn't good enough. In a business context, if Paul negotiates a small level of compliance on four issues, he's usually successful. But with Meg, if he fulfills three of the four, he can be sure that she'll remember the fourth one in all subsequent arguments. In business, Paul can negotiate creative options. But at home, there isn't much creativity in relating to in-laws or how to change their son's diaper. Her expectations are that all four issues will be resolved based on standards she has set. Three out of four isn't good enough.

Why are expectations and needs more difficult to negotiate in interpersonal negotiations than in business negotiations? What would you do if you were one of the two adults in this scenario?

---

may no longer live in the home. Unclear boundaries contaminate negotiation processes. In contrast, business negotiations generally involve specific issues that have beginnings and endings in terms of both substance and timing. Box 7.6 illustrates the challenge of setting boundaries in a relationship.

A relationship factor that greatly affects the development of interpersonal conflict and negotiation is a principle we might term *captive audience*. Who else do we have to talk to about our frustrations, disappointments, fears, inadequacies and needs? Our closest relationships serve as a captive audience in that it is difficult for them to escape our moods. At work, colleagues can go home at the end of the workday, take a long weekend, or take a vacation. It's difficult to get a vacation from close friends or family. They're trapped.

Two problems tend to occur. Our frustrations may be with events elsewhere, but our listeners may believe they are the target of our feelings. Second, if our listeners believe that they need to provide an answer to our problem or fix the issue, we may react negatively against their solutions. Now, they *do* become the target of our emotions. We have two problems: the personal frustrations we began with and the relationship problem created through discussion. If both our goal and our listeners' goal was to understand the issue instead of fixing a problem, our energies would be more constructively directed.

Solutions to this situational problem begin with the listeners, the captive ones, approaching discussions with an attitude of "What's the real problem here?" For speakers who resist addressing underlying issues, listening requires a great deal of patience. In addition, listeners may help the situation by focusing on how the speaker is experiencing the problem. For example, to a friend who complains about many small issues, the response might be, "It sounds as though you're angry about many things today." To a spouse who abnormally fixates on issues of money, the response might be, "You're feeling the pressures of our finances a lot more than usual today. Are there some unusual pressures there?" To get to real problem solving and negotiation, we often have to demonstrate a great deal of patience in getting the speaker to move from superficial issues to the underlying issues generating frustration and anger.

Communication

Because of the high importance of friendships and relationships with family members and neighbors, parties in these contexts tend to avoid discussion of issues that may provide high tension. Parties put off discussion of problems to maintain relationship harmony or in hope that the problems will go away on their own. Gottman and Silver (1999) estimate that in both healthy and unhealthy couples' relationships, 80% of the time, men avoid discussion of difficult issues. The perception is that the absence of open dispute is a better condition than emotional verbal interaction.

People avoid discussing true feelings if they believe discussion might escalate the problems or if they believe their comments will not be valued. Rejection can be a worse fate than solving a problem. Sillars, Colett, Perry, and Rogers (1982) estimate that about 50% of problems are not discussed. This can be a significant issue for friends or colleagues who want to solve problems as they occur. A common statement by people dealing with interpersonal disputes is "I can't get him (her) to talk about it" or "I didn't know anything about this until now."

The key to inviting discussion with parties who avoid problems begins with providing a safe climate in which sensitive issues can be discussed. Questions that demonstrate active listening and empathy create a climate where such discussion can occur. Probing, inviting questions look for this hidden information. If the other party is overly quiet, *meta-communication* (that is, making an observation about how we're talking about the issue) might help bring hidden issues to the surface. Meta-communication involves comments such as "It would appear that you're avoiding this subject. Am I right about this?" or "I find it difficult to work on this problem with you if you won't tell me what's important to you." Acknowledge the impasse and ask for help from the silent partner.

The privacy of interpersonal discussions can influence the intensity of emotional statements. Because needs and expectations are strong for relationships, *emotions* have greater impact on the direction of discussions. Emotions such as fear, resentment, anger, or rejection can make disputants more positional and more demanding than they might otherwise be. When one party believes that the other side cannot be trusted or is trying to achieve more than is fair, emotions rise. People feel angry when they are vulnerable or their ego is bruised. For example, a gentleman in his 70s once said to me, "My brother took the girl I wanted to date to the high school prom. I've not spoken much to him since that time." He expressed this strong emotion despite the fact that this event had occurred 55 years earlier and he had been married to his current wife for 50 years. Negotiating issues where trust has been broken requires a great deal of venting of feelings.

When others express strong emotion, we first need to lower the intensity of the situation. This involves statements that show respect for feelings and validation of people's right to feel the way they do. People lower their emotional intensity if they feel that they are valued and someone is trying to understand. Use comments such as, "We're going to get through this. What's important to you in all of this?" or "Help me understand. Tell me what's behind the way you feel now." Respect, validate, and then focus on information. In addition, we recommend that you do the following:

- Listen with empathy.
- Look at the problem from the others' point of view.
- Point out that your interest is not to do harm but to look for a better way to do things.
- Share your own fears, doubts, and anxieties in a nonthreatening manner.
- Ask if there might be a better time to discuss the issues.
- Help others save face by giving them room to back off from positions.

Managing one's own emotions in the context of negotiation begins with a principle called *living with intentionality*. This principle involves responding in ways that we know we want to respond instead of engaging in knee-jerk reactions to something someone says. Just because we *can* get angry or explode with insults doesn't mean we should. When we feel emotions building, we need to ask ourselves, "How *should* I behave to get the most out of this situation?" Living with intentionality requires us to manage our emotions rather than allow them to sabotage our best interests.

In both interpersonal and organizational contexts, emotional displays of anger or disappointment may serve as tactics designed to manipulate. They're intended to keep others off balance and preoccupied with emotions rather than focused on the issues. An effective response by negotiators is to allow for the expression of the emotions, but without concessions or unreasonable flexibility. Flexibility needs to be a strategic move based on interests and goals, not a response to emotional outbursts.

Another factor that distinguishes the contextual dynamics of interpersonal negotiation is a greater tendency to *personalize the issues*. Negotiators make each other the issue. They assign blame, either to themselves or to the other parties. Blaming others takes the form of depreciating comments, assigning responsibility for remedying the problem, or scolding statements. When people personalize an issue, there's generally some other issue beneath the surface that's the more important issue, one that they are resisting dealing with.

Self-personalizing occurs when someone feels "threatened, anxious, devalued, insulted" and when "[saving] face becomes an issue which overwhelms the substantive grounds of conflict. Self-defense is the first priority and leads to impulse of fight or flight, for competition or withdrawal" (Dallinger & Hample, 1995, p. 273). When a problem is self-personalized, parties pay less attention to the information they hear or focus more energy on defending their actions and formulating counterattacks. Any of these behaviors escalates destructive cycles.

Responding to people who personalize the issues may begin with questions asking them to explain more about how they view the issue. Seek a deeper understanding about *why* the person is upset about the problem. Another tactic might be to write down the issues; sometimes, changing the form in which the problem is expressed—for example, from verbal to written—pulls others away from the need to blame because they can *see* the problem. If continued attempts to move others away from personalizing the issue fail, it may be necessary for a neutral third party to help with the discussion.

Understanding plays a greater role in interpersonal negotiation than in other contexts. People will tolerate a great deal of sacrifice and delayed gratification in relationships if they understand why something is important. For example, a 10-year-old child asks to attend a party on a school night. Because the child is normally not allowed to go out on school nights, permission to go will largely rest on the child and parent arriving at a mutual understanding about the importance of the party, parental supervision at the party, and the time the child will be home. The parents may make exceptions to their rules if they can negotiate an understanding about the party. Without understanding, problem solving becomes either distributive negotiation (bargaining) or manipulation.

Understanding is also vital in marriages. During 2000, more than 100 scholars, religious, and civic leaders founded the Coalition for Marriage, Family, and Couples Education. The professionals signed a statement pledging to begin a movement to reduce divorce in the United States (Marriage counselors see new directions, 2000). Researchers studying marriage found that both healthy and unhealthy marriages had conflict over the same kinds of issues: money, sex, children, time, in-laws, coworkers, and friends. The factor that most distinguished longevity of the marriages was *how* the couples handled their disagreements. People don't become incompatible after 3 years of marriage; they tire of the way their partners approach conflict. The implication is that to reduce divorce, couples require more effective negotiation when differences occur. They require greater skill in the following:

- Sharing information about underlying issues
- Allowing others the right to have different interests
- Valuing the expression of ideas, even though they may differ from our own
- Approaching issues from a collaborative rather than a forcing perspective

Demanding that others think as we do, share the same goals as we do, or feel as we do creates resentment that is difficult to overcome with any kind of negotiation.

Gottman, Notarius, Gonso, and Markman (1976) look specifically at problem solving and negotiation in the context of couples' relationships. In studies involving 250 couples, they found that men and women in distressed relationships labeled 36% of their partner's behavior as positive compared with 57% in nondistressed relationships. Positive behaviors included displays of empathy, relaxation, forward leans, and eye contact. Partners in distressed relationships used a greater number of negative behaviors—such as whining, blaming, sarcasm, pointing, and smirking—in their problem solving than nondistressed couples did.

Gottman (1994) compared the communication patterns of couples who lived in what they described as satisfactory or unsatisfactory marriages. He found that couples who negotiated differences during marital problems and demonstrated higher levels of support for each other described their marriages as the most satisfactory. Couples who described their relationships as unsatisfactory demonstrated less willingness to listen to each other, used more positional statements during exchanges, complained more often, and used labels for their partner's behaviors.

Nonverbal behaviors during negotiation involve cues, which signal a level of involvement, acceptance, liking, and commitment. Because many people in close relationships focus first on these nonverbal cues before focusing on substantive issues, these cues play a significant role in setting the climate for constructive conversation. For example, the concept of *immediacy* describes the level at which our nonverbal cues communicate our focus on the here and now or our engagement with the issues. Higher levels of immediacy—characterized by behaviors such as a forward lean, a steady eye gaze, or open stance—facilitate higher levels of trust and commitment. Lower levels of immediacy—characterized by behaviors such as avoidance of issues, looking away, or folded arms—communicate disinterest in a settlement.

Based on more than two decades of research, Gottman and Silver (1999) state that with 91% reliability, relationships fail not because couples argue—they fail because of the *way* couples argue. The couples whose relationships fail share common characteristics. They begin their discussions in a harsh manner; they become defensive; they stonewall potential solutions; they overwhelm each other with criticism or use statements displaying contempt; and they repeatedly fail to repair the damage they've done in their discussions. Gottman and Silver provide the following advice for couples when they engage in problem solving:

- Take turns when discussing issues.
- Don't give unsolicited advice.
- Stay focused on your partner with head nods, genuine eye contact and questions.
- Communicate your understanding.
- Be supportive. Take your spouse's side. Don't side with the opposition.
- Express a "we against others" attitude.
- Let the other know that his or her feelings make sense to you. (pp. 88-89)

In earlier studies, Gottman et al. (1976) found that the most important skills for promoting healthy communication and constructive problem solving were listening, validation of verbal comments and expression of feelings, openness about issues, and negotiating agreements. They proposed the following priorities of negotiation in couples' relationships:

1. Establish regular weekly meeting times to openly discuss issues.

2. Express and listen to nonattacking gripes and frustrations about specific issues.

3. Build an agenda of a few specific issues to discuss in more detail.

4. Turn specific gripes into positive suggestions about how to remedy problems.

The factor that most resembles negotiation in other settings is the search for creative options to overcome polarized positions. A 10-year-old child asks Mother for transportation to an after-school soccer game followed by an evening school choir rehearsal. Mom has plans of her own and resists the role of family chauffeur. With the help of the parent of another child, they negotiate a ride arrangement in which Mother takes the children to soccer;

the mother of the other child takes the children to choir rehearsal; and the first child's mother now picks the children up after choir rehearsal and shuttles them home. All party's interests can be met through creative problem solving. This kind of scenario plays itself out daily in homes across the United States.

Interdependence

One factor that makes interpersonal negotiation especially difficult is greater *interdependence of emotional and psychological needs*. In business negotiation, parties may have interdependence of interests and goals, but interdependence in interpersonal relationships is more complex. This interdependence may involve issues of intimacy, love, emotional support, control, power, or internal needs, all existing in subjective perceptions and expectations. Mischel and DeSmet (2000) explain that "the interdependence coming from interpersonal closeness creates the very situation where emotions are strong and the tendency to react impulsively in hurtful, damaging ways is greatest" (p. 262). Although concrete issues may be the visible components of a negotiation, parties are simultaneously negotiating how close they want to be to each other, how much to depend on each other, and the balance of power for making decisions.

Interdependence can be an especially challenging factor in relationships between neighbors. It's difficult to exert legitimate power through neighborhood associations without creating animosity that will extend to other issues. The daily exchange of communication, relationships between families, and a shared neighborhood can make negotiation of problems difficult. Box 7.7 describes a neighborhood where interdependence defined as living in the same neighborhood becomes challenging.

Of all the different contextual factors that influence interpersonal negotiations, the interdependence of issues may be one of the easiest to overcome. When parties become aware that they are dealing with multiple issues, they generally will respond favorably to requests for narrowing discussion to one problem at a time. Most people don't like the frustration of being overwhelmed by complex issues and appreciate greater focus on specific, solvable problems. In addition, most people are willing to discuss sociopsychological issues such as dependence, power, or control separately from material issues. Often, discussion about how each of these factors is experienced in a relationship alters how they are demonstrated, creating a more mutually satisfying balance for the parties.

Power

Family is one of the few contexts in which we all have experience. For some, the experience may be summarized in comments such as, "There was

Box 7.7

NEIGHBORS AREN'T NECESSARILY NEIGHBORLY

Barking dogs, tree branches over a property line, noisy cars, trashed yards, delinquent youth—all are issues that neighbors fight about. The outcomes range from neighbors not speaking to lawsuits. Most of the cases appear comical to outsiders and intensely serious to partici-pants. For example, a father built a 55-foot-high baseball batting cage, supported by 21-foot aluminum poles, in his back yard. To build the cage, he needed to remove part of the home's roof and cut down a tree. It took a 40-signature petition by neighbors, a city lawsuit based on building codes, and 2 years to reach a court settlement to tear down the batting cage. By then, the neighbors had moved. In another case, a woman stored junk in her front yard, including a rusting car, a washing machine and dryer, a sofa, shopping carts, an old metal table, chairs, several bookcases, and cement. After neighbors complained, she hired workers to build a 30-foot-high fence around her front yard to shield her yard from view of neighbors. Fortunately for the neigh-bors, city officials prevented completion of the fence (Russell, 1998).

Recently, a member of a neighborhood association board said, "The trouble with coercive action against neighbors is that retaliation often makes the conflict worse than when it began." Resolving disputes requires diplomacy and discussions based on positive relationships.

no discussion. Mom and Dad told us what to do" or "Mom and Dad made rules, and we figured out how to get what we wanted in spite of the rules." Much of the difference between negotiation in families and in other settings is that families tend to be more hierarchical. When parents raise their children, communities expect them to teach and enforce respect for authority and culturally appropriate behaviors. Many behaviors are rarely negotiated, such as whether or not children will go to school. In other settings, parties have greater equality with regard to power and decision choices. In families, power rests primarily with parents, and problem solving is limited to specific subject areas.

In some families, children learn that their parents lack power in govern-ing family activities. The children in these families use that power to their advantage with behaviors such as refusing to eat their meals, refusing to go to bed at the appointed time, or refusing to perform other appropriate behaviors. When these children discover that they have power, the family hierarchy breaks down, power becomes equalized, and parents must negotiate with the children to gain compliance. Because of the use of many coercive tactics, the family discussions become very distributive in nature. Parents offer children rewards for finishing their meals, bribes for going to bed, and threats for not obeying directives. The parents find themselves searching for ways to persuade their children to get better grades or, in some cases, just to go to school.

Power can be a subtle but significant factor in marital relationships. The partner who earns the greatest income might control decisions about how money is spent. For example, in one marriage, a husband's comment to his wife makes a statement about power and interdependence in their relationship: "My sales job pays for our house and cars. I need a break from it once in a while. I'll go hunting whenever I choose and with whomever I choose."

Power from outside a relationship must occasionally be negotiated. In Box 1.2 in Chapter 1, the daughter-in-law was conducting a kind of negotiation with her father-in-law about the kind of power he was to have on his son's decision making. Box 7.8 illustrates a couple for which a mother-in-law exerts a subtle form of power to control events.

Negotiating with family members may at times be unproductive because of cultural norms and role expectations. Some patterns of behavior can be difficult, if not impossible, to change. Knowing when to bring up an issue and when to leave it alone can be a difficult guess.

Similar choices occur in approaching problems with neighbors. Lehrman (1997) advises that before complaining to a neighbor, a homeowner should first assess the likelihood that the problem will be recurring. If a loud party or noisy cars are temporary, it might be best to ignore the issue. If the problem is recurring, think about a fair and reasonable solution before approaching the neighbor. In addition, Lehrman recommends the following strategies:

- Think about the impact of your words before approaching the neighbor.
- Keep the tone of the conversation cordial, nonaggressive, and understanding.
- Ask other neighbors if the problem bothers them.
- Follow up discussion with a cordial, unthreatening letter with proposed solutions.
- Assess your rights with a call to the zoning or planning departments.
- If discussions fail, get a mediator to help with a negotiated agreement.

Box 7.9 describes a dispute between neighbors that escalated to an appearance in court and retaliation.

SUMMARY

Interpersonal disputes, ranging from friends and family to neighbors, involve many subjective factors based on relationship needs. The need to be listened

---

Box 7.8

MOTHER KNOWS BEST

A few days before Thanksgiving, Phyllis phoned her daughter-in-law, Diane, to invite her and Phyllis's son to Thanksgiving dinner. Phyllis began, "What time would you like to have dinner on Thanksgiving?" Diane answered, "Ken and I would like to eat early in the afternoon, maybe around 2:00 or 3:00, because we have a lot to do on Friday. We'd like to get back home early." Phyllis responded, "Hmmm. The football game will be on at 2:00, and I don't want dinner to be interrupted if people want to watch." Diane restated her need: "We can sit down for dinner and turn off the TV. I really don't want to eat at 5:00 or 6:00 because the rest of the family will be coming later for dessert, about 6:30, and then we wouldn't be leaving until 8:00." Phyllis countered, "What about 5:00 then?" Diane answered, "How about 4:00?" After consulting with her daughter, who also wanted dinner at 4:00, Phyllis agreed.

Diane called on Thanksgiving morning to confirm the plans. She reminded Phyllis that the rest of the family would arrive about 6:30. Phyllis said, "I'm running a little behind schedule. Looks like we'll eat about 4:30. That should still be okay." When Diane and Ken arrived at 3:00, Diane noticed that the turkey was still cold in the oven. It hadn't been in long. They eventually ate at about 6:30. Dessert occurred at 8:00, and they didn't leave for home until 10:30.

Diane says, "Phyllis does that all the time. She begins by pretending to negotiate to get buy-in and make you feel you have options, but then she does what she wants anyway. She has a great deal of power because it's her home, and she controls when she turns on the oven and when she serves the meal."

Phyllis's role as mother invests her with power that makes negotiating with family members difficult. What do you recommend that Diane do when she's involved in future negotiations with Phyllis?

---

to or understood may overshadow other issues. The high emotional quality of interpersonal conflict can escalate situations quickly and polarize parties to a point where defensiveness or resentment inhibit problem-solving efforts. Recognizing the antecedent conditions that later escalate becomes essential for negotiating solutions before barriers become insurmountable.

Box 7.9

WHEN BEING ENVIRONMENTALLY FRIENDLY BECOMES UNFRIENDLY

1997 during National Bird Feeding Month, Suzanne bought a 6-inch by 12-inch wooden birdhouse and installed it on a pole on the side of her house. A few days later, Emma, one of Suzanne's neighbors, reported the birdhouse to the Board of Health.

A Board of Health inspector visited Suzanne's home. He told her that the birdhouse was a health hazard because of the bird droppings and seeds that fell to the ground below the birdhouse. He told her that she needed to build a platform around the base to catch the droppings. In compliance, Suzanne asked her brother-in-law to build a 4-foot square plywood platform around the base.

The same evening the plywood base was completed, a police officer visited Suzanne's home. He handed her a criminal summons for building a housing structure without a building permit. The summons included a fine of $250 or 15 days in jail. The policeman took her to the courthouse.

The summons was based on Emma's complaint that as many as 25 pigeons land on her house at one time. Because of the large number of pigeons, Emma had to power wash the side of her house to remove bird droppings. Another neighbor complained that when it rained, the water ran off into his back yard, potentially spreading diseases.

Suzanne fought the complaint and summons in court. The judge acquitted Suzanne based on an interpretation of the city building code that the birdhouse did not qualify as a building structure. Suzanne sued Emma, who had filed the initial complaint, claiming false arrest and malicious persecution.

Do you think the judge made the right decision in this case? What would have been a more constructive way to resolve this dispute without going to the Board of Health or the police?

Especially challenging in this setting is a perceived need to get even or retaliate for violating expectations. When people feel their trust has been betrayed, it's often insufficient to simply right the wrong. They frequently want revenge for loss or emotional suffering.

Awareness of the needs generated by contextual factors in interpersonal relationships becomes important if parties want to avoid frustrating problem-solving efforts. Internal conflict and avoidance influence the ability to focus attention on specific issues. Erosion of trust and historical antecedents of the conflict are old business that must be dealt with before moving on to new problems. Emotional venting and personalization of issues inhibit attempts to set an agenda for discussing issues. Lack of clear boundaries and inter-dependence of needs create complex issues that are difficult to separate for problem solving.

Because of the emotional element and greater psychological needs of relationships, interpersonal negotiation may be one of the most difficult contexts in which people have to problem-solve, as evidenced by the high divorce rate and high rate of family violence in the United States.

Because of the need for enduring relationships, family and neighbor negotiations can be especially challenging. When needs and expectations are high, emotions escalate conflict quickly. Parties become polarized based on perceptions of entitlement: "I am your mother. Therefore, I deserve more," "I am your friend. Of course you'd do this for me," or "Neighbors wouldn't do that to each other. You owe me."

During negotiation of interpersonal conflicts, the need for understanding is greater than in other contexts. The ability to listen longer, ask more questions, and search for creative options determines the success of problem solving. Tradeoffs of valued interests involve more issues of relationship than in other settings. The lack of clear boundaries between issues generates perceptions that problems never end. Clear markers that specific issues have closure may be necessary. And, finally, a great deal of attention must be given to process and how we talk about the issues, and less to tangible outcomes. In most cases, *process* will be the issue.

PROFESSIONAL PROFILE

MARJORIE BRIBITZER, LCSW, ● FAMILY THERAPIST

Modeling and Teaching
Negotiation Skills to Family Members

The following interview echoes many of the findings referenced in this chapter. Families come to therapy because they have practiced avoidance and need a neutral third party to facilitate dialogue. Often, members hold unreasonable expectations that do not account for the needs of other members. The interviewee focuses on her work with families of teenagers as an example of systems where interdependence is a given, the audience is captured, and emotions are high.

Family therapy is a useful way of helping family members in emotional distress. Family members are capable of addressing problems in their relationships with each other and solving conflicts within the family. Identifying the problems, clarifying each member's point of view, generating options for resolution, and arriving at mutually satisfactory agreements is the work of negotiation. Not all family members or even therapists label such processes negotiation skills. However, looking across contexts, the dynamics of negotiation in families demonstrate more similarities than differences with negotiation in other contexts. Marjorie Bribitzer is a Licensed Clinical Social Worker who discusses her work with families in terms of negotiation.

Introduction to the Practitioner

Marjorie received her MSW (master's degree in social work) degree from the National Catholic School of Social Service in Washington, D.C., and interned as a family therapist with Northern Virginia Family Service in Falls Church, Virginia. A special interest in treatment of adolescents and their families led her to a position as a therapist and supervisor at a shelter and counseling service for teenagers and their families in Virginia.

Marjorie is now in private practice as a family therapist in Hampstead, North Carolina. She deals with a wide variety of typical family issues. She attempts to teach and model negotiation skills for her clients because she views negotiation as an important skill for living in harmony with others. She is also able to provide an emotionally safe environment in which family members can practice and refine those newly acquired negotiation skills.

Marjorie's philosophy is that within conflicts, there is a middle ground where family members can find solutions. She notes, "In order to be successful, all participants must share the belief that such a middle ground exists, and all must benefit from finding it."

Success is also dependent on the ability of participants to define what they hope to achieve through negotiation. She explains, "Often, family members have fuzzy ideas of how things 'ought to be.' Yet that lack of specificity does not stop them from resisting another member's definition or preference." Success is often promoted by the therapist assisting family members to develop more specific ideas of their own goals, as well as encouraging them to become more open to the goal statements others may make.

Marjorie identifies certain skills that are critical to her practice. First, "I put myself in the family system to be able to recognize the emotions driving each member. Then, I do the opposite—that is, I observe the family system from outside to see what aspects of its operation have caused it to become stuck in the current impasse." Second, Marjorie considers what kind of statement or question will expand a person's viewpoint or, conversely, what might push someone into a rigid defense of his or her original viewpoint. Work with families requires that the therapist be willing to show respect for each person's position.

Finally, the person assisting families in conflict must have the ability to view the situation broadly as their work together progresses. The neutral observes whether goals have been subtly altered, whether any hidden agenda appears, whether any member pretends to work toward conflict resolution but isn't truly invested. The skilled negotiator understands the importance of monitoring these three critical success factors.

Insights About Negotiation

In terms of preparation, Marjorie explains, "Negotiations are done in the context of an ongoing therapeutic process. A thorough assessment of the family is done initially, and the family is continually assessed throughout the course of therapy. Before we begin, I am aware of the issues to be negotiated and the history behind them. With this information, I am able to assist family members in clarifying their goals prior to the negotiating process."

For Marjorie, a typical session involves a set of parents and a teen who won't do his or her homework, is failing in school, or is insolent at home. In the exchanges that take place before they go to a therapist, the parents charge the teen with being lazy, and the teen accuses the parents of being mean. The school has suggested that the student needs medication for attention deficit disorder. Everyone involved is looking for the magic bullet.

In the course of obtaining information in the first session, Marjorie asks about the family rules that deal with homework, school, and behavior. The parents assure her that the teen knows the rules. However, the teen retorts, "They don't tell me what they want. Nothing I do is good enough. They don't want me to have what I want. They'll never give it to me." Marjorie might suggest, "If your parents agreed to let you go out with your friends on Saturday night if all your chores and homework are done by Saturday noon, would that be a good deal?" Dealing with one issue at a time is usually the most effective approach, because magic bullets are few and far between.

Another typical occurrence in family negotiations is that teens talk a lot about their rights. In family negotiations, Marjorie attempts to encourage people to discuss privileges rather than rights. Until they reach certain ages, defined by law in each state, teenagers do not have the rights to which they often express entitlement. Marjorie explains, "For example, they don't have the right to unlimited curfew, to manage their own money, or to decide where to live or whether or where to go to school. Even when they do reach the legal age for making a particular choice, if they continue to live with their parents, sensible parents will expect and require them to fulfill obligations to the household. However, anyone in the family should have the right to have their opinions heard and respected, and the opportunity to be a party to negotiating the family rules."

Successful family negotiation depends on several assumptions. Marjorie reports, "Family members must buy into the idea that what they are getting is what they want. Furthermore, they must be willing to work for what they want." Often, this work involves changing established habits of speech or behavior. As is the case in other negotiations, parties must be satisfied that the agreement is more desirable than other options. It is not always possible to convince family members to arrive at settlements, because the therapist is not always able to help members find something one wants that the other is willing to give.

A power struggle between marital partners is one of the toughest challenges that Marjorie faces. In such cases, negotiations with teens are seldom effective. Sometimes, nothing the therapist tries is effective, although encouraging partners to clarify their own bottom lines may help. Success in resolving family conflicts is less likely when parents have not resolved their own power struggles.

When negotiations break down within families, the results are dramatic and sad. Families split up, children leave home at an early age, couples separate. Therapists cannot prevent every divorce or bridge every broken relationship between parents and teens.

Contextual Differences

Family negotiations may endure over a longer time than those in other contexts. Also, they often involve a large range of topics with high personal salience to family members. In Margaret's opinion, "Sometimes a therapist, due to her relationship with the family members, can still be of assistance after breakups or even assist the members in continuing with further negotiations. In these cases, the therapist/client relationship adds a different dimension to the process than the relationship one might have with a negotiator who simply works briefly with several parties around a single issue."

Changes and Conflicts

Marjorie states, "Therapists sometimes differ about the extent to which the neutral party should be directing clients toward specific negotiation outcomes. Don't see yourself as the negotiator; see yourself as the mentor of others learning to negotiate. If the negotiation fails, it is not because *you* failed to find a satisfactory solution. Don't get invested in what seems an ideal solution to you. You are looking for *their* solution." This view of nondirective intervention contrasts sharply with the sentiments of some (such as Freund), who assist business negotiations and see themselves as deal makers.

One does not need to change contexts to find differences of opinion about the best approaches to negotiation. Marjorie cites topics of disagreement within her own field of practice. She identified two disputes: "First, therapists debate the extent to which mental health problems are internal to individuals, rather than existing and being amenable to change in the context of a relationship." To the extent that practitioners hold the latter view, they would be more likely to emphasize the importance of negotiation in relationships and to use negotiation to explore particular issues.

Second, therapists debate the need to hospitalize or remove a child from the home to some other institution. Those who see institutionalization as a way to cure a mentally ill child are less likely to work first at solving interpersonal issues among family members. In Marjorie's view, "Institutionalization, even for a short period, should be a last resort, when, for example, a family cannot manage a child's violent or suicidal behavior. Even when a child is hospitalized for sound mental health or safety reasons, continued involvement of the family in the therapy is essential. After all, the goal is to restore the disturbed person to the family and to society."

Whether family conflicts involve young children, teens, parents, or grandparents, negotiation is a critical skill for problem solving. Those who assist family negotiations help members to define their interests, listen to the other members' needs, and explore tradeoffs. Those who model and teach negotiation in the course of such problem solving leave clients better equipped to deal with future conflicts. Marjorie Bribitzer is one of those teachers.

PROFESSIONAL PROFILE

CHRISTINE A. COATES, JD, ●
ATTORNEY MEDIATOR FOR FAMILY CONFLICTS

Negotiating Divorce: Interpersonal
Dynamics in the Shadow of the Law

There are few human experiences more painful than divorce. The losses may be staggering in terms of income, home, way of life, companionship, support, contact with children, and other crucial issues. In particular, one spouse is often not as ready for separation as the instigating partner or has not had the time or motivation to work through the difficult personal issues that accompany the dissolution of a marriage. Although divorce may be the ultimate answer to marital difficulties, or will even eventually improve the welfare of all parties, the process is frequently painful.

Husbands and wives who navigate this troubling transition are not usually known to be in their most logical, reasonable states. Emotional attachments to each other and to the vital issues at stake often leave adults handicapped when it comes to acting as effective negotiators. Previous partners may be unable to describe their own interests accurately, much less offer unbiased appreciation for the interests of the other. One or both parties may be too angry to seek solutions whereby both sides could improve their situations. Either or both may be distracted by a desire for revenge or may agree to a settlement that fails to consider adequately the children's welfare. Arguments over the worth of property may become such a stumbling block that assessment by an independent third party is necessary to break the stalemate.

Divorce negotiations are not improved by taking these conflicts to court. Indeed, most divorcing partners testify that sides become even more polarized by litigation. One alternative to divorce litigation is mediation, in which an independent neutral assists the negotiations in an attempt to produce a settlement that is fair and lasting. In many courts of the United States, judges will not even hear divorce cases unless the husband and wife can demonstrate that they have at least attempted mediation. Thus, mediation in divorce negotiations becomes mandatory. Other divorcing couples, recognizing that they need help, seek out assistance on their own. Results of assisted negotiation have been positive, and this trend is growing.

Introduction to the Practitioner

Christine Coates is known to her colleagues nationally through her role as President of the Association of Family and Conciliation Courts. Her fellow attorneys in Colorado know her as a member of the Board of Governors of the state Bar Association. In 1986, that body named her Outstanding Young Lawyer in the area. Students at two law schools in the region—The College of Law at The University of Colorado and the College of Law at the University of Denver—call her professor. For the majority of her clients (husbands and wives attempting to keep their divorce out of the courts), Christie is the coach who facilitates their negotiations.

Christie focuses on the settlement of family conflicts. Her concentration in law school was family law. In 1984, early in the institutionalization of mediation, she received mediation training. She specializes in helping couples who are divorcing, although she does deal with other areas of family conflict, such as intergenerational and parental rights. In 1996, she was named Mediator of the Year by the Colorado Council of Mediators and Mediating Organizations and was recognized for her advocacy of children by Voices for Children, a national organization.

Insights About Negotiation

"Children's issues must be kept in the forefront of divorce negotiations," Christie says. Advocacy for children's issues is fundamental to effective negotiation in family mediations. Several other elements are also essential to success, especially an attitude of compassion. "Those who assist divorcing parents must be aware of the dynamics of family systems. These are the issues that strike the deepest chords. No matter how bizarre the issue may seem, very real human emotions have promoted that and must be respected. In addition, showing respect for the parties builds trust in the neutral. It takes a lot of courage to come to the mediation table and involve me in the issues."

Effective negotiation assistants must be aware of not only the interpersonal dynamics of family conflict, but the legal aspects as well. Although family law offers a large latitude of solutions, there are boundaries, and an effective mediator understands where the shadow of the law begins and ends.

Christie notes several characteristics of effective neutrals in divorce negotiations that apply to many other contexts. Her overall template is an interest-based process. In terms of guidelines, she exhorts neutrals to "uphold the basic ethical standards that mediators have of confidentiality and impartiality and neutrality. . . . It's never possible to totally avoid bias, but recognize that bias and don't let it interfere."

Professional preparation for a divorce mediation begins with intake (filling out forms) by Christie's secretary. Before the clients arrive, Christie says, "I don't do a lot. I don't do conflict analysis; this is more case specific preparation." She looks at the file "to ascertain whether there are children involved, what stage of the process they're in, and to make sure that I haven't represented any of them in the past. In my practice, there is a web of connection, and I need to make sure that all parties know when I have worked with any of them in the past."

In terms of personal preparation, Christie relates, "One thing I try to do prior to each session is to make sure that I have taken a few minutes to center myself." She speaks of the need "to be present instead of being back in my day. It's easy to be very stressed. These are often very emotional sessions." Her typical daily schedule includes two divorce mediations, but that total may go to four if necessary. A short meditation, focusing on being helpful rather than harmful, helps Christie personally prepare for negotiating divorce settlements.

Sessions of a typical divorce mediation are held every other week over the course of several months. Christie says this makes sense in her experience, "because I've felt in the family area, it's much more helpful if people have time to do their homework, to think about what they're doing." Most sessions take about two hours. Christie may even be consulted before an initial separation takes place. In subsequent sessions, "I review the file so that I can see which issues we've resolved, which ones still need work, so that we can pick up where we left off."

The definition of success in this context is important to establish. Although many in the field look at numbers of settlements, Christie does not. For her, "Success means that the parties are making effective decisions, that the children's issues are covered, for the parties to be able to negotiate, for them to enter into interest-based negotiation. I try to help them look beyond what their original positions have been." Christie assists them in expressing why certain issues are important to them and assists the other person in listening to what is behind their partner's requests.

Christie builds toward success by giving a brief overview of interest-based negotiation in the first session. "I know they may not always hear it, because people are often so stressed and fearful then. But I can refer to it later in the way mediators do, by using questions such as, 'I'm hearing you say you want the house. What I'm not hearing you say is why.'" She then tries to draw the reasons out of the party requesting the house, while helping the other to listen.

Success also implies better communication in the future, because divorcing parents will need to maintain a relationship relative to the children. "What I think is so powerful is making people aware of their communication styles so that they can interact more effectively in the future," Christie says.

"Together, we try to discover 'What's going to help you two communicate better?'" She talks to them about what to do differently: "'Jane, whenever you shake your finger in his face, you've lost him; he's gone.' I do try to help them because I think mediation can have a profound effect on relationships in the future." Christie's goal is to help the spouses develop negotiating skills so that they will be less likely to need a neutral to assist them.

There are a number of challenges in divorce negotiation that can lead to a breakdown of the process. Post-dissolution clients who are stuck in their conflict present the most challenging situation for Christie. "They are at an impasse. Negotiation between the parties is not effective, and they need psychological or mental health intervention." Sometimes, people are operating out of extreme anger. Christie says, "They are really not able to understand what the other needs; sometimes, they are not even able to articulate their own needs. They are unable to focus on the good of the family or even the children's ultimate good."

Occasionally, mediation will fail because one spouse is not ready, or not as ready as the spouse who initiated the process. The initiator has had more time to reflect and work through issues of grieving. The surprised spouse is shocked and unable to be an effective decision maker. In addition, the involvement of a lover (that is, the situation of a romantic triangle) often complicates negotiations. Finally, great discrepancy in the valuation of an asset can stall or even abort divorce negotiations.

Contextual Differences

Rich and complex interpersonal dynamics set the family context apart from areas in which Christie mediates. She enjoys intervening in conflicts where issues are vitally important for most people, such as how their children are parented. She also observes a difference is her own intervention style: "In nonfamily cases, I'm much more directive. When there's litigation involved, the mediator is expected to be more directive and evaluative."

Other differences also pertain. "In family negotiations, typically people are present without counsel. Whatever the current dispute, they're going to continue to have a relationship." Christie contrasts family mediations with personal injury cases, "where you are basically just cutting a deal, and everyone just walks away when it's done."

Changes and Conflicts

There are new and emerging trends in family negotiations. The transformative movement has been an interesting discussion, but it hasn't really changed family mediation substantially. "What I see that is new is some hybrid processes that have grown out of mediations that failed. For instance, for the high-conflict couple who are not able to move on, mediation alone is not enough." Christie mentions processes that she conducts because she can see that standard mediation doesn't fit all families: parenting coordination, coordinating among professionals involved, med-arb (where the parties agree in the beginning that the mediator will make decisions if they cannot), and special masters who do intensive work with families over time. For those with high-conflict needs, the growth of options keeps people out of court and coaches them in new skills.

Experts in the field of family negotiation share the standard debate that most mediators have: How directive should the neutral be? Variations in this context take the form of "Should the mediator be an advocate for the children?" or, if mediators see parents making suboptimal agreements concerning the children, should they suggest better ways of solving standard kid issues? There are also differences of opinion about whether the neutral should be strictly facilitative, somewhat therapeutic due to the complexity of interpersonal dynamics, or frankly transformational.

Within the tension of these professional debates, Christie Coates represents the experience of an attorney mediator who has learned to deal with difficult interpersonal dynamics within the shadow of the law. She faces the challenges of the family context, is stimulated by the intellectual challenge of the complex issues, and is moved to compassion by the depth of emotions involved. Her role is to assist divorcing spouses so that their negotiations are interest-based. She accomplishes this through coaching the parties, hoping that not only will they reach better settlements for the family, but that they will practice negotiation skills to use in their ongoing parenting relationship.

PROFESSIONAL PROFILE

● **JOHN (SAM) KELTNER, PHD,**
PROFESSOR AND ADR CONSULTANT

Neighborhood Issues:
You Can't Negotiate if You're Anchored to the Bottom

The following interview about negotiation among neighbors touches on the same boundary issues that were discussed earlier in this chapter, including fences, noise, and access to property. The interviewee points out that neighborhood conflicts often sound silly to outsiders but are serious and emotional issues to those experiencing them. He advocates using communication skills such as listening, reframing one party's language to sound less antagonistic, and summarizing the main ideas of the session.

Introduction to the Practitioner

Sam Keltner could be profiled in almost every chapter of this book. In the preface to his 1994 book, *The Management of Struggle: Elements of Dispute Resolution Through Negotiation, Mediation and Arbitration*, Sam writes,

> "The negotiation process has been part of my life since the beginning. It has been a basic tool in the everyday process of growing up, department administration, teaching and training, conducting a consulting business, and dealing with the affairs of living." (p. ix)

In 1957, Sam was engaged by the Federal Mediation and Conciliation Service (FMCS) to provide training to federal labor-management negotiators in his specialty, communication. He became so interested in the mediation process that he left his university faculty position to become a mediator with the FMCS. He later returned to academic life and incidentally became an arbitrator in labor-management disputes. He continued to practice various forms of alternative (appropriate) dispute resolution as a consultant. He has written, taught, and trained students, colleagues, and others interested in negotiating and facilitating dispute resolution.

Sam's consulting practice has encompassed a wide range of disputes, including family, labor-management, divorce and child custody, commercial, intra- and interagency, and neighborhood dispute resolution programs. This last area is the focus of the following interview. Sam became involved in neighborhood disputes when he assisted in founding a dispute resolution center for the city of Corvallis, Oregon, where Oregon State University is located. Corvallis is a city of approximately 50,000 people; the center serves approximately 50 neighbors annually, with 30 trained mediators available. The purpose of the center is to assist neighbors who had been unable or unwilling to negotiate neighborhood disputes without intervention. If parties are willing to negotiate with assistance, they may be able to resolve their problems without resorting to more costly forms of dispute resolution, such as arbitration or litigation.

Insights About Negotiation

Sam reports that "the content areas of neighborhood disputes are wide and varied. We hear about barking dogs, people making noise at night, where the property line is, who has a right to the driveway, where the driveway goes. Sometimes feuding neighbors are referred by the police, sometimes they seek the service on their own." Originally funded by a combination of city, state, and county funds, the dispute resolution center is now part of a community outreach program.

Success depends on attributes of both negotiators and their assistants. Neighbors must offer a willingness to talk and consider various options for resolving their problems. Those assisting negotiation as mediators must demonstrate a complex skill set. Sam lists the following important skills: "Listening, reframing, summarizing, feedback, developing empathy with the parties, et al." Additionally, mediators must "assess where the parties are in the process of negotiation. They must understand the difference between a fight and a negotiation. Really, what it gets to is understanding the nature of the struggle spectrum."

Sam names a number of characteristics salient to each stage, such as problem-solving behaviors, relationship between the parties, goals, decision making, and possible outcomes. Understanding these aspects of a conflict enables a third party to determine whether or not negotiation may be useful to any given neighborhood problem. According to Sam, "If those assisting negotiations don't understand the struggle spectrum, they don't know whether their intervention is going to be useful or not."

Sam notes that "other than the basic training and experience I've had, preparation for neighborhood negotiations involves a case development period, which is prior to the time neighbors come face-to-face. The neutral party gets in touch with each of the parties in conflict, finds out what the struggle is all about, covers a bit of history—that's what we call case development." In the course of these conversations, the neutral party also establishes a relationship with the parties in conflict so that the parties feel a commitment to make a good-faith attempt at assisted negotiation.

In a typical first negotiation, neighbors or landlord-tenants agree to meet, and the mediator sits down with them saying, in effect, "Now, what's the problem?" Each is encouraged to state their positions. At this point, the mediator may attempt to get them to address each other, saying, "Now, don't tell me, tell each other," Sam says, "In that process, they will begin to engage each other. As the process goes on, they may begin to see possibilities, or the mediator may intervene, saying 'Am I right? Let's see if I can state this accurately . . .' to help reframe parties' positions. Or, the mediator will just shut up—stay out of it. I encourage mediators to stay out of the discussion unless the neighbors are simply unable to proceed."

The length of sessions may depend on the type of the dispute. "At one extreme, neighbors might settle in an hour or two. One neighbor might say, 'That's okay with me, let's get 'er done.' At the other extreme, we've had negotiations go through several sessions and total up to 12 to 24 hours."

The most essential element in success is that the neighbors are willing to talk to each other and to work with each other. In orientations for neighbors about to negotiate, Sam explains, "This is your chance to work this out for yourselves rather than have someone else decide for you." In his mind, the principle of self-determination is the hallmark of negotiation through mediation.

Sam finds that the most challenging negotiations are those where the neighbors hold deep emotional involvement. The deeper this involvement, the more difficult it is for negotiators to maneuver. Sam gives examples of deep emotional involvement, such as "cases which involve their families, where there's heavy money involved, personal pride is threatened, or long-standing traditions are challenged." For instance, in one small city, two neighbors had quarreled for years about parking practices that blocked each other from using a common driveway. In 1999, one of them waited 6 hours in an alley until his neighbor returned, whereupon he shot both the neighbor and his teenage daughter.

Sam gives an example of a challenged tradition that resulted in protracted negotiations: "For years, Pete has used an access road across Joe's property that is between the main road and the river. Without this access, Pete's property was worthless. Joe opposed continuation of the access for several reasons: It bisects his land, creates a drainage problem, and interferes with his cattle, who have become isolated on half of Joe's property. Encouraged to consider possible problem approaches, Pete proposed that if Joe would allow continued access, he would purchase the property required by a road, fence it, and build a tunnel under the road to enable Joe's cattle to graze on both sides of his property. Settlement was achieved."

Sam recounts an example of threat to personal pride by recalling a landlord who had spent substantial time and money maintaining a house that at one time had been his home. "Student renters did not keep up the house to his satisfaction, and he was angry. They were messing him up." The students countered that he had not attended to some of their complaints. Negotiations had to deal with both the property and the relationship issues between landlord and tenants.

When negotiations break down, Sam says, "The parties separate, the battle goes on, the conflict either moves on to the judicial phase, or they may begin to get into fights. You go back to the struggle spectrum, and you can track this as a failure to use negotiation, even with the help of a third party." Although it's shootings that make the newspapers, there's a great deal of other violence that results from unresolved neighborhood issues. Sam says, "The most common violence is property damage, such as tearing down fences and digging up yards. A major difficulty is that people don't know how to talk to each other about problems. They tend to figure that their solution or position is the most practical one, and it's hard to get them to sit down and discuss the problem with somebody else. Once that happens, negotiation can proceed, but that threshold of *being willing to talk* is critical."

Contextual Differences

Sam's considerable experience in a variety of areas gives him an edge in assessing how neighbor negotiations are different from those in other contexts. "Number one, neighbors aren't necessarily tuned in to negotiation processes, whereas in the labor-management venue, these are skilled negotiators. They've been at it for many years, they've had training, they know how to do the deed. Skilled negotiators meet face to face, they respect each other's skills, and they may even put on a show. Some people are very skilled at negotiations. Neighbors usually haven't had the experience of problem solving through give and take, generating options, and so on. And, of course, they get caught up in the emotion of the thing." Third-party neutrals in this context do not try to teach negotiation skills or expect that the neighbors will be better at negotiating future issues as a result of their experience with the dispute center.

Changes and Conflicts

The practice of neighborhood negotiations has not basically changed. However, "A number of the larger cities have instituted dispute resolution centers to assist in settling neighborhood conflicts. All over the country, there are neighborhood policing projects. Corvallis, for example, gets a number of referrals from the Police Department, where they have been called in. In general, the processes are growing—more and more cities and counties are cooperating with independent agencies offering community dispute programs."

Neutrals assisting neighbors may disagree about how much information you ought to have about the issues before you can facilitate. Sam asserts, "My position is, if you are skilled in the process, it isn't necessary for you to be a specialist in the content. There's a running argument between those who espouse the evaluative and those arguing for a facilitative approach. I prefer the facilitative approach. I do not agree with the evaluative process wherein the neutral judges the quality of presentations and content of the dispute. I do not think that a neutral is in any position to monkey around with the content of a dispute. That approach belongs in the field of arbitration or the courts. If the parties are having trouble with the content, I simply refer them to specialists."

Sam also advises that mediators assisting neighbors should steer clear of practicing law: "They should make no references to legal decisions or give legal opinions. They should make no presumptions about what would happen if they went to court." However, he says that a mediator may suggest that the neighbors be aware of legal issues and seek legal advice.

Sam gives the following advice to neighbors in conflict:

1. Take a look at the alternatives. Keep your mind open. You can't negotiate if you're anchored to the bottom.

2. Try to get behind the other's eyeballs, understand the other person's point of view.

3. Don't hold back. Don't be afraid to express your own opinions, interests, and feelings on these issues.

Whether they're down the hall or over the next valley, all of us have neighbors. Because of shared interests, conflicts between neighbors are both inevitable and resolvable. Sam's advice to us is grounded in his years of negotiation practice generally, as well as his experience with neighborhood disputes specifically. His three pointers will go a long way toward helping us keep our anchors out of the mud.

CHAPTER 8

CONSUMER NEGOTIATION

Striking a deal is like striking a balance. It entails that mysterious, teetering point at which a buyer is willing to buy and a seller is willing to sell.... Your input as for where that point lies is going to depend, in large part, upon two factors: the attitude you adopt and the goals you set.

— Bredenberg (1997, p. 3)

S hopping malls, online shopping, and credit cards influence a great deal of modern American life. Shopping for many is as much a recreational activity as participating in sports. The two activities become integrated for "mall walkers," a group of people whose exercise consists of brisk walks around a mall. The importance of buying and selling in American life dates to Colonial days, when "consumers of the gentle and particular 'middling' classes began to purchase an unprecedented number and variety of manufactured goods and to use many of them in conspicuous displays of leisure, social ritual, and status affirmation (or arrogation)" (Axtell, 1999, p. 85). In 1771, Connecticut parents instructed their children "to practice verture [virtue] and industry [work ethic] with good economy, which will naturally supply the individual with abundance . . . and render them useful, respectful, and independent" (Breen, 1999, p. 120).

Consumer negotiation possesses the most unusual set of contextual factors of the five settings we explore in this book. Structurally, the negotiation may involve only two people, a buyer and a seller, who negotiate in just about any setting in a timeframe that varies. The parties may possess no relationship history and, outside of cultural expectations, no tacit or formal understandings about behavior. They may be linked by no more than a short-term interdependence, and the interests of the negotiation are largely economic. Communication can range from civil, honest, and open to uncivil, dishonest, and closed. Power generally favors one of the parties.

Although distributive behavior characterizes a great deal of consumer negotiations, both sellers and consumers interested in long-term relationships will engage in more integrative tactics. Integrative consumer negotiation tends to favor common interests ("I want to sell and you want to buy"), shared understandings ("You will get the best deals from me"), and creates a mutually beneficial interdependence. Stores such as Kmart and Target learned long ago that giving dissatisfied customers their money back without hassles was good for business.

Because the six variables we apply to contexts vary so much in consumer negotiations, we've had to add additional variables that explain a great deal of the dynamics that occur in this setting: the impact of choice, the lack of loyalty, the perception of entitlement, the importance of public relations, and the growth of consumer groups. These five factors exert a great deal of influence on the power possessed by buyers in the consumer setting. In addition, to create a sense of interdependence, sellers—such as department stores, car dealers, and small businesses—invest a great deal of energy in building relationship through goodwill and customer service.

The impact of choice, expanded by e-negotiations, influences tactics used by both buyers and sellers. Attempts to create loyalty influence businesses' need to invest efforts in customer relations and resolve customer problems. The growing shadow of identity fraud and the complexity of contracts create a need for consumers to be more aware of financial dangers. Each of these issues, extensions of the five principles discussed next, are discussed later in the chapter.

● THE IMPACT OF CHOICE

Several factors define the buyer-seller relationship in the United States. The first is the many *choices* that are available to consumers. Waldman (1999) describes this factor as the "tyranny of choice" (p. 359). Americans buy because they can and because things are there to buy. Some automobile bumper stickers reflect the American preoccupation with shopping:

- Shop till you drop.
- I shop, therefore I am.
- Gone Shopping.
- When the going gets tough, the tough go shopping.

Many people buy impulsively without much thought about the sellers or the product, raising the probability that something may go wrong. Choice also leads to greater consumer power in negotiating prices in situations where sellers have room to bargain. In addition, the growth of the Internet has provided a great deal of information to supplement the greater number of choices. Consumers are able to investigate many of the claims made by advertising and sales. Because there are more choices available to buyers, there is a greater independence between buyers and sellers and less investment in relationship.

THE LACK OF LOYALTY •

A second factor that characterizes the buyer-seller relationship in the United States is that choice *erodes loyalty or commitment.* People change their minds, decide that they wanted a better model, or learn that they could have gotten a better bargain elsewhere. Competitive prices, the growth of generic products, and product promotions create a buyer's market for many kinds of products and services. Consumers possess more BATNAs than sellers, providing them a great deal of power in their selection of services and merchandise.

When a consumer has no potential for a future relationship with a seller, it's easier for them to make statements without worrying about the consequences. For example, a consumer buying a car may make aggressive or rude comments to a salesperson, knowing that after the sale, he or she won't have to speak to the salesperson again. Similarly, a buyer who returns an unwanted purchase may be rude to a salesperson, knowing the relationship need not be protected; there are many other stores at which to shop. Shopping becomes depersonalized, resulting in a greater number of distributive tactics during problem solving. In the buyers' minds, sellers become objects whose role is to satisfy personal needs.

THE PERCEPTION OF ENTITLEMENT •

A third factor involved in American consumer buying is *entitlement,* a factor discussed in the context of interpersonal negotiation in Chapter 7. Entitlement involves an attitude such as "I bought it. If I don't like it, I deserve a full refund." Many people rationalize, "This small loss won't hurt the budget of that large company." For example, a woman stood before the clothing counter of a major department store. Her overweight 16-year-old daughter stood by her side. In an aggressive, hostile tone, the mother said, "We bought this winter coat just a short while ago, and the zipper broke. We want a refund." The clerk said, "Do you have a receipt to show that you purchased the coat here?" She responded, "No, I thought the quality of your merchandise was better than this." The daughter interrupted, "Momma. We bought this coat 4 months ago." The mother said to the daughter, "That's just fine. Let me handle this." The clerk said, "We could have that zipper fixed for you." The mother became angrier. She demanded, "Don't you guarantee your products? I want a refund."

Many buyers approach shopping with this entitlement perspective, which influences how they manage a problem. Often, in negotiating a sale, consumers may ask sellers for extras to close the agreement. A perception of entitlement contributes to the use of language and tactics that would not fit the norms of other contexts. For example, buyers may believe that the use of aggressive statements and demands is okay because they believe it's the best strategy to get what they want.

● CONSUMER GROUPS

A fourth factor, linked to entitlement, involves the *growth of consumer groups* during the 1980s and 1990s. The rise of consumers' rights transformed consumers in the marketplace into a power with which to be reckoned. More than 90 consumer groups protect, educate, and warn consumers. Consumers exert their power through consumer newsletters, support for consumer legislation, and product boycotts. During the 1990s, consumers participated in more than 100 national boycotts of products or companies (Friedman, 1999). Representatives of consumer groups make about 19% of the appearances before U.S. House or Senate hearings (Maney & Bykerk, 1994). During the last third of the 20th century, consumer groups, led by figures such as Ralph Nader, tilted the balance of power toward consumers, altering consumer perceptions about rights and entitlements.

● CUSTOMER RELATIONS

The large number of stores that compete for customers creates a great deal of power for consumers. For every restaurant that opens in the major cities, an established restaurant closes. *Customer relations* becomes a significant aspect of every store's work. Many managers are aware of the industry findings that dissatisfied consumers will tell between 8 and 10 people about bad service, and 1 in 5 will tell 20 people (Barlow & Moller, 1996). Pleasing customers who have a great deal of choice becomes a drama when customers

---

Box 8.1

AT TIMES, PLAYING CAN GET A LITTLE ROUGH

Two women became engaged in a fight in a toy store. The incident, which was broken up by a security guard, involved two women interested in the same scooter. With the permission of a sales clerk, Ruth took a scooter off a display and headed for a checkout counter. As she moved down the aisle, Andrea stopped her. She asked, "Just where do you plan on going with that scooter?" Standing next to her 10-year-old daughter, Ruth answered, "It's mine. We've been looking at it for days, and now we're buying it. My daughter had her heart set on this one." Andrea countered, "No, you're not. I've just come from the manager, who said that I could have the last scooter, the one on display. Get your hands off of it. It belongs to my son."

Tension grew as discussion became more heated. Ruth told a store clerk who came running up, "I'll punch her lights out if she doesn't get her hands off my scooter." As Andrea swung her purse repeatedly at Ruth, Ruth's daughter bit and chewed on Andrea's arm. Andrea pushed the little girl aside. The two women wrestled from the bikes and scooters aisle to the doll aisle before the security guard broke up the fight. Both women were issued summons to appear in the city municipal court. Neither one took the scooter home.

The store manager needed to intercede early in the dispute. He needed to reduce the attacks and blaming, which involved accepting some responsibility. He might have said, "I believe we've made an error here. Let's see if we can solve this problem in a way that both of you ladies get what you need."

---

are dissatisfied. For example, a customer in a computer software store expressed dissatisfaction with some software he bought. The manager validated the customer's concern but pointed out signs on the wall that said that there were no refunds for used software. The man became angry and more boisterous. The manager, concerned about the impact of the man's complaints on other customers, ushered the man to a private office to discuss the matter. To compete for customers, many stores have to devote a great deal of energy to maintaining good customer relations.

Consumers who lack negotiation skills tend to become positional and emotional very quickly, as illustrated in Box 8.1.

● SELLER TACTICS

Negotiating in the world of consumer buying involves maximizing resources and opportunity. The power granted by choice gives the buyer advantages that should not be easily relinquished. Sometimes the power may be misused, as evidenced by the woman returning a well-worn coat, but in most cases the power can be used as a constructive tool. Food delivered cold in a restaurant serves neither the buyer's nor the seller's needs. A product that breaks after one use undermines a brand name and potential future purchases. The consumer-buyer relationship is an important one for the good of both parties.

To help buyers understand what they might expect when they make major purchases, Skopec and Kiely (1994, pp. 133-134) list tactics sellers use to raise selling price. Sellers will do the following:

- Make a first offer in the high end of the price range, expecting to later demonstrate flexibility and compromise
- Let unknowledgeable shoppers make the first offer to discover their starting points
- Boost the price as much as possible while stripping away extra-cost options to maximize the profit margin
- Increase the perceived value of a purchase by emphasizing superficial features
- While comparing the price and product to a competitor's, advise, "Our price is a little higher but our quality is significantly higher"
- Promise the buyer additional incentives (of little or no cost to the seller) to raise the perceived value of a deal
- When preparing for a sale, sell the highest-priced item first and then promote low-cost add-ons, which will then seem insignificant in additional cost
- Promote buyer emotional investment by getting a small commitment, such as trying on a new suit or test driving a new car

Sellers sometimes use terminology that needs to be looked at carefully. For example, sellers use a *scarcity strategy* when they encourage a buyer to purchase *now* while a product is "on sale" or "while supplies last." Bredenberg (1997) points out that department stores sell 60% to 80% of all merchandise on sale. The word "sale" may be more manipulative than real. Sellers attempt to minimize a perception of risk by telling buyers that a product is "low maintenance" or "can be operated by a 12-year-old child." The large number of flashing lights on living room VCRs because the clock isn't set (which is the state of VCRs in the majority of all homes) would seem to counter some of these claims. Sellers build on consumers' aversion to risk through promotion of "extended warranties," which are expensive and often are of limited value to customers. Buyers calling the toll-free customer-service

---

Box 8.2

PLAYING A GAME WITH CUSTOMERS
WHO COME TO BUY A GAME

If you were a billiard-table dealer, which would you first show a potential buyer—the $329 model or the $3,000 model? You would probably promote the lower-priced item and hope to interest customers in the higher-priced item when they come to buy. But G. Warren Kelley, a new business promotion manager at Brunswick, says you could be wrong. To prove his point, Kelley has actual sales figures from a representative store. During the first week, customers were shown the low end of the line and then encouraged to consider more expensive models—the traditional *trading-up* approach. The average table sale that week was $550. However, during the second week, customers were led instantly to a $3,000 table, regardless of what they wanted to see, and then allowed to shop the rest of the time in declining order of price and quality. The result of selling down was an average sale of more than $1,000 (Cialdini, 1993, p. 47).

---

numbers are met with a series of voice mails—rarely a live person. A common consumer complaint is that when buyers actually try to collect on a warranty for an automobile, computer, or real estate, they hear, "That's not covered under the limited warranty" or "The warranty doesn't cover normal wear-and-tear items." Box 8.2 illustrates a *contrast strategy* designed to push up the price buyers are willing to pay. For many kinds of sales, the standard is for salespeople to make at least three attempts to get a buyer to purchase more items.

Consumer advocates Ralph Nader and Wesley Smith (1995) point out three commonly used sales techniques designed to influence buyers:

- *Just say yes.* Salespeople ask a series of questions designed to get a "yes" response from buyers, predisposing buyers to say yes to later seller requests.
- *Put buyers on the defensive.* A salesperson will counter buyer reasons against a product or reasons why the buyer can't afford a product. Buyers succumb to what they perceive is the better judgment of the seller.
- *Use an emotional appeal.* Sellers promote impulsive buying by emphasizing the emotional appeal of particular features of a product.

● BUYER TACTICS

Sandler (1998) laments, "Some people happily pay thousands more than they should for a car, buy televisions and VCRs at list price, . . . pay twice as much as the guy in the next seat for an airplane ticket, and throw away a good portion of their income on unnecessary or improper insurance" (p. xiv). Consumer negotiation isn't a technique to outmaneuver salespeople; it is a process to get fair prices based on respectable standards of market value. Sellers deserve a fair profit, and buyers deserve a fair price.

Getting the best deals on purchases involves many tactics, all of which begin with research. Prenegotiation is important in many contexts, but it is essential in consumer negotiations. Knowing the market value of an item and what the seller needs to get out of a deal sets the boundaries for discussions. Real estate competitive analyses, consumer reports, and buying guides play important roles for leveling the consumer-buyer playing field. Market research serves as the foundation for offers and counteroffers. Highly successful consumers do their homework and know their product better than salespeople. Some specialists recommend carrying a computer printout of comparative data with you as you begin negotiations. In addition, Schaffzin (1997) advises,

> In the event that you don't have the time or the resources to research carefully the industry statistics or the objective basis of any agreement, you have one more line of defense: Ask the other side where they get their numbers. By making them explain their reasoning, you will, at a minimum, get to see any way in which they skewed the figures they present, to your advantage." (p. 22)

A second tactic to get the best deals is an understanding of the seller's reputation and the sales strategy you might expect. Engel, Blackwell, and Miniard (1995) point out that 23% to 40% of consumer complaints cite the retailing merchant; only 5% cite the manufacturer. About two-thirds of the problems associated with online shopping involve complaints about sellers. Some businesses train their salespeople to use distributive tactics, whereas others promote mutual gain. For example, a statement used in negotiation training for J.D. Edwards managers illustrates the kind of integrative norms some companies set for staff who interact with customers:

> J.D. Edwards is committed to maintaining the highest level of integrity in business dealings with stakeholders, employees, customers, suppliers, local communities, government at all levels and the general public wherever we exist. J.D. Edwards has an outstanding reputation for honesty and integrity . . . we take great pride in our ethical reputation and commit ourselves to its continuation as the basis of our future success. (J.D. Edwards, 2001)

Choosing the right business and right salesperson with whom to do business may be one of the most important aspects of successful negotiations. It may take three or four visits to automobile showrooms to find a salesperson with whom you feel comfortable. Many in the real estate industry recommend interviewing at least three real estate agents before selecting one to sell your home.

Knowing the markup strategy or negotiating range of the seller can be useful to buyers. Sandler (1998, pp. 11-12) lists some of the generally accepted above-cost markups of products:

- Automobiles: 5% to 12%
- Real Estate: 10% to 15%
- Appliances: 15% to 25%
- Computers: 10% to 25%
- Clothing: 50%
- Furniture: 50% to 100%
- Books: 50% to 100%

All of the margins are dependent on factors such as time of month or year, general market conditions, and what competitors are charging. The implication is that making offers significantly outside the negotiating range of the seller without reasoning and justification will probably be ineffective. Buyers need to understand the range that sellers may have and work to maximize gains within it.

Just as in the other negotiation contexts, questions during the actual negotiation serve as an important tool for maximizing gain. A few of the useful questions include the following:

- Is this the best price you can offer me?
- Is there a discount for cash?
- When do you expect that this item will next be on sale?
- This is a higher price than I intended to pay. Is there anything you can do to make this work for me?

In negotiating the terms of the contract, buyers need to be aware of subtle tactics used to minimize perceptions of actual cost. For example, here are some things sellers might say and their translations:

- "The percentage rate on your credit account is only 1.85% a month," which is in reality 22.2% a year.
- "The monthly payment for this car is only $300, and you had said you were willing to pay as much as $325 per month." However, the payment will now be for 4 years instead of 3 years, which means you'll have to pay $2,700 more over the long term.
- "Our workers will repair your roof for $20 per hour, whereas others will charge you $30 per hour." The important question is, how many hours does it take the lower-priced worker to complete the job?

■ "We can build this house for $250,000, a lot lower than our competitors at $285,000." But the offer does not include a lot premium ($10,000), a basement ($15,000), double-pane windows ($5,000), front yard landscaping ($7,500), better carpet than you'd expect in a warehouse ($5,000), and an overhead roof for the front porch ($5,000), all items included in the competitors' price.

When a cost is spread out over many months and the actual expenses are numbers on a contract, we tend not to spend as much time considering the specifics of the deal. The add-ons seem insignificant compared with the large expense to which we're already committed. We're already invested in the commitment to purchase and minimize the impact of the details. However, some of the most important aspects of negotiations are the details.

Koren and Goodman (1991) provide tactics often used by salespeople that buyers can use to equalize the playing field. For example, sellers who invest a great deal of time in explaining, demonstrating, and advising a buyer will be more willing to cut a better deal. They don't want all of their efforts going to waste. So buyers need to get sellers to invest time in them. Sellers prefer to do business with buyers they like and those who speak in a pleasant, conversational tone. Just like sellers, buyers need to promote relationship. Negotiators who focus on facts, figures, and precedent reduce manipulation through emotional appeals or distortion of fact, which derail constructive discussion. Personalizing the buyer-seller relationship and depersonalizing the issue promotes greater seller responsiveness. Sellers tend to be more flexible with buyers who request help and information. Like buyers, sellers want to be valued.

● E-NEGOTIATION

"Negotiation needs computers about as much as the hummingbird needs snowshoes. Or so many negotiators specialists seem to think" (Wheeler, 1995, p. 169). Historically, negotiation has been understood as a face-to-face, problem-solving interaction. Reading the nonverbal messages on the faces of other parties or the interpersonal behaviors that indicate trustworthiness or credibility were important aspects of the processes. Between 1995 and 2000, more than 800 consumer online auction sites encouraged buyers to make offers on a large number of products. The biggest online site, eBay, did $2.8 billion in sales in 1999, and online auction sites are expected to reach $6.4 billion in sales by 2004.

Most of the online auction sites use similar styles of negotiation, largely distributive negotiation (value claiming) that focuses on a single variable: price. Buyers engage in bidding (such as on eBay and Priceline), make offers and receive counteroffers (makeusanoffer.com), or compete in games against computer opponents (Hagglezone). Buyers' willingness to negotiate varies by product. Hobson (1999) observes that a buyer's willingness to negotiate online is related to the frequency with which the buyer purchases the product, the value of the purchase, and the level of involvement the buyer wants to have in the purchase. For example, buyers are more inclined to conduct online research or make online deals for infrequent purchases such as home mortgages, automobiles, or real estate, and they are less inclined to make online purchase of commodities such as groceries or electronic equipment, where there are many stores to compare prices.

In e-negotiation, there is little or no problem solving, sharing information, or relationship building. Parties make price offers with no attempt to uncover underlying interests. Power generally favors the buyer. There is not much sellers can do to create a desire to negotiate. They lack information about a buyer's interests or timing for making a purchase. However, when bidding begins, the results favor the seller. Hobson (1999) points out that 20% of buyers end up paying more than market price. He explains, "The excitement of the auction may distort a buyer's analysis of his or her willingness to pay" (p. 216).

In most negotiation contexts, price is not the only factor driving negotiations. Other factors—such as trust, relationship, and quality of product or service—may be just as important to consumers. Raisch (2001) argues that skilled negotiators are not satisfied with passive exchanges, the kind found in most e-negotiations. For online negotiations to be successful, the process will need to be humanized. Raisch says, "Buyers will negotiate price, deliver time, condition of goods and payment terms. In future online negotiations, the process will be designed to provide the digital equivalence of a handshake and a look in the eye" (p. 7).

Compared with face-to-face negotiation, negotiators using computer-aided communication experience the following:

- More positional orientations
- More negative expression of emotions
- Greater time for reflection
- Fewer expressions of status differences
- Better outcomes in competitive or individualistic climates
- Reduction of effects of organizational climate
- Depersonalized communication

Some cautions exist in the use of computers as a communication tool for negotiation. In text-only mediums, communication appears to have fewer inhibitions (these inhibitions are normally regulated through nonverbal cues), so parties are more likely to make negative statements that emphasize differences (Siegel, Dubrovsky, Kiesler, & McGuire, 1986). Online negotiation provides more time for negotiators to question the motives of others and to respond with tougher statements. Text-only media tend to encourage a higher conflict intensity in messages. Poole (1991) concludes that using text-only media makes it more difficult to achieve integrative agreements.

On the other hand, a significant place may exist for computer-aided negotiation. If as much as 80% of negotiation is actually preparation (prenegotiation), then negotiators can engage in a great deal of preparatory discussion, information gathering, and identification of interests and goals online. In two negotiations, Spangle asked parties to begin by e-mailing him interests prior to face-to-face discussions. Without names attached, the interests were arranged in lists and returned to the parties. The parties then prioritized the interests and returned the new lists via e-mail. At the beginning of negotiation, a summary of the prioritized lists served as a central element of negotiation. The same procedures can be created for sharing goals or brainstorming options. In either case, dissociating names from ideas provides a freer exchange of ideas and trims hours of discussion from the negotiation.

At a minimum, Wheeler (1995) proposes that a computer database or spreadsheet could pool information for the use of all parties in a negotiation and provide a forum for developing a single text for an agreement. Interests, options, or market analysis could all be explored with a common set of data, and parties could spend more time focusing on the problem instead of on each other.

The most far-reaching ideas for computer-aided negotiation involve decision making or economic analysis computer programs designed to elicit each side's preferences, evaluate proposals, and suggest mutually beneficial agreements. The goal of these programs is to minimize emotional, subjective elements of the process that might influence choices. Conceivably, the computer program could factor in such elements as BATNAs, expectations, or assumptions. Samuelson (1995) proposes, "Such a system would seek to identify an agreement that is efficient (gets the most for both parties); equitable (balances the interests of both sides); and stable (promotes long-term relationships)" (p. 142).

● CONSUMER PROBLEMS

Case Western Reserve University in Ohio conducted a survey of thousands of households to determine the frequency of buyer dissatisfaction and typical responses to dissatisfaction (Singh, 1990). They looked at problems associated with grocery shopping, automobile repair, medical care, and banking services. About 30% of the households recalled dissatisfying experiences. According to Singh, of those who were unhappy,

- 37% wanted to resolve the problem without further escalation;
- 28% wanted revenge and retribution;
- 21% said nothing to the sellers but told others about their problem; and
- 14%, though unhappy, kept shopping at the store where they had encountered problems.

A federal study reported that only about one in 25 people who were dissatisfied with a product or service actually complained. The Better Business Bureau in 1996 ranked the following consumer complaints in order of source and number of occurrences:

1. Auto dealers: 14,668

2. Auto repair: 9,728

3. Home furnishings: 7,792

4. Services, miscellaneous: 7,129

5. Home remodeling contractors: 6,829

6. Used-car dealers: 6,164

7. Computer sales: 5,733

8. Telephone companies: 5,682 (Source: Green, 1998)

Buyers who are dissatisfied can become unruly, as demonstrated by an unhappy car owner in Marin County, California (Barlow and Moker, 1996). A Volkswagen owner became so dissatisfied with his vehicle that he placed a sign with large letters on the side of his VW van that read, "VW, the Very Worst Car." Below the words, he listed unresolved defects he'd had with the vehicle. Below the list of defects, the owner displayed a large chart of consumer automobile complaints in order of frequency, with VW at the top. In addition, the sign included a blowup of a quote from an automobile magazine. It would have been in VW's best interests to find a way to address this customer's complaints before such a significant escalation of dissatisfaction.

A similar consumer response occurred in Walnut Creek, California (In the end, the customer is always right, 1995, pp. B1-B2). Jeremy Dorosin went into Starbucks to buy an espresso machine. He understood that when he bought the machine, he would receive a half pound of coffee free. The staff refused to give Jeremy the extra coffee, claiming that he misunderstood. Jeremy became angry. Later, he said that he'd felt embarrassed in front of the other customers. To make matters worse, the coffee machine malfunctioned when Jeremy used it at home. Although Starbucks' staff tried to rectify the coffeemaker problem, Jeremy remained unhappy. He ran an ad in *The Wall Street Journal* that began, "Had any problems at Starbucks Coffee?" He ended the ad by calling himself "one mistreated customer" and included a toll-free phone number people could use to talk to him about troubles they had had with Starbucks. Before the ordeal was over, Jeremy said that the only thing that would make him happy would be Starbucks establishing a center for runaway children in San Francisco. Occasionally, in cases such as this, the customer's need to save face or prove a point is greater than the need to resolve a problem.

Researchers estimate that sellers have the ability to resolve about 75% of consumer problems (Williams, Drake, and Moran, 1993). In most cases, sellers maintain a higher business reputation by negotiating solutions to problems with unhappy buyers. Sellers may use many of the same tactics used by buyers to resolve problems. These tactics include gathering facts about the situation, asking a lot of questions before saying what you are willing to do, demonstrating respect for the other party, expressing commitment to a solution that is mutually acceptable, and determining what the other party wants. Attempting to understand the other party precedes the generation of solutions.

Whether buyers write a letter of complaint or discuss the issue face-to-face appears to be a function of the kind of business with which buyers have the problem. For example, Fulmer and Goodwin (1994) report the results of a 3-year survey that looked at complaint letters written to 77 industries, predominantly airline, hotel, restaurant, bank, credit card, auto-sales, and car-rental businesses. Overall, customers received responses from the businesses about 41% of the time, ranging from no response by some restaurants, credit card, and auto sales to 90% by banks and 83.3% by car rental agencies. Hotels were third in response rate, at 73.7%, but only about 9% of the hotel responses addressed the issue directly. Airlines and banks showed strong inclination to respond specifically to the issues. The average time it took for buyers to receive a response was about 17.3 days from the date of their initial letter. This study suggests that complaint letters will be more effective with businesses that value continuing relationships and less effective with businesses that primarily do one-time sales with customers.

Rather than characterizing the way consumers handle problems as complaining, we would suggest that the process be framed as problem solving or negotiation. We believe that both buyers' and sellers' needs would be better served. We propose the following process for buyers in this context:

1. Before approaching a seller about a problem with a product, consider whether it will be worth the hassle. Driving across town to return a $10 purchase may not be a good use of time. Getting a home builder to fix a sticky window or replace a gasket in a faucet may not be worth the stress of convincing the builder the work needs to be done.

2. If you decide that it's worth the hassle, return to the place where the purchase was made. Face-to-face discussion raises the probability of satisfactory resolution of problems.

3. Gather the facts. Prepare to present relevant documents in an organized fashion.

4. When expressing dissatisfaction, manage the tone and inflection of your voice. Curtis Loewe, manager of Consumer Services for the Minnesota Attorney General's Office, suggests, "Don't personalize the process. It's a business, so distance yourself and treat it that way"

(Bredenberg, 1997, p. 25). Describe dissatisfaction with an item or service and ask if someone can help you.

5. If the salesperson provides no help, do not hesitate to push the problem to the next level. Be firm about your interests, but work with organizational hierarchy.

6. Demonstrate a willingness to negotiate a solution that works for the best interests of both buyer and seller.

When we have a problem, we should not alienate potential allies, such as sales clerks, office assistants, or customer service representatives, but work to get them on our side. Pollan and Levine (1994) suggest three principles for making allies of these first-level employees:

1. Let the person know that you recognize the limitations of his or her position.

2. Acknowledge that the person has done the job in a responsible manner.

3. Give the person an opportunity to help you in whatever way he or she can.

These principles also apply to navigating our way through organizational systems, when finding the person with the power to help us can be challenging.

Sandler (1998) points out that "in most situations you have the right to cancel a deal and receive your money back because of nonperformance, unacceptable quality, or even a limited right to merely change your mind" (p. 26). Most businesses have a greater need to protect a relationship with a buyer than to make the small profit gained on many products. On major purchases, such as houses or cars, where a great deal of money is at stake, buyers must be aware of the fine print about the costs of cancellation in the contract.

For 20 years, Harris County (Houston), Texas, District Attorney Russel Turbeville investigated and prosecuted problems associated with consumer fraud. He summarizes many of the insights that he's learned through the years (R. Turbeville, personal communication, December 8, 2000):

1. If it sounds too good to be true, it probably is. Be suspicious and careful before engaging in any consumer transaction where you seem to be getting a lot for very little. Hunters catch prey; fishermen catch fish; and con men catch victims by baiting traps. Don't get caught.

2. Contracting is a two-way street. Generally speaking, under the law, consumers are legally stuck with deals once they're made. There is

no "3-day cooling off period" for the vast majority of consumer transactions. Many reputable merchants allow consumers to return goods and cancel contracts, but that is their policy. It's not a legal right. Many times, once a consumer pays for an item or signs a promissory note for services, he or she has bought it, and the money need not be returned.

3. Seeing is not necessarily believing. Just because a consumer sees a product or service advertised on television, hears it on the radio, or reads it in the newspaper or on the Internet, the offer is not necessarily real. Generally, media will take any ad and run it until and unless they know the offer is fraudulent and, by that time, it's too late for the buyer. Don't rely on the media policing their ads.

4. Deal with tried-and-true merchants. Established merchants with large capital investments in their businesses almost never commit intentional fraud. They generally want to correct any serious problems to preserve customer loyalty and their business reputation.

5. Don't do business with "Lone Rangers." When you send money or credit card numbers to people who solicit business through phone calls, newspaper advertisements, or the Internet, it is difficult to investigate a crime. When the seller cannot be identified, it's almost impossible in a court of law to prove who is responsible for a crime or who has misused a credit card.

6. Avoid prepaying for anything you don't have to. Clever crooks often persuade victims to make a substantial deposit or full payment for merchandise or services that are to be received later. Any time a buyer enters into an agreement for a significant purchase, he or she needs to get some type of document that memorializes the agreement so that a third party, knowing nothing about the transaction, could after the fact understand the terms of the agreement. If the promise made is not in writing, it doesn't count.

7. There is no free lunch. In the real-world marketplace, sellers don't "give" you anything. In some way, whether the cost is absorbed in the purchase price or in the financing, the buyer pays for all that is received.

8. Avoid high-pressure sales. Don't allow yourself to be pushed into buying the wrong thing at the wrong price because you've been manipulated into believing that this golden opportunity won't last forever. High-pressure sales tactics are specifically designed to overcome the buyer's good judgment. Unfortunately, under the law, most of the time buyers are stuck with the deal, even if they change their mind.

9. The guarantee is as good as the one who makes the promise. Consumers seem to feel a lot more comfortable in parting with their money when the seller provides a written guarantee. A guarantee is just a promise. If the person taking the money is lying, the guarantee is just one more lie.

10. Use an ounce of prevention. Remember that the cheapest deal is not always the best deal. Quite often, it's just bait. If you allow yourself to be scammed, even if the case can be prosecuted, you probably won't get your money back. Even if the offender goes to jail, you still lose your money.

IDENTITY FRAUD •

Criminals who practice identity theft unlawfully make purchases using another person's name, credit card number, Social Security number, checks, driver's license number, or signature. Currently, this is the number one consumer fraud problem in the United States. The Federal Trade Commission's Identify Theft Clearinghouse reports that more than 69,000 complaints of identify theft involving credit cards, phone calls, bank accounts, employment, and loans occurred between November, 1999 and June, 2001 (Federal Trade Commission, Identity Theft Data Clearinghouse, n.d.). Identity-fraud thieves rent apartments and buy cars as if they were the person whose name they use. Although she was the victim, a woman in Savannah, Georgia, spent 18 months in jail until officials resolved the problems another person had caused for her through identity fraud. In Massachusetts, an imposter used another's name to get a $14,000 loan from the General Motors Acceptance Corporation.

Under the 1996 Electronic Fraud Transfer Act, the consumer's liability for unauthorized use of a credit card is $50 if the consumer notifies the bank within 2 business days. The cost jumps to $500 if the consumer fails to notify the bank after the 2 days but within 60 days. After 60 days, the consumer has unlimited liability. But no such liability limits exist on a great number of other types of fraud that can be committed against consumers. Box 8.3 illustrates a theft that required many negotiations to resolve.

Consumers who are the victims of identity theft need to first contact the police department to file a report. They then need to have a fraud alert added to their credit report through the three major credit bureaus: Equifax, Experian, and Trans Union. Then the negotiation begins. Each of the businesses with bills outstanding will have to be contacted. Green (1998) recommends sending the businesses "a copy of the police report and any documentation that shows you are the victim of fraud . . . Write letters, make follow-up calls, and personally check credit reports to be sure it's been restored" (p. 644). Next, negotiate the best deal you can to reduce the costs of the fraud. Howard and Meltzer (2000) lament,

Box 8.3

THEFT THOUGH NOTHING DISAPPEARS

Bill and Susan are a young couple who live in the suburbs of a major city. Recently, they received their phone bill, which included $150 of charges made to a 900-prefix sex line. They were furious and called the customer service representative at the 900 number to complain. The representative said, "The calls were made from your phone number. You are responsible." Bill argued, "But they weren't. Is there anything you can do for a fraud such as this?" The representative agreed to take the charges off the bill.

The next month, Bill opened his phone bill to find $150 worth of charges to various 900-prefix sex line phone numbers. The phone company came out and checked his phone lines but found nothing. Bill changed the locks on his house and put a lock on his outside phone terminal box. He called the 900 numbers and managed to get $75 taken off the bill. He had to pay the balance. Bill asked each of the services to block his number from any further calls.

Bill was suspicious of his next-door neighbors' teenage son. He went over to talk to the boy's parents. They said that they had similar charges on their phone bill. They found that their son had made the calls, but he agreed to make no more such calls. Bill had no evidence to further accuse the boy.

The next month, Susan cautiously opened the phone bill. It listed $225 of 900-number phone calls. Bill immediately called the police. An officer came to their home and investigated but soon left, saying, "There's nothing we can do. The calls are coming from your phone." Bill told the neighbor that he was involving the police now and expected the phone calls to stop. About a week later, Bill checked windows in the basement and first floor to make sure they were locked. The only place he could even remotely expect someone to get into the house was a little dog door on the side of the laundry room. He put a lock on the laundry room door. Following negotiation with the 900-number representatives, he agreed to pay $150 of the latest phone charges.

The next month, the phone bill was free of any unauthorized calls. Was it the dog door? Did involving the police make a difference? The couple never found out, but they did discover that they were liable for any calls charged to their phone bill. They were victims of theft even though nothing was taken. Fortunately, they were able to negotiate so they had to pay only about one-half of the charges.

There's virtually nothing you can do to keep thieves from stealing your identity because the 1974 Privacy Act allows the three major credit bureaus to invade your privacy at will, and gives you no control over how they make your Social Security numbers and personal information available. (p. 218)

CONTRACTS •

Gotbaum (1999) observes that in the United States "more than in any other country, a contract is sacred. It is considered a final document by all signers, and its authority is a bedrock principle of American democracy, serving as a protection of our values" (p. 170). Contracts such as those associated with prenuptial agreements, home mortgage payments, or automobile financing reduce a great deal of uncertainty for consumers. Major sports figures who sign multiyear contracts view the agreements as protection against loss of income due to injury or changes in plans by ownership.

Consumers should read all contracts closely to avoid detrimental repercussions. Used-car lots that carry their own financing can lock car buyers into exorbitant prices for the life, and sometimes beyond the life, of a car. A renter who signs a 1-year lease for an apartment may decide that he doesn't like his noisy neighbors, but he is liable for paying the rent for a year, regardless of whether he lives in the apartment or not. A young couple signed a contract with a real estate agent to sell their home. The home didn't sell in 2 months, so they took the home off the market. They didn't like the way the agent marketed their home. Two months later, the couple decided once again to sell the home. They discovered that their contract with the agent bound them to him for 6 months. They could sell the home, but he still received a 3.5% commission for the duration of the contract.

Earlier in this chapter, a statistic from the Better Business Bureau identified auto dealers as the largest source of consumer complaints. If a sales contract reads "sold as is," the consumer becomes liable for defects even if the seller failed to disclose them. In one case, a buyer received a great deal on a 5-year-old Mercedes convertible, which he drove away from the seller's property. After several days of cleaning oil off of his driveway, the new owner took the vehicle to his repair shop. He discovered that the car had a cracked block and needed a new engine, which would cost thousands of dollars. The bill of sale received from the seller provided no protection for vehicle defects.

Occasionally, consumers enter into contracts with businesses that eventually enter bankruptcy. This may not matter on small purchases but, for buyers who expected upgrades for their computers, repairs for their new home, or services that they paid for, the costs can be significant. One business invested $10 million in a computer data system. A year later, the firm from which it bought the system went bankrupt. The business remained liable for the costs of the contract even though it had to spend tens of thousands of dollars yearly on consultants to keep the system running efficiently.

The contract is an essential element of negotiations. As statements of legal obligations, contracts aren't perfect, but they can reduce some of the uncertainty and a few of the risks for consumers. The first and most important priority for consumers is to pay close attention to the details of contracts they sign. One buyer tells about how he negotiated with a car dealer for an anti-theft alarm system to be included in the deal for his new car. The buyer managed to get the price down from $2,000 to $1,200. Later, at home, when the buyer was reading the contract he had signed, he noticed that buried in the list of numbers was a cost for the alarm of $60 per month for 3 years, an actual cost of $2,100. When reading the details of the contract, some of the basic elements we should pay careful attention to include the following:

- A list of specific obligations of all parties involved in the agreement
- Explicit instructions about time for completing responsibilities or for making payments
- Explanation about how an offer or agreement may be terminated
- A process for remedies or penalties if either party fails to fulfill obligations

Although buyers who are emotionally involved with decisions do not expect that they'll change their mind, they should allow for that possibility in the contract. The length of the contract and penalties for default must be discussed and sometimes even negotiated. Losing $5,000 in earnest money on the purchase of a home because of unforeseen circumstances may be a high price to pay for not including an escape-clause provision in the contract.

Belli and Wilkinson (1987) summarize many of the principles that consumers need to understand with regard to their rights and legal obligations:

- The terms of a contract are generally binding even if provisions in the written document differ from what one party understood them to be.
- A contract may be accepted in person, over the phone, by mail, or over the Internet by promising to do what the offer requires.
- Contracts may be modified by an oral agreement, even if the contract is a written agreement.
- To be enforceable, the written contract needs to contain only three requirements: the names of the parties, the subject matter, and when the contract is in effect.
- Once a contract is made, changes can be made only if both parties agree.
- The legal criteria for evaluating satisfactory performance involves performance that would be acceptable by any "reasonable person." If a reasonable person would be satisfied with the results, a buyer cannot refuse to pay the agreed-upon price, even if the performance didn't measure up to their standards.

- Mistakes in a contract need not invalidate the contract. The mistakes would have to be significant and disagree with the "heart of the agreement."
- A contract can be rescinded if the sellers can be proved to have committed fraud or misrepresented facts. The cancellation must occur soon after the seller discovers the fraud, not 6 months or a year later.

Negotiation doesn't end when buyers and sellers reach agreement. The process is not complete until the contract is written, read, and signed. Many times, if there are going to be problems, they will occur because the contract didn't say what the consumers thought they had agreed to, the cost of getting out of the contract was high, or remedies for nonperformance or failures were not clearly stated. Negotiation over the terms of the contract are as important as negotiation for the initial sale.

SUMMARY ●

Consumer negotiation differs from negotiation in other contexts in large part because of the greater emphasis placed on price and satisfaction of economic expectations. Consumers often have a narrower range of expectations for economic negotiation than they would for interpersonal or organizational negotiation. Few hesitate to take a purchase back to a store if performance is unsatisfactory. Although relationship can improve the dynamics of many consumer negotiations, relationship is not as important a factor as others. In a society with decreasing brand or store loyalty, an increasing choice of merchants or service providers, and little commitment to community, much of consumer buying becomes depersonalized.

Consumer negotiation differs from problem solving in other settings because of more frequent use of distributive tactics. Sellers make high-end offers expecting to compromise, provide misinformation that favors their product, and attempt to manipulate buyers with emotional appeals. Buyers sometimes use the following strategies: hiding relevant information (recall the shopper whose daughter wore a coat an entire winter before returning the coat for a refund), bluffing ("I can buy this at your competitor for a cheaper price"), or demanding ("If you don't give me what I want, I'll speak to your manager").

Effective consumer negotiation involves a great deal of prenegotiation planning and research. Buying from the stores or sellers with good reputations minimizes the potential for later problems. Clarifying a store's return policy or the exit provisions from a contract is an essential element of many negotiations. The art of questioning assumes importance for uncovering price breaks, flexibility in terms of contracts, and additional alternatives that provide greater opportunity to maximize gain while minimizing cost.

Although relationship plays a secondary role in buying, it plays a central role in resolving problems. Sellers often prefer to make things right for buyers who seek help for a problem or for buyers they like. Studies suggest that many problems are best handled face-to-face, yet buyers who are coercive and demanding may receive resistance from people who might otherwise provide help. Additionally, consumers have more success negotiating problems if they focus on attributes of the service or product they dislike (depersonalize the issue), recognize the limitations first-line workers have in solving problems, and affirm the positive contributions sellers make in efforts to provide help.

Computers can aid negotiation processes through the sharing of information. The information may involve listing of interests, goals, alternatives, or potential agreements. Computer messaging is most effective when negotiators manage unconstructive displays of emotion, craft messages that emphasize interests rather than positions, and demonstrate listening and understanding about the needs and interests of others.

And finally, most buyers treat contracts as afterthoughts or extras that should be completed as quickly as possible. In actuality, the contract is a continuation of the negotiation. Negotiation is not complete until provisions in the contract are read, discussed, negotiated, and signed. Many consumers sign away their rights to compensation for damages or ability to get the service they paid for because they have not fully read the contract. The contract phase in major consumer purchases may actually be the most important phase of negotiation.

PROFESSIONAL PROFILE

BARBARA BERGER OPOTOWSKY, ●
FORMER PRESIDENT,
NEW YORK CITY BETTER BUSINESS BUREAU

Negotiating Returns or Repairs:
Be Calm, Patient, and Reasonable

The most frequent opportunity consumers have to practice negotiation comes when we attempt to repair or return products that are unsatisfactory in some way. We may have changed our minds about the color of the sweater we want, Aunt Tillie in the nursing home needs the pajamas in a smaller size, the plumbing continues to leak even after repair, or the new car is a lemon.

Sometimes our consumer needs are accommodated on the first try. Other times, we are transferred from one department to another or, worse yet, there is no response to our complaint. Occasionally, a business we thought legitimate is "missing in action" when problems occur. Although not all variables in such situations are under our control, we can greatly enhance the occurrence of successful negotiations by following the advice of Barbara Berger Opotowsky, former President of the New York Better Business Bureau. Barbara's experience there provides consumer negotiators with concrete suggestions for achieving satisfaction.

Barbara agrees with a number of the suggestions mentioned in this chapter. For instance, she mentions the importance of buying from a legitimate, established business in the first place. In complaint negotiation, the consumer should make reasonable requests, manage emotions, and present adequate documentation. Dissatisfied consumers must be willing to spend time and be patient in negotiations with organizations. Well-run businesses regard complaints as an opportunity to build a customer relationship.

Introduction to the Practitioner

Barbara's career began with the private practice of law for a few years, but she soon moved on to the Department of Consumer Affairs, an agency of the City of New York. She terms this period "a wonderful experience." For the next 17 years, she was President of the Better Business Bureau of Metropolitan New York, a private nonprofit where she dealt daily with consumer issues. She is currently the Executive Director of the Association of the Bar of the City of New York.

The first skill that Barbara thinks consumers should have is lack of ego. She advises, "These disputes are not about you personally, or about the other party personally—it's about the dispute. The more the consumer's ego is involved, the harder it is to solve the problem." Another similar skill is to be dispassionate.

Third, Barbara emphasizes the importance of being organized, saying, "Put together the information that you need to make your case. Then you have to be adaptive. You must be open to alternative solutions. For instance, I recently attempted to return an item to a store whose policy, 'No refunds,' was prominently posted. Legally, in this state, they do not have to return any money. However, I was upset with my choice and tried to return the item the next day. They refused. I didn't get angry—I asked why. They explained that the reason for the policy was because it cost so much in terms of credit card costs. I offered to pay the credit card costs and receive the balance. The credit card costs are only a few percentage points, and I much preferred to lose those few dollars than hundreds of dollars. They said, 'Of course, that's fine.' I couldn't get a return in the usual sense, but for a modest amount of money, they were only too happy to keep me a satisfied customer." Bill Ury (coauthor of *Getting to Yes*) would see this process as getting behind the store's position to discover their interest and creating options for a "yesable" proposition.

Barbara notes that she never uses her job or title as leverage in negotiations. She believes that any of us could use the same skills to advantage. She asserts, "Most retailers and manufacturers who are in business any period of time know that the complaining consumer represents an opportunity for repeat business. Secondly, they want goodwill. Obviously, people are not going to take enormous losses on your behalf but, if it's a reasonable request, most people in business want to agree. They want to be liked and respected. This is why the great majority of consumer complaints are resolved. The cases you hear about from the media are the exceptions, the bad situations in which consumer disputes are not resolved." It's important to remember that most businesses do want satisfied customers and will make reasonable accommodations to build customer loyalty.

Insights About Negotiation

Preparation begins with choosing a retailer or manufacturer that is reputable. Barbara suggests, "Do your research before you buy. You can check out organizations through your local Better Business Bureau or by accessing their national web site at www.bbb.org. If applicable, there may be a licensing organization that assures minimal standards of practice. Or, your purchase might be within an industry that is regulated by a government agency." These are some official channels of quality control. It's also appropriate to ask for references from individuals you know who have used the product or service.

Next, assuming that you have researched the retailer or manufacturer, let's say you then find it necessary to return or repair an item. Successful preparation depends on getting all the facts clearly organized. Barbara elaborates, "To the degree that you can gather documentation such as receipts or repair orders, do so. You might take photographs of a faulty product. Putting the materials together in an organized way is very helpful. I recently handled a claim for a friend. The problem was that the store had charged her again for the item she'd bought and then returned. I went to the store with her American Express receipts. The salesperson totally denied the claim. However, when I produced each of the receipts, it was very hard to refute her claim." By sticking to the facts, having them well documented and ordered, Barbara was successful in resolving her friend's dispute.

Barbara discusses problems with car purchases as an example of a typical consumer negotiation. A common scenario is, "You buy a new car. It breaks down. You have it fixed. It breaks down again. The dealer fixes it again, only to have it break down a third time. You're feeling frustrated and have little confidence in the dealer at that point. The dealer may not have any obligation to you other than repair but, unfortunately, you at that point are getting rather tense. You've spent an enormous amount of money for this major purchase; maybe they'll fix it, maybe they won't. You must keep very careful records—who you spoke to, what they told you, what happened next, etc. Laws differ around the country, but the third breakdown might well trigger a 'lemon law.' You say, 'This is unacceptable, I want a new car.' Things have improved in this area, but problems still happen." Readers who have bought "lemons" understand how upset most consumers are when their cars repeatedly break down.

Barbara states that at this point, consumers must pose several questions to themselves:

- *Should you give the dealer another opportunity to repair the car or insist on a new one?* "At some point," Barbara says, "the consumer decides, 'This is not acceptable.' You take it back to the dealer, or possibly the manufacturer."
- *To whom do you talk in each of these situations?* According to Barbara, "Initially, you should always talk to the person you've been dealing with. There's no reason to go to third parties initially because, in fact, you always have that to lean on if you can't resolve it yourself. If you're still not satisfied, work your way up the chain of command in a calm manner. Some people write a letter to the chairman of the board and carbon every officer. Never send 5 or 10 copies around;

being on the receiving end, I can assure you that with multiple copies, no one feels they're responsible. Find out who is best equipped to handle your particular problem and direct your letter there. This will vary across jurisdictions. For instance, if there's a licensing law for car dealers in your area, I would go to that specific agency, such as a motor vehicle department. The Internet is a good source of information on this topic."

■ *When do I go up the line?* "If you are not satisfied after repeated efforts to resolve the problem, be aware that many car companies have strong executive-level complaint handlers," Barbara relates. "If you get to this level, you will find a more sophisticated operation than the typical customer service. When you go to a regulatory agency, you will have a much better case if it's clear that you've tried to resolve it and that you gave them an opportunity to respond. The agency will then take your complaint more seriously."

Complaints are not necessarily a problem from a business perspective. Barbara notes, "If a consumer comes to your business with a complaint, and you resolve that complaint in a good fashion, they will be a much more loyal customer than if they had never raised the complaint. Sometimes a business will put in a complaint system and be anxious about the larger number of complaints they receive. It's not true that those who didn't complain before were happy; they were angry, and you were just losing them." Feedback is critical to retaining customers and building continuing relationships.

There are several elements of successful consumer negotiations. Barbara reminds us, "There have always been, and there will always be, problems with some purchases. The only choice is how you handle them. For instance, my former partner at the law firm called to ask if I could help with a faulty washing machine. Instead of turning this over to the complaint department, I made the phone call. I was still dealing with that complaint a week later. The reality is that it takes work and perseverance."

Consumers can enhance their chances of success by appreciating that returns and repairs involve active negotiations. Seldom does a store or manufacturer accept a return without at least asking some questions. Barbara specifies, "Be prepared for some back and forth, some give-and-take. Sometimes, when people don't get instant gratification, they become a little edgy, a bit more aggressive. In most cases, the biggest error people make is thinking that they should come on aggressively. I *firmly* believe that the best thing you can do is to be calm and respectful. If someone is abusive to you, that's different. But, in the vast majority of cases, if you assume they want to do the right thing and you set it forth in a balanced manner, you will do much better." Consumer negotiations seldom involve instant gratification. They do require work and perseverance; in the case of car repairs and returns, negotiations could last as long as a year.

Barbara recommends beginning the negotiation at a reasonable price. She explains, "Some people try to overreach and ask for more than their complaint is worth. This strategy assumes they'll be negotiating down from this original inflated position. I don't think that is particularly effective. I think that being direct and candid about what is fair gives you a credibility and a strong foundation for getting a fair response from them." Again, the advice about where to begin negotiating is consistent with the general guideline of being respectful and assuming the other party wants to do the right thing.

Barbara understands the challenges that consumers face. The first one she names is frustration with not being taken seriously. An organization may be so bureaucratic that its representatives are not responsive to complaints; some other department or unit is always at fault. Another challenge is when people don't say they're sorry. In her view, "People understand that things may go wrong. What upsets them is when no one says they're sorry. An apology goes a long way, and it's also the right thing to do." Both lack of attention and not getting an apology are frustrating to consumers.

Contextual Differences

Barbara notes that it is not only the consumer who may be challenged. In her experience, "There are people who make careers out of disputes. They are so personally angry at how they have been treated that it's very hard to resolve the dispute. They have ceased to be realistic. They want someone to be hung by their fingernails because they treated them so badly. The reality is that this isn't going to happen." Businesses may be very challenged by consumers who are too angry to be realistic in their demands.

When negotiations break down, consumers may go to regulatory agencies or to court. Barbara continues, "This is painful for me to admit, but in most of these instances, a lawyer doesn't want your case. There's usually not enough money involved to justify attorney fees. Some years ago in New York, there was much attention paid to enhancing car buyer's rights. The attorney general's office worked very hard to staff a panel to take these cases. However, there is another option. For instance, problems with appliances often end up in the small claims courts, which work well if you're dealing with a reputable company. However, one of the biggest problems with small claims court is that you get a judgment, but you can't collect because the company can't be located. Consumers seldom have to wait longer than a few weeks to be heard in small-claims court."

Another response to the breakdown of negotiations is appeal to government regulators. Barbara urges, "When you complain to a government agency, you are accomplishing something more than just helping yourself. To the degree that complaints from you and others start to show a pattern, there is some underlying problem. It could be fraud; it could be bad business practices. Whatever it is, when a pattern starts to show up, someone can take action. Reports are compiled and available to warn future consumers of potential problems." Consumers can look at reporting as both satisfying their own needs and as the opportunity to make a difference.

Over the years, there were a number of complaints about moving and storage companies in the New York area. These companies didn't want people to complain because they didn't want a bad report from the Better Business Bureau. Barbara recalls, "One of my staff was offered a bribe to change a report from bad to good. I reported this to the DA's office, which followed up, and there was a conviction. So, on top of the unsatisfactory record on the company, there was a note about the bribery conviction. That was one of the better moments!" Never minimize the importance of speaking up.

Negotiation in consumer complaints differs according to whether it is business to business or private consumer to business. Barbara explains, "When my organization makes a purchase from another organization, negotiations regarding repairs or returns are rather impersonal. When individuals are involved, there is often more impact for the consumer. When something goes wrong, it really hurts their life. If my PC goes down in the office, I'm not happy, but I borrow one from another office. If my car breaks down and I can't get to work, I lose a day's pay. If my refrigerator goes out, I lose the dollar value of a great deal of food. It's a constant irritant, and it has a direct impact." These elements contribute to the passion an individual brings to the consumer negotiation context.

Changes and Conflicts

What has changed in consumer negotiations? Barbara believes that "over the last decade, business has become more sophisticated in managing consumer complaints. They recognize that it's better to recognize problems than to play hardball." The consumer negotiator is more likely to be heard and responded to within the complaint context.

Barbara notes that there are many more laws on the books protecting consumers than there were 10 years ago. However, she cautions, "The problem is, laws are not an answer—they are a step toward an answer. If you don't have aggressive enforcement, laws can be ignored. This varies according to jurisdiction, but we don't always have the resources we need committed to enforcement of consumer protection. People take comfort in the fact that there is a licensing agency, when all that may mean is a business has paid $100. There may be no oversight function by the agency. Even in the professions, which are more highly regulated than the sale of cars, there is seldom aggressive enforcement." Consumers should not become complacent because of the addition of new laws.

One topic about which advice givers might disagree is the use of informal methods to resolve disputes. Barbara says, "A lot of people think very highly of methods such as arbitration; others do not. The answer is in the details—for instance, is the program one that really has an impartial arbitrator? I lean toward informal dispute resolution generally, not just for consumer disputes. I think that we litigate far too much. I'm a special master in the Appellate Division in New York, and I am stunned about what people are fighting about. I favor alternative dispute resolution, but not everyone agrees with me." Practitioners who advise consumers differ in their opinions about how best to handle failed negotiations.

Barbara Berger Opotowsky offers advice to all of us who must return or request repair of purchases. Start by buying from legitimate, established businesses. Document and order all transactions to present a clear and convincing case. Contact the person who made the sale originally. Make a request that is reasonable and fair under the circumstances. Expect some give and take. Don't expect instant gratification. Do expect that a calm, reasonable, respectful approach is most likely to ensure success. In today's sophisticated business climate, problems are likely to be seen as an opportunity to build consumer loyalty.

PROFESSIONAL PROFILE

● **CHRISTINE BEARD,**
TRAVEL AGENCY OWNER

Using Negotiation to Get Off the Ground

Few business or leisure travelers have been able to avoid the experience of being grounded. We have personal histories that connect with the phrases "mechanical problems," "weather problems," "overbookings," and "flight cancellations." Travelers who thought they were going to Chicago may be rerouted to Milwaukee. Airline delays result in missing the boat—literally— when the travelers' flights don't put them in Miami in time for the cruise ship's sailing. A change in the business schedule or the death of Aunt Matilda may mean we are stuck with a nonrefundable ticket. Are we at the mercy of a deregulated system, or could we use our negotiating skills to be more effective managers when travel plans implode? Christine Beard offers advice to assist travelers and their agents in becoming more successful negotiators in the not-so-friendly skies.

Like Opotowsky, Christine recommends that travelers do business with an established agency, because that agency will have the leverage with airline sales representatives to get the traveler on the next flight. She also advises the consumer to come to negotiations with adequate documentation. However, these two experts offer contrasting opinions about emotional management. When it comes to face-to-face negotiations in airports, it's often the obnoxious complainer who gets his way.

Introduction to the Practitioner

Christine has worked in the travel industry for 25 years. The first 10 of those years she was employed as a flight attendant for Continental Airlines. Subsequently, she lived overseas for several years. Upon returning to the states, she started working for different travel agencies in Houston, Texas. Soon, she decided to open her own agency, called Absolute Travel and Tours, which has been in operation for 15 years. Her agency is part of a consortium of other travel agencies that use their combined volume to leverage the best prices in the travel industry. Approximately 70% of her agency's business consists of corporate accounts; the rest of her business comes from individual clients. Christine is very active in community affairs.

Christine remembers travel before deregulation: "Everything seemed normal up to 1976. There were two classes, first and coach, and every ticket was refundable. Continental Airlines added an economy class that offered travelers a lower price than the coach fare. At the same time, the economy fare allowed the traveler to purchase a snack for a nominal fee. Airline service changed radically when deregulation was instituted in 1976. Airlines became more competitive; business class was added." Today, travel agents are allowed to collect 5% of every domestic ticket, up to $50, and 5% of overseas tickets, up to $100. Some international carriers still allow 8% to 10%, with no capping of the commission. These rates of return are significantly lower than they were before deregulation. In Christine's opinion, "Basically, the airlines are trying to put us out of business. Still, travel agents account for 80% of all travel-related transactions."

Insights About Negotiation

Christine negotiates with clients, providers of travel services, and others in her agency's consortium. She describes her approach: "Make sure you have all the facts. I document everything. I have notebooks that I keep for years, because you never know when you might need the information in order to help a client—for instance, when an airline has not issued a refund to the client. While working on each record, I use a computer that has direct access with the airline's computers, thus narrowing the possibility of any errors or miscommunication."

Christine also believes negotiation works best when people can trust each other. Her rule of thumb is to "be as truthful as you can. Sometimes the truth will hurt but, eventually, people will come to believe in you. You must also make sure your client is being truthful. Not long ago, a client went to Mexico and was still there when I had a call from American Express inform-ing me that the client had declined the airline charge. In those cases, the travel agency is stuck with the charge. I located the client in Mexico and he admitted that he did purchase the tickets through me. As a result, American Express was able to confront the client and pursue him for the charges. I make sure that I have all the facts before pointing the finger at anyone."

Relationship building is another important negotiation strategy. Christine explains, "I try to go to as many travel shows as possible, not only to meet the tour operators, cruise representatives and airline personnel, but to continuously stay informed of all the ongoing changes in the industry, as well as learning new selling techniques. I ask them, 'What if I were traveling with a group and ran into trouble—how could you help me?' After I meet the reps at these shows, I write them a note the following day, letting them know that I'm looking forward to working with them. That way, when a client gets into trouble, I have a contact who may be able to help them."

In a typical negotiation, Christine intervenes with the airlines on behalf of her clients. She offers the following example: "One of my corporate accounts is headquartered in Houston and Germany, with a high volume of travel to and from the states, so there's lots of transatlantic travel. Recently, I had to call the airlines as my client was driving to an airport that he was not familiar with and missed his flight. You are allowed 4 to 6 hours to board another flight before the airlines will assess a penalty. The airlines were accommodating and waived the penalty. In another instance, I had a client who finished his business in Hong Kong 2 days early and wanted to return as quickly as possible. I was able to get him on the next flight, and the airline waived the penalty fee." Airlines differ tremendously in what penalties they assess and how amenable they are to waiving them. Travel agents who are effective negotiators begin with the knowledge of each carrier's requirements.

Christine recounts her most challenging situation. A large corporate account with a lucrative business located in several states decided without warning to change agencies. Christine had both personal and professional relationships with the officers. She remembers, "Then, there was a changing of the guard. A new employee was hired by this company and convinced the management to use the travel agency where the employee had a personal contact. The leverage used to convince this company was that the officers would have elite status with one of the major air carriers. Elite status would entitle them to a better chance at first-class upgrades. If I had been informed, I could have negotiated the same entitlements. However, nothing was said. When I inquired about the lack of business I received, there was no response. At this point, all communications with these corporate clients ceased. Finally, I realized that this had become a no-win situation for me. It would have been helpful if I had been informed of why I lost the account. I found out I'd lost the business through another employee of that company. That was the worst part." For Christine, the worst experience was when an account wouldn't communicate or negotiate about the job her agency was doing.

A negotiation breakdown usually results in the termination of business between an agency and other tourism services. When a cruise line or different tour operators are unable to meet commitments, Christine will not send them further business unless the client insists on using that particular company. If the breakdown occurs between the travel agency and an airline she must continue to work with, Christine may compensate a good client to retain their business. Before coming to that point, she says, "I go through as many channels as possible. For instance, many of the airlines have executive help desks or sales representatives who are willing to work with travel agents when problems arise. One must try to use as many avenues as possible with the different carriers to try and satisfy your clients."

Advice to the Consumer

First of all, Christine advises negotiating for lower fares or other benefits whenever possible. The worst thing that can happen is that the carrier will say no. Christine has advice for successful negotiation when one's flight is cancelled or significantly delayed. Her strategy involves maximizing the traveler's leverage when problems do arise. In her view, "Start with a travel agency that has been in business for a number of years. The tenure of the agency provides leverage with sales representatives in getting the consumer on the next available flight. Second, call your travel agent. If it's after hours, get in line for the next available flight, and use your cell phone to call the airline directly on one of their 800 numbers. The airline representatives will be able to help you more quickly than the time it takes for a plane load of people to get to the gate agent. If you still haven't received an answer from either the travel agent or the airline representative by the time you arrive at the head of the line, deal with the gate agent." While you are making these calls, keep your eye out for supervisors who are designated to problem-solve. For instance, Continental Airlines keeps supervisors on the floor in bright red coats so that travelers needing assistance can spot them more readily. Some airlines provide a Care Desk to deal with problems.

In addition to maximizing leverage, a traveler increases the chance of success by possessing documents that provide the information needed to change tickets between airlines. Christine explains why a paper ticket versus an electronic ticket provides superior information when a flight is cancelled, delayed, or if an airline goes on strike. Using paper tickets involves a uniform process utilized by most airlines, whereas each airline has its own system for electronic ticketing. After the airlines have an integrated system for electronic tickets, that type of ticket will become more compatible across carriers. In her words, "Airline systems are different, so that if you have an electronic ticket from one airline and need to book a flight on another, your price can't be confirmed on the computer of the second airline. You have no proof of your fare basis. Especially during the summer months when planes are full and when you are traveling out of the States, you can save yourself a half to a full day of backtracking and frustration if you have the paper ticket." The bottom line is that if you purchase your ticket over the Internet, a travel agent cannot help you. Travelers may achieve some savings by buying an Internet or wholesale ticket, but they should be aware of the risks they are taking if changes in the itinerary are required.

If you're thinking of a cruise, it's always a good idea to include your airfare with the purchase. Christine explains, "You might be tempted to use your frequent-flier points to get to the ship. However, should some delay arise and you miss the sailing, it is totally up to you how to connect with the ship's next port and how to pay for that additional expense. However, if you buy a package and the air is delayed, it's the responsibility of the cruise line to get you to the ship."

Christine also mentions purchasing travel insurance packages and cautions close reading. For instance, "Look at whether or not the package covers preexisting conditions. What does your protection plan consist of? I had a client who was called back into the military, but the insurance that he purchased did not cover the return flight that was required to comply. When the military shortened his leave, he was under the impression that his travel insurance covered such a contingency. It was very hard for him to cover this unexpected cost."

Interpersonal negotiations reflect a context in which emotional extremes may work to one's advantage. In Christine's experience, "It's the squeaky wheel that gets the grease. Instead of being proactive about a travel-related problem, customers who turn into obnoxious complainers usually get their way. Sometimes, tears help. People do really get upset and, when they start crying, the usual reaction of the staff is, 'We need to take care of this person immediately.'"

Christine continues, "Airline policies reflect the fact that some travelers are not honest in their dealing with airlines. One example is buying a ticket for a flight that is continuously full or oversold in order to become a 'volunteer' who will take a later flight in return for receiving vouchers for future flights. It used to be that the airlines would offer higher revenue vouchers to get volunteers, who would then keep upping the ante until the number of seats needed was met. As more and more passengers bought tickets they never intended to use, the airlines became aware of this pattern and gradually lowered the value of the vouchers."

Another example of passengers dealing dishonestly relates to bereavement tickets. These tickets offered discounted rates to family members who had to fly on short notice. Such tickets have been basically discontinued due to passenger scams. Passengers would check the obituaries in the destination city of their choice, note the name of the deceased and the funeral home, and order a bereavement ticket, claiming to be a member of the family. The airlines could check with the funeral home but had no way beyond that to verify who was using this fare legitimately. In 2002, the bereavement fare is approximately the same as the 7-day advance fare but is not necessarily the lowest fare available.

Contextual Differences

Compared with other negotiating contexts, the biggest difference in negotiating in the travel business is the nonrefundable aspect of tickets. Christine reminds us, "People complain all the time. You can choose to purchase merchandise at most retailers and can take it back and receive a refund or store credit without penalties. There are some companies to whom you can return a purchase a year later and still receive a refund. Just about any commodity we buy, including credit card purchases, is refundable. The airlines started this nonrefundable policy some years ago because they were losing money on the no-shows." As long as the airlines continue the policy of nonrefundable tickets, negotiating in this context will involve more constraints than the usual commercial negotiation.

Changes and Conflicts

Christine finds that although the travel business has changed enormously, negotiating with clients and travel providers remains essentially the same. She concludes, "You make your contacts over the years and the more benefits you can provide, the more solid your business will be. Getting those benefits for clients requires thoughtful negotiations with the airlines and other carriers."

In another trend, travel agencies seek the advantage of size in negotiation. There is the growth of travel consortiums like the one Christine's company is a member of. Some of the smaller agencies join together to gain greater leverage in dealing with the airlines, tour operators, and different vendors in the travel business. Then there is the consolidation of travel agencies into fewer large ones, gaining some of the same advantages in negotiation. And a vast number of large corporations have their own agencies in-house.

Consolidations aid travel agencies. They in turn can assist the consumer through the influence they have as a source of continuing business. Coping with travel problems can be less difficult when we rely on an organization with pertinent information and a preestablished relationship with the airlines and travel vendors. Christine advises that there are also steps we can take for ourselves, such as using a reputable travel agent, buying paper tickets as long as electronic systems are not compatible among airlines, and pulling out the crying towel when all else fails. Her experience and insight on the travel agency industry provide an edge for negotiators who operate in rather unfriendly skies.

PROFESSIONAL PROFILE

● **RUSSEL TURBEVILLE, JD,**
DISTRICT ATTORNEY FOR CONSUMER FRAUD

Negotiator Beware:
English Common Law is No Match for Con Artists

Russel Turbeville has been dealing with consumer fraud in the Houston, Texas, area for 20 years. His observations about typical scams will assist negotiators in becoming more discerning about protecting ourselves from fraud and in being more aware of when to withdraw from questionable negotiations. This chapter lists what Russel calls his "Ten Commandments for Consumers" at the end of the "Consumer Problems" section.

Because Russel describes consumer negotiations secondhand in this interview, the usual list of interviewee questions does not apply. However, the same flow of topics will be followed: first interviewee background, then typical negotiations, and finally predictions about the future.

Introduction to the Practitioner

Russel grew up in Houston and went to law school there as well. He claims that "most of the people I grew up with became either police officers or criminals." He began his career in the criminal division of the Harris County, Texas, District Attorney's office, coping with street crimes—drug dealing, robberies, murder, sexual assaults and the like. Russel left state government to practice law as a defense attorney in private practice but discovered that he really didn't like it. The District Attorney's office welcomed him back but, at the time, their only vacancy was in the economic crime division, where he expected to serve for 1 year before moving back to street crime. Twenty years later, Russel describes his long tenure in this office as "atonement for having quit my job in the first place. I guess it was like Brer Rabbit being thrown in the brier patch. I seemed to like the work, and I seemed to do well at it. Like I'd been born and raised in the brier patch." Russel's career path appears to have veered onto an assignment that Russel initially found unwelcome, but one in which he has ultimately found success and satisfaction.

Russel's attraction to studying economic crime derives from several sources. He explains, "We receive complaints from citizens directly. With our resources as a police agency, we're able to file our own cases in court. We have more product control in that, compared to other units, we do our own investigations and don't inherit problems associated with faulty investigations compiled by some separate unit." Another reason Russel chooses to remain in law enforcement of economic crimes is that consumer fraud cases "make you think. You have to analyze situations and put them together. These investigations are extensive and quite detailed. With white-collar crime, you're dealing with lots of paperwork and many witnesses. A murder file might be an inch thick. Typical consumer crime files take up boxes and boxes of records you've gathered. It's challenging work."

The broad impact of consumer fraud also attracts Russel. In his words, "Whenever we're brought in, it's like an airliner has crashed. Some business situation has crashed—it's failed. Someone hasn't performed their promises. Citizens are not always able to articulate the harms. All they know is that they have paid money to someone who hasn't delivered the desired goods or services, and they've been hurt. Under our law, in order to convict, we have to prove that the contractual default was intentional. We have to come in and show that the business didn't fail—it was murdered. And, we have to convince 12 people of this beyond a reasonable doubt." Building persuasive cases demonstrating intent to defraud the public is appealing work for Russel.

There is an inordinate amount of publicity attending consumer fraud and its prosecution, but this is not one of the reasons Russel enjoys his work. The four major television networks and several local stations each have a reporter specifically assigned to follow this topic. Russel notes, "It's a very competitive market for stories, so there is lots of publicity around our cases. We don't seek it. They call us. The stories have some pizzazz. People joke about how often I'm on TV. I never even watch."

Insights About Negotiation

Typical categories of fraud involve automobiles, home remodeling, and investments. According to Russel, "The most common complaint from people who buy vehicles is that they can't get title. The reason that they can't get title is that the entity that sold it to them doesn't own it. Most used car lots don't own their inventory. Many of them get into trouble because they misspend the money, don't pay whoever is holding the title and, therefore, can't get it."

Russel explains, "People who are poor credit risks pay exorbitant down payments to buy used cars at 'Tote the Notes Lots.' In these negotiations, the buyer has little leverage and usually no power in negotiating price or the terms of the contract. The used car lot finances itself or finds outside financing, and the buyer pays them biweekly or monthly." Russel notes, "Most of those lots don't own their inventory and, even though law requires that a nonnegotiable title be given that shows the lien, most of those lots don't give a title." These customers have a poor BATNA, because they typically need a car to get to work.

Russel explains the win-lose ending of these negotiations: "Only on the rare occasion that someone completely pays for a car and has complied with all the egregious terms of the contract does the lot go find who does hold the title and pay them off. These lots operate on the theory that buyers are going to default and will never pay the car off." After default, the lot repossesses the vehicle, places it back on the lot, and secures a new down payment from the next poor credit risk. The used car becomes a readily renewable inventory resource, and the consumer loses all the money previously paid.

One of the most serious types of complaints Russel's office receives involves allegations of construction fraud. Commonly, a contractor obtains a construction contract (generally with the low bid), receives the initial and some progress payments, and begins the job using subcontractors and material men. Later, the contractor defaults on payments to the subcontractors and, after having gotten as much money as possible from the property owner, "walks" the job. Russel recounts, "The more sophisticated scam artist will continue to profess good intention, spin a litany of sad stories and excuses, hoping that the owner will become so exasperated and discouraged that she or he will order the contractor off the job. Then, the contractor can argue that the property owner was the one who breached the contract." In construction negotiations, the homeowner has more leverage than the poor credit risk vehicle buyer but makes an error that leaves him legally liable.

In a recent case, Russel is convinced that the contractor started making sexual advances toward the owner's wife after the job was in trouble in an effort to make the owner lose his temper and order the contractor off the property. Russel asserts, "A good crook will frustrate you so badly that you will have a knee-jerk reaction and do something that will breach the contract. Then, they can come into court and blame you." Russel recalls Gene Wilder's first movie, *The Producers* (Brooks, 1968), wherein viewers learn that a good crook can make more money out of a failure than an honest person can make out of a success.

Investment fraud may manifest itself in various guises. The vehicle can be oil wells, inventions, stocks and bonds, gold mines, or cattle. The "opportunity" can be advertised, offered at auction, made by telephone, or available on the Internet. The number of victims may range from a handful to thousands. However, Russel surmises that "what all the fraudulent investment opportunities have in common is that they are Ponzi schemes."

In a Ponzi scheme, the purported investment is fictitious either in whole or in part. Russel explains the typical scenario: "The promoter convinces investors that the promoter can earn substantial profits. Monies are taken in from earlier investors, and early investors sometimes receive their investment back, plus 'profits.' This builds confidence and, inevitably, the early investor reinvests the money and tells all their friends to invest also. What is happening is a pyramiding of debt and, inevitably, the amount of investment principal that might have actually been spent on some investment vehicle subsides inversely in comparison with the total amount of money owed to the growing investor base. Ultimately, the promoter depletes his potential investor base, cannot obtain enough new money to pay interest, and the fraud collapses. Investors believe there is an investment vehicle that's churning profits and don't realize they're just participants in a pyramid scheme that will soon collapse." In investment negotiations, the typical consumer failure results from not asking enough questions or exercising healthy skepticism of seller claims. As the adage goes, "If it sounds too good to be true, it probably is." (This is also the basis of Russel's first commandment earlier in this chapter.)

Scams involving automobiles, home remodeling, and investments are just a few instances of negotiations in which con men represent themselves as legitimate. However, the reader can see how each of these illegitimate practices captures buyers from different layers of the economic spectrum. Russel emphasizes the variety of victims who thought they were negotiating in good faith. He says, "It all depends on the opportunity. There are people stealing from every strata of society by posing as businesspersons. There's fraud in every marketplace. There are equal-opportunity crooks; everyone's money is green."

Russel does highlight the vulnerability of doctors to con artists. In his estimation, "They're making so much money, they're working so many hours, they don't have any time to manage their investments. They're always putting their money with some investment advisor or some broker who's just churning it. For example, we had a complaint from a successful doctor who'd been investing for 18 years. As I asked the history of his investments, he told me about investments in apartments, in oil wells, in raw land; over the years, this guy had lost no less than $75,000 per year. Finally, I come to the complaint he'd brought to us, and I said, 'Doctor, what kind of investment was this?' And he said, 'It was another 4 D investment.' 'What's that?' I asked. 'Another damn dumb doctor deal.' Was the response." All of us are vulnerable, including our doctors.

In contrast to the demographic variety of victims, the profiles of fraudulent negotiators are quite similar. Russel reports, "Inveterate con men have the same mentality, the same kind of personality. They are outgoing because they have to solicit people. They're good promoters. But what's unique about them is that they are sociopaths. They have a perverted view of themselves and society. They regard themselves as superior beings. If they are smart enough to swindle you out of your hard-earned money, they must be more worthy than you. They are predators and you are prey. They have no compunction about hurting you; indeed, they get a vicarious thrill out of it because it reinforces their feeling of superiority, of being at the top of the food chain. They all think that way. They care nothing about what they're destroying. They would kill the goose who lays the golden egg if they wanted feathers today." In Russel's view, there can never be a reasonable deal struck with such persons.

Russel notes that con men habitually return to the predator pattern. In his experience, "It's just like the pedophile. It's what they know. It's what they've done well. It's your classic cheater. They can look you straight in the face and lie to you. Think about the 18-year-old kid who comes up to you on the street and says, 'Give me your money or I'll blow your head off.' There's a basic honesty in that transaction. He's not asking you to trust him. He's not pretending to help you. He just told you what the deal is and you can take it or leave it. Whereas, the con man comes up to you and says, 'I like you. Let me help you.' And he intentionally fosters a relationship of trust so he can screw you to the wall like a molly bolt. That's his psyche." Although honest negotiation thrives on trust and relationship building, con men use those elements to snare the buyer.

After these crooked transactions take place, people may choose to report them to the Office of the District Attorney. The Houston consumer fraud office has been visible for many years and averages 1,200 complaints annually. Russel scans complaints every morning, looking to see whether they are worth pursuing. Approximately 25% of complaints are closed immediately by responding to the complainant in a letter that explains why his office cannot help with a particular case. Russel then assigns the remaining complaints to other attorneys in his office who oversee the development of the subsequent investigations.

Throughout, Russel is aware of instances where there are multiple complaints about the same "business." In his opinion, that is the strongest indicator of fraud. He explains, "There are seldom any problems with established businesses in the community, so when we see several complaints about a group that's just sprung up, we try to focus on them very quickly. A crook who sets up as a business doesn't steal from just one or two people. He tries to advertise and steal from as many people as possible. Usually, our office will hear about such activity in fairly short order. We identify a large part of the fraud in our community."

The District Attorney's Office sometimes works with other agencies, such as the Better Business Bureau or other data sources. As soon as possible, an attempt is made to establish whether this is a one-shot contractual default or a problem of fraud. In Russel's experience, "A civil contractual default and a criminal contractual default look exactly the same to the persons being defaulted. They paid money, and they didn't receive the goods or services promised. We cast investigative nets to try to gather as much information as we can, in the shortest possible time, to determine whether or not fraud was involved. We run a lot of search warrants on business records, sometimes in a matter of days. After 20 years in this work, I can tell very quickly from looking at the company books whether this is a legitimate operation." What appeared trustworthy to a gullible consumer is a painfully obvious fraud to an experienced district attorney.

Russel's office typically prosecutes about 10% of cases reported—about 120 per year. Of these, approximately 10 cases per year result in trials, with the rest leading to negotiation. Over 20 years, his office has received only two "not guilty" verdicts of cases brought to trial. There could be between 5 and 300 plaintiffs in a case.

In terms of the plea-bargain negotiations, there are several considerations. How much harm has been done, how many people were victimized, how much money has been lost, and what is the ability of the defendant to rectify that? Russel reports, "Typically, the plaintiffs are more interested in getting their money back than in what happens to the criminal. That's not controlling on us, but it's certainly influential. Also, prior criminal history or lack thereof of each defendant is considered. There is a wide range of punishments. Approximately 33% to 40% of the criminals are incarcerated." What began as a negotiation with criminal intent by one party ends in a negotiation about the penalty for that same party.

Changes and Conflicts

The future for con men looks bright. Consumers might ask why those who do not negotiate in good faith are allowed to continue to operate. According to Russel, the answer has a great deal to do with laws that are written to reflect a laissez-faire attitude toward business regulation. In many states, the legislature responds to those who lobby and contribute to political campaigns. Business participates in this way; consumers do not. Therefore, it should be no surprise that legislation usually supports business interests and practices. Often, this means a minimum of consumer protection legislation.

Russel states, "I'm not a bleeding liberal. I believe in regulating and licensing as little as possible. We should not interfere with good business. But we need intelligent laws that would be tools for law enforcement. The laws would exempt good business practices but create a hostile environment for bad business practices. That's what I would like to see happen. One of these days, it probably will." Until then, a laissez-faire approach to protecting consumers will characterize the laws of many states.

When laws do exist and are broken, there still may be loopholes for fraudulent groups. For instance, in the case of investments, states have laws based on U.S. Securities and Exchange Commission guidelines, and agencies must assess securities according to these guidelines before the securities may be offered to the public. However, according to Russel, groups can make offers to "35 or fewer sophisticated investors, provided all material facts are disclosed." This is the typical claim made by fraudulent investment groups that maintain they are exempted from surveillance by state agencies. Russel summarizes, "They lie. Crooks disguise public offerings as private placements."

In addition to a laissez-faire legal posture and loopholes in existing law, consumers negotiating at a distance make it difficult for law enforcement to prosecute crooks. Russel is clear when he states: "When you respond to a media solicitation, or a cold call, or send your money off into cyberspace to buy something off the Internet, you make it impossible for law enforcement to effectively investigate and prosecute the crime. You've never met and can't identify the person who stole your money. Give law enforcement a chance."

There are technical advances that assist scamming. Russel reminds jurors, "The pen is mightier than the sword—by which I mean that ideas are more powerful than force in persuading consumers to submit to scams. Telemarketing is a great medium for crooks because they don't have to deal with anyone face-to-face. They don't give their real names, you won't be able to recognize them, so they can't be identified. And the really smart crook won't steal from anyone in the state where he's operating. He'll get a 1-800 number, and there's no DA's office in the country that can afford to bring in people from all over the country to prosecute him. He'll run a boiler room for several months and then pick up and move. What we've seen in recent years is that most of the smartest telemarketers have moved to Canada. They're soliciting United States citizens from Canada and getting away with it nicely for several reasons. First, Canada is essentially provincial, and there's no effective national law enforcement. Second, since the victims are not Canadians, why would local law enforcement spend its funds to protect U.S. citizens? The crooked telemarketers have found a successful way to be a Hole in the Wall Gang."

During the last decade, the federal government began to get involved in prosecuting economic crime that crosses state lines. Russel recalls, "We worked a lot of cases together in the last 8 or 9 years that were really federal cases, but our office could assist with search warrants and identification. They did a very good job of cleaning up the boiler rooms in Houston, which used to be a mecca for them. However, since 1999, we're seeing a meaningful amount of fraud over the Internet, with all the private auctions. With the technology now, you can have a server in Madagascar, and the ability of local law enforcement to cast that investigative net is minimal. A good crook will be in one place and have a server in another. There are many private carriers and phone companies that make investigation more complicated."

The power of the mouse will produce more and more fraud in the marketplace. Russel points out, "Internet markets are still developing, evolving, and changing so fast that it's difficult to set up any kind of regulations or standards. However, there are some Web sites where consumers can alert each other to faulty products and services. The Better Business Bureau has a Web site. EBay has a staff of fraud investigators. They care about their market, and it's bad for business to have fraud on eBay. They research their databases and identify crooks. However, every time crooks were found, they moved on under a different name. They're like viruses mutating. As soon as you get some kind of vaccine, the virus mutates and turns up in a different form somewhere else. Any crook worth his salt can get back on in minutes." The mouse that empowers us to enter auction negotiations worldwide also leaves us even more vulnerable to fraud in those transactions.

That vulnerability is fundamentally based in English common law. As Russel sees it, "Our criminal law centers around witnesses coming to the courtroom to identify the person who committed a crime. Unfortunately, our lives have changed. We don't live our lives face-to-face. The law no longer applies to the situation where one man steals another person's horse. Now, we have crooks stealing incremental amounts from an infinite number of people who never see them. Our rules of evidence are not designed to deal with the proof of that crime."

Russel continues, "We have stepped into a virtual world. When crooks put out a fraudulent solicitation and take money from people around the world, how can local law enforcement respond? The laws need to change to respond to this virtual world. We need to be allowed to offer evidence the same way the crooks stole it—through cyberspace." He also points out that it will be imperative that we have local, federal, and international law enforcement units working in concert. In reality, we are a long way from that ideal situation. The virtual world requires consumers to be even more discerning in transactions than ever before.

Russel Turbeville has been combatting economic crime in Houston for 20 years and explains how all consumers can easily be marks. A condition of trust, so essential to most negotiations, is used by predatory con men to effect a total win-lose scenario. State legislatures tend to favor business interests and pass the minimum of consumer protection. English common law was designed to prosecute entirely different kinds of crimes and is virtually helpless against telemarketing and Internet auctions. Caveat emptor!

CHAPTER 9

ORGANIZATIONAL NEGOTIATION

The requirements for getting work done reside less in the exercise of authority and more in the ability to communicate and negotiate with a wide variety of members of an organization.

— Donnellon and Kolb (1997, p. 162)

Conflict and problem solving exist in the very fabric of organizational structure and processes. Negotiated understandings become important in organizational climates with changing structures, values, and roles. Competing priorities and competition for limited resources create a context where the quality of negotiation serves as a good predictor for organizational effectiveness. Putnam (1997) points out that negotiation in organizations functions as "a catalyst for identifying and defining problems and reaching understanding by enabling members to negotiate the meaning of organizational events" (p. 153). An example of this function occurred in a large sales organization. The manager wanted to improve relations with large clients, so he told his staff that he would have an open house. He wanted staff to lead the clients in games, use lots of balloons, and create some skits to demonstrate products and services. The staff resisted to the point of refusing to cooperate. During a staff discussion, the staff aired their complaints about producing a program "better suited for adolescents." Together, the manager and staff negotiated the purpose for the client visit, goals for the program, and activities that would be regarded as more professional. Negotiation served as a tool for achieving understanding about how to best relate to clients.

Many conflicts in organizations have a source in identity needs of the organization's members. For example, an unhappy worker negotiating a job description may say, "I would like to be proud of what I do." A volunteer on an advisory board may threaten to quit, stating, "I don't feel recognized or appreciated for the work that I've done." Gossip that damages reputations, lack of clear roles, and us-versus-them attitudes create a need for people to negotiate shared understandings about how people should work together.

A complicating factor in many organizational disputes is when substantive issues and interpersonal issues occur together. For example, a bank employee became involved in a dispute with one of his bank's managers. The employee, tasked with the responsibility for establishing a database, said, "This manager needs to stay out of my work; let me do it my way." The manager responded, "I've worked in this bank a long time, and I know how things should be done." Both agreed on the role of the database but disagreed about how the job should be done. In this case, the two employees needed to develop understanding and relationship if they were going to be open to negotiating a way of doing things.

In many ways, organizations resemble families. For example, both contexts possess histories that cast shadows over current discussions. In both settings, the personalities of members influence group dynamics. As membership of the groups changes, so do the dynamics. Members in both contexts engage in rituals having to do with accomplishments or comings and goings. Both organizations and families possess behavioral norms to which members are expected to conform. And, finally, both contexts develop shared codes for communication, complete with jargon that only in-group members will understand, with which they talk about issues and solve problems. Some of the factors identified in interpersonal and family negotiations apply to organizational settings as well.

Negotiation in organizations also possesses distinct differences from negotiation in other settings. For example, values such as efficiency, quality, and profit influence goals. Differences in power and authority create territory and ego boundaries that influence the sharing of information and decision making. Even though a goal may be clear, conflicting priorities tend to make negotiation appear more distributive than integrative on many issues. In the interview with Linda Putnam in Chapter 5, she pointed out the difference between negotiation and other organizational processes: "Negotiation is not simply joint problem solving. A lot of issues are better handled by putting a group together to decide how to address a problem. In joint problem solving, people seldom come to the table with predisposed positions." Box 9.1 illustrates attempts by

Box 9.1

NEGOTIATION ENTERS DEEP FREEZE

In 1997, a major Texas manufacturing firm bought a Midwest company with a long history of producing high-quality refrigerators. Early in 1998, the Environmental Protection Agency (EPA) issued new guidelines for product energy consumption and the use of freon. The guidelines required compliance by all U.S. companies by July 1, 2001.

In the past, the refrigerator firm's engineering department originated product improvements, and those changes were based on function and efficiency. But because the new owners set as priorities higher profits and a greater share of the market, they asked marketing to make recommended changes in accordance with the new EPA guidelines and based on refrigerator cabinet designs that sell best in the marketplace. The new owners asked all other units to support the new design.

Marketing completed its set of recommendations in July 2000. It took another 3 months for the design shop to create new electrical and mechanical specifications required for the new cabinet models. Engineering received the new specifications in October 2000. After several months of work, the engineers determined that at least 24 different parts would not fit in the new models recommended by marketing. Engineering asked marketing to reconsider its recommendations.

At this point, operations reminded engineering, "If we don't complete our prototype by March 1, we'll not make our July 1 production goal, and we will have to send our 1,800 factory workers home." The company's vice president of finance told all departments, "Keep change costs down. Costs are hurting the profit margins." Marketing told engineering, "The model designs we gave you are the ones that will sell. We'll not change them." The new owner said, "We've invested over $100 million in this new product line. We don't intend to lose our investment." The design shop told engineering, "The 24 changes you gave us will cost hundreds of thousands of dollars more and many hours of overtime for our staff to design what you requested." Engineering said, "We need the changes *now*. Even if we have the changes, our staff will have to work a great deal of overtime to meet the deadline."

The web was complex, involving every department of the company. As you might expect, the personalities of the different department managers influenced negotiations a great deal. What are the most important factors fueling this conflict? What would you do?

management of a Midwest appliance company to integrate company goals with each department's need to complete its responsibilities.

Structure

Structure in organizations defines not only the formal roles and relationships established by organizational charts, but also the decision-making procedures and designation of agents who negotiate within and on behalf of the organization. Structure sustains a culture in which members link their identities to the roles and values established by the organization. Structure regulates social interaction by supporting norms that determine *who* is authorized to talk to whom and *about what*. For example, supervisors remind workers to honor the chain of command and not to try to negotiate solutions to some problems on their own.

Shared understanding of symbols supports staff identities and authority for conducting negotiation. Suits, ties, titles, corner offices, nameplates, and meeting rooms with oak tables influence perceptions about authority and the language of negotiation. An employee negotiating a salary raise may find the language of negotiation different when the negotiation is conducted in his or her office compared to in the supervisor's office or in the vice president's suite.

Diffusion of decision-making authority and processes can create a lack of clarity about *who* makes decisions. The diffuse, often unclear decision-making processes of organizations require negotiators to develop a great deal of patience with inconsistencies and occasional roadblocks. Most of us find it frustrating to negotiate an agreement with a car salesperson, only to hear him or her say, "Now I have to go see if my manager will accept your offer and these terms." Yet this dynamic is commonplace in many settings. Department managers enter into agreements with clients or staff, aware that a higher authority can overrule their decision. Sales staff, monitored by sales managers, make agreements with customers based on policies. The distribution of decision-making authority across many levels of management hierarchy is very much a part of the fabric of organizations.

Diffusion of authority creates a problem for people outside the organization negotiating with agents of the organization. Although agents may want a great deal of flexibility, normally they have to work within the limits of policies and procedures defined by the organization. This can create conflict for someone negotiating with the agent. For example, a teacher might say to a parent, "If it were up to me, I'd let your child skip these exams, but the principal and the school district require the exams." A customer service representative may say to a customer, "I personally don't believe you should pay the late charge, and several of our managers agree with me. But our director won't relax the policy." In cases such as these, decision-making authority rests elsewhere in the organization, not with the agent with whom we are negotiating. McKersie (1999) explains, "The challenge faced by all agents arises from the negative range that often develops between the expectations of the clients and those of the organization. The divergence can occur over both the substantive agenda and the social contract" (p. 185). The inability to fulfill the substantive agreement may influence the social contract (continuing relationship). Box 9.2 provides an example of the importance of coordinating decision-making processes into an agreement with shared expectations.

When negotiating with people within an organization or between organizations, we need to do so with several questions in mind:

- How much authority does this person have in making agreements?
- How much information is this person able to disclose about the shape or possible terms of an agreement?
- Would disclosure of the decision maker influence the nature of agreements we want to make?
- How much flexibility does this person have with respect to potential options or implementation?

The number of parties involved in a negotiation influences the language and communication in an organizational negotiation. Negotiation between friends or family members generally involves a small number of people who possess a shared history, tacit understandings about rules for interaction, and knowledge about trustworthiness. In organizations, all three of these factors may be lacking. Information is revealed slowly while each party reduces uncertainties about the other. Parties ask questions about the other's background in the organization to establish credibility and trustworthiness. The greater the number in the negotiating group and the shorter their shared working history, the longer the parties will require to create a climate of safety and trust.

Kolb and Putnam (1992) argue that organizations contain both private and public forms of disputes, each with different procedures. Private forms occur when responses to differences of opinion take the form of avoidance, tolerance, accommodation, or camouflaged agreements. Publicly, parties appear overly cooperative and harmonious, but, privately, they argue issues in the break room or at lunch. Often, private disputes establish antecedent conditions for intense negotiations, which occur at a later time.

Public disputes occur when differences of opinion are openly expressed in conformance with processes and norms that are sanctioned by the organizations. Managers, human resources personnel, employee-relations specialists, and ombudsmen may serve as facilitators of these open negotiations. Other elements, such as organizational status, power, and manner of communication (e-mail, phone, face-to-face), may influence how negotiations

Box 9.2

HAMMERING OUT AN AGREEMENT

Western Millwork provides cabinetry, railings, and woodwork for corporate offices and upscale restaurants. Contracts once began with an estimator for the firm visiting business owners involved in the process of constructing a new building. Based on requirements established by the business owners, the estimator bid on the project. At the time of bidding, the estimator worked with ideas that would later become blueprints for the internal design of the building. From this point, the estimator hired subcontractors who would actually perform the work.

Recently, Western Millwork's CFO met with the senior estimator about losses occurring on many of the projects. The costs submitted by the subcontractors, including the change orders occurring on the projects, totaled more than the amount received for the project. The CFO asked, "Why are the estimates hundreds of thousands of dollars low?" The estimator responded, "I have to bid the project as low and accurately as possible to get the contract. The subcontractors are not paid a fixed rate. So when changes occur or designs can't be completed as planned, costs go up. The changes are unpredictable, and the actual work required often turns out to be different than we planned. With a labor shortage of millworkers, we have to honor our commitments."

Western Millwork had to redesign its negotiation process. It now requires that the clients provide a full set of blueprints for a subcontractor to review before a contract will be formally signed. It also requires a fixed price with the subcontractors, with changes to be submitted to the client for approval, before the work is completed. The client must pay the cost of changes from the original design. In short, although it involves more work initially, the new process ensures that the three parties involved in every agreement coordinate their decision systems to meet project expectations.

occur to resolve disputes. In addition, private disputes may serve as the hidden negotiation in public disputes.

Norms and Values

Both the formal rules and tacit understandings contained in organizational narratives influence organizational processes such as negotiation. During the first week of employment, a new staff member will hear stories about employees who have failed and who have been successful. Mythic tales circulate about how the founder's vision formed the organization. Values drawn from the vision teach new employees about how, to whom, and about what to communicate within the organizational culture. Postings on walls list norms and values by which employees are expected to conduct business. Walton, Cutcher-Gershenfeld, and McKersie (1994) emphasize the importance of understanding the underlying norms and tone of relationships that influence attitudes about negotiation. Some norms generate fears, whereas others establish rules about openness to diverse opinions. Norms manage internal differences and shape attitudes about the organization and staff relations. They influence how consensus is built and how people talk about issues.

Cultural norms within organizations can range from highly integrative to highly competitive. A sales representative for a software sales company states, "I would like to engage in integrative negotiation, but my manager wants to see profits. I need to make that deal come out in our favor, or I won't have a job." The organizational climate is highly competitive. An organizational climate is the collective attitude, the global set of expectations and beliefs that influence the members of groups. It's the conceptual orientation or shared perspective that links people in a common culture (Carbaugh, 1985). Climates may be cooperative or competitive, supportive or critical, friendly or unfriendly, open or closed, trusting or suspicious. Negotiating in an open and trusting climate involves a great deal more constructive problem solving than negotiating in a closed and suspicious climate.

Within organizations, departments may have distinctly different climates, despite the fact that they belong to the same company. For example, in Nauta and Sanders's (2000) study of manufacturing firms, marketing departments demonstrated many more contending and fewer yielding behaviors than members of planning departments. The type of work, goals, and priorities all influence the organizational climates. To fit in or get ahead, people adopt the qualities characteristic of the climate.

Because organizations possess multiple climates with different codes of conduct, as well as different goals, ground rules reduce uncertainty and build a common set of expectations. The ground rules may include agreements such as seeking to understand before criticizing, being open about interests, needs and goals, promoting shared interests, or honoring commitments to time allocations and responsibilities. Ground rules enable negotiators to achieve a higher ground in negotiations—principled behavior that might not otherwise occur. Box 9.3 describes a firm in which overlapping projects and priorities require a common set of ground rules.

Relationship

Organizations are networks of members intertwined by roles, relationships, and processes. Competition for control of resources, enhanced

---

Box 9.3

REFEREEING ORGANIZATIONAL PRIORITIES

Internet Technology Systems (ITS) provides development and support for organizational Internet networks. ITS helps organizations define their system needs and network requirements. An ITS department then translates these requirements into a specific system design for the company and develops a timeline for its implementation. Later, the operations department will install, test, and debug the system to make it fully operational.

Occasionally, tension arises among the sales department, which creates the contractual agreements; the design department, which develops the system; and the operations department, which implements the system. Tension occurs over several issues, including additions that the client wants after the initial design, changes the system requires after implementation, and fixing problems that occur later. Staff who implemented a particular system may be involved in different projects when clients need repairs to that system. New large clients may be given higher priority for installing a system, which means that smaller firms must wait. System additions that were not anticipated must somehow be woven into scheduling.

To handle project scheduling and changes, ITS established a department whose sole responsibility is to mediate the varying needs of the clients. The department established ground rules for change orders, additions, delays, and moving clients up in the priority lists. Without the ground rules, the competition for limited resources would turn the negotiations into distributive battles for priority.

---

status, and financial reward creates boundaries between departments and us-versus-them polarizations among members. Negotiation functions as a tool for spanning boundaries and for creating linkages or strategic alliances. Negotiation serves as a medium for exchanging ideas that enable members with opposing views, agendas, and priorities to achieve both symbolic and actual coalitions for accomplishing organizational objectives.

Parkhe (1991) argues that *strategic alliances* between departments within an organization or between organizations foster the kind of cooperation that might make negotiation more successful. These strategic alliances are "relatively enduring cooperative arrangements involving flows and linkages that utilize resources and/or governance structures from autonomous organizations for the joint accomplishment of individual goals linked to the corporate mission of each sponsoring firm" (Parkhe, 1991, p. 581).

Strategic alliances enable groups to increase the power of their resources through supportive relationships. In a study that involved 11 manufacturing firms and 126 employees, Nauta and Sanders (2000) found that increasing interdependence between departments fostered more constructive negotiation behaviors because employees realized that they needed each other, both now and in the future. Interdependence in terms of alliances abounds in business. Toyota maintains 77 Asian and 97 U.S. alliances with parts suppliers. Chrysler is involved in about two dozen similar alliances. Alliances replace sales reps and buyers. In addition to enjoying lower transaction costs, Toyota has to spend only 20% of its contact time with suppliers negotiating contracts. Chrysler spends about 21% of its time negotiating compared to General Motors, which spends as much as 47% of its time devoted to negotiating contracts. Dyer (2000) argues that the corporate winners of the next decade and beyond will be those organizations that develop a collaborative advantage through alliances:

> Rather than maintaining a bargaining orientation, the firms in the enterprise focus their energies and resources on how they can optimize the performance of the entire system. In short, rather than focusing their energies on splitting the pie, they focus their energies on expanding the size of the pie, so that all parties are better off regardless of their percentage share. (pp. 181-182)

Strategic alliances depend on the ability of partners to share information about interests, needs, strengths, and weaknesses. For example, in Box 9.1, each of the appliance firm's departments needed an understanding of the timeline needs of each of the other departments to work effectively with them.

Communication

Because of multiple communication channels (face-to-face, fax, phone, e-mail, memo), the influence of climate (e.g., trusting or nontrusting, competitive or collaborative), and networks of relationships, a political element is more visible in organizational negotiation than in other contexts. When people speak, their status and role influence our interpretation of their messages and our responses. A colleague who tells you, "I won't compromise on this" will have a different impact than a supervisor who speaks the same message. Negotiation between departments can be influenced by the amount of resources controlled by each department or the current importance of the department to the CEO. In national or international organizations, managers who work in the home office may have stronger bargaining power than the managers dispersed in other regions.

Access to information and willingness to share information can be sources of power both within and between organizations. Information passed up a chain of command arrives incomplete or distorted, affecting the quality of decisions. Box 9.4 illustrates how structure, power, the dissemination of information, and the lack of interdepartmental relations influenced problem solving in one major corporation.

Concerns about organizational identity, with implications for both status and authority, heighten the importance of saving face in organizational negotiations. The more important loss of image or reputation becomes, the more we might expect to see defensiveness, longer time to reach agreements, and lower joint outcomes. According to Brown (1977),

> In some instances, protecting loss of face becomes so central an issue that it swamps the importance of tangible issues at stake and generates intense conflicts that can impede progress toward agreement and increase substantially the costs of conflict resolution. (p. 275)

The more a negotiator can avoid language choices that create a need for others to save face or protect reputation, the greater the potential for developing shared understanding and achieving negotiation objectives.

Negotiation research reveals that systematic bias and faulty judgments that affect decision making can prevent negotiators from reaching optimal settlements (Bazerman, 1983; Neale and Bazerman, 1993). For example, Thompson and Lowenstein (1992) found a tendency among negotiators to "make egocentric interpretations of fairness" (p. 184). Negotiators assess fairness with a bias that favors the groups to which they belong. They tend to overestimate the rightness of their own perspective and underestimate the perspective of others. Each side tends to exaggerate information to support its arguments. Thompson and Nadler (2000) warn that the implication is that, "if the partisans in a conflict perceive their differences as greater than they really are, then they might be overly pessimistic about finding common ground" (p. 221). It is important for negotiators to be aware that exaggeration and bias occur frequently during conflict. To reach an attitude of negotiation, both sides need to discuss the nature of their beliefs, concerns, and assumptions to reduce perceptions of being unreasonable or extreme.

A second bias is the tendency for members of contending groups who are negotiating to view negotiation as a forced choice between competition and cooperation. This perspective is probably linked to an organizational need to maintain identity and distinction from other groups, evidenced by the difficult negotiations of Republicans and Democrats, labor unions and management, environmentalists and industry leaders, or marketing and engineering. Each group pictures the others as competitors with distorted views of the facts. Pruitt and Carnevale (1993) report a study, conducted at State University of New York at Buffalo, in which researchers found that groups were more likely than individuals to choose competitive over cooperative tactics

Box 9.4

MORE THAN THE ROOF IS LEAKY

General Electronics is an electronics company with more than 7,500 employees and multiple corporate sites. The company's testing lab houses millions of dollars' worth of specialized equipment, which calibrates high-tech machinery before it is delivered to clients in the aerospace industry.

The facilities department decided it was time to repair the 20-year-old roof of the testing lab building. Company policy required the department to notify the lab supervisor and post notices announcing the days of work. Bob, the lab supervisor, asked Tom, the facilities manager, for a delay to complete a project, but Tom said, "We have a yearly schedule that we stick to, and we won't change it." Bob asked Tom to reconsider his decision, but Tom wouldn't budge. Bob asked his manager, Steve, to intercede on his behalf, but Steve said, "Solve your own problems with them. Just be sure that the equipment isn't damaged."

The facilities crew began its work on the scheduled day but quit about 4 p.m. when snow began to fall. About 5 p.m., Bob called Tom to tell him the roof was leaking. Tom responded, "Based on your description of the leak, it won't spread across the room to harm your equipment. Anyway, we're too busy trying to solve the power outages across the plant." Bob called Steve to give him an update. Bob told Steve, "Tom said not to worry about it because of the location of the leak."

The leak continued to spread across the ceiling. Tom said he was too busy to do anything about it, and Steve wouldn't intercede. Bob spent the next few hours trying to reach the beams of the building so that he could hang tarps to protect the equipment, but he couldn't find a ladder tall enough or a lift that didn't require power.

The next day, inspectors found that the equipment had been damaged. At the interdepartmental staff meeting, to which Bob was invited, he was asked about the damage to the equipment. Although Bob explained that he followed company policy by notifying both the facilities department and his manager, he was told that he was negligent in protecting the company's equipment. He protested but found that anything he said made Steve, his manager, look negligent. Two weeks later, Bob was demoted to the level of lab technician based on "incompetence" demonstrated as supervisor.

Politics, interdepartmental relations, and poor communication processes created a situation in which Bob was not able to negotiate solutions to problems he faced. What communication processes could have prevented this problem or resolved it after it had occurred?

when given choices for dealing with conflict. The impact of a competitive bias is felt in the great number of lose-lose outcomes ("If I can't have it, neither can you."). Thompson and Hrebec (1996) found that in an analysis of data involving 5,000 participants, lose-lose outcomes occurred about 20% of the time.

A third bias of groups is the practice of making oversimplified, stereotypical assumptions about people in other groups. Fisher (2000) explains,

> In intergroup relations, there is a tendency to see out-group members as personally responsible for negative behaviors, rather than this being due to situational factors. In addition, the personal characteristics that are the focus of attribution tend to be group qualities that are embodied in the negative stereotype. In contrast, undesirable behaviors by in-group members tend to be attributed to external conditions for which the member is not responsible. (p. 171)

Ng and Ang (1999) provide several reasons why these biases occur: The attributions support defensive, self-protective orientations; information differs upon which judgments are made; the focus of attention differs; people base judgments on their own experience; and people tend to overemphasize negative information about others. Ng and Ang (1999) recommend that countering attributional bias involves the following:

■ Focusing on common interests
■ Acknowledging the other party's perspective
■ Developing a *Teflon* personality by ignoring unhelpful responses
■ Focusing on positive aspects of the other person's comments
■ Floating possibilities for other reasons to explain situational dynamics
■ Expanding the range of normality beyond the other's experience (pp. 382-384)

Box 9.5 provides an example where comments that may have been intended to be humorous were interpreted as demeaning. The negotiations that followed turned out to be very difficult. Do you think the problems are solvable? What should the parties do to overcome their stalemate?

Negotiating agreements that address underlying issues can be difficult in work groups where members believe that dissenting opinions are not appreciated. Raising issues of concern in these contexts demands a great deal of courage. Many managers enforce norms for compliance to maintain a perception of consensus or esprit de corps.

Janis (1989) describes *groupthink* as artificial consensus when members withhold dissenting opinions. In some organizations, employees say, "I wouldn't share my opinion at a staff meeting. Openness is retaliated against later." In other groups, you might hear, "Why speak up? It won't make a difference. The decision has already been made." The organizational climate suppresses openness that disagrees with the manager's or group's predispositions.

Box 9.5

NEGOTIATION THAT FEELS LIKE A SHELL GAME

Sixty-five employees from diverse backgrounds work at a government office. Management provided both diversity and sexual-harassment training and promoted those principles in organizational policies. Yet employees occasionally bantered among themselves in deprecating ways.

Juan began one Monday morning by complaining about coming to work. Ralph, who didn't like Juan, said in jest to Juan, "Why don't you wetbacks go back to your country?" Juan was incensed at the disrespect and reported the incident to his supervisor. Based on organizational policy, Juan was offered the option to go on leave (without pay) until the incident was fully investigated. He chose to take the leave. After a 3-week investigation, Ralph received a written reprimand, and Juan was told to return to work when he was ready. Management told Juan that when he returned, the staff would meet with him to discuss ways of "making the situation right for him."

When Juan returned to work, management called a meeting to negotiate a resolution to the problem. Many were present, including Ralph, Juan, the union representative, and several senior managers. The negotiation produced many agreements: Staff training in harassment would be provided again to all employees; Juan would be moved to a new, better job; Juan would be paid for his time off work and assured that vacation benefits would not be interrupted; and all employees would be monitored for the next year to maintain compliance with organizational policy.

Juan asked for a short recess to confirm the agreement with the union representative. Thirty minutes later, after the meeting resumed, Juan stated, "I fully support the agreement, but I also want $100,000. During the 3 weeks that I was off, I was not able to make my house payment. That hurt my credit. I had been planning on starting a business that would carry into my retirement. I was denied the loan because of my status. I want to be compensated for these inconveniences. Management should have acted faster on my complaint. Three weeks was too long." One manager said, "We've got only $25,000 available for these kinds of problems." The union representative responded, "Looks like this is going to court."

Disasters such as the Challenger space shuttle or the flawed Hubble telescope prove that groupthink can have detrimental consequences. The impacts of groupthink decisions that occur daily in industry can also be significant because of poor choices and decisions that lack careful scrutiny. (Callaway & Esser, 1984; Fodor & Smith, 1982; Leana, 1985). To reduce groupthink, Turner and Pratkanis (1997) propose the following tactics: "the establishment of norms favoring the expression of opinions, doubts, and uncertainty, the consultation of relevant sources (including those who are likely to disagree), the implementation of solutions rather than the zero-sum choice procedures" (p. 65).

Among the many strategies we might try in an effort to reduce groupthink and promote high-quality negotiated agreements are the following:

- Structure the discussion so responsibility for identifying issues that may have been overlooked in discussions rests with selected members or subgroups.
- Structure the discussion so that a member(s) serves in the role of devil's advocate during the discussion. The role may rotate.
- Ask the group members to assume the perspectives of constituencies with whom the group negotiates.
- Create a group norm in which diverse opinions are appreciated.
- Before negotiations are complete, ask respected outside sources about additional alternatives or to assess the quality of an agreement.
- After an agreement has been reached, ask group members to second-guess their solutions.

Ethnic diversity is a prominent value in many organizations. Theoretically, this value may have strong support from staff but may be difficult to implement operationally, as demonstrated in the staff dispute described in Box 9.6.

The problems depicted in Box 9.6 involve different perspectives on many issues, including values involving what it means to cooperate and problem-solve as teams. Fine (1991) argues that management's responsibilities involve creating discussion processes that facilitate open expression of diverse opinions in problem solving. He describes the responsibilities as follows:

- Resisting *privileged discourse*, language that creates division between employees or between managers and employees
- Promoting *harmonic discourse*, discussion that recognizes language differences and integrates differences for the good of the group

Facilitators of problem solving or negotiation of multicultural groups need to create respect for both language differences and the values that come from different cultural perspectives about problems. Integrating multiple perspectives involves a great deal of reframing of issues to find common ground and common understandings.

Box 9.6

WHEN DIVERSITY *IS* THE ISSUE

Sixty accountants worked for the accounting department of a large organization. Organizational values promoted the hiring of people from many ethnic backgrounds who brought multiple perspectives to the staff's work.

The work of the accountants was done in teams of six. Each team would work on a project for a few weeks and then move on to other projects. The teams would shift in composition based on availability of workers, skills, and department priority for variety.

Conflicts within the teams occurred over many issues, including value of organizational rewards, commitment to team goals, work ethic, family interruptions, management tactics, and communication styles. Disputes between team members began affecting cooperation and timely completion of projects. A member of one ethnic subgroup said, "Those people work too slow. They think slow and are unable to keep up the pace we need to complete projects." A member of a second ethnic subgroup said, "Those people want to spend too much time with their families. To do this job, it is expected that we will all work some evenings and weekends." A member of a third such subgroup responded, "Some of the workers are too independent. They don't know what 'team' means or how to talk with us about coordinating activities."

The whole department—made up of 60 accountants, including managers, of five ethnic populations—met for a half-day retreat led by a facilitator. Before the retreat, the managers told the facilitator, "You know they won't talk in the big group. They're accountants, and they worry about what the managers will think." To reduce the impact managers would have on small group discussions, the facilitator divided the 60-member staff into two groups. Each of the groups sat before a chalkboard turned away from the other group. The facilitator told one group, "List on the chalkboard the things that work well on your teams." He told the other group, "List on your chalkboard the things that don't work on your teams."

After the groups completed their lists, they turned the chalkboards toward the other group. Each side took turns reading a point from the list, accompanied by discussion.

After groups completed the lists (about an hour), the facilitator asked each of the groups to list on its chalkboards creative solutions to the most important problems that had been raised. As the lists were read to the full group, participants were asked, "What would it take to make this suggestion work?" The teams left that day with an agreement about action items and a new appreciation for their diversity.

In addition to coordinating the work of the teams, what other factors were the team members negotiating?

Interdependence

The interdependence of departments and staff creates a need to continually negotiate processes, the use of resources, and priorities. Budget structures, separation of workers into departments, and different priorities create natural rivalries in organizations. Salaries are drawn from a common pool. Positions, supplies, funding for projects, and office space create predictable tensions among competing groups. Negotiators work on specifying the nature of their interdependence through the exchange of proposals and the choice of language that manages tensions. The language that frames the importance of issues or parameters for discussion establishes levels of autonomy, control, and power between the parties.

At a theoretical level, the managers may all agree about the importance of creating value that can be mutually rewarding but, at a tactical level, when personal interests are at stake, claiming value takes precedence. For example, senior executives from a major national department store had trouble understanding why stores in a particular region resisted sharing ideas and resources until the store managers pointed out that rewards for store managers were based on the individual store's performance. Rewards reinforced competitiveness. In a university, department chairs were given additional faculty and funding based on the number of students who registered for their courses. Predictably, faculty from the department provided little support or encouragement for students who considered other majors or who spoke about taking courses outside of the department.

The problems of the refrigerator firm discussed in Box 9.1 illustrate the complex nature of competing priorities experienced in many organizational settings. A sales department wants rapid production and quick delivery. Manufacturing wants a slow enough pace to reduce errors and produce quality products. Marketing wants both rapid production and fast sales. Daniels, Spiker, and Papa (1997) explain, "When human values and the goals that arise from these values come into conflict, the result can be anything from rivalry and feuding to all-out warfare" (p. 271). Organizations with conflicting values, goals, and priorities must engage in continual negotiations to align their processes.

In many settings faced with scarce resources, problem solving faces fewer barriers if negotiators can establish *superordinate goals,* which require all parties to look beyond their differences and cooperate. For example, a major marketing firm reduced competition among its departments by basing rewards on 50% organizational performance and 50% departmental performance. This established organizational success as a superordinate goal, which the firm hoped would facilitate more interdepartmental cooperation.

Organizational negotiations require a great deal of effort to establish *common ground.* This common ground may include factors such as solutions to common problems, interests that may be mutually beneficial, or long-term benefits of working together. For example, in a recent negotiation, department directors agreed to trim their operating budgets by 10% to avoid cutting staff members from any of the departments. At a diabetes research center, the medical staff found that to get sufficient patients for their studies, they had to extend the clinic's office hours earlier in the morning and later in the evening to accommodate patients' work schedules. The common goal—to get sufficient patients for the studies—served as a factor that motivated staff to share responsibility for the additional hours. When Apollo 13 became disabled in space, "bring the astronauts home safely" became the common ground, the shared goal, which prioritized all work efforts at NASA mission control. The more complex the issue and the larger the organization, the greater the need to negotiate priorities during early stages of negotiation. Box 9.7 describes a situation in which parties agree about priorities but differ on the interpretation of a school policy.

Because priorities vary between departments or between organizations, parties need to use differences in priority to fashion agreements. McKearnan and Fairman (1999) frame the process with a question: "What could we give you on the issue you care more about that would allow you to live with the proposed agreement on the issue you care less about?" (p. 340). For example, a manager agrees that his department can take on additional tasks with the provision that the manager can have a longer timeline on other projects. An employee negotiates an agreement with his or her manager to work the next few Saturdays to meet project deadlines in exchange for a new work computer at the beginning of the next fiscal year.

Power

Although power is an issue in most settings, it plays a highly visible role in organizational politics and problem solving. Kochan and Verma (1983) argue that "any organizational analysis that considers negotiation to be an important phenomenon will need to consider power as an important source

---

Box 9.7

A SCHOOL WITH LEARNING PROBLEMS

Eastridge Middle School is located in an affluent neighborhood. Tensions have grown steadily between parents and teachers over the student absence policy. The policy reads: "If a student is gone for any reason, the student or student's parents must notify the teacher about the absence and arrange for making up all missed work."

Teachers believe that the policy is fair and clear. Enforcing the policy is another matter. Frequently, during the school year, when parents have vacation time, they take their children on extended trips. The teacher is rarely notified and, when students return, the students resist doing any extra work. Accordingly, the teachers give these students low or failing grades.

Parents complain, "You're penalizing my child unfairly. They get more education on one of our trips than in the classroom." The principal asks the teachers to go easy on the extra work, but teachers emphasize the importance of all students completing district policy curriculum goals. In their letters to the school board, parents threaten to have the principal fired. The parent-teacher advisory board for the school sides with the teachers and principal, perhaps because the principal selected the board's representatives. So the board is in a standoff with the students' parents.

Parents, students, teachers, and administration are all members of this organization. All agree that educating children is a priority, but they differ about what constitutes learning. What do you recommend to help this group negotiate resolution to its escalating conflict?

---

of influence and part of the dynamics of decision making" (p. 20). Status and position power influence openness in communication, the level of trust that occurs, and the willingness to consider options. For example, in a telecommunications firm, staff members engaged in weeks of discussions about how to improve cooperation on their cross-functional project teams. During the fourth session, a unit director decided to join the discussions. Staff members who before were quite verbal now spoke little, deferring judgments to the director about how things would be done.

Demonstrations of power in organizations occur in many forms, including the authority to control resources, the ability to enter into or block agreements, or the ability to influence others who can make agreements. Often, formal, public negotiations parallel informal, private negotiations. A relevant question for negotiators is the following: "If we're going to reach our goals, who else do we need to speak to before we can announce this agreement?"

Often, parties attempt to increase their negotiating power by adding or withholding resources. For example, a major software development company provided several million dollars of work for a client. The client refused to pay a portion of the bill—$430,000 for consultants to repair the client's system so that it could effectively use the software. The software company believed its power was weak in getting the client to pay the bill, even though the bill met contract expectations. During negotiations over the money owed, the software company argued that it could not provide upgrades to the system or maintenance without payment of past-due bills. The potential for major expenditures on the client's part in future years equalized the power so that there was a greater willingness on both sides to resolve differences.

Box 9.8 illustrates a situation at Harvard University where interdependence, relationship, and power became factors in reaching an understanding about employee pay.

Closely linked to power is the concept of *territory*. People feel compelled to become more competitive if they believe the groups they are responsible for are being threatened. Department heads regularly engage in distributive tactics for scarce resources when they believe the resources are necessary for *their* department's success. Negotiation will need to link potential gains to specific interests valued by others. For example, McKearnan and Fairman (1999) describe how a potentially positional discussion between community leaders can be framed in mutually beneficial terms:

A mayor may state his position as, "The health clinic has to go in my town." If other participants ask why, it may turn out that the mayor's underlying interest is for the clinic to be easily accessible to the large number of elderly residents of the town. Knowing this, the group can consider other ways of meeting this mayor's interest, for example, by providing low-cost transportation from the town to the clinic or providing a mobile health van that visits the neighborhoods where elderly persons are concentrated. (p. 330-331)

Addressing issues of territory often involves meeting the underlying interests that leaders hold for their groups. The interests need not be tangible resources. At times, respect for the leader's authority, concern for the group's needs, or inclusion of the group's opinions in the decision-making process may be sufficient to generate agreement.

Power-focused, positional, or aggressive negotiators can be difficult to work with, especially if you can't afford to lose the organization they represent as an ally or as a client. Their aggressive style may reflect their

---

Box 9.8

HARVARD'S LONGEST SLUMBER PARTY

For 3 weeks during April and May 2001, more than three dozen protesting students staged a sit-in in the president's office at Harvard University. The students claimed that in spite of Harvard's $19.5 billion endowment, the school paid only $6.50 an hour to many of its sub-contracted employees.

Harvard administration countered that many of the lower-paid employees were custodians, food service workers, and maintenance personnel who lacked high school diplomas. In addition, administrators explained that no more than 400 of the 13,500 employees earned less than $10.25 an hour, the minimum wage for working in the city of Cambridge. Harvard's president argued that the workers could help themselves by improving their job skills or participating in literacy programs.

Nevertheless, the students continued their protest, demanding that the school pay a "living wage." Powerful sources came to the support of the students. At student rallies involving more than 1,500 students, Massachusetts Senator Edward Kennedy, former U.S. Labor Secretary Robert Reich, and the American Federation of Labor-Congress of Industrial Organizations (AFL-CIO) president John Sweeney announced their support for the protest.

A few days before graduation, Harvard's president announced an end to the protest. The school's administration agreed to form a 10-member committee, made up of faculty, administration, students, and workers, to make recommendations about the school's employment policies. In addition, the administration agreed to a moratorium on outsourcing jobs and to retroactively raising the wages of some workers.

What factors influenced the administration's willingness to negotiate? What impact did the setting, Harvard University, have on the actions of the parties involved?

---

beliefs about how to achieve their interests or may be the style promoted in their organizational climate. Keiser (1999) provides several strategies that might be useful in drawing the other party into more of a problem-solving partnership:

- When under attack, listen.
- Keep track of issues.
- Summarize what's been accomplished and sketch out what still needs to be discussed.
- Assert your company's (department's) needs.
- Commit to a solution only after it's certain to work for both parties.
- Save the hardest issues for last.
- Don't be emotionally rattled into concessions you wouldn't otherwise make. (pp. 414-417)

Keiser (1999) summarizes, "The essence of negotiating effectively with aggressive customers is sidestepping their attacks and convincing them that a common effort at problem solving will be more profitable and productive" (p. 418).

● SALARY NEGOTIATIONS

Many people say that negotiating salary for a new job or for a raise in a current job may be their most difficult type of negotiation. Some people link the level of pay to self-esteem, value to the company, payback for years of experience or preparation, or worth as a professional. Any of these reasons creates an emotional component that can make negotiations difficult. Based on *Wall Street Journal* interviews of executive recruiters, Silverman and Dunham (2000) point out that job hunters sabotage their own efforts by appearing too polished or arrogant, spending too much time focused on their own needs, or making wrong assumptions about the company.

A necessary piece of work for job hunters is researching the worth of their skills in comparable jobs before negotiating for the job they want. A colleague told me about his interview for a faculty position at a major eastern university. When he was asked about what he needed for a starting salary, he responded, "$125,000." The interview ended shortly after that. Knowing what the market pays for similar jobs is essential information.

The ability of employees to negotiate higher salaries or raises depends on the type of organization. Schools, hospitals, nonprofit organizations, and similar contexts have little flexibility in what they can pay employees; the pay scales are tied directly to inflexible budgets. Similarly, it may be just as difficult to negotiate with organizations that are large or old and established; these firms place high value on parity of employee salaries and human resources-driven pay scales. In 1999, most raises in the large organizations averaged 3% to 5% (Uhland, 1999). The older companies are more bound by precedent, policies, and procedures. Negotiating higher initial salaries or raises has greatest potential in small businesses or start-up companies that have greater budget flexibility.

An additional factor in salary negotiations involves how easy or hard it is for organizations to hire particular expertise. In industries where demand is high for a particular skill, such as often occurs in technical fields, it's easier to negotiate higher salaries. Raises for high-demand positions can be several times higher than in low-demand positions, which are easier to fill.

Negotiating with an organization can be difficult if the hiring manager does not negotiate. But, assuming that there is a need for the skills you bring to an organization, that the manager is willing to talk about salary with you, and that you've researched comparable worth in the industry, we propose the following principles for negotiations:

- Be prepared to list qualities that you bring to the organization that have value.
- Display commitment and genuine interest in the position. Don't make it appear that the position may be short-term or only a stepping stone to another job; doing so may decrease your chance of getting an offer.
- Consider the entire compensation package. Extra vacation days, lower-cost health insurance, or flexible hours can be more valuable than small increments of salary.
- Be careful with the trick question "How much do you want to earn?" Frequently, this question is used to eliminate people who are too expensive. Respond with something like, "A specific number depends on many factors. I'd like to hear about all aspects of the job and the compensation package before getting too specific."
- Don't let personal reasons support claims for a raise. The business is not responsible for subsidizing your lifestyle. Stay focused on the values you add to the organization.
- Reduce your emotional investment in the process by separating what you would like to have from what you must have. The industry may not bear what you want.
- Proceed with questions that allow flexibility in response, such as "Would you consider . . . ?" "How much room do you have to move closer to . . . ?" "What does your firm pay for comparable positions?"
- Prepare to give a little on some issues if you expect to get something on others.
- Understand what your best alternative to no agreement is, but do not use it to threaten or coerce. Coercion generally leads to positional responses. Yet having alternatives may be your best tool for asking what you're worth.

Box 9.9 provides the insights of Gordon Miller, author of *The Career Coach: Winning Strategies for Getting Ahead in Today's Job Market* and founder and CEO of Delta Road, the largest corporate and career coaching organization in the United States. At Delta Road, more than 300 coaches have coached over 100,000 individuals in their search for jobs and negotiation for salaries.

Box 9.9

GETTING THE JOB AND SALARY YOU WANT

Career coach Gordon Miller argues that the old strategy of submitting resumes to a large number of job postings in a job search is less effective in a market where good jobs are highly competitive. Stacks of resumes grace every hiring executive's desk. Miller states, "Job applicants must do something that distinguishes them from the masses and gets their resume to the top of the stack" (G. Miller, personal communication, April 26, 2001). The same is true of interviews. The old strategy of showing up with a college degree or a few years of experience no longer means entitlement to a job. Miller believes that as employers interview candidates, they ask themselves, "What value does this candidate bring to help us accomplish our goals that I can't get from someone else?"

Miller recommends a new strategy to get the job you want:

1. Choose five businesses or companies where you like the kind of work they do and the values they stand for.

2. Research the company. Connect with someone in the company who can tell you what is working and what isn't.

3. Find a way to meet a decision maker in the company and explain how you can help them better accomplish their goals and that you'd like to talk to someone more about it.

4. During the interview, Miller advises, "Don't say, 'Tell me about your company' or 'Tell me about the position.' You should already know that information. Brand yourself as someone who loves changes, who possesses the skills that will address their needs, who thinks creatively and likes problem solving. Position your skills in alignment with the needs of the company. Tell them you can make a difference in 90 days and are willing to provide a plan that describes how you can make a difference."

When negotiating salary, begin with an understanding of the market rate. Speak about compensation packages and limit discussions that are solely about pay. Look at other benefits that the business has to offer, such as stock options, flexible hours, bonus plans, telecommuting, 401K contributions, or performance-based pay incentives. Miller concludes, "Today's companies are looking for great people—people who understand the new ways of doing business. Applicants should express a passion for working in the business and provide specifics about how they will add value to the company."

SUMMARY •

Negotiation serves as a catalyst for organizations to reach understandings about the meaning of organizational events, structure, role, and processes. Each discussion that involves conflicting interests or competing goals serves as a forum for negotiating language that creates culture, levels of independence, norms for organizational communication, relationships that serve as alliances, and power, which will control direction or resources. The ritualistic discussions in staff meetings serve as a symbolic process for managing tension and coordinating activities because each discussion provides cues about the appropriate way to approach issues. Members learn that it is acceptable to cooperate or compete, to listen to or to ignore others, and to engage in compromise or to remain positional.

The term *organizational climate* describes the milieu in which negotiations take place. An unfriendly, cold, untrusting organizational climate makes integrative agreements difficult to achieve. Through open sharing of information and the use of listening behaviors, effective negotiators build a relationship that fosters a climate conducive to integrative agreements. The success or failure of a negotiation may be determined in the first 10 minutes of a discussion based on the climate established by negotiators.

Frequently, negotiation becomes easier when negotiators are able to create strategic alliances with peers, clients, or other departments, creating a spirit of "We're in this together; how can we help each other?" These alliances will be most effective if they can be established *before* they're actually needed. Emphasizing a superordinate or shared goal can often be the motivation for partnership.

Organizations can be difficult settings in which to negotiate because of the systemic influences. Decision processes may be slow, priorities may be unclear, interpersonal skills may be weak, agendas may be hidden, egos may be big, resources may be limited, and expressions of power are real. The context requires negotiators to manage their emotional triggers of impatience or frustration and remain focused on achieving mutually beneficial gains for all parties. Finding opportunity to build relationship prior to negotiating may be the most important prenegotiation strategy. People tend to share more information, demonstrate greater trust, and cooperate with people with whom they have a positive relationship history.

PROFESSIONAL PROFILE

● **JOSEPH RICE,**
CHAIRMAN OF CLAYTON, DUBILLIER & RICE

Negotiating Leveraged Buyouts:
Simply a Job, Not Personal Combat

Few of us negotiate the sale of businesses worth millions of dollars, but our jobs and our purchases are often affected by those sales. This interviewee provides an insider perspective on such negotiations: who is involved, what is the process, and which approaches lead to success. The term *common ground* discussed in this chapter relates to the leveraged buyout; negotiators in this context look for common ground where the buyer and seller have an overlapping range of opportunity. Common ground is limited by the buyer's preset range of net return (their stake in the ground). Displays of emotion between negotiators are rare. In this business, negotiations must be conducted on a face-to-face basis, even when that requires international travel. In the practitioner's opinion, awareness of objectives, perseverance, and objectivity are success factors in this context. Despite the high stakes, successful negotiators in this arena use many of the same processes and practices recommended for other organizational settings.

Introduction to the Practitioner

Joe Rice has been active in leveraged buyouts for most of his career. Educated at Williams College and Harvard Law School, he spent a few years practicing law with a large New York law firm. While there, he represented a client of the firm who did a leveraged buyout; Joe decided he would enjoy that work much more than practicing law. When Joe's firm, Clayton, Dubillier & Rice, was formed in 1978, the first business bought was worth 7 million dollars. In 2000, the last investment was for 1 billion dollars. Joe notes, "The firm's growth has been a linear progression. As time has gone by, both the capital to be invested and the transactions have grown."

Joe defines the leveraged buyout business as "the purchase of an *economic entity,* and I use that phrase to connote a subsidiary or division of a corporation, or a corporation in its entirety, on a basis where the entire ownership of the business is transferred to the acquiring entity. The capital that's used in payment of the purchase price is provided through a combination of both debt and equity, and it is the term *leverage* which connotes that we use debt in our capital structures. If we are successful in doing what we're trying to do, this will give us leverage on the return."

A negotiator must be very skilled to be successful in this arena. Reflecting on the skills that he developed as a lawyer, Joe says, "I think there are two: one is a knowledge of the law of contracts, since inevitably there is a contract between buyer and seller. Negotiating the sale and purchase of a business can be a complicated process and inevitably involves a great number of contractual intricacies. An understanding of the impact of contracts and how they establish obligations between a buyer and a seller is a necessary skill to have. The second skill is a recognition that negotiating the purchase of a business can be a long and demanding process in which you have to be patient and persistent. In addition, skill in financial measurements is desirable so that what you're trying to achieve is clear." Joe has no special training in business, so his financial and analytical skills were acquired on the job.

Insights About Negotiation

The first step in the negotiation process is establishing a price range within which both buyer and seller are willing to negotiate. Joe explains, "Unless there is an agreement on price, you don't get to the question of negotiation. Our firm has a number of benchmarks that guide our business. We have said to our limited partners (the institutions which provide us with capital) that we expect to generate a 30% compound return net to them. Since I take 20% of the gains, it means that you have to generate around a 36% to 37% compound return on our equity investment. That benchmark helps me establish how much I can pay for a business."

The next step in establishing a price range is to develop a view of that business and the likelihood of success of reaching the benchmark. Joe describes his approach: "We prepare a 5-year plan that reflects what we think the outlook for the business is. We look at how the business might perform in a variety of economic environments. We develop a capital structure that reflects the existing state of the financial markets and the capital needs of that business. Some portion of that capital structure will be debt, and some portion will be equity. I place the capital structure in a frame that says, 'On the basis of the projections that we've developed, I want to generate a 30% compound return net to the providers of the equity capital.' That is the stake in the ground. I will negotiate up to that price but not beyond it."

Assessing the value of the asset to be acquired reflects good negotiation practice in most commercial contexts. Joe explains, "Although not every commercial negotiation requires benchmarking a particular return, if return on investment is important to one of the parties, there must be some 'stake in the ground' that limits a negotiator's participation in a transaction. Although many of our dealings involve time frames shorter than 5 years, the basic approach to determining whether buyer and seller have an overlapping range of opportunity is the same."

After a price has been established, much of the negotiation that follows is an effort to preserve that price. The representations that Joe asks the seller to make are designed to assure Joe that he is assuming responsibility for only those liabilities that he has knowledge of and has factored into his pricing.

Joe distinguishes between being a buyer and a seller. He explains, "If I am the buyer, I want the seller to represent to me a host of things about the quality of the business. If I am the seller, I basically want to say, 'I will give you the opportunity to look at this business as long as you want to, but once you buy it, it's yours, and you have no remedies against me.' Now, those two positions are mutually exclusive, and I recognize them as being mutually exclusive. But, they are nevertheless the most advantageous positions a buyer, on one hand, and a seller, on the other hand, can take."

There are other traditional approaches to preparation that apply to leveraged buyouts. Joe speaks about studying the business in preparation for the negotiation. He mentions the importance of avoiding expectations about the length of negotiation. In his experience, "It can move very speedily if the seller wants it to, or it can move with great difficulty if the seller and the buyer don't agree on how the transaction ought to be structured."

The typical leveraged buyout negotiation for Joe's firm involves a business that is in the manufacturing, distribution, or service industry. The firm does not deal in commodity or high-tech businesses. These limitations are driven by the background and expertise of the operating partners. Joe explains, "We have both operating and financial partners. We are always trying to invest in businesses that our operating partners understand because that gives us the opportunity to impact the value-creation process, rather than be simply passive observers. We also look at business sectors that have the potential for organic growth."

Joe explains why the firm does business in only the United States and Europe: "We have limited the scope because we do best in jurisdictions where the rule of law prevails, where people abide by contracts, and where there is a legal system that permits us to enforce a contract. We don't do well in jurisdictions where there are great political aspects to the sales process, or where there is tremendous volatility in the economic cycle. We have limited our activity to the U.S. and Europe because we feel these regions have such characteristics."

Joe describes the initiation of a typical negotiation: "We manage a pool of capital that is 3.5 billion dollars in size. We are recognized as a credible and consistent buyer of large businesses so that if there is such a business for sale, we will often be approached." An investment banker who is associated with a potential seller initiates the typical negotiation for the seller.

If due diligence establishes it is a business in which there is interest, the firm presents to the seller a proposed contract that would govern the transaction. Joe says, "It would be a very full contract that would provide for a variety of representations about the condition of the business, such as representations as to the ownership of assets and historical financial performance. The contract would provide a series of conditions for the closing, the most important condition being that the representations made in the contract are true at the closing date and that there has been no material adverse change between the signing and the closing."

A typical time frame in the leveraged buyout business is difficult to identify. Some negotiations have lasted as long as a year. Usually there is some time pressure. A single session might last from 2 hours to all night. Ideally, the negotiators would meet every day, but there are often 1-day interruptions for the lawyers to write up agreements reached. Joe offers an example: "We bought a business unit from IBM, where IBM was both a customer and a supplier to the business. There were 73 different contractual arrangements between the two entities, and each had to be separately negotiated, so this was a time-consuming process."

A conventional negotiating session involves a small group. According to Joe, "There might be three people from our firm, two or three of our lawyers, and a comparable number from their side—roughly a dozen people in all." An operation such as the sale of the IBM unit might keep 10 professionals busy for a year. However, it's important to understand that the firm operates on a team basis. There is a legal team, an accounting team, an environmental team, and an insurance team, all of which are out-sourced. As Joe says, "This means that our firm's job is to a certain degree a management job, coordinating those separate organizations."

The people at Joe's firm measure success by whether they have met the firm's principal objective, which is to make money for their limited partners at a rate that equals the 30% compounded mentioned earlier. In terms of successful negotiation strategies, Joe believes, "First of all, you must understand what your objectives are and have that stake in the ground that you can go back to."

There are many important intangibles, most importantly perseverance. Joe advises, "Negotiation can be a very tedious process. It can go on for hours and hours and hours. In some respects, the party who is willing to stay at the table longest wins. The opponent who felt strongly about a point at 3 p.m. is often more amenable at 2 a.m. My own lawyer stays all night at the table if she needs to."

Joe continues, "Next, success depends on the ability to handle the negotiation process in a way that doesn't allow the process to become inflamed— that is, to permit you to move forward by approaching it simply as a job, not as personal combat." Among many other considerations, awareness of objectives, perseverance, and objectivity are success factors in this context.

Joe's example of a major challenge in negotiation was the IBM negotiation mentioned previously. He remembers, "Taking a piece of a business out of a larger corporation is always a difficult thing to do. It's hard to anticipate all the interrelationships between the two. There can be supply contracts, purchase contracts, questions of ownership of intellectual property. For instance, in most corporations, patents and trademarks are generally shared. So, when you take a smaller part out of a larger business, you must be aware of how dependent the smaller part may be on the property of the parent."

For instance, in the IBM case, Joe's firm asked for use of the IBM logo for the new separate entity, a request that IBM had never granted before. It was a matter of great concern to the corporation because its reputation is tied to the products that carry that logo. In Joe's opinion, "Such a situation is bound to be difficult because both parties have very legitimate claims to that single asset. This can be a very long, involved, and demanding process, and one that has in it the seeds for very contentious negotiation."

As is true of other types of negotiation, occasionally typical leveraged buyout negotiations fail. For instance, "Someone may approach us and, after investigation, we may be unable to agree on a price. As mentioned earlier, there are basic contradictions between the philosophies of buying and selling. It may well be that the seller won't agree with our assessment of what we find appropriate for a sale. However, negotiation breaks down more often over the terms of the contract than over price." For instance, Joe's firm might ask for a representation that the financial statements are true and correct. If the seller refused, the firm would not be interested in buying the business, and the negotiations would end.

Contextual Differences

Leveraged buyout negotiations differ from negotiations in other contexts by virtue of the complexities and the amount of risk involved. For instance, in negotiating for real estate, a buyer can get a good title by ordering a survey of the property and title insurance. Joe summarizes, "It's pretty cut and dried. The property will have good title or it won't. An independent authority can establish the *fact*. I don't ask the seller to do anything; I simply go get title insurance and a survey. Whereas in buying a business, I'm asking the seller to make a whole series of representations. That's the difference."

Buying a business from a corporation is also very different from buying a family business, where the relationships involved tend to produce a high level of emotion and unpredictability. In Joe's experience, "With a corporation, if the boss says. 'Sell the business,' that business will be sold. With a family business, often you're not sure the business is going to actually be sold until the contract is signed."

Changes and Conflicts

The financial firm as a buyer of business has become a very well-accepted phenomenon in the United States, and the process has been exported to Europe. Reflecting on the future for European business, Joe says, "This situation has not fully matured yet, meaning it holds further opportunities and greater risks related to different languages and accounting conventions." Despite the linguistic and cultural differences, Joe's firm approaches the negotiation process in exactly the same way in Europe as they do in the United States.

Global competition has driven more business sales and has stimulated more mergers and acquisitions. Joe explains, "The impact of foreign competition on the U.S. has had a very dramatic effect on the way people feel about their businesses. As we became truly a global marketplace, U.S. corporations in the mid- to late 1980s recognized that they had to focus on the businesses that they managed well and divest themselves of the business that they didn't manage well. Noncore businesses were sold."

Joe continues, "We are well advanced in the process of divestiture. U.S. corporations are more focused and efficiently managed today than they were 20 years ago. The process is just beginning to take hold in Europe; they are 10 to 15 years behind us in the evolution of their thinking about how to manage their businesses. You can look at Europe and say to yourself, 'I can see where they're going and, therefore, I can see where the opportunities are.'" The firm has an active European office located in London, where Joe spends 1 week of every month.

Among negotiators involved in leveraged buyouts, there is debate about whether there are greater opportunities in the private or the public sector. In Joe's opinion, "There are a great number of U.S. corporations that are selling at very low multiples. It is commonly thought that this condition affords great opportunity. I think the theory is true, but trying to implement the theory has proven more difficult than anyone expected. The differences in the way you approach a public versus a private transaction are sufficiently great that you want to weigh them. For instance, in a private transaction, when I negotiate with a selling corporation, for some period of time after the closing date, the representations that are made in the contract will survive. In a public transaction, because there is no single entity that you can point to as surviving the transaction, those representations will expire. That's a very great difference between the two."

Joe continues, "In addition, while it's true that multiples are lower in the public sector, converting that into a transaction hasn't been done very successfully. Boards of Directors have proven reluctant to approve a transaction at a significant discount to the market high, even though it represents a substantial discount to the current weaker price."

Joe's firm uses e-mail and the Internet to exchange documents but never to substitute for face-to-face negotiation. In his opinion, "Being across the table from the other party allows a negotiator to understand the nuances of the other person's position. You're not going to get very far without personal interaction. I believe that effective negotiation can only be done on a face-to-face basis."

Joe Rice has been an effective negotiator in the leveraged buyout business for many years. He has both observed and contributed to tremendous growth in this arena. Many of his observations about the process and success elements of negotiation apply not only to this context but also to commercial negotiations in general. In this interview, Joe teaches by example and also leaves us with a reminder: "The art of negotiation is to find a middle ground that is satisfactory to you and the person with whom you're negotiating."

PROFESSIONAL PROFILE

Bargaining Within Respectful Relationships

No negotiations have been more widely reported than those in labor management. However, recent changes in both corporations and unions have impacted the way such negotiations take place. In particular, there is a trend toward mergers and acquisitions for both corporations and unions because increasing in size allows them to amass more resources. In 2000, US West, one of the so-called Baby Bells, was acquired by a wireless company called Qwest. There is speculation that this combined organization is positioning itself to merge with an even larger communication company, possibly in Europe. In the following interview, Annie Hill reflects on how these events and others have changed labor-management negotiations.

As this chapter discussed, the organizational need to maintain identity and distinction from other groups affects labor-management negotiations. Annie Hill and the practitioner in the next profile have both observed a trend in the nature of labor-management relationships: They are becoming increasingly less cooperative and more competitive. From 1980 to the acquisition of US West by Qwest, many of the recommendations made in this chapter were enacted in that organization: focus on common interests, acknowledging the other party's perspective, and building on the positives of the other's proposals. The practitioners' comments about organizational climate reinforce this chapter's discussion of climate. An organizational history of no strikes was interrupted by a bitter, 15-day strike in 1998, and the tone of subsequent negotiations became more competitive. Business acquisitions play a large part in positioning union-management negotiations along the competitive-cooperative spectrum.

Introduction to the Practitioner

Annie Hill served as the president of her local union in Oregon. In 1990, she became a staff representative for the Communications Workers of

America (CWA), an assignment that included being the bargaining agent for her union for contracts with small corporations, such as cable and sign companies. Annie's experience as a staff representative was grounded in good working relationships. While Annie held this position, there were no strikes.

Annie lists skills she believes are critical to her bargaining and negotiation practice: "Knowing what your issues are, knowing when to compromise, having a lot of patience, being able to sell your issues—not only with passion but also with facts. This is true whether I'm selling to members and leaders of the union or to representatives of the company."

Annie also describes a mindset that is important to labor negotiators. She says, "You must accept that you'll never make everyone happy. If you're not okay with that, you're in the wrong work. For instance, with the results of bargaining over an overtime issue, union response varied from 'That's good' to 'It wasn't enough' to 'How could you do this to us?'" A skilled negotiator takes these criticisms in stride.

Annie says it's also important "that the elected reps keep members informed. As much as you try, as much as you're on the phone, the message changes. You just have to keep repeating and repeating so that people don't feel left out of the loop."

Insights About Negotiation

"Pray" is Annie's response to how to prepare for contract negotiations. On a more mundane level, the union collects information. "We will send out a survey to 64 local unions, and it's up to them how they assemble the information," Annie explains. "They prioritize their issues and send us their top 10 about 6 months before the contracts expire. It helps us to know more clearly what membership wants so we don't go into negotiations with a laundry list. We compile that information into a document for the prebargaining period. We begin negotiating 60 days prior to contract expiration. Both the union and US West were comfortable with this process—will the new company want changes?"

In the typical contract negotiation, Annie relates, "Early on, it's quite straightforward. Both sides are presenting their proposals and asking clarifying questions." Recently, the experience has been that the union has completed its proposals in the beginning of the bargaining period. In the last several negotiations, the company has offered parts, but not all, of its proposals in the beginning, largely due to executive turnover shortly before the start of the negotiations. There have also been delays getting input from the benefits committee, which provides vital data, especially about complex health care benefits.

Usually, management and labor send the same number of representatives to the negotiations. In the case of US West, there were 6 from management and 6 from labor. On the management side, there were a number of people supporting their negotiations, usually from labor relations and human resources departments. They do a lot of the legwork. On the union side, Annie says, "We really don't have that. We have our union secretaries. If we have to go back to specific groups for information, the elected representatives will assist."

Annie explains the climate as the negotiations draw to a close: "As you get toward the end of the negotiations, it becomes much more intense. Even with our prioritization, we know we're not going to get everything. We give signals when there are issues we really care about. Some trading goes on."

Discussing what is essential for success in contract negotiations, Annie reflects, "Both parties must want to get there. Be realistic about what you can accomplish. There must be an established relationship [with negotiators on the other side] in which you can talk about the tough issues. You need to know where the other person is coming from. In the past, union and company leaders knew each other well and respected one another. They were able to work through difficult issues and prevent disruptive events, such as strikes."

Annie emphasizes the value of relationship to success in contract negotiations. She explains why it matters: "Let's face it—both parties are coming to the table with needs and wants. If you don't have a sense of what separates those two categories, you're on a collision course. You need a strong relationship to work through the tough issues. You need to have a working relationship with the person you're negotiating with. I don't think you have to like them, but you have to respect them."

Annie's toughest challenge comes from changes in the character of the workplace, which in turn influence labor-management relations. In the 1980s, movements such as quality of work life and partnering moved those relations in a collaborative direction. Company-wide training and contract language reflected this collaborative tone. However, this atmosphere changed in 1994 when the company tried to restructure.

Annie describes what happened to collaborative labor-management relations when re-engineering was introduced: "It all started to crumble and fall apart. The next period was more confrontational than it had been. Now, we're more likely to be stuck in our positions, and the art of compromise has been lost. Now, there are more issues which go to arbitration; in the past, we would have found a way to fix that."

Annie notes, "You can't just pick a date and say, 'Everything changed then'; it's really evolved over a period of time. But it does make you relate differently, and it does make negotiations look very different. Of course, in 1998, we had a strike. Typically, when you get down to the last few days, you only have a few language things left. In 1998, we had 40 to 45 items left to resolve when the contract expired. That is highly unusual! Not only from a negotiating standpoint were we miles apart, but we had many angry people at US West. A lot of people weren't ready to go back. For the rank-and-file members, they'd been pushed so hard by the company that the strike was like a vacation." Exhaustion from overwork enhanced the value of the strike for employees.

In the 1998 negotiations, overtime was a critical issue. Annie explains, "It's one of those tough issues because workers have very different priorities. We have people who would sleep at their workplace so that they can get every single hour and minute of overtime, and then there are others who want to do their 40 hours and then go on to other things. Of course, that's not unique to our workplace. We were able to get some caps on overtime (10 hours per week), which will be phased in. The cap will be reduced to 8 [hours per week] next year."

It's clear that the labor-management relationship in 2001 is quite different from that of 1994. Now that the acquisition by Qwest has occurred, no one knows where that relationship is headed, although contracts expired again in 2001 and were renewed. However, Annie is hopeful about the new leadership: "They're actually doing some positive things, such as bringing the president to meet with the union leadership. We've met them; they've said a lot of the right things. The CEO knows what he wants and has experience dealing with labor before."

Annie worries, "The problem is, some people [union members] don't want to give them [the executives] a chance. They've read critical things about the new leadership in the paper. I think we should give them a chance; then, if things aren't working out, you can always alter your course."

Challenges also arise from executive-level issues. Lack of relationship between the leaders of the two companies that merged has negatively affected interactions with the union. The leaders started off with joint meetings, and then those fell apart. When senior management is divided, it is more difficult for the union to conduct productive bargaining.

Contextual Differences

Differences in corporate cultures often affect relationships between the merged unit and the union. In this case, Annie says, "Their [Qwest's] style is much, much different because they're a start-up company. They're movers and shakers. Seniority is different; there are many young people, and in 2 years they get a lot of stripes. Like many of the other Bell companies, US West has a monopolistic history and is struggling to come out of the old ways. And we have a lot of senior employees who have 25 to 30 years of service. So, from the union standpoint, it's challenging, because the senior workers and the Gen-Xers don't have the same needs and desires." These differences make representing labor's perspective a more complex problem.

According to Annie, challenges may be caused by overly assertive approaches: "Some people come in with big chips on their shoulders, so everything they present is said in an angry, antagonistic way. Every now and then, we all lose our tempers. But what I see is that, for the most part, the people who get listened to are people who can present their positions in logical order, respectfully and calmly. People who are nasty and mean get attention for a short time, and then people close their ears. My experience is that you may occasionally get nasty to emphasize that this is an important issue but, if you do that all the time, you're not going to be very effective."

Because of the 1998 strike, Annie can certainly speak to what happens when negotiations fail. "After the strike began, we divided up the issues. The leaders on both sides took the 12 most important issues and worked on them in separate, closed sessions." This meant that negotiations on the major issues were resolved between the chief negotiator for management and the chief negotiator for the union—two very stubborn, strong-willed persons—with no record of discussion about their reasoning.

During this summit meeting, the rest of the negotiators from both sides continued to work together on the remaining issues, sometimes breaking into smaller groups. Annie recalls, "We worked on contract language, which allowed us to have quite a bit of conversation. We probably spent more time than we would have had there been no strike. Everyone was a little more serious about what's really important." Finally, a settlement package was assembled from the two groups.

The breakdown of negotiations creates enormous pressure for union negotiators. Annie felt "*huge* responsibility. Through my decisions, 75,000 workers and their families were put at risk." Union leaders and members also experience public reactions, which may be very unpleasant. Annie remembers, "As we were picketing during the strike, people would drive by and yell, 'Get back to work!'"

After a strike ends, Annie explains that the aftermath is a difficult time: "We're still dealing with some of the events that happened during the strike. There's still a lot of baggage about that. It's a tough situation; it's a lot of pressure." Issues within the union have continuing repercussions. And many workers continued to be angry with the company when the strike was over. Annie reasons, "A lot of those people don't understand that, when you negotiate, and it's over, you have failed miserably if you have one total winner and one total loser. Both sides have to walk away feeling that they got something. People have to be in a position to save face. You can't just kick people when they're down."

Changes and Conflicts

Annie points to the trend in corporate restructuring—that is, large companies merging into mega-companies: "US West-Qwest is valued at $80 million to $120 million. This is judged to be not big enough—probably, there is another merger on the way. Therefore, there is less time to develop and build relationships, less ability to gauge the reactions of negotiators from management or anticipate what they'll do next. The speed of changes, turnover related to mergers, and the corporate giants which emerge make relationship building across the labor-management divide rather problematical."

Another trend related to mergers relates to the combination of different work cultures noted earlier. Annie muses, "The other thing that will impact us is, how are you going to represent members of the wireless company, whose needs and wants are so different? They are not so interested in lifetime employment as those who joined the telephone company. For instance, pension issues are troublesome. When vested workers leave the company, they do not receive their pension money until they are 65. That doesn't go over very well with younger people, who want to have more control over their money."

A third trend influencing negotiations is low unemployment. "There are not enough people out there to fill all the slots," Annie notes. "And health care rates are skyrocketing. So, having a solid health care plan gives our company an advantage in hiring and retaining workers." These national trends in employment and health care costs give additional leverage to unions in contract negotiations.

Finally, as companies merge, unions are merging. Some union mergers are for survival, whereas others take place to provide unions with more resources. In addition, the scope of union concerns has expanded. Annie gives an example: "For instance, our union includes not only telephone people, but newspaper people, manufacturing people, nursing home workers, and state employees." Jurisdictional lines within unions are blurring.

There are a few areas of disagreement among union negotiators. Annie says that her colleagues often debate the question "To what extent should the union be a partner with the company?" Annie previously strongly favored partnership, "But after living through one cycle, I'm more cautious. Some negotiators favor a relationship-based approach; others are more hard line."

Unions also differ in how they conduct their internal business. "Our union has a reputation for being very democratic," Annie says. "Others are more autocratic." Unions that use a democratic approach have a more complex job in convincing membership to accept proposals worked out at the bargaining table.

In the 12 years Annie Hill has negotiated union contracts, she has seen enormous changes. Up until 1994, labor-management relationships with her Baby Bell employer were marked by a high degree of collaboration. Few issues went to arbitration, and the longest strike lasted one day. Since re-engineering in 1994 and the merger with a wireless communication company in 2000, there have been more arbitrations and a strike which left many scars. The labor-management relationships that supported constructive contract negotiations in the past are at risk. As this book goes to press, Qwest struggles with a $26 billion debt load and numerous federal investigations of its accounting.

PROFESSIONAL PROFILE

KAREN GRAVES, ●
FORMER DIRECTOR OF LABOR
RELATIONS, QWEST COMMUNICATIONS

Management Side: 12 Months of
Preparation for 60 Days of Negotiation

Introduction to the Practitioner

Karen Graves loves to negotiate. And she believes that negotiating union contracts was the best part her job as Director of Labor Relations for US West (now Qwest), one of the Baby Bells. Karen came to this position after serving in the human resources department of one of US West's founding corporations, Mountain Bell. Before she joined a bargaining team to conduct contract negotiations, she was a management representative for grievance reviews.

Karen characterizes the effective negotiator as someone who "knows the issues completely and thoroughly, so you can determine whether there can be compromises, or whether the two sides are so far apart that you'll never reach an agreement." In addition, there must be "complete understanding by both parties of a give-and-take relationship. Neither party can go into negotiations saying, 'It's my way or the highway.' You've got to be able to bend and flex."

Karen continues, "Good listening is the skill most critical to the practice of labor negotiations. Listen to be sure you understand the needs of the company, the needs of the employees, the needs of the institution. In addition, you must have confidence in your ability to present your ideas and to convince the other side that what you need is just as important as what they need." Last but not least, Karen emphasizes the importance of physical and mental endurance. "You can't wear down. I don't think a good negotiator can become weary and then say, 'Okay, I'm tired, let's end it for the day.' If the topic under discussion is still relevant and still at issue, you have to keep going." Contract negotiators listen carefully, possess confidence in their persuasive abilities, and maintain stamina.

Insights About Negotiation

Karen describes 12 months of extensive preparation that preceded 60 days of contract talks. Karen explains, "At US West (now Qwest), we started about a year ahead of time. You really have to start that far ahead. We began by meeting with all levels of management, from vice presidents to the first-line supervisors. We used interviews and focus groups—whatever worked best for the organization. We attempted to discover what things in the contract were not working well for them or needed to be changed. We took it from the ridiculous to the sublime, asking what they would like. The interviewing process could take from 3 to 6 months." In an organization with hundreds of executives, managers, and supervisors, these procedures are lengthy.

The department of labor relations also reviews conflict history. "We did an environmental scan as part of the preparation. We looked at the number and type of arbitrations during the current contract period—what we won, what we lost. We examined whether there were any contract changes needed as a result of arbitrations experienced under the past contract. We looked at what grievances reached the third step [formal adjudication] and asked whether there was anything in that group of grievances we needed to consider during negotiations." Although this review is necessary, arbitrations and grievances didn't play a substantial part in generating issues for negotiation.

Karen described the next phase of preparation: "Then, with the labor attorneys, we [the management team] charted all of the wish lists, all of the needs, all of the desires, and then we inserted our two cents' worth. That process worked very well for us—not so much to determine what the issues were as to determine where our training needs were. In the interviews, we found that people would put things on the wish list that they could already do under the current contract, and that helped us identify where we had training needs. Then, if we could, before we went into bargaining, we went to those same groups and trained them so that they were comfortable we didn't ignore their ideas, but their bargaining team knew the contract before we went into negotiations." In large organizations, preparation involves creating a common understanding of the current contract as well as what is proposed for the next one.

Karen concludes, "The bottom line is, by the time we sat down to have the first negotiation session, we had our team lined up, we had a contingency planning team lined up, we had the bargaining team well versed on what the issues were and the leadership team clear on which issues we were pursuing and in what order. And we knew what our marching orders were and in what priority order we would pursue our needs. Until then, we weren't ready to sit at the table. It takes a long time to get all that together and then, of course, some issues are moving targets. Two weeks before bargaining, some issues may change because the business has changed."

Respectful communication typifies labor-management bargaining. Karen reports, "I've been at the table five times [five sessions lasting for 60 or more days each], and 99% of the time I've seen professional negotiations. We are a professional organization on our side of the table, and the union is a professional organization. We're generally very respectful of one another. There's no sense for either side to get nasty. We're both trying to get the best contract for our company and our employees so, while we don't always see eye to eye, we have a common goal. Between 1% and 3% of the time, I have seen unprofessional behavior, such as screaming and hollering. What I've found is the best way to deal with that is to call a recess so the emotions can subside, and then we get back together." Karen's experience of respectful negotiations is congruent with that of her union counterpart, Annie Hill.

There is an underlying assumption by both union and management that technological changes will cause frequent modifications in their communications business sector. In Karen's words, "Technology has moved so fast and we've worked well together. The union had a healthy understanding that we're not going to keep doing things according to the dark ages of technology, and that helped us in the provisions of the contract we negotiated. We both believe that members are treated fairly." Such a shared understanding would be an advantage for any organization's negotiations.

Karen has worked on teams with union representative Annie Hill three times: in 1992, 1995, and 1998. Karen remembers, "In that last round, she and I were both cochairs [for our respective sides] at the negotiating table. I was the spokesperson and led the majority of the negotiations for management." Many negotiation experts would conclude that the lengthy relationship between these negotiators would also be an advantage in bringing the negotiation to a successful conclusion for both parties because the women have had time to develop an understanding of each other. Trust and respect marks their relationship.

Karen notes the timeline for typical contract negotiations: "We gave ourselves 60 days to reach agreement and, since our contracts expire in mid-August, this means a typical session starts in mid-June. I called the first week 'Getting to Know You.' The executives from the company came in to give a state-of-the-business report. It was a two-way dialogue in that the union asked questions. These sessions lasted from 2 to 4 hours." Unlike Annie and Karen, some of the negotiators will not have known each other before this first week.

Karen continues, "The second week, we would start receiving all the union proposals. The process is that the union presents all of its proposals before the company does anything. This took from 2 to 4 days, including questions of clarification. Then, the company responded to the union proposals, as well as presented their own. When we got into the serious part of negotiation, it was generally an 8-hour day at the beginning and whatever it took at the end. Other than the Fourth of July holiday, we met every day. Sometimes there was a 3-day weekend toward the end of July. Then, the last week or 10 days before the contract expires, you're working against the clock." Clearly, momentum builds as the two sides move closer to the contract expiration date.

Numbers of issues on the table vary from session to session. Karen recalls, "The most issues I've ever seen were 300 proposals from the union in 1992. And it was everything from the ridiculous to the sublime. They have to propose what their membership asks for. In 1998, they culled it down to approximately 100 issues. Management has a much smaller number of issues—at the most 50. Of these, there may be close to 25 top issues. The rest of the time, we're responding to them."

Karen is emphatic that success depends on complete respect between the parties for each other's issues. She remarks, "If you're going to respond, 'What you proposed was B.S.,' you might as well not be there. But if each side goes in [saying to themselves] 'Okay, we're going to get some things that we think are stupid, we are going to get some things that we can probably agree with,' then we can manage. I've been in individual sessions where we were practically holding hands, and I've been in sessions that ended in a strike." Karen's union counterpart, Annie Hill, also prioritized respect for those across the table as the most important variable in the success or failure of contract negotiations.

Contextual Differences

Karen does not judge trust a critical variable in successful labor-management negotiations. She argues, "I don't think that trust between the parties has anything to do with success because, when you get right down to the actual proposals, they are based on facts. When we have a need, we have to have the facts to demonstrate that need, and the same goes for the union. They have to [rely on] something of substance rather than questions of trust. Where I think trust comes in is the atmosphere. If you don't trust the person you're talking to across the table, the atmosphere is very bad."

A critical variable in successful contract negotiations is anticipated agreement from the constituents who are not at the table, such as union members and boards of directors. Karen notes, "We have to keep in mind that everything we do at the table must be ratified outside. We do as much as we can working through the management teams to determine: 'Is this going to fly? What do you think the employees will think about it?' Something that both sides may think is terrific may result in employees throwing up their hands in disgust. Then, we have to go back to the table to make revisions."

Karen's toughest challenge came in 1998 when the union called a strike. She remembers, "It felt to me like they were gunning for us. It didn't matter if we gave them a million dollars in cash across the table, they were going to strike. That was tough, because I'm a very honest negotiator and that last 24 hours, it didn't matter what I said. I could give them the Taj Mahal and they still felt they needed a strike. Their philosophy was 'give us what we want' and mine was 'give and take.' I took that personally for about 24 hours." Challenge in this case takes the form of a situation in which the management negotiator has no control over whether a strike will occur.

Karen reflects on the breakdown in negotiations that led to the strike: "The management negotiation team took the position that the management runs the business. Over the years, the perception was that the union had gotten too involved in running the business. It was a philosophical position that manifested itself in practical ways that the union didn't like. The union was determined to walk out. They had to show some muscle, regardless of what was on the table. Therefore, some time had to pass before a settlement could be reached. Politically for them, they couldn't just call a strike and then run right back and agree." In this case, the strike lasted 15 days.

US West called in a federal mediator. In Karen's opinion, "The mediator ran back and forth between their side and our side carrying messages. Frankly, I didn't see that it was worthwhile. I didn't see that the process moved us along."

Karen believes that the breakthrough came when the chief negotiator for the company said to the mediator, "This seems to be moving awfully slowly; I'm going to start meeting one-on-one with the union's chief negotiator." In her view, It was the discussions between those two that created the impetus for resolution. There were about a dozen issues they worked on and then assigned to a group to work out the details. She thinks that "the mediation was very valuable for our public image, showing that we did all work toward agreement. Bringing in a federal mediator showed an honest effort to work through the issues and minimize the disruption for our customers. The mediator did not settle the strike, but he pointed us in the right direction and created the atmosphere to achieve a settlement." Mediation was helpful in an indirect way.

Because of economic pressures, employees became more receptive as the strike continued. Had it lasted one more day, their health care benefits would have been cut off. The union does have insurance policies that cover such events, so if someone had lost their health care and needed surgery, their insurance would have covered that. Karen reflects, "I never felt we were cutting anyone off at the knees because they would have been covered, at least for the big stuff." However, potential loss of health care benefits was part of management's leverage in ending the strike.

Karen assesses the residual effects of the breakdown of negotiations, saying, "There is still ill will 2 years later [as of 2001]. It's not trivial. As I said, I took the strike personally because I'd worked with these people forever, and I thought, 'How could you do this to me?' And then I realized, this is a lot bigger than me and them. I think the union is still stinging from the strike because some of the issues they fought for are not popular with their members. The union leadership read it wrong, and they're still getting jazz from the locals. Also, there were a few political ramifications for union leaders. There were some local presidents who chose not to run again, and there were a few leaders who were defeated in a subsequent election, purportedly because of the new contract." Failed negotiations may result in rancor and damaged relationships not only between labor and management, but within union ranks.

Changes and Conflicts

Karen does not perceive any new trends in labor-management negotiations. In her words, "We've been doing it the same way for so long."

One area of disagreement that Karen highlights is telecommuting. In her words, "We think that telecommuting makes sense. We have a program called Home Office to supply anyone who's working from home with the latest and greatest technology. We would like even more of our employees to telecommute. The union does not agree. If we have employees who have serious family illness, and they could work but couldn't leave home (such as caring for a sick child who had to be nursed every 2 hours), the union has agreed to work with us on a case-by-case basis." Karen anticipates that telecommuting may be a significant issue in future negotiations.

Karen explains, "The union's philosophy about telecommuting is that they wouldn't have the control over their membership that they have when everyone is in the same workplace. And they want 'all for one and one for all'—that is, equal conditions for everyone. The union hasn't had enough serious pressure from members to change its position against telecommuting." It's also possible that Occupational Health and Safety (OSHA) regulations could greatly complicate the issue of telecommuting.

Whether making sense out of past negotiations or anticipating future issues, Karen Graves offers a thoughtful, experienced perspective. She generates and presents management proposals that are grounded in extensive preparation. She approaches her union counterparts with respect. Her final thought about contract negotiation is "I love it. It was the best part of my job."

PROFESSIONAL PROFILE

JUDY TOWERS REEMSTMA, ●
PRODUCER OF DOCUMENTARIES FOR TELEVISION

Negotiation in TV Production:
Dealing with Multiple Parties

We are vaguely aware that the television we watch represents an investment of many hours and many dollars. Actors, technicians, directors, and other skilled assistants have contributed to the programs we see. However, before all the shooting begins, there is a producer whose ideas initiate the program and who must negotiate with financial sponsors to guarantee production. Before filming a documentary, the producer negotiates with the persons and institutions whose stories will be featured. During the shooting, the producer negotiates with the technicians whose shots bring his or her ideas to vision. And, after the shooting, there are negotiations with executives who must approve the film before it airs. In this interview, Judy Towers Reemstma describes the different negotiations necessary to produce a high-quality documentary. Her production skills are clearly complemented by her skills as a negotiator.

With so many persons and departments involved, it is not surprising that many of the contextual factors for organizational negotiation explored in this chapter apply in this context. Producers compete with each other for limited resources available to fund video and film production. The nature of artistic involvement and the lengthy nature of projects mean that the level of emotional attachment to one's position may be high. The producer with a proven track record has more power than does the novice in this organizational setting. The artistic aspects of production mean some issues cannot be compromised in negotiation.

Introduction to the Practitioner

Many successful productions and awards have marked Judy's career. She produced several videos with Bill Moyers, including *People Like Us*

(Moyers & Reemstma, 1983) and *Healing and the Mind* (Moyers & Reemstma, 1993). At CBS News, Judy produced videos with Walter Cronkite, Charles Kuralt, and Marlene Sanders. At NBC, she produced programs for MacNeil/Lehrer, including a series with C. Everett Koop, MD. As an independent producer, Judy has made films for Turner Broadcasting and several public television stations: WETA in Washington, D.C., and WNET in New York City. She has received national awards for writing and producing, including three Emmys and the Columbia Dupont Writers Guild and Sidney Hillman Awards.

A modest beginning preceded these achievements. During her summer vacations from Wellesley College, Judy worked at a TV station as a "vacation relief secretary." Despite her lowly status, Judy reflects, "This allowed me to see how various parts of a television operation worked and how much fun some of the people were having. Willard Scott was there doing a talk show, and Jim Henson was there making the puppets which were the prototypes for the Sesame Street puppets." Later, Judy moved to New York to work for CBS, where she began to participate in research and writing. Following a typical career track for television documentary makers, she later advanced to associate producer and eventually to producer.

Insights About Negotiation

Judy identifies several negotiation skills needed when working with the different people involved in documentary production. Certain skills are necessary for almost everyone, from young cameramen and camerawomen to senior executives. The first useful skill is to listen carefully. Judy explains how complicated the listening process is in her industry: "Producers like to think that they are in total control, but the fact of the matter is that you're producing for broadcast, and there are *layers* of people who have to look at it and pass on it. The process for a typical 1-hour documentary is that you usually have an executive producer who looks at your rough cut and makes some changes. Next, when that person is satisfied that the documentary is as good as it can get, the president of CBS news screens it. That was a helpful system, because you didn't have to confront the top brass alone—you had your executive producer who'd already worked out one level of editing." In the sessions with the top network brass, a new round of negotiations is held until the film is ready for release.

Judy comments on her reaction to the feedback offered by network executives, saying, "My own experience is that these transactions, which are in effect a kind of negotiation, were 85% to 90% helpful. That is, others will see something you did which was either a downright mistake or, more often, you structured the story in such a way that you understood it because you were so familiar with the material, but a first-time television viewer would have been lost. For the most part, I had the good fortune to work with terrific senior producers and senior executives at CBS. If there was a hole in the film, they would catch it." A producer must listen very carefully to what people are saying, because incorporating their feedback ensures that what goes on the air is of very high quality.

Judy continues, "There may be a 10% to 15% range where the producer believes that the feedback is wrong. A boss will be insisting on something that you believe won't work because you know the story and the people involved. In that case, you pick your battles. I was very fortunate for most of my career to work for people who listened, and I did not fight everything. So, when I did pick a battle, they knew I wasn't picking it just to have my own way. Then, the boss would most likely say, 'Okay, if you feel that strongly about it, I respect your judgment.' One of the big keys is knowing what to negotiate and not trying to negotiate everything." Reserving her resistance to executive feedback to a few important instances gave Judy more credibility and therefore more leverage in these negotiations.

Judy notes the importance of knowing with whom you're negotiating. She recalls, "I was in two situations over the course of my career where it [negotiation] broke down. In one instance, I couldn't negotiate because someone else needed to take almost complete control. There was no way to negotiate. In one instance, the executive had never done a film like the one I'd shot, so I was trying to negotiate with someone who hadn't had the same experience I had. I'd shot the whole thing, and then he felt very strongly that he wanted to edit it. At a certain point, there's not room for two people in an editing room. I simply backed out of that one, and he took the material." The final approval meeting was where Judy occasionally found the toughest negotiating challenges. Coworkers who are collegial and have respect for each other are essential to the success of negotiations in the TV production arena.

The fourth negotiation skill Judy notes concerns the ability to work as a team member. Sometimes, documentary crews fall short of their best work because experienced producers do not respect the opinions of younger members, such as cameramen and camerawomen. Judy believes in using the talents of all members of the crew, saying, "The cameraman must understand your vision, and you must respect his calling the most effective shot. When working with younger people, a producer must make sure they are heard and that their views are incorporated in the filming. Don't ever assume they don't need to be heard." Again, Judy emphasizes close, active listening as a skill that will encourage constructive feedback and lead to a better product.

Judy comments on what's required for success in negotiating with the subjects of a documentary: "First, you have the story idea, then you research possible people or institutions who are living examples of that story. Once you decide on a group, you have to persuade them to let you in. In this preparation phase, there are always fears on the part of those persons about how their story will be portrayed. If there's a story, there is something *raw*. In addition, people get anxious when they see camera and sound crews tromping into their house with all that equipment." A documentary producer must deal with several compelling reasons why the potential subjects of a documentary may be reluctant to be filmed.

Judy negotiates with potential subjects in the following way: "The main thing is to explain to these people why this story is important, why you want to do it, why you think their story in particular is important. The only way you can justify barging into someone's life is to convince that person that the film may be helpful to someone else. Usually, people are responsive to that. You also have to give them a sense that you are trustworthy, that you're not going to make something out of the story that it isn't. If the film were made the wrong way, it could be harmful. The biggest part of negotiating with potential subjects is quelling their fears. Also, they must have faith in your skills." Similar to negotiating in other contexts, success depends on establishing trust within a personal relationship.

In an institutional setting, as opposed to a family or personal setting, knowing who has the authority and persuading them to grant access is critical to success. The strongest argument for institutional participation is that there is some good that will come out of filming this story. Judy acknowledges, "Sometimes, this is a risky decision for an institution to make. In a film we wanted to make about nursing, we were fortunate in finding a forward-looking dean of the Nursing School at the University of Pennsylvania. She made it possible for us to have all kinds of access in that health care system." Other producers have thought they had institutional agreement to shoot, only to have the organization back out at the eleventh hour.

Judy hands off the job of negotiating with film crews and assistants regarding financial arrangements. She feels it is better to separate the artistic and the financial relationships. She comments, "I know who I want to work with and I know what the budgets are. I find it's better not to have financial conversations with someone you are having artistic conversations with. Typically, there's a production manager on documentary projects who will handle booking crews, contracts, and payroll."

Judy's typical production job involves several different phases and takes considerable time to film. Network executives approve a brief proposal and provide a budget, typically ranging between $250,000 and $300,000. Production of a 1-hour documentary often requires 6 months but could take as long as a year. Judy explains, "You shoot a story over a period of time because the narrative develops with time. I like to try to figure out a story that is in its beginning. When we start, I won't know exactly what the middle and end are going to be. So, it's a bit of a high wire act." Given that the nature of a proposed project is sometimes sketchy at the outset, one assumes that Judy's reputation provides considerable leverage toward executive acceptance of the proposal.

Judy recounts the research period that preceded filming of *What Shall We Do About Mother?* (Reemstma, 1980), a film she produced that won several Emmys. The film is about middle-aged children taking care of parents. She recalls, "In September, I called every institution that had to do with nursing homes. In addition, I must have called 100 families and interviewed a number of them. Lord knows, I went all over the country searching for the right family for this story. I was looking for one where elderly parents were about to go into a nursing home, where it was clear there was going to be change in the next several months." In this field, before negotiation with the subjects of the documentary begins, extensive research and information gathering takes place.

Judy continues, "I identified a family in Pittsburgh where one parent was just about go into a nursing home. There was another set of parents who were living with a child, and it was clear that they could not continue to live there much longer. There were events in this family that were consequences of this kind of stress. I thought to myself, 'This might work.' But, in the conclusion of the first interview, a family member informed Judy, 'If you think I've got a problem, you should talk to my daughter's husband's mother! She's got her two parents and his one parent.' One of the most important judgments in my business is to know when you have a story and when the material should go into the wastebasket. A producer must wait until the right version of the story presents itself."

After a suitable family has been identified, the producer's next job is to persuade them to participate and to negotiate the conditions of that participation. Judy remembers, "It took a week to persuade this family to allow us to make them the subjects of our documentary. I had to do some fast talking; however, they seemed amenable, and they seemed to see why there was a reason to allow this nuisance in their lives. Shooting took 6 months, and I was editing over the next 3 months." Although there is a uniquely artistic element involved in recognizing what version of the story to pursue, preparation for a project is similar to negotiation in other contexts, where problem definition and timing are critical to success. When the shooting is about to begin, participants sign contracts signifying their willingness to be involved.

Network executives who may approve the project don't look at the film until it's in rough cut form. Judy notes, "Actually, I approached these negotiations not with a rough cut, but with a film that was as good as I could get it at that point. That seemed to work well." Judy came to that table with her best material.

The production process is sometimes a challenging one. Judy deals with several types of frustrations. Occasionally, she goes so far as to remove her name from a project after months of shooting: "I can think of issues that were worked out in discussion, but when it gets down to basic stuff, somebody's got to be in charge. For instance, you must edit a film in the way that reflects reality as you know it from your prior involvement with the subject. In the documentary business, you're part filmmaker, but you're also part recorder, and you've got to have your facts straight. Obviously, the truth walks in many sets of clothes. But, you [the producer] have studied the situation, interviewed people, and think you have a grasp on it. When someone wants to make changes in such a way that is not true, it just won't fly. So, if you feel you can't get the facts as you know and understand them across to someone, you're really *skunked* in that negotiation." Judy believes that most things in her business are negotiable, but faithfulness to the facts of the story is a nonnegotiable issue for her.

A second type of frustration Judy encounters relates to obtaining funding for public television documentaries. In her experience, "You write and you write and you write proposals, and then you write scripts, and you haven't shot a damn foot of film! In one of the most frustrating experiences of my life, I, along with partners, tried to produce a series on World War II in conjunction with the 50-year anniversary of the end of that war (1995). We had a total of 20 Emmys between us. We had a board of advisors that included Doris Kearns Goodwin and Stephen Ambrose. We had professional fund-raisers working with us. Everyone said, 'This is a natural!'"

Judy identifies where the partners were successful and where they reached impasse. "We received money from the Corporation for Public Broadcasting, and we got a lot of money from the National Endowment for the Humanities. That was a treadmill that takes 2 years. But we could not raise any corporate money." This project failed because Judy and her partner were not able to get all the necessary players–in this case, corporations—to come to the table.

One frustrating aspect of this impasse was that Judy still doesn't know what she did wrong, saying, "I haven't a clue!" She wishes she could take a lesson from this failure, but she still can't puzzle it out. She laments, "That's the worst part. It's a good thing that the people who fought World War II were more successful than the people who were trying so hard to produce a series about them. I said to them at the time, 'You just wait. There will be a BBC series.' Of course there was. The British preempted the United States."

A third challenge is maintaining professionalism during the shooting of the film. Judy narrates the scenario: "You're been involved in a film for the better part of a year and you are working pretty hard. You're on location, away from home, or even out of the country for extended periods. You can get quite emotionally entangled in the production, and your ability to negotiate intelligently may be compromised. I have learned how important it is to disentangle my own emotions from the film but, even so, I was not always completely successful." Similar to negotiation in other stressful contexts, emotional control in this setting enables the negotiator to build her best case.

Contextual Differences

Negotiation in the service of film production differs in a significant way from other contexts. According to Judy, "All negotiations share the necessity for two-way communication. However, as a producer, there are issues about which I cannot negotiate. One can't compromise journalistic values. In many other kinds of negotiation, there can be tradeoffs. For instance, in personal relationships, there can be compromise. She watches the football game with him, then they both attend a sappy movie." Although some issues in personal relationships may be nonnegotiable, the artistic and journalistic aspects of documentaries set negotiation in this context apart.

Changes and Conflicts

Judy is not aware that the process of producing documentaries has changed in any substantive way since she has been in the business. She notes, "There are always new technologies, but those seldom change the nature of negotiations. The basics remain as they have been. The business has expanded onto the Internet and cable television. Therefore, the networks have less dominance than they did previously."

Producers differ with regard to negotiation style. Judy says, "You would find that there are some producers more confrontational than I am. However, negotiating success has to do with whether or not you're respected on the basis of your record. If you are respected on your record, if you can be trusted, you will be heard." A producer with a portfolio of acclaimed documentaries achieves leverage in negotiations, regardless of style.

Judy Reemstma has established a record of films that are highly regarded in her industry and well known by documentary viewers. She was mentored by some of the best-known names in the business and has gone on to make her own mark. Her achievements reflect talent, expertise, and the skill requisite for negotiating from proposal to broadcast. Although the artistic aspects of production mean some issues cannot be compromised, the elements of success and challenges she identifies may be found in many other negotiation contexts.

CHAPTER **10**

COMMUNITY NEGOTIATION

*It is no longer acceptable for such decisions to be made by
a few powerful leaders who purport to act on behalf of the
many but who refuse to involve the many in their deliber-
ations. . . . Unless the public's demands for involvement
are heeded, decisions can prove meaningless in the face of
the public's apathy or active opposition.*

— Thomas (1995, p. 1)

During the past two decades, many organizations and businesses flat-
tened their organizational structure. Leaders placed a greater priority on
inclusion of organizational members in decision-making processes. The
benefits were significant, including greater buy-in during implementation,
more information on which to base decisions and, in many cases, higher-
quality decisions. In many settings, hierarchical structures gave way to more
horizontal, inclusive systems that emphasized values such as fairness, openness, responsibility, and integrity. Described as consensus building, the same
shift occurred in public discussion of issues.

The roots of this shift to greater public participation lie in the cultural
diffusion of power away from central authority and in changes to the legal
and congressional landscapes. Special-interest and citizen groups gained

systemic acceptance and a great deal of clout in getting their agendas before Congress. Government and legislative organizations found that early inclusion of people who will be affected by policy decisions reduced resistance and costly court battles.

Sources of tension in community negotiation are identity needs, such as respect, reputation, self-image, and belief that the opinions of community members are valued. People want to know that they have a say about who their neighbors are, how they're treated by others, and decisions that affect their community. Issues that can cause community conflict include noise levels in a neighborhood, proximity of industry development, location of low-cost housing, or the creation of a home for troubled adolescents in an established neighborhood. Homeowners argue that, as taxpayers, they should have some say about decisions that affect housing values, safety, privacy.

CONTEXTUAL FACTORS ● FOR COMMUNITY NEGOTIATIONS

Structure

The most visible aspect of community groups is the large number of participants, largely volunteers, held together by a common purpose. A great number of tangential discussions take place because negotiations occur over many months and participants change from session to session. Negotiations stall as new negotiators express priorities different from those of previous negotiators.

Defining the relevant publics can be a prominent concern in community problem solving or negotiation. Who should be included in the discussions? Having strong feelings about an issue is insufficient reason to be included in the negotiations. The following are among the types of people who should be included:

- People with information that provides understanding about issues
- Representatives from groups who would be affected by decisions generated by agreements or decisions
- Parties who could later block or sabotage agreements if they are not included in discussions
- If public acceptance of decisions is necessary, inclusion of parties favored by the wider public

Thomas (1995) advises,

The risk of being too exclusivist in the initial definition is probably greater than the risk of being too inclusive. . . . Public decisions may be threatened more by interested groups that were overlooked than by uninterested groups that were not. (p. 60)

To foster inclusiveness, community groups involved in the problem solving of public issues frequently choose to select members from a broad base of interest groups. However, because of the potential for polarization or barriers created by hard-liners, Zartman (2001) advises such groups to select members who possess both an openness to a diversity of ideas and sufficient power to counter tactics by hard-liners who seek to prevent agreements. Inclusive membership must balance diverse membership with the ability of participants to function collaboratively.

One strength of organizational or interpersonal negotiation is that parties have a continuing relationship. Parties invest in processes and people because they know they will have to deal with the same people again at another time. In community negotiations, discussions rely on *involvement of volunteers* who may have little commitment to others involved in the negotiation. They can make positional statements without worrying about the impacts the statements may have on the group. In addition, the citizen representatives may lack adequate negotiation skills or awareness about the differences between integrative and distributive outcomes. In one land-development discussion, one of the parties complained about a representative whose only concern about zoning issues was whether fire trucks would have adequate access to the land in the event of a fire; the representative was by day a construction worker and by night a volunteer firefighter. Another representative encountered a different problem: "When I come to our community negotiations, I have to dumb down to people who find it difficult to look critically at issues. Their interests are very specific and may miss the broader picture." Crowfoot and Wondolleck (1990) explain, "Strategies stressing collaborative problem-solving, negotiations, and consensus decision making confront many citizen organizations with unfamiliar options and requirements for information and skills they may not possess" (p. 4).

After volunteers are recruited, coordinating and supervising their involvement can be difficult. Brudney (1990) explains, "Given the relative autonomy of volunteers, a heavy-handed approach to supervision can be expected to elicit antagonism and attrition, rather than compliance" (p. 109). Obtaining the positive contribution of volunteers requires leaders who employ techniques akin to persuasion and coaching rather than coercing. Mismanaged volunteers who believe that they are not heard or that their contributions are not valued can become a substantial emotional drain on both leaders and group processes.

Lack of a sense of community can be an issue in some community discussions. Collaboration by diverse groups of people in public settings can be difficult if people feel distant from their neighbors or distrust people from another part of town. Building a sense of community sometimes involves choreographing the seating arrangements for group negotiations. Groups sitting opposite each other or around square tables may be more adversarial than those sitting side by side. Fisher, Ury, and Patton (1991) observe,

> The physical reinforces the psychological. Physically sitting side by side can reinforce the mental attitude of tackling a common problem together. People facing each other tend to respond personally and engage in dialogue or argument; people sitting side by side in a semi-circle of chairs facing a blackboard tend to respond to the problem depicted there. (p. 61)

Building a sense of community through either seating arrangements or structured discussion may promote a sense of working together on common problems.

The slow pace of large group negotiations can be a difficult factor for many participants in community negotiations. Long, drawn-out meetings and a series of many meetings with slow progress can test the patience of group members. Susskind and Cruikshank (1987) explain,

> The stakeholders in public disputes tend to feel increasingly threatened as the dispute drags on; they are more and more likely to posture and "grandstand" as events get beyond their control. As the conflict intensifies, they are less likely to listen seriously and think clearly. . . . It is easy for disputing parties to lose control of the circumstances. (p. 93)

Compared with interpersonal and organizational negotiations, community, neighborhood, and church disputes have greater need for predictable processes and leaders who effectively facilitate the processes. Effective negotiation cannot occur if disputants get bogged down in disagreements about data, tangential arguments triggered by emotional reactions, or less important issues. The pace and progress of negotiations must provide participants with sufficient confidence that their interests will be addressed in a fair and timely manner.

Norms and Values

In organizational negotiations, damage to reputation frequently is sufficient penalty to prevent personal attacks or intense displays of emotion. Formal organizational norms govern which messages are shared and which are withheld. Community groups often lack similar norms, permitting more uninhibited displays of emotion about subjects that parties care about deeply. A common complaint in many community groups is the inability to control unproductive comments made by some of the group's members. The facilitator functions more as a referee than a process coordinator. Innes (1999) states that consensus-building processes stand a greater likelihood of success if the group "follows the principles of civil discourse . . . face-to-face discussions in which all participants are respected and listened to, have equal access to information, and are able to learn about each other's interests" (p. 648). Large-group discussion frequently becomes chaotic when participants use community meetings to further their personal agendas, interests, and goals. Agreed-upon ground rules are essential for healthy functioning of community discussions.

Both as participants in and as leaders of community-based discussions, we should encourage the discussion and development of norms that will discourage unproductive and polarizing behavior. These norms should emphasize respect for differences and openness to other points of view. Norms or guidelines serve a similar purpose that rudders do for ships: They keep the group on course in intended directions. A few of the norms that promote successful group negotiations include the following:

- Explain and clarify information as it is shared.
- Build relationships by using language that facilitates trust and commitment to working together.
- Listen without interruptions, even if you don't agree with what you're hearing.
- Acknowledge the hearing and understanding of information as it is shared by others.
- Promote language that demonstrates mutual respect as parties explore issues of concern.
- Generally, it is best to provide full disclosure of information early. Discovery of information at a later time can create doubt and mistrust, which can become barriers to agreement.
- The group shall view conflicts as mutual problems to be solved.

Community negotiations involve a great deal more value discussions than negotiations in other contexts. Carpenter and Kennedy (1988) state,

> Nearly all public controversies entail divergent beliefs about what is right and what is wrong, what is just and what is unjust. Many policy decisions are essentially choices among competing values, and some of the most heated of all public controversies result when someone's fundamental beliefs about what is important are threatened. (p. 10)

Discussions in these contexts often involve competing values, such as quality of life versus economic development or individual needs versus community needs. Environmental negotiation may weigh the opening of forest terrain ski runs or recreational activities against danger to animal habitats. The Environmental Protection Agency (EPA) or State Health Department might establish levels of safety for drinking water or soil contamination, but community members approach the issue with their own beliefs about levels of safety based on their value for the land. A 1996 survey of American attitudes reflects the ambivalence many Americans have about which values should have priority in discussion of public policy; 31% of adults believed that we should protect the environment even if it means the loss of economic benefits associated with development. However, within this 31%, 56% said "only some protection" and 17% said "hardly any" (Mitchell, 1998). Value discussions can be some of the most difficult disputes to resolve because they involve positional orientations to problems with little room for compromise.

In some negotiations, stakeholders' interests may be incompatible. In these cases, the goal of negotiations may be to create and sustain dialogue and promote understanding between parties rather than to settle disputes. In essence, the disputing parties agree to disagree and learn to live with an unstable situation. These kinds of understandings can exist between neighbors who do not like each other, homeowners and factories, or Israel and Palestine.

Relationship

Searches for solutions to problems that involve many parties in a community can be especially challenging because of a growing *distrust* citizens have about public institutions and political leaders. Every 2 years, The National Opinion Research Center in Chicago conducts a national face-to-face survey that asks Americans about their attitudes on a number of issues, including government, public issues, family, and religion.

Table 10.1 summarizes the center's 1996 survey of 2,900 adults. The data provides information about the level of confidence that many Americans have in their leaders. Since 1976, regardless of gender, confidence in leaders in Congress, the executive branch of government, and the press has been in a steady decline, whereas the confidence level for leaders in the church and major industry has remained relatively stable.

The Kettering Foundation conducted similar surveys using a series of citizen focus groups held across the United States (Kettering Foundation, 1991). It found that a growing number of Americans don't believe that their leaders understand the needs of citizens. People complained that leaders entrusted with the public's interests "neither connect with the concerns of citizens nor make any sense to them" (Kettering Foundation, 1991, p. 4). People in the focus groups reported that they felt disconnected from the political process in three ways: the setting of political agendas, the framing of issues, and how issues are discussed. They perceived that special-interest groups, professional politicians, political action committees, lobbyists, and the media dominate public-policy discussions. This distrust of leaders and processes can make negotiation of community issues especially challenging. Instead of focusing on integrative goals, citizens promote distributive goals and make statements emphasizing values and rights.

Table 10.1   American Attitudes About Its Leaders

Confidence Level in:	Percentage of Americans		
	Great Deal	*Only Some*	*Hardly Any*
Congress	8	43	46
Executive branch	10	43	45
Supreme Court	28	50	17
The press	11	48	39
Church leaders	25	51	19
Major companies	23	59	14
Education	23	58	18

Based on information from Mitchell (1998)

William Potapchuk (1995), executive director of the Program for Community Problem Solving in Washington, D.C., argues that overcoming public cynicism and distrust of politics requires processes designed to promote inclusiveness through multiple avenues of participation. The success of community problem solving will involve proactive planning that encourages open deliberation of all dimensions of the issues. This priority explains, in part, the positive effect that between-meeting planning and building relationships had on the ability to reach agreements in the Hispanic-Mexican national neighborhood described in Box 10.2 later in this chapter. In addition, Potapchuk (1995) lists the following factors, which build trust and relationship, as contributing to the success of community-based discussions:

- Involve stakeholders at the earliest possible stages of problems.
- Provide an early, proactive response to potentially contentious issues.
- Involve stakeholders in shaping the agenda for the problem-solving discussions.
- Create an opportunity for stakeholders who are not involved in the task force discussions to express opinions.
- Seek common ground and balance between stakeholder solutions and government protocols and decision-making needs.

The success of community negotiation will be a function of the quality of relationships developed by group participants. Breaking down stereotypes, assumptions about what others think and believe, and misunderstandings will promote relationships conducive to problem solving. Groups who develop a history together and shared understandings will be more successful than those who don't.

Communication

Several assumptions negatively influence communication in some community groups. The first is the following assumption: "If I just tell them, they will understand." Parties engage in a great deal of telling without providing explanations that may be necessary for understanding. Group effectiveness improves as parties are invited to "unpack" their assumptions, generalities, and claims to help others understand their meaning. A second assumption is "There is no need to talk about it." Parties want to move right to the generation of solutions without ample discussion to understand the problem. Or, the parties assume that decisions have already been made and that they lack the power to change them. Community groups need to focus efforts on what they have the power to change and limit conversation about issues over which they lack power to influence decision makers. A third assumption is "There is no harm in venting emotions." In some cases this may be true, but in many instances, venting emotions turns into blaming and proliferation of issues. The venting of emotions must not be the sole focus of discussions; there must be a balance between expression of frustration and anger and focus on substantive issues.

Because community negotiations involve many parties with vested interests in outcomes, discussions frequently involve many conflicting perspectives. Parties disagree about what the problem is or what an acceptable agreement might look like. Touval (1989) explains, "The larger the number of participants, the greater the likelihood of conflicting interests and positions, and the more complex the interconnections among the parties" (p. 163). As groups grow, diverse preferences and goals make communication more difficult.

In many situations, conflicting perspectives are fueled by negative attributions, which exaggerate differences between groups. Parties lose objectivity in their perceptions of the problem and perceived motives of adversaries. Amy (1987) describes this behavior as stereotyping:

> [When stereotyping, parties] tend to justify the use of the most manipulative or deceitful political tactics. In its essence, stereotyping is a way of dehumanizing one's opponent, a way of turning them into objects. And it's much easier to coerce, manipulate, deceive, or mistrust objects than real human beings like oneself. (p. 49)

Stereotyping occurs when industry regards environmentalists as long-haired hippies, homeowners regard city leaders as insensitive bureaucrats, or developers regard community groups as roadblocks. Overcoming conflicting perspectives generated by negative attributions requires a negotiation process that promotes relationship between disputing parties so that they have a greater willingness to examine the unproductive stereotypes. Breaking down stereotypes, which promote distorted interpretation of information or false assumptions, is a central goal of negotiation in community settings. Processes must emphasize specifics that facilitate deeper understandings than those contained in vague generalities or stereotypes.

The meaning and relevance of information can be the source of contention in many community discussions. Dueling occurs when two experts look at the same data and come to different conclusions. The conclusions closely align with the ideological perspective of the group each represents. For example, one expert can judge that the thinning ozone layer over the North Pole is a sign of dangerous global warming, whereas another can characterize the phenomenon as an expected cyclic event in Earth history. One expert looks at new construction as a prelude to overdevelopment, and another looks at it as an opportunity for economic growth. Groups will disagree about which information is important, how accurate the information is, and how best to interpret the information. Carpenter and Kennedy (1988) recommend that when disagreements about data create impasse, parties need to "return to the reasons why they want to solve the problem and what they need in a solution. . . . Going back to their original reasons for participating in dialogue dislodges parties from frozen positions about sets of figures they demand to be accepted" (pp. 263-264).

Gotbaum (1999) states, "There is just no substitute for knowledge. You must recognize that negotiating is not just a process; you must know the facts" (p. 113). If you are negotiating in a large-group context and lack information, you will be at a significant disadvantage. In public discussions, information about past practices, potential for harm or benefits, cost, impact of decisions on other decisions, and potential alternatives serves as a considerable source of power. In the university parking dispute in Box 10.1, the withholding of information damaged a university's reputation and resulted in a harsh temporary solution to a problem it had with neighbors.

Many forms of facilitated public discussion structure conversation in ways that promote both understanding and collaboration. For example, in 1987, 40 participants from 15 countries participated in an open public discussion at the Congress of the International Physicians for the Prevention of Nuclear War (Chasin and Herzig, 1988). Using a technique known as *circular questioning*, subgroups generated assumptions they believed groups held of one another. The participants then indicated which of the assumptions were least widely held by their own group. Each of the participants then constructed a one-sentence refutation about what they believed was erroneous in the assumptions. The final step involved sharing information generated by the small groups in structured large-group discussion. The process produced dialogue, which facilitated understanding, clarified misperceptions, and identified areas of common ground.

Similar discussions occurred in the early 1990s between American and Soviet filmmakers, between peace activists and defense analysts in the United States, and between American pro-life and pro-choice advocates. Other programs designed to facilitate community discussions include the Listening Project, created by the Rural Southern Voice for Peace; the Community Building Workshop, created by the Foundation for Community Encouragement; the National Issues Forum, sponsored by the Kettering Foundation; and the Policy Jury, developed by the Jefferson Center for New Democratic Processes.

Box 10.1

WE LIKE THE STUDENTS BUT DON'T LIKE THEIR CARS

In its early years, 100-year-old City University was on the edge of a large city, but development eventually engulfed the school. As the school grew to almost 12,000 students, parking expanded well into the neighborhoods around the school.

During the last 3 years, the growth has created a parking problem. Neighbors began to complain about the increased traffic, noise, and lack of privacy. The university argued that parking problems occur around schools all across the United States, and the neighbors would have to adjust. Neighbors interpreted this response as insensitivity to their needs.

Two neighborhood groups formed—one on the west side of the university and one on the east side. Both appealed to the city's Office of Neighborhood Response. The ONR facilitated eight meetings, held over many months, at which parties attempted to negotiate a solution to the problem. Representatives in the negotiation included the city director of parking and safety, the community response officer for the police department, a university vice president, a representative from the school fraternities, the director of parking for the university, and representatives from each of the neighborhood associations. The neighbors were told that the city would not act on the parking problem unless 75% of the members in each of the neighborhood associations achieved consensus on a solution.

During the negotiations, neighbors complained about loud fraternity parties and potential safety issues. Some neighbors complained about walking several blocks from their car to get to their home or the lack of parking for their visiting friends. One homeowner gave an impassioned plea focusing on her need for weekly chemotherapy and the lack of parking for the ambulance that picked her up. One representative brought up the sorority house that was turned into an office for school programs; the house, which once housed 22 sorority sisters, now provided lectures for hundreds of students, and these students required parking. When university officials argued that no one could be sure that the people parking were students, one homeowner asked where the university's 1,200 employees park. Parking was not provided for this group on campus. The university parking director pointed out that the school encourages students to ride bikes to school. A homeowner countered, "Then where are the bike racks?"

At the end of the eight meetings, participants were able to negotiate resolution to all of the issues except one: the school's future parking plans. Homeowners asked about parking for the new university sports arena being built and for the proposed performing arts center, which would be completed in 3 years. Although the school assured the homeowners that parking would be available, they could provide no plans that could account for all the cars that would need to be parked. Privately, the university planned to use the proceeds from a capital fund-raising campaign to pay for a new parking structure, but this would not occur for several years. They withheld this information from the community group.

The university was confident that the homeowners couldn't achieve the 75% vote required to influence city policy. They guessed wrong. Someone leaked information that the university had no plans to build a parking facility for several years. Although the long-term university plan included a parking lot, the university representatives' unwillingness to discuss the plan supported the misinformation. The neighborhood groups became outraged at the university's apparent dishonesty during discussions. They might have been willing to discuss interim measures had the university been straight with them, but not now. A new vote requesting the harshest of measures—the posting of 1-hour parking signs in the neighborhoods—surpassed the required level of consensus. The city responded by posting and enforcing the new regulation. Permits would be granted to homeowners or their guests for longer parking times.

Students were notified immediately of the change. Many had to park far away from school and walk long distances. Some women in evening classes complained about the long walks on dark streets back to their cars after class. Many students who believed the law would not be enforced received tickets. The school began immediate plans for a new parking structure and methods for improving its damaged public relations.

Interdependence

The *complex nature of conflicting interests* is often challenging to groups attempting to forge common ground or to focus on common goals. A homeowner who doesn't want a jail in the community will be in direct disagreement with state officials who find a location in the homeowner's town economically the best decision for the state. State officials can talk of more jobs and more community development, but homeowners can counter with needs that involve less noise, less traffic, and greater safety. Both may be right and at the same time incompatible. Dukes (1996) explains,

> Disputes are not solely clashes of interests. They also involve struggles for recognition, identity, status, and other resources less tangible that are not immediately apparent. Disputes are not fixed. They are instead socially constituted, dynamic organisms, whose actions, issues, and consequences are invariably shaped and transformed by the means available and used to contest them. (p. 138)

Interdependence can be an important factor in forging a climate open to negotiation in community settings. For example, in one community, homeowners competed each year to see who could create the largest light display during the Christmas season. Elaborate displays involving thousands of lights decorated three community homes. A television station ran a special, displaying pictures of the homes. The displays became so well known in the city that Grey Line buses regularly toured the street with loads of tourists. Every evening, thousands of cars paraded through the neighborhood. The displays made the neighborhood distinctive, but many of the neighbors complained about the constant traffic, lack of parking on the street, and the exhaust fumes that blanketed the neighborhood. Several of the neighbors complained to the city council, which called a meeting of the homeowners and the local businesses. The three homeowners with displays asserted their right to celebrate the holidays in any fashion they chose. The nonparticipating homeowners asserted their right to privacy. The facilitator, seeking common ground, asked if the health of the neighbors was important. They all agreed. He asked if it was important that they worked cooperatively on this problem, because they had to live as neighbors the other 11 months of the year. Once again they agreed. After considerable discussion, the manager of the Safeway store on the corner agreed to let people park in the parking lot and walk down the street during the holidays. The television station agreed to run another story that discussed the agreement with Safeway. Additionally, the homeowners agreed on a curfew time when all the lights would be turned off. The interdependence of people living and working in the community contributed to both understanding and a successful resolution to the traffic problem.

Power

Public disputes often begin with the following question: "Do we really have the power to do anything about this situation?" Some community members view multinational corporations as sources of unlimited money, political clout, and difficult opponents with which to have fair discussions. Some view government as unduly influenced by special-interest groups. From these perspectives, power resides in authority over public policy, access to information, ability to influence legal processes, and ability to make and implement decisions. Dukes (1996) points out that "underlying many disputes are struggles over power. . . . Ordinary disputes are often the manifestation of deeper societal divisions . . . [and] the disparate power that favors relations of dominance among these divisions" (p. 173). Many people who work with public-policy discussions believe that a balance of power must be achieved before meaningful negotiations can begin.

Coalitions may serve as one tactic to equalize perceived power imbalances. By agreeing to work together, two or more parties believe they stand a better chance of achieving their interests or controlling outcomes than if they approach problems individually. When a neighborhood comes together to discuss an issue of drugs being sold in a corner house or a dangerous dog in a yard, the goal is to exert power either socially or legally over the errant homeowner. When community members, elected representatives, and business leaders join in discussions about environmental damage in a community, the goal is to create sufficient power to take on the perceived power of the company. Community groups can put pressure on organizations they perceive as powerful through legal threats, attempting to influence leaders through letters and information sent to newspapers. Amy (1987) concludes, "Disputing parties are only willing to negotiate and compromise when a balance of power prevents them from getting what they want on their own" (p. 81).

Box 10.2 describes a community negotiation in which homeowners struggled with lack of power in getting help with a community problem. The potential for a grant to address community problems, support from the police department, and collaboration between meeting times facilitated agreements in the community meetings.

In some public discussions, coalitions can inhibit negotiations. United by ideology or narrow interests, coalitions may frustrate negotiation processes and adversely affect the possibilities of agreement. Hampson and Hart (1995) explain,

> Coalitions are unwieldy entities and typically arrive at a negotiating position only after hard bargaining among the members of the group has taken place. Having developed a position, a coalition may be reluctant to change or modify it, since doing so may lead to conflict within the coalition, perhaps even causing the coalition to break up. (p. 30)

In settings characterized by a willingness to look for broader-based solutions or those in which compromise or tradeoffs may be necessary for agreements, coalitions can be significant stumbling blocks for negotiations. Concerns about values, rights, and group solidarity can be more important

Box 10.2

FINDING A WAY TO
DEAL WITH AN UNRESPONSIVE NEIGHBOR

A group of families applied for a $2,500 grant from their neighborhood association to clean up their neighborhood. The neighborhood was composed of two groups of families: Hispanic and Mexican nationals. Historically, the neighborhood association had refused to work with the two groups because of ongoing conflict between the groups. The association agreed to consider the grant if the two groups met together to negotiate solutions to their problems. The families agreed to meet for four sessions to resolve common problems.

About 30 people attended the first meeting. Led by a core group of 10 Hispanic families, the meeting turned into a chaotic discussion. Hispanics alleged that the Mexican national families were responsible for graffiti on walls, cars on lawns, illegal numbers of families in homes, noise, drug dealing, garbage in the front yards, and a free-roaming barking dog. Many families complained that absentee landlords were allowing the nationals to destroy the neighborhood. Representatives of the Mexican national homeowners argued that they had no control over the transient renters who caused most of the damage and should not be held accountable. Both groups agreed that the city leaders were incompetent, untrustworthy, and unhelpful. They pointed out that city neighborhood inspectors did nothing to help and that the state assemblyman refused to help because neither of the groups had good voting records in the elections.

The core Hispanic group realized that they were sabotaging their own efforts, so they agreed to meet before the next meeting to establish a goal and prioritize interests. In addition, they invited the chief of police to attend the meeting. With about 40 people and the chief of police in attendance, the interim meeting was well focused. The discussion was limited to three properties where most of the problems occurred. The neighborhood inspector agreed to perform random drop-by inspections, and the 10 core families agreed to draft a letter of complaint against the landlords of the properties.

Because many of the families didn't speak English, a translator attended the third meeting. About 40 people, many of whom were different than earlier participants, attended the meeting. City officials pointed out that the letter, drafted by the families, was a legal liability because of its accusatory tone and lack of evidence for claims. The participants became angry, and the meeting once again turned to chaos.

The new participants, who lacked a history with the group, argued that the city's response once again demonstrated its unwillingness to help. The city officials agreed to draft a new letter, which would be reviewed at the next meeting.

The fourth session was once again well focused. The neighbors agreed to the city's wording of the letter to the landlords. The inspector presented a detailed report about her inspections of the neighborhood and the number of citations she issued for failing to comply with city safety standards. The chief of police agreed to support the efforts of the neighborhood resource manager, who was responsible for addressing community problems, and the inspector. The neighbors conceded that the yards appeared a bit cleaner since the inspector began issuing citations and agreed to quit complaining about the city's leadership. The neighborhood association approved the request for the $2,500 grant to educate the neighborhood about safety and health issues.

The hidden outcome of the community meetings was the building of understanding and the ability to work together among the neighbors. The act of talking together created relationships that would be valuable in solving other issues.

than resolution of problems. Box 10.3 illustrates how a meeting designed to promote appreciation of diversity erupted into a shouting match between competing coalitions.

Coalitions need not be a negative influence on multiparty discussions. Hampson and Hart (1995) point out that coalitions "greatly facilitate the exchange of information by reducing the number of core positions and interests to a manageable number" (p. 352). In addition, dealing with representatives who are skilled in integrative negotiation may reduce the conflict-escalating dynamics that occasionally occur in large group discussions. Facilitators may focus efforts on skilled, cooperative leaders who can bridge differences between groups.

Working with coalitions involves highlighting similarities and minimizing differences. It involves focusing on common interests and potential areas for mutual gain. In addition, Watkins and Rosegrant (1996) propose five principles for negotiating within and between coalitions:

- Approach the parties that have strongly compatible interests early.
- Emphasize common ground around similar deeply held values.
- Create analogies with similar experiences.

Box 10.3

FACILITATING RESPECT FOR DIVERSITY CAN BE DIFFICULT

In 1995, meetings titled "One America" were held across the United States. Community leaders and national figures, including Duke professor John Hope Franklin, led these community-based discussions. The goal for the meetings was to promote better race relations through greater appreciation of ethnic differences.

In Denver, about 800 people attended one of these meetings. During the evening discussion, about 50 Native American protesters in ski masks and bandanas drove the leaders from the stage. Protesters demanded to know why no Native American was on the stage. African Americans shouted back that history demanded that their needs be given priority in the discussion. Despite pleas from the Denver mayor and the U.S. Energy Secretary, the two groups escalated their argument over which group suffered the most. One protester shouted, "One America, that's the lie we're trying to speak to tonight," while the U.S. Energy Secretary shouted back, "We're all human beings here. We can either have a dialogue or a shouting match." Afterward, one member of the audience said, "We're all members of one family. We all have the same needs; we share the same concerns. It seems like tonight the ego got in the way. It was me, me." One frustrated participant said, "If I wanted to see a fight about racism, I would've stayed home with my sisters and cousins."

In this community dialogue, the needs and interests of two strong coalitions collided in a way that sabotaged constructive discussion. If understanding was the goal, all sides lost. How do you propose that members from different cultures in situations such as this begin the task of building shared understandings?

- Highlight common threats and potential losses.
- Work with relationship networks.

COMMUNITY NEGOTIATION PROCESSES ●

A well-planned discussion process improves the likelihood of successful negotiations. Agreeing on a set of procedures can reduce unfocused discussion and maintain momentum toward desired outcomes. Typical community negotiations involve the following elements.

Prenegotiation:

1. Select representatives from interest groups.

2. Decide whether a third-party neutral is necessary to facilitate the negotiation. Identify funding source for facilitator and select facilitator.

3. Establish times, location, and duration of the meetings.

4. Assemble background materials, historical documents, and potential ground rules that will be shared with participants prior to the meeting.

First phase of negotiation:

1. At the first meeting, establish the purpose for the negotiations.

2. Introduce participants and reason for their involvement.

3. Agree on roles: convener, recorder, facilitator, and logistical support.

4. Establish objectives or goals for the negotiations.

5. Propose, discuss, and agree on agenda.

6. Discuss and agree on ground rules for the negotiation.

7. Agree on the method by which decisions will be made.

Second phase of negotiation:

1. Identify issues that generated the need for the negotiation.

2. Discuss interests that each party considers important.

3. Create task groups to research data, potential options, or handle problems that are better managed in small groups.

4. Generate options for achieving desired outcomes.

5. Establish criteria for measuring the appropriateness, desirability, and acceptability of options.

6. Apply criteria to existing options.

7. Discuss implementation procedures.

8. Create monitoring system for evaluating success of implementation. Include penalties for violations and procedures for renegotiation of unsuccessful elements.

Third phase of negotiation:

1. Draft agreement for review by all members.

2. Reach final agreement.

SUMMARY •

Community negotiation occurs in many contexts, including neighborhood meetings, public policy discussions, environmental advisory boards, and homeowner associations. Group dynamics create a different context for negotiation than is found in interpersonal and organizational negotiations. Leaders of community groups possess less leverage with which to promote cooperation. Volunteers may lack knowledge about integrative processes and be less committed to mutual gains outcomes. There may be few incentives to hold participants to a slow, time-consuming process.

In community meetings, participants often adopt positional or value-driven orientations because of high investments in outcomes. Parties become emotionally involved in discussions that involve *their* neighborhoods or *their* communities. Group discussions can become contentious as participants attempt to further their personal goals and interests. Of all the settings, community negotiations have the greatest need for a third-party neutral, mediator, or facilitator to lead discussions. The large number of participants and the tendency to get bogged down in tangential discussions can seriously impede progress. Well-designed decision-making processes can keep participants involved and focused on integrative outcomes.

Success will be largely determined by the ability of groups to agree on procedures, negotiate in good faith, and support mutually beneficial outcomes. In addition, the presence of incentives and deadlines may provide the motivation participants need to cooperate.

Negotiating in large-group contexts involves different skills than in one-to-one, family, or organizational contexts. Because of the presence of coalitions, the large number of conflicting interests, the many perspectives, and the frequent presence of positional orientations, community negotiations often possess many of the dynamics of labor negotiations. Attempting to identify and address group interests and hidden agendas involves skills associated with mediation and facilitation.

Early planning about the structure of a community discussion plays a significant role in promoting the success of a group. If decision makers who can block implementation of agreements are not present for discussions, agreements may be meaningless. If one party believes that it has more chance of getting what it wants in court, that party may have insufficient incentive to be fully invested in negotiations. The lack of deadlines often slows group progress, so much so that participants may lose interest.

Based on a 10-year research program on community mediation in the United States, Pruitt (1995) found that the factors responsible for short-term successful community problem solving differ from the factors responsible for long-term successful problem solving. Short-term success is related to immediate relief from the tension created by conflict and by achieving specific interests. Long-term success is linked most to the improvement of relationship and the capacity for parties to work together. Specifically, the presence of joint problem solving predicted long-term success for the complainants who initiated the need for community discussions. The presence of procedural fairness predicted long-term success for the respondents (those whom the complaints were about).

Figure 10.1 summarizes many of the factors that contribute to group effectiveness in community groups.

Participant-related factors
    Identification and involvement of affected parties
    Direct involvement of decision makers
Process-related factors
    Agreement on procedural issues
    Presence of sufficient incentives to negotiate
    Ability to satisfy each party's interests
    Maintenance of constructive working relationships
    Negotiation in good faith
    Presence of deadlines
Content-related factors
    Agreement on the scope of the issues
    Agreement about interpretation of data or relevant facts

Based on Bingham (1986)

Figure 10.1   Factors Influencing the Likelihood for Success

PROFESSIONAL PROFILE

JOHN FISKE, JD, ●
ATTORNEY, NEGOTIATOR, AND
MEDIATOR FOR MUNICIPAL CONFLICTS

Negotiating Conflicts in the City:
When Your Neck Is on the Block

Negotiating in municipal matters involves a variety of city government services, such as police protection, roads, and libraries. Often, an overlay of state and federal regulations must be taken into account. Other layers of government, such as water districts, may have interests related to the municipal conflict. Citizens may be involved as individuals, as homeowner associations, or as neighborhoods. Nonprofit groups that have interests in the issues at stake may also come to the table; if the spotted owl is in jeopardy, the Audubon society wants to be heard. Clearly, the number of governmental entities and regulations that impact municipal negotiations make this one of the more complex areas of negotiations.

This complexity is often joined by a high level of citizen emotionality. Although it may be difficult to get the typical citizen interested in topics such as campaign reform or foreign affairs, municipal conflicts often affect citizens directly. The demonstration that blocks a busy highway at rush hour, the condemnation of private property in one's neighborhood, the threat of the sex offender moving in next door—these are but a few of the conflicts that raise the emotional ante in city negotiations.

The practitioner in this profile reinforces several points discussed in this chapter. He notes that multiple perspectives and conflicting interests make community negotiation complex. He agrees with the researchers that the parties to negotiation must not only be skilled negotiators, but they must be able to control their constituencies. John finds that the likelihood of success is greatly influenced by the willingness of the parties to enter into negotiations in good faith, particularly to avoid violence. In city negotiations, prenegotiation involves many meetings with the separate parties, and eventually with both parties together, to agree on ground rules for public demonstrations.

Introduction to the Practitioner

John Fiske is a negotiator who combines the intellectual acumen to handle complexities with a temperament adequate for the high emotionality of city conflicts. John is a graduate of Yale University and the College of Law at Michigan University. One of John's first jobs out of law school was first assistant corporation counsel for the city of Boston. Later, practicing both law and mediation, he assisted negotiations in Weston, a suburb of that city. John has served on various town boards and understands the workings of municipal governance.

John was one of the first attorneys to perceive the applicability of mediation to family disputes and to alter his practice accordingly. For years, he has been active in developing and volunteering for professional organizations that promote the use of mediation in family conflicts. In addition to their active practice in dispute resolution, John and his partners have trained many mediators in New England. John has made significant contributions to principled negotiation directly through his practice and indirectly through training others and building institutions.

"The skill of connecting" is John's first thought about what negotiators in municipal conflicts must be able to do. By this phrase, he means the ability to establish a credible relationship with both government officials and citizens. John believes that anyone who attempts to negotiate must persuade others that he or she is playing a useful role. In his words, "Through these connections, the negotiator achieves credibility, currency, status, influence. In concrete terms, when you call the town official, he returns your phone call."

A second critical skill is projecting honesty and the motivation to achieve a fair solution. Those at the table and their constituents must believe that the negotiator has integrity. John says, "People have to believe that you aren't going to shortcut or hoodwink them in any way."

Third, John cites the analytical skill of being able to understand what is wanted. Finally, there is the skill of discerning common ground. John advises, "The effective negotiator has the ability to see that folks who demand very different things actually have a lot in common." Whether in the city or the suburbs, John asks, "What is it that we all have in common?" John has honed these skills for himself and has trained other negotiators to exercise them.

Insights About Negotiation

John uses his analytical skills in preparing for negotiation. For instance, the negotiator may have some control over which persons will represent their groups in a municipal negotiation. One significant criterion for selection is the relationship of parties to their constituencies. John finds, "Skilled or not, if persons cannot control their constituencies, they won't be able to effect settlements."

John also uses compatibility among representatives as a selection criterion. His strategy is "to find reasonable people [among the groups in conflict] who would be compatible. Then, I talk to each of them, asking, 'What's most important to you?' Next, I go back around to the others, saying, 'Here's what's most important to [each party].' Finally, I get them to sit down together."

One of the most volatile types of city negotiations involves confrontation between citizen demonstrators and police. In 1968, when John was just a few years out of law school, he was appointed by a bright but also very young mayor [Kevin White] of Boston to be the city's counsel to the police department. John had been at his desk on the sixth floor of city hall only a few months when Dr. Martin Luther King, Jr. was gunned down. Shortly thereafter, the Ohio militia fired on students at Kent State, killing several, and, in June, Robert Kennedy was assassinated. Campuses all over the United States erupted with protests against the war in Vietnam, and universities in the Boston area were no exception. John remembers, "Harvard was finally boarded up, because it was getting trashed by demonstrators every day. Demonstrators seized the office of the dean of students and carried him out to the yard, in his chair." In this maelstrom, John began his negotiating career as legal counsel to the Boston police department.

In a typical negotiation, John spoke with the leader of an antiwar demonstration, such as John Gage, head of the People's Coalition for Peace and Justice, who did not want violent confrontation with the police. Fiske says of Gage, "He was a very level-headed, sensible person. He told me that he could organize 100,000 peaceful demonstrators if I could keep the Boston police peaceful." Violent demonstrations did occur in some other cities at that time.

At that point, John had worked in the Boston police department for 2 years and knew who the key people were. He then searched for a member of the police department who was willing to sit down with demonstrators beforehand. Many of the supervisors were not willing and said, "John, you're just a liberal flake." Finally, he found Warren Blair, a supervisor who said, "If you can find demonstrators who won't throw rocks at my men, I'll go anywhere, anytime."

Over the course of 10 sessions, John then helped Blair and Gage plan a demonstration that was peaceful. He then took them to the office that licensed demonstrations and helped them fill out the forms in a way that was consistent with their plans. He recalls, "As a result of that, [Senator George] McGovern came to speak on the Boston Common to 100,000 people, and there was a grand total of three arrests. It was the second-largest demonstration in Boston's history. The police were totally under control and there were no surprises. It was unbelievable."

Other demonstrations were also peaceful but effective. John was pictured in the *Boston Herald* standing next to the police superintendent who was arresting protestors one by one. John describes the scene: "At the South Boston Army base, some of Boston's most prestigious citizens came from offices in the city and homes on Beacon Hill to protest the war. We would say, 'Okay, Mr. Lowell, we're about to arrest you now. Is that your wish?' And they would say, 'Yes, please arrest me.' It was all very civilized."

John believes that there are several elements that determine success in city negotiations. First is the willingness of parties to enter the process in good faith. For instance, some demonstrators may intend to be violent, and no amount of negotiation will budge them from that position. John describes the violent protestors in the 1999 Seattle riots: "Those were thugs who took over the demonstrations [against disparities in the global economy]. The peaceful demonstrators were furious! They had come to exercise their first amendment rights. They were sitting quietly when suddenly these people come running in, throwing rocks and stealing things out of store windows." Success hinges on involving parties who wish to explore alternatives to court or more violent solutions.

Another essential for success in resolving city conflicts is identifying common ground. Parties tend to focus on what divides them and must be constantly reminded that they share certain values and interests. An effective negotiator knows that common ground requires repeated emphasis.

Finally, John speaks of taking the time to know and be known by the important parties in the negotiation. "During the 6 years I represented the police, I was never home until late at night. I'd work in city hall until 5 p.m., I'd take the "T" [underground transit] over to the police department and sit and schmooze with the police commissioner for 2 hours." John is convinced that without this considerable investment in the relationship, the police would not have endorsed his idea for their supervisor to sit down with demonstrators and make plans for peaceful demonstrations.

The toughest challenge for John was being stereotyped and attacked by all the sides he was attempting to reconcile. For instance, his legal colleagues at city hall thought he had been co-opted by the police department. They concluded, "Fiske, you've become a radical, hard-hat police redneck," whereas, "To everyone at police headquarters, I was this wide-eyed liberal from city hall. I was too educated, my father was not a police officer, and I wasn't even Irish. While they liked having me on their side, they didn't know how to deal with me. Demonstrators thought I was the mayor's spy. After all, to them I represented the establishment. You have to remember the hatred and alienation toward anyone in authority at that time." The municipal negotiator isn't likely to make friends on the job and may even be bad-mouthed by everyone involved.

John continues, "Everybody hates the peacemakers. They don't have any position. If you're an angel, you're on the side of good, and if you're a devil, you're on the side of evil. But the people who remain neutral and try to facilitate the survival of civilization are hated because they don't belong to either side."

When negotiations break down, John observes, "Civilization crumbles. When negotiations fail, the law of the jungle takes over. The law of self-survival takes over. The law of me-first takes over. It's sad for the negotiators whose best efforts were unsuccessful." Student demonstrators interrupt their studies and may lose their places in prestigious universities. In the case of a town, when negotiations fail, there may be bad feelings between citizens, some of whom might move away, and civic resources are not used to their maximum potential.

Contextual Differences

The contrast between municipal negotiations and private practice is striking. As John puts it, in municipal negotiations, "My neck is *so* far out. No matter what you say, you're offending someone." In addition, the negotiator's work is subject to intense scrutiny that leads to a stronger leadership role in the municipal context. John reflects, "I'm always conscious of serving the public interest, regardless of my formal role. I need to consult with others in order to discern just where the public interest lies." Municipal negotiators must take a stronger leadership role, exposing themselves to criticism as they try to discern and serve the public interest.

Changes and Conflicts

John reports on recent changes in clashes between police and demonstrators: "I see much more municipal awareness of the importance of preparation [for demonstrations]. Because national conventions were coming to their cities in '00', police from Philadelphia and Los Angeles were present for the World Trade Center meeting in Seattle in '99. And, boy did they learn a lot from Seattle. Those police thought they were prepared, but they were overwhelmed. Because it's been a bad time for demonstrators the last 10 years—everybody's too happy. Now, all of a sudden, the malcontents are discovering that they can get public attention again. That's an oversimplification, but there is an element of truth to it."

Technology has produced interesting changes in the way demonstrations are organized and led. Tom Ginsberg, reporting for the *Philadelphia Inquirer* (Ginsberg, 2000), notes that there have been radical changes in the way demonstrations are organized. The structure is decentralized, groups are small, and leadership is diffuse. The absence of a central leader has both tactical and philosophical advantages. The belief system of the demonstrators may stress grassroots leadership, and the lack of one central person leading removes an obvious target from their enemies. Instead, there are many coordinators who walk the streets, staying in contact with the small groups by cell phones. In this way, demonstrations can be mounted with maximum flexibility and timeliness.

Ginsberg notes that, in 21st-century demonstrations, a coordinator offers options to a small group. For instance, its members might surround a building, block a street, or protest outside an office where a sensitive meeting is being held. The coordinators provide the information that allows small groups of demonstrators to be successful, such as maps and building exits. The group then elects the target it prefers, begins the demonstration, and is monitored by the coordinator, again by cell phone or Palm Pilot. The absence of a central leader, although strategically powerful, would make John's approach to negotiation with the police much more difficult, if not impossible, to employ.

This use of technology by demonstrators in Philadelphia provoked some very unorthodox responses from the police there, Ginsberg reports. More than 300 demonstrators were jailed during the 2000 Republican convention. Law enforcement targeted citizens who were using cell phones and Palm Pilots because they looked like demonstrators to them. The charges were for using an instrument of crime. For this misdemeanor, bail was set at 1 million dollars. After the convention delegates returned home, most of the high bail amounts were considerably reduced. The police response was rather heavy handed, relied on stereotypes, and was more likely to polarize parties than to lead them toward negotiation.

Fiske explains that the major differences among city negotiators are attributable to a range of opinion about how much formal authority to exercise. Some negotiators are more prone to the use of force and regulatory power, whereas others favor the development of more voluntary compliance whenever possible. For instance, many members of the Boston police department in 1968 believed, "The only way to deal with these people is to lock them up." Evidently, this same sentiment prevailed among Philadelphia police in 2000.

As the reader may have gathered, John Fiske favors the development of voluntary compliance. His success in city negotiations is based on personal integrity, relationships developed between and among other key parties, and establishing the interests of the various parties. Whether the unit is a small township with issues of property or a major city encountering demonstrations, the same negotiation rules apply.

PROFESSIONAL PROFILE

WAYNE CARLE, PHD, ●
FORMER SCHOOL SUPERINTENDENT

Negotiating Teacher Contracts:
What Is Best for the Most

Whatever differences separate us as readers, chances are that the vast majority of us live in communities served by kindergarten through 12th grade (K-12) public schools. Regardless of whether we have children attending them, the great majority of us pay taxes supporting these schools. Because the greatest expense of any school is salaries and benefits for teachers, we have a vested interest in the negotiations between school districts and teachers.

Our local and national media report on this type of negotiation. Teachers are often represented by the American Federation of Teachers (AFT) or the National Education Association (NEA). Such reports feature traditional bread-and-butter issues such as salaries and benefits, but, more recently, the media are also noting pedagogical issues—such as class size and student performance—as part of the contract talks. These negotiations may be smooth or acrimonious, although the latter is the type that tends to draw more media attention. The great majority of these negotiations are conducted privately; the press is excluded, so we read secondhand information. In this profile, a school superintendent takes us behind the scenes to view educational negotiation from the perspective of an insider. His opinions about the changing character of school negotiations relate to comments in this chapter about power and coalitions.

Introduction to the Practitioner

Dr. Wayne Carle has witnessed incredible changes in K-12 public school education since he began his career 50 years ago. Among other changes, he has observed and worked with an array of negotiation approaches used to bridge the gap between community resources and teacher salaries. Wayne's negotiating experience began with a rather informal "meet and consult" approach in the 1950s and continued through the introduction of confrontive techniques in the 1960s. This led to a more formalized process first known as professional negotiations, then collective bargaining, and culminated in the current trend toward a collaborative, problem-solving approach.

Wayne Carle had just begun his first teaching job in Utah when he was tapped to be a teacher's representative with the state education association. Wayne was promoted to school superintendent in Dayton, Ohio, and served there from 1968 to 1973. Wayne's effectiveness as a negotiator was recognized by the Dayton Urban League, which sent a plaque engraved as follows: "In recognition of devoted and selfless consecration in service to mankind by persistent efforts in desegregation for quality education in the Dayton Public Schools." From 1973 through 1975, Wayne was again a school superintendent, this time in Hammond, Indiana.

Shifting from administration to teaching, Wayne spent 12 years in higher education settings where, along with other responsibilities, he taught negotiation. Eventually, he returned to administration, becoming assistant superintendent and later superintendent for the Jefferson County school district (located in Colorado, this district had 90,000 students in 2001). Wayne's length of service, his exposure to negotiation in different parts of the country, and his period of teaching negotiations qualify him to speak with considerable authority on the subject of negotiations between teachers and school districts.

Insights about Negotiation

The skills critical to negotiating between public school teachers and administrators are, Wayne states, "obviously, good judgment and a sense of fairness. Then, in any high-stakes negotiation, beyond the issues is the importance of relations with stakeholders. For instance, both sides consider, 'How will the public see this tentative settlement? How will the state legislature view it? How will it impact future relationships between the teachers and the administration, teachers and the community?' School administrators ask themselves, 'How will provisions of the proffered contract be financed? What are the long-term economic consequences of going forward with current proposals? What impacts will it have on instruction?'"

Wayne reports that negotiators prepare by debriefing from the previous year. Although everyone espouses win-win settlements, more than likely, the last round of contract negotiations has resulted in a win-lose compromise. Most teacher contracts are for 1 year, and even those written for longer periods usually include enough circumstances under which a contract might be reopened that it is easy enough to provoke annual negotiations. For the educational system, Wayne says, "contract negotiations are disruptive. They are the annual shadow under which administrators operate."

The typical educational negotiation runs from 12 to 20 meetings, Wayne explains. Although most sessions last several hours, it is not unheard of for final negotiation meetings to be 24 hours in length. The typical negotiation team consists of five to eight administrators on one side and five to eight teachers on the other. School board members are advised against taking an active role, although a board member might be assigned to listen during talks. Each team has a leader; for administration, the assistant superintendent of schools typically takes on this function. For the teachers, the leader is often the association's executive. Attorneys will be consulted frequently, but they are less likely to be asked to participate than they were in the recent past. The current negotiation model is based on the assumption that those more directly involved in the issues are most qualified to make decisions about them. Also, there is more emphasis today on good-faith efforts from both sides and a problem-solving, as opposed to an adversarial, approach.

At the first meeting or meetings, Wayne says, both sides agree to the ground rules of the negotiation, in which the following questions are answered: "How frequent should negotiation sessions be? Will teachers be given released time to attend them? What will constitute an impasse? What will constitute an agreement?" The parties will decide whether the press may attend. Typically, the teachers do not want the media there, whereas the board may favor press attendance. It may depend on who perceives an advantage in having bargaining positions publicized. Thus, there usually is an agreement on when and how news releases will be made and by whom. After such issues are decided, proposals are offered by both sides at the next meeting. From then on, counterproposals and discussion follow until either a settlement or an impasse is reached.

Wayne defines success in two ways: "An agreement, of course. Also, it's when both parties believe they did the best they could under the circumstances." Sometimes this belief arises naturally, but sometimes it takes a member of one of the teams to persuade both sides that they have arrived at this point.

Challenges arise from several areas. "First, negotiating is difficult where there are deep ideological splits," Wayne explains. "For instance, the public holds the perception that smaller class sizes promote more learning. Teachers, focusing on the best economic result for their members, may accept larger classes for better pay." A second challenge is the issue of performance pay. This is difficult to work through for many teams because it flies in the face of traditional step-and-level pay scales. Third, racial differences may present a challenge. When Wayne was school superintendent in Dayton, some schools were staffed completely by African-Americans, and others were staffed exclusively by Anglos. "Through inviting the teacher's association to assist in the planning of integrated staffs, over 700 teachers changed schools. This was the largest voluntary movement of teachers in any school system in the United States."

Finally, adversarial relationships are challenging. Wayne concludes, "Unless administrators, school boards, teachers, and parents can build and maintain collaborative relationships, not much is accomplished." Although many of us might find collaboration laudatory, legislatures may find it threatening. In the past, legislatures have held power partly through the fractionalization of these parties. Legislatures that do not favor unions see union collaboration with other interested parties as creating a situation that Wayne says is "out of control."

Challenges may result in impasse. Although strikes by school personnel are usually prohibited, they happen occasionally. Obviously, strikes harm a number of parties—most directly the students, who suffer a loss of instruction and continuity. When districts have attempted to bring in substitute teachers or parent volunteers to fill the gap, community relations suffer. Parent-teacher associations generally have opposed this tactic. Another possible response to failed negotiation is binding arbitration. However, Wayne says, "School boards shy away from binding arbitration; elected representatives are not eager to give away their constitutionally required decision-making power."

Contextual Differences

As a school administrator, Wayne had many opportunities to engage in informal as well as formal negotiations. In fact, he relates, "As a school administrator, I was *always* negotiating with one or another group. For instance, I negotiated with chambers of commerce about tax issues. I needed to know what level of taxation they would support in order to make a reasonable proposal. In one case, negotiations about mill levies was tied to performance pay in that the chamber would only support a tax increase if it were tied to performance pay for teachers."

Internal negotiations also were significant. "There are frequently negotiations with students, parents, and teachers within the context of an agreed-to policy, where someone(s) needs or wants an exception made. In fact, I learned a valuable lesson from a student senate in my first superintendency. I announced that the district would fund intramurals next year. Receiving only tepid response, I talked to a student leader afterwards and asked why. 'Don't give us anything we don't ask for,' he advised." Finally, there are groups such as the district accountability committee that require extensive meetings and negotiations.

Asked to contrast these types of negotiations with contract negotiations, Wayne is quick to reply, "Informal negotiations are easier and more pleasant. They can often lead to more effective decisions. They are usually not subject to the same level of nitpicking." However, he does note that one advantage of formal negotiations is that once agreement is reached, "We have clear marching orders and everyone can get back to the job."

Changes and Challenges

Wayne names several recent trends in contract negotiations. First and foremost, "There is an increased interest in the problem-solving approach to negotiations. Secondly, superintendents at national and state levels—also school boards and teachers—are increasingly impacted by legislatures. Issues that used to be decided in the professional domain are now publicly debated and often legislated. For instance, both state and federal governments are discussing how to influence student performance standards. Presidents and presidential candidates propose educational changes decided at the federal level."

Wayne points out that many states are pushing for merit pay for high-performing teachers and proposing new rules for teacher preparation and licensure, and new bills to alter the levels and methods of school funding. Some state legislatures are close to acting on these issues; others have already done so. For instance, California mandated additional teachers so that all first-grade classes in the state are capped at 20, thus creating a temporary shortage of both teachers and classrooms. Governmental intervention in educational policy has significantly increased in the recent past.

Wayne is aware of a number of issues educational professionals disagree about. One question directly related to contract negotiations is how to inject civility into a process based on adversarial relationships. Some administrators see teachers as allies and want to pursue the collaborative approach to negotiations. The benefit of healthy relationships among community members seems obvious. Wayne asks, "What is the guiding value of adversarial negotiations? They can become totally disconnected from the reality of schools." Other administrators prefer the use of professional negotiators within an adversarial context, explaining that the happy settlement of economic issues may not adequately represent the community's interests. That is, school boards and teachers might be satisfied with a settlement on pay and benefit issues, but educational outcomes may suffer as a result. Such negotiations have limited success, in that they may not deliver what Wayne terms "the best for the most."

Pay for performance is another area of disagreement. Some argue that rewarding good teaching would encourage it and raise student achievement. Others feel that setting some teachers apart would result in unhealthy competition.

These disagreements engage not only professional educators, but all citizens who have to pay for and benefit from public education. Contract negotiations between school administrators and teachers will continue to be widely significant, not only for settlement of the issues on the table, but for the ongoing relationships among community members and the educational outcomes which flow from them. Wayne Carle has contributed in this context for many years, conducting, teaching, and modeling effective negotiations. As the mayor and other civic leaders wrote when he left Dayton, "You have caused us to dream new dreams—you have made us turn our faces and reach our hands toward the future with new resolution and deep commitment."

PROFESSIONAL PROFILE

● **CHARLES CURRIE,**
PRESIDENT, THE ASSOCIATION
OF JESUIT COLLEGES AND UNIVERSITIES

Higher Education: Surrounded by
Wall-to-Wall Toes Waiting to Be Stepped On

According to Father Charles Currie, president of the Association of Jesuit Colleges and Universities, leaders in higher education and religious organizations are *always* negotiating. In his words, "You're always trying to get people to work together, to get agreement on issues, and occasionally serving as negotiator for larger communities." In the opinion of this practitioner, preparations prior to negotiation in higher education and religious settings emphasize strategizing similar to those in other multiparty disputes. As recommended in this chapter, identifying who should be at the table is a critical step. In addition, negotiators should have as much information about the disputes and the other negotiators as possible, and negotiators must have the support of their constituencies. In higher education, there are not only multiple issues and multiple parties to negotiation, but there are also certain sensitivities, especially to justice issues.

Introduction to the Practitioner

Fr. Currie, who has been twice a college president (Wheeling Jesuit College, 1972 to 1982, and Xavier University, 1982 to 1986), currently oversees an association of 28 colleges and universities. In this context, negotiations might involve the faculty and staff of a given college, faculties of a number of institutions, or a university and its outside constituencies. He says, "Currently, there are 24 colleges and universities involved in a Jesuit distance education network, 26 are working on a joint MBA program in China, and all 28 are participants in an immersion experience in El Salvador." These collaborative projects require considerable amounts of attention and coordination.

In addition, there are negotiating opportunities outside the traditional job description of college leader: "College presidents are frequently called upon to act as negotiators or mediators in community disputes," Fr. Currie explains. "For instance, in West Virginia, I was involved with the coal industry, and, in Cincinnati, the university tried to broker the relationship between two communities upset by an interracial killing. Then, when I was at Georgetown, I was involved in efforts to bring about peace in El Salvador. While the United Nations was the official broker, there were behind-the scenes-efforts as well."

Fr. Currie prepared for his role as negotiator the way many leaders do— which is to say he has had no formal training. His undergraduate and graduate major was chemistry, and he also took many courses in philosophy and theology. His skill in negotiation is a product of years of experience and what he describes as "wanting to help people." For him, the approaches and techniques are just common sense.

Fr. Currie judges good listening as the number one skill an effective negotiator possesses. Second, he names analytical ability, saying, "Being able to identify just what the issues are helps the parties recognize and find new options. A good negotiator creates win-win strategies for all parties. There must be genuine respect for each person involved. Finally, there must be some minimal level of trust." Although he has not been formally trained and has not read deeply in the negotiation literature, his description of effective negotiation skills is consistent with that of principled negotiation.

Insights About Negotiation

Fr. Currie's preparation involves getting to know as much about the situation as possible, including information about the people he is working with. It's also important to identify all the parties who should be at the table and to persuade them to come. Having negotiators who are credible to each party is helpful.

In addition to the "what" and the "who" of negotiations, Fr. Currie also speaks about the importance of where they are held. He advises, "Try to find the best setting for the conversations. For instance, in the negotiations relative to El Salvador, we were trying to get all segments of Salvadoran society together. However, the U.S. State Department wouldn't let us bring the guerillas to Washington, D.C., so we held the negotiations in Costa Rica.

"More generally speaking, it's getting the right place and establishing the right climate for the discussions. Depending on the people involved, if the meeting place doesn't make much difference to one side and does to the other, you can hold the negotiation where the latter is comfortable. If turf is an issue for both, obviously you need a find a neutral spot. Normally, it should be as pleasant and congenial as possible—I've heard stories about labor negotiations where they lock the doors and don't feed people until they come to agreement. I wonder how successful that approach is?"

Knowing the people involved and what their sensitivities are leads to the selection of a setting that promotes success.

Certain preparations in religious groups are likely to contribute to the effectiveness of negotiations. Fr. Currie explains, "First, when you're working with faith-based communities, it's always helpful to begin within a spiritual context. Whatever the setting might be that will dispose people as positively as possible, that should be chosen. Sometimes, that's talking over a meal or refreshments. Obviously, one has to be careful in including drinks. Second, it's always good to try to get people first to say something positive before they get into the negatives. As a Jesuit, I've been brought up on Ignatian spirituality, where there is a great emphasis on discernment as a lifestyle. Part of that is to see things in a positive light before you start concentrating on problems. To the extent that that's possible, I think it's helpful to introduce that practice into any kind of a negotiation." The attempt to establish a positive disposition of the parties is a worthy goal in both religious and secular negotiations.

A typical negotiation involving colleges and universities could be centered on distance education, a topic that is debated among educators. Although most administrators, faculty, students, alumni, and others are open to the basic idea of distance education, they differ in their opinions about how it relates to traditional education, what programs and courses will be offered, how quality can be maintained, what the role of faculty should be, how cost-effective distance education can be, and many other questions.

Fr. Currie recalls, "The idea for a Jesuit network (Jesuitnet) was first endorsed by the deans of continuing education from the various institutions. It was obvious that some other constituencies on campuses did not share their enthusiasm for distance education, so it became a question of broadening the base of support for the idea. Once we had the first group of deans, we reached out to other academic administrators, then the informational technology folks." Emphasizing the importance of getting the first group to support distance education, Fr. Currie points appreciatively to their willingness to "let go" and bring other people along to move the project forward.

After the group of early adopters signs on to an institutional change, Fr. Currie advises negotiators to "keep expanding your base of support. Identify the right people on campus, the opinion leaders, and work to get them on board. I work with them as individuals and as part of a group. For instance, there were some vice presidents who felt that distance education cannot provide quality education. Some faculty members felt that replacing face-to-face contact with students violates an essential element of education. In addition, we had to address budgetary issues implied by this change. Finally, with a few isolated people who I knew were particularly opposed, I tried to address their concerns. Some I was able to win over; others I haven't yet." Each group brings different concerns and questions.

The process of negotiating change in higher education can take a long time. Fr. Currie says, "In the case of distance education, 24 of the 28 institutions have agreed to participate in the distance education network after a year of negotiations. We're still in the process of fleshing out that commitment in terms of specific activities on each one of the campuses. Schools have committed a sizeable amount of money, so we know they're serious. Still, we're developing interest and support on the campuses." Intensive and continued efforts are required to negotiate changes in large systems.

Fr. Currie names a number of factors for successful negotiation when he illustrates how different conflicts call for different approaches: "First, make sure that folks are informed of the issues. Some will want more information than others, but they all should have whatever is required to participate in an informed manner. Second, be sensitive to people's self-interest. If you know what gets people excited, you try to be sensitive to that in the way you develop the conversation. For instance, the Cincinnati situation followed the murder of a white woman by a black serial killer. There were two communities involved—one predominantly white, the other mostly black. We brought the top dozen leaders from both communities together in a conference room near my office. We let everyone scream at each other for several hours and, after they vented their anger, we worked out some strategies and things calmed down."

A third success factor is finding areas of agreement. Fr. Currie offers this example: "In the Salvadoran situation, our task was to discover areas of agreement for two sides who had been shooting at each other for years. We did so, and the negotiation worked on expanding the areas of agreement." Fr. Currie believes that when parties are stuck, a neutral third can assist by reframing the situation from a different perspective. Establishing a context larger than the dispute is one way to find and expand areas of agreement.

A fourth success factor is establishing trust. Speaking of the coal mining dispute, Fr. Currie offers, "There were new safety regulations which scared both the company and the miners. The coal company thought there would be roadblocks in their attempts to hire people, and the miners thought this was another hoop they'd have to jump through. We spent a lot of time reassuring each side that their fears were not justified. Then, we had to make sure that was the case and it did work. Animosity was reduced, and the program is still operative 20 years later." Fr. Currie sees that a minimal level of trust (although a higher level is desired) is necessary for successful negotiation.

Identifying and addressing the correct problems is a fifth success factor. He explains, "Generally speaking, you're always trying to get people to say 'yes' without violating their principles. It's essentially developing a win-win situation. You've got to show them that it's possible for them to do something and still remain faithful to their principles. No red-blooded American wants to lose, so you try to show them how their ideas are part of the larger settlement." Identifying and addressing the correct problems is especially important in the negotiations that involve multiple institutions of higher learning.

As noted earlier, there are many challenges in negotiations within higher education. Fr. Currie summarizes, "The length of these negotiations is challenging. They may go on for years. You need to be patient when what you think will take 6 weeks takes 6 months. And then, I think the biggest challenge is something that's not working at all. When someone is not going to change in any way, shape, or form, despite all sorts of efforts to find a way to agree, it is frustrating."

When negotiation breaks down, Fr. Currie attempts to prevent people from saying a final "no," or even from using the words "final" or "last." However, he acknowledges, "That's not always easy. Nor is it always possible. I've seen this with couples and parents in a different form of negotiation. If it gets that far (the final 'no' is said), it's very hard to bring people back to the table. What you try to do is chip away and, depending on how final it is, you've got a chance to get the negotiations going again. If the 'no' is an emotional outburst, they may talk again after they've calmed down. Though you may always hope that over a period of time people will change, it may not happen."

Fr. Currie also addresses breakdowns in international affairs. He recalls that in the Salvadoran conflict, it appeared that negotiations would break down until one side was willing to take the risk of putting down their arms. That was a critical stage in the process. Fortunately, that breakthrough occurred when enough people outside the situation assured the guerillas that they would be protected if the risk backfired. Fr. Currie draws the following parallel: "That same problem can be seen in Ireland, where the IRA [Irish Republican Army] is afraid to lay down their arms. Someone has to take the first risk in order to achieve a breakthrough in negotiations."

Contextual Differences

The higher-education context influences the practice of negotiation in several ways. Fr. Currie observes, "One of the things that sometimes grinds things to a halt is that folks bring so many issues to the table that it's difficult to sort them all out." A number of writers note that negotiations about one issue, such as monetary damages, are difficult to deal with (in Chapter 4, see reference to Froman & Cohen, 1970; Mannix, Thompson, & Bazerman, 1989). Fr. Currie notes that in academia, the opposite may also be true, in that a large number of issues may overwhelm negotiators.

In addition to multiple issues, the higher-education context involves multiple sensitivities. Colleges are sometimes described as "wall-to-wall toes waiting to be stepped on." Fr. Currie remarks, "On a college campus, you have a very high level of idealism. Students especially are very easily disheartened when they perceive an injustice. They have such a keen sense of justice that sometimes makes it hard to get through to them. Faculty members have heightened sensitivities in a number of areas. This very high level of sensitivity is complex and nuanced." In academia, negotiators must exercise great care in identifying and responding to sensitivities related to injustice.

When the colleges are religious ones, sensitivities are even more intense and pronounced. In Fr. Currie's experience, "People who want to make their point say, 'How can you do this in a Catholic college?' Sometimes that's a fair question; sometimes that's a loaded question that's covering up some other issue. If you profess higher ideals, and you're not living up to them, there's a problem. Bad feelings are created. For example, if a school is talking a lot about social justice and isn't paying their faculty a decent wage, there's a credibility problem there. Sometimes there is a significant gap; sometimes there's a misunderstanding." When higher education is religious in character, expectations for justice among students and faculty are even higher than in secular contexts. Demands for justice may be sincere or specious, but they are an implicit part of this negotiation context.

Changes & Conflicts

A new social phenomenon is making negotiations more difficult. Fr. Currie finds "widespread polarization in society generally. We see it in politics; we see it in the church. It can also be found in the academic setting. Many politicians who once were capable of multiple alliances have adopted the new politics of polarization. In the church, there is polarization between conservatives and liberals. One side demonizes the other so that they don't have to take them seriously. In a negotiation, you try to get one party to understand the other so that there's a certain amount of empathy for a position, even though you might not agree with it. It's very difficult to do that if people are totally polarized." Whatever the context, polarization and demonization of parties will certainly make settlement less likely to occur.

It's ironic that just when negotiations are increasingly complicated, the parties are less able to find solutions because of their polarization. Fr. Currie says, "Issues are so complex today, you need the best wisdom from all perspectives to resolve them. Any negotiation, if it's to be successful, must involve give-and-take. Too often today, parties take nonnegotiable stances. Everything that they believe is right, and everything that you believe is wrong. That's pretty tough to handle." The loss of civility throughout our culture affects negotiators in every arena, including higher education.

Fr. Currie attributes differences in negotiation practices among academic leaders primarily to style. He draws the distinction in this way: "There are some folks who are much more directive than others, who like to take charge more than they like to facilitate. I've seen examples where each has worked, so I can't say one approach is better than the other. I have known negotiators (and psychiatrists) who have been Dutch uncles, rough and tough. And, I knew of others who offered TLC [tender loving care] and were mild in their manner. So, depending on what I thought folks needed, I suggested one or the other."

Fr. Currie concludes by remarking that he wishes he had time to study the negotiation literature to see what the experts have to say. Lacking that viewpoint, he has relied on common sense and interpersonal skills. In his words, "I like people, and I like to see them working well together." The higher-education system generally and Jesuit colleges specifically have greatly benefited from his work and his wisdom.

CHAPTER 11

INTERNATIONAL NEGOTIATION

Bargaining in the international arena is intrinsically positional. Negotiators from various countries arrive at international meetings with carefully crafted marching orders—from which they are not supposed to deviate in any way. Their standard "positions" are, for the most part, not open to revision.

— Susskind, Chayes, and Martinez (1996, p. 19)

The birth of globalization occurred as the result of many factors, including the development of high-speed communication technologies, the integration of world trade markets, the loosening of trade barriers, the rise of multinational corporations, and the end of the Cold War in 1989. In the past decade, international business generated four out of five new jobs in the United States. With more than 153 major corporations doing world trade, the United States continues to be the most active nation in international business. The U.S. Postal Service has facilities in nearly every foreign country. Acuff (1997) points out that "the days of producing and selling products and services mainly on your own turf are gone forever. It's hard to imagine many organizational scenarios that won't include an international aspect over the next few years" (p. 4).

Perhaps no negotiation context has as many elements outside the control of negotiators as international negotiation. Negotiators attempt to fashion agreements in the presence of cultural and ideological differences, foreign-policy restrictions, complex political relationships, and changes in market conditions. Every agreement will be subject to refinement or veto by people and forces that are not involved in the negotiation. American negotiators who are used to reaching agreement in a few days or weeks must become accustomed to agreements requiring months and sometimes years of negotiation. Relatively insignificant elements in a process, such as approval from a manager, can delay progress in negotiation for months. The importance of norms and values, relationship, interdependence, and power is clear in the problems encountered by the church that wanted to rebuild in Jerusalem (Box 11.1).

In transformation theory (see Chapter 3), negotiators attempt to transform or rearrange elements of a situation to fashion new understandings in a context. Attitude shifts create different expectations, ways to communicate about an issue, and norms for relationship. Parties re-evaluate their policies based on their changes in attitude. Zartman (2001) argues that transforming attitudes is at the heart of international negotiation. Attitudes that portray the opponent as an enemy or adversary to be beaten need to be transformed so that the problem becomes the enemy. Such a transformation occurred in South Africa when the South African government and the citizens in opposition shifted their attitudes toward each other.

A second shift in attitude regards the stakes of a negotiation. Parties must re-evaluate their interests and resources in a new way, one that permits trade-offs and joint outcomes. "Trading economic for political payoffs in the unification of Germany . . . and providing economic incentives for Russia in German reunification are examples of each of these approaches" (Zartman, 2001, p. 7).

A third shift that can occur involves the norms for conduct that govern the relationship. Problem solving may replace complacency or confrontation. Processes that prevent escalation of issues may replace reactive approaches. For example, in 1986 at the Vienna Convention on Early Notification of Nuclear Accidents, negotiators "developed a mechanism for the rapid exchange of information when nuclear accidents occur to avoid the spread of misinformation and the generation of crisis" (Spector, 2001, p. 215).

● CONTEXTUAL FACTORS FOR INTERNATIONAL NEGOTIATIONS

Structure

When two parties from different nations negotiate an agreement, the negotiation is described as *bilateral*. Most international business discussions fall into this category. Negotiations that are *multilateral* involve three or more parties from different nations who attempt to reach consensus on

Box 11.1

NEGOTIATIONS THAT REQUIRE A LITTLE FAITH

A 35-family Christian church led by U.S. clergy in West Jerusalem serves primarily Israeli Christians. The location of the church in Jerusalem and its mission to convert Jews led to a bombing and fire that destroyed the church building. After the cleanup, the church members vowed to rebuild the church on the same site.

Unfortunately for the church's membership, some of the same people who bombed the church had influence over the city committee, which granted building permits. Many civic leaders resisted the presence of Christians in Jerusalem, making it difficult for the church to get approval to construct another building. The church's leadership appealed to a U.S. congressman, to the mayor, and eventually to the Israeli Supreme Court. During the Supreme Court discussions, one justice asked, "If we give your group 3 1/2 acres somewhere else in the city, will you give up the 2 acres where you want to rebuild?" Though the offer was attractive, the group decided to continue with its plans to build on the site. Eventually, after many months, the city officials granted the permit, providing the church's plans met with the approval of the church's neighbors.

A second round of challenges began when the church's leadership met with the local neighbors. Many of the neighbors did not want a foreign-style building in their neighborhood. Some complained that a steeple would prevent them from viewing their own holy places. Others worried that they would lose more of their street parking. Once more, the church leaders began intense negotiations.

After months of discussions, the church leaders agreed to construct a building that architecturally resembled a synagogue, with no steeple, and with a parking lot that the neighbors could use during the week. Four years passed from negotiations about the permit to the first phase of building the church.

The pastor of the church explained why he believed the church was successful in achieving its goal: "The Israelis highly value someone standing up for what they believe and not backing down. They don't respect someone who gives in easily. The membership was willing to suffer for what they believed in. The Israelis respected the church's determination. Second, the church was clear about its interests. Members expressed their interests firmly and with little compromise, another factor that matched the Israeli negotiation perspective." The members could have taken the 3 ½-acre compromise and avoided the struggle, but they didn't give in. The church was successful because its leaders demonstrated values and principles valued by their Israeli counterparts.

many complex issues. They approach the issues with a variety of values and perspectives. The size of multilateral groups can vary from as few as three countries, as in the North American Free Trade Agreement (NAFTA), to an unlimited number of nations, such as the 75 nations that from 1988 through 1992 negotiated the Intergovernmental Panel on Climate Change (IPCC) or the 100 nations from 1986 through 1993 that negotiated the General Agreement on Tariffs and Trade (GATT) ratified in 1996.

Whether bilateral or multilateral, international negotiations generally use agents to negotiate business or government agreements. Agents function as more than passive observers; they serve as tacticians who attempt to influence both supporters and opponents in a negotiation. Negotiating with agents requires sensitivity to the pressure of decision makers not at the table, as well as hierarchies and bureaucratic processes that might influence decisions being made.

Hall (1976) differentiates cultures as either high context or low context. High-context cultures, such as Japan or China, possess collectivistic tendencies. Norms for behavior rely on high concern for others, inclusion, and obliging. Avoiding and collaboration styles of communication occur in greater frequency. Norms favor behaviors that are relationship-sensitive, face-saving, expressive, inclusive, and systemically interrelated.

Low-context cultures, such as the United States and Canada, possess individualistic tendencies. Norms emphasize concern for self and autonomy. Confrontational, competitive, and problem-solving conflict management styles occur with greater frequency. Norms tend to favor greater self-disclosure, straightforward communication, and the ability to separate people from the problem. Perhaps the high-context surfing community described in Box 2.2 in Chapter 2 found the low-context newcomers an intrusion on their domain.

Jandt and Pederson (1994) provide a series of insights to differentiate low- and high-context cultures. We've paraphrased in the following lists a few of these insights that specifically apply to negotiation.

Low context:

- Conflict and negotiation processes are often resolved in private.
- Settlements are usually devoid of ritual.
- Participants frequently avoid dispute resolution strategies in favor of court settlements.
- Face-to-face negotiation is preferred.
- Resolution of differences is defined by individuals involved in the conflict.

High context:

- Methods of resolution are defined by the group or culture.
- Although conflict may occur in private, it must be made public before discussions to resolve problems.

- Participants emphasize preventative measures and monitoring of problems.
- Settlements are frequently accompanied by ritual.
- Dispute resolution through intermediaries is preferred.
- It is regarded as failure when court resolution is required.

Although high- and low-context distinctions are normally used to distinguish differences between Western and Eastern negotiating orientations, mutual gains negotiation combines elements of both orientations in an integrative approach.

Respect for personal space during negotiations varies among cultures. Respecting individualism, Western cultures allow for a lot of personal space during conversation but, in both Mexican and Arab cultures, the preference is for close physical proximity. "Africans get physically close to complete strangers and stand even closer when conversing" (Richmond & Gestrin, 1998, p. 95). Physical expressiveness may be reserved in Asian cultures, but in business, they appear to be comfortable with closer space than Americans (Acuff, 1997).

Even seating arrangements during negotiations can be influenced by culture. Americans tend to sit directly opposite their counterparts, symbolic of direct, getting-down-to-business negotiations. Japanese base seating on hierarchy or status, with the most important person sitting at the head of the table. In Korea, the one sitting on the right is the one granted status or honor.

One of the oldest topics in the study of international negotiation is the use of time across cultures. Usunier (1996b) writes, "Among all the dimensions of culture which have a significant but almost invisible impact on business negotiations, time patterns are probably the strongest" (p. 153). Time influences negotiations in how promptly meetings begin, the pace of introducing and discussing issues, and the timing of concessions.

Many Western cultures view time as *monochronic*, which anthropologist Edward Hall (1983) describes as linear, segmented, and manageable. Viewed in economic terms, time is to be saved, not wasted, and should be used efficiently. Events proceed linearly along predictable sequences. In contrast, many Eastern cultures view time as *polychronic*. Time is defined by natural rhythms rather than events limited by the clock or calendar. Time is holistic, and activities begin and end when people are ready.

The way a culture views time influences the behaviors of its negotiators. Western negotiators move methodically, sometimes with haste, through a planned agenda toward an agreement. Middle Eastern and African cultures move slowly, with many interruptions, toward potential agreements. Adler (1986) points out that Eastern negotiators sometimes use the differences in perception of time strategically:

Americans' sense of urgency disadvantages them with respect to less hurried bargaining partners. Negotiators from other countries recognize

Table 11.1   Use of Time by Different Cultures

Region	Pace of Negotiations	Decision Making	Punctuality
North America	Fast	Fast	High
Western Europe	Moderate	Moderate	High
Eastern Europe	Slow	Slow	High
Latin America	Slow	Slow	Moderate
Middle East	Moderate	Slow	Low
Far East	Slow	Slow	High

Adapted from Acuff (1997); Samovar & Porter (1997)

> Americans' time consciousness, achievement orientation, and impatience. They [non-Western cultures] know the Americans will make concessions close to the deadline in order to get a signed contract. (p. 162)

In Latin America, negotiators are expected to show up late for appointments as a sign of respect. Indonesians do not want to be hurried; they treat time much like rubber, something that can be stretched as needed (Harris & Moran, 1996). In Africa, people move slowly, because those "people who rush are suspected of trying to cheat" (Ruch, 1989, p. 278). Tung (1996) points out that Japanese negotiation processes can be slow because 90% of lower- to middle-management-level negotiators seek group consensus before making decisions. Chinese negotiations may be slow, but for a different reason; Chinese negotiators must contend with a great deal of government bureaucracy, requiring long periods of time to obtain approvals.

Perhaps because of their turbulent history of treaties and agreements, Israeli negotiators tend to focus a great deal on the present. Morrison, Conaway, and Borden (1994) explain, "Successful deals in Israel must promise an immediate return. Long-term guarantees and warranties are rarely selling points" (p. 191). Table 11.1 summarizes the cultural perspectives in the use of time in pacing during negotiations, decision making, and punctuality of meetings.

The level of formality differs among cultures. In Great Britain, traditions and cultural heritage are important. Negotiation involves greater formality and attention to protocol. Negotiators describe British managers as casual, diplomatic, reasonable, and willing to seek compromise. They engage in a lot of small talk and rarely exaggerate or display emotion. Japanese negotiators demonstrate a style that is polite and nonaggressive. They value first contact by a third party who can speak honorably about the parties with whom they will be negotiating. As with many Far East nations, Chinese place high value on respect for status and protocol. The negotiation processes will be reserved and dignified. They value honoring appointments and being punctual.

Table 11.2 Priorities of Cultural Orientations

Individualistic Cultures	*Collectivistic Cultures*
Solution oriented	Relationship oriented
Prefer independent decisions	Prefer group decisions
Approach issues directly	Avoid conflict
Value autonomy	Desire social approval
Emphasize cause and effect	Appeal to authority
Greater interest in personal needs	Greater interest in group needs

Norms and Values

Many scholars distinguish between individualistic and collectivistic orientations of cultures, arguing that these perspectives will influence factors such as worldviews, expectations, and the choice of language in negotiations. Table 11.2 lists many of the differences between these two orientations.

Culture provides its members with a set of norms by which the value of agreements is measured and by which relationships are conducted. Individualistic cultures, such as the United States, Canada, Great Britain, Netherlands, and Australia, emphasize autonomy, independence, and concerns about self-interests. Collectivistic cultures such as Japan, Korea, Mexico, and Taiwan emphasize conformity to group norms, interconnectedness, relational harmony, and concern for in-group interests. The culture of the country a negotiator is from will have a profound effect on his or her willingness to deviate from group norms and to take risks. For example, Lee and Rogan (1991) report that members of collectivistic cultures "place more emphasis on maintaining harmony than accomplishing tasks" (p. 184). This factor alone would create a great deal of tension for a U.S. negotiator who does not take time to build relationship with a Chinese counterpart.

Negotiators from collectivistic cultures deal with conflict differently than their counterparts in individualistic cultures. For example, to save face, there will be greater avoidance of open discussion of conflict and more accommodating behaviors. In an argument, there is a greater tendency to appeal to authority for answers or clarification.

In contrast, negotiators from individualistic cultures speak more directly about problems, offering statistics or reasons why things should be done in a particular way. There is greater emphasis on achieving solutions and agreements in shorter time frames. Box 11.2 describes a conflict in April 2001 in which the United States and China both needed to assert identity through statements of power. It also illustrates the cultural differences in communication expectations and the importance of saving face.

Collectivistic cultures react to uncertainty differently than individualistic cultures do (Hofstede, 1980). Members of some cultures demonstrate a greater tendency to control environment, events, and situations. Belgium,

Box 11.2

WHEN TWO CULTURES COLLIDE

The collision of American and Chinese planes about 65 miles off the China coast in April 2001 highlighted the cultural differences between the two countries. The Chinese called for a U.S. apology to "the Chinese government and its people." The U.S. responded that it had nothing to apologize for and demanded return of its plane and its crew.

The Chinese response focused on damage done to them collectively as a nation. Claiming their sovereignty and dignity had been insulted, Chinese depicted themselves as victims of American espionage. One Chinese diplomat criticized the United States as "arbitrary and unreasonable" and involved in "a gangster type of hegemonism" [aggressive expansion of nations]. One Chinese leader accused the American representative of "displaying an arrogant air." Another diplomat asked for the U.S. to "do something favorable to smooth the development of Chinese-U.S. relations, rather than make remarks that confuse right and wrong."

The U.S. representative argued that the U.S. plane had a legal right to fly and conduct routine "surveillance" as long as it was over international waters. Another American official said that Americans were looking for a "common understanding" through an "exchange of explanations." The U.S. stayed focused on rationale about why it had nothing to apologize for but, to allow the Chinese to save face, it eventually showed a willingness to express regrets for the accident.

Later, the U.S. increased "regret" to "sorrow" and eventually to being "very sorry" about the disappearance of the Chinese pilot and "sympathy" for his widow. After 11 days, China released the U.S. crew, claiming that the Chinese people had received "a form of apology" from a nation "that talks big but is inconsistent."

The cultural exchange demonstrated that issues of respect for national identity were as important to the collectivistic Chinese as solutions to a problem. They responded in a predictable condescending, parental manner. In contrast, the individualistic Americans looked for quick decisions based on logic and legal definitions of international space.

Japan, France, and Russia display a strong need for controlling uncertainties. Other nations, such as Denmark, Sweden, and England, tend to "accept and handle uncertainty without much discomfort and show a relatively greater tolerance for opinions different from their own" (Kale, 1996, p. 27). Nations such as the United States, Spain, and Greece fall somewhere in the middle.

Graham, Mintu, and Rodgers (1994) compared the negotiation behaviors of 11 nations, including the United States, England, China, France, and Germany. They looked at problem-solving approaches, profits, and satisfaction with outcomes. The scholars found negotiators from the more individualistic cultures were more competitive and antagonistic than problem solving. Researchers confirmed the preferences of collectivistic nation negotiators for maintaining harmony and avoiding open discussion of conflict.

Western cultural groups highly value linear completion of tasks and formal agreements. Contracts tend to be written, specific, and formal. Contracts specify who does what, when, and how, and they include benefits or penalties for implementation in an agreed-upon time. But this perspective is not shared by all cultures. Sonnenfeldt (1986) states,

> Americans often feel uneasy if a negotiation does not conclude with a completed document, signed, sealed, and delivered. This is not the case with the Soviets. They have often been prepared to engage in endless talks and negotiations without conclusion and still attempt to promote their interests through that process. (p. 24)

Acuff (1997) quotes the manager of contract administration from a global corporation as saying, "Many feel that having a contract with the Chinese is a joke because when you get right down to it, the Chinese do not view the contract as binding" (p. 61). Pye (1986) explains that Chinese negotiators prefer informal agreements with loosely worded statements expressing mutual cooperation. On the other hand, negotiators from Western Europe, North America, and Australia have a high need for contract specificity. Knowing what your counterpart expects in terms of contractual arrangements might in itself be an important phase of negotiation. Table 11.3 summarizes a few of the perspectives about the level of specificity or ambiguity expected by negotiators as they move toward agreements.

Spector (2001) argues that creating a cooperative relationship – one that prevents escalation of conflict – involves building leadership that observes adjusted norms or new norms that govern behavior of parties. These norms may involve factors such as participation of nontraditional parties, new coalitions, consensus formation, or policies regarding the assessment of information. Spector cites as an example the Zambezi River system negotiations. The discussions "led to the creation of a regional regime to manage the economic development of shared water resources among eight riparian states" (p. 215).

Table 11.3   Level of Specificity of Contracts and Agreements

Region	Level
North America	High
Western Europe	High
Eastern Europe	Moderate
Middle East	Low
Latin America	Low
Asian	Low

Adapted from Schuster & Copeland (1986)

Relationship

During the fall of 2001, the importance of the relationship between the United States and Pakistan or the United States and Tajikistan could not be underestimated in the negotiation for the use of air bases, intelligence information, and airspace in the war on terrorism. The relationships are no less important in the creation of corporate alliances in the business world for the building of computers, televisions, or automobiles. Relationship may serve as the bond that maintains cooperative attitudes during times of difficult choices and tradeoffs. Unless sufficient relationship exists to transform the way parties view each other or the issues, even potential economic gain will not help the negotiations to succeed. A case in point is the ongoing inability of the Palestinians and Israelis to sustain agreements, in spite of many potential gains.

Within a negotiation, culture may play a significant role in how much negotiators value relationship during a negotiation. Both British and French negotiators tend to precede relationship building by dealing with business matters first. Similarly, German negotiators get down to business, moving right to the agenda without a lot of questions or warmup (Morrison, Conaway, & Borden, 1994). They have a reputation for being hard bargainers and value relationship less than some of the other cultures do (Acuff, 1997).

Prenegotiation ritual, after-hours socialization, or establishing credibility based on geography or family history serves as a method for building relationship. Relationship serves as a vehicle for overcoming early resistance. In East Asia, many believe that who you know is more important than what you know. This is referred to as *guanxi* in China, *kankei* in Japan, and *kwankye* in Korea. Each of the words refers to the importance of building relationships or connections with individuals who may influence the course of a negotiation (Tung, 1996, p. 378). Box 11.3 describes the importance of relationship in one negotiator's experience working with both profit and nonprofit organizations in the former Soviet Union.

Communication

One of the most visible aspects of negotiating across cultures is the difference in communication styles. For example, direct, personal questioning

---

Box 11.3

NEGOTIATING WITH RUSSIANS

For 4 years, Steve Reiquam conducted contract negotiations in the former Soviet Union's Central Asian republics of Kazakstan and Kyrgyzstan, as well as Muldova. He believes that business negotiation in the former Soviet Union is heavily dependent on building relationships. He states, "No relationship, no business. There are reasons for those 3-hour lunches. As a matter of fact, business is often no more than the consequence of personal relationships" (personal communication, April 12, 2001).

In terms of problem solving, Reiquam observes, "It's very top-down in the organizational context. The boss makes the decisions, and others appear to willingly accept his (usually it's a he) authority." Typically, the Russian negotiation style involves stating "extreme initial positions and later making concessions that don't amount to much." In the use of time, Reiquam says, "Russians seem to have all the time in the world, operating as if no decision is the best decision. Indeed, not making decisions is virtually all that it takes to botch up your project or deal."

Reiquam concludes that negotiators who work in Eastern Europe must possess a great deal of patience and flexibility. "Lower your expectations about how quickly you can reach agreement," he says. "In addition, invest in relationship."

---

may be acceptable in the United States but regarded as threatening to French, Thai, or Italian negotiators. Direct eye contact may be valued as a sign of genuineness by American negotiators but regarded as aggressive by East Asians. The ways we communicate, a function of our cultural heritage, influence how we act and respond during negotiations. Usunier (1996a) states that "the capacity to cope with very different communication styles is the key to successful international business negotiations" (p. 112).

There's been a great deal of research about average tendencies in cultural communication of negotiators from different nations. For example, Chinese and Japanese negotiators tend to be receiver-oriented, as demonstrated by behaviors that display respect and sensitivity. They ask a lot of questions, focus on listening, and use a great deal of silence. Japanese negotiators share less information than U.S. negotiators do (Brett & Okumura, 1998). German negotiators use a high percentage of self-disclosure statements and a low percentage of questions (Graham, 1996).

Table 11.4   Display of Emotion in Negotiation

Region	*Level*
Africa	High
Latin America	High
Middle East	High
United States	Moderate
Western Europe	Moderate
Eastern Europe	Moderate
Asia	Low

Like many African and Eastern nations, China will strategically "provoke, develop, and exploit potentially conflicting views in deliberate fashion . . . through the use of ambiguous formulas, and allusive or paradoxical statements . . . designed to make the 'water muddy to catch the fish'" (Faure, 1998, p. 141). The lack of precision in language allows for maneuverability during negotiation, changes in direction, and occasionally for saving face. Strategic ambiguity can serve as a tactic for creating common ground between highly polarized adversaries. Japanese negotiators avoid saying "no," preferring instead terms such as "inconvenient" or "under consideration" (Richmond & Gestrin, 1998).

Culture may explain some of the different expectations with which negotiators approach negotiation processes. German negotiators place a great deal of emphasis on planning and order in their negotiations. They value logical explanations. German negotiators tend to be direct and blunt and expect counterparts to be well prepared and knowledgeable about the issues. Russian negotiators are status-conscious and want to negotiate with key decision makers. They "regard compromise as a sign of weakness; it is morally incorrect" (Morrison, Conaway, & Borden, 1994). French negotiators, who value precision and clarity, conduct business principled by Napoleonic Law. Their style is often described as autocratic. Graham (1996) states that "the style of the French negotiator is perhaps the most aggressive of all the groups. In particular, they used the highest percent of threats and warnings . . . used interruptions, facial gazing, 'no' and 'you' more frequently compared to other groups" (p. 83). Box 11.4 provides the perspective of a Canadian negotiator who works with both French and British industries.

The kind and level of displays of emotion vary among nations (see Table 11.4). Eastern nations such as China, Thailand, Philippines, and Malaysia speak with little emotion and quiet, peaceful tones. In direct contrast, Latin American negotiators are verbally expressive and will use loud displays to make their points. Foster (1992) explains, "In general, Latins might permit their display of affection, warmth, anger, frustration, sadness, disappointment, and joy at the negotiating table to a greater degree than would be appropriate for Americans" (p. 160).

In addition, Foster (1992) points out that many older cultures in Western Europe and Asia place "a special quality of expressiveness on the high art of

---

Box 11.4

VIVA LA DIFFERENCE

Canadian Shelley Slater serves as a contract administrator whose primary responsibility is working with companies across Canada and in France. She says, "Canadians want to be seen as independent from the United States, so they value their identity a great deal in negotiations. They display this priority in the way they make a big deal out of every little deal. In addition, they will compromise more than most American negotiators" (personal interview, April 5, 2001).

Slater describes French negotiators as possessing a high concern for the law. They tend to be highly bureaucratic and socialistic, making the pace of negotiations slow and tedious. She laments, "We negotiate when to negotiate. Things never get done. There's never a 'yes' or 'no,' but lots of maybes and shrugged shoulders." The French, she says, use indirectness and demonstrate a lot of tentativeness. "The French place a high value on status and protocol and show little respect for women with whom they negotiate. When decisions are to be made, instead of making the decision, they look for a male in authority to tell them what to do. They're very chauvinistic." She adds, "When they're rude, you just have to ignore it. Respond with humor and earn their respect. You have to win them over."

---

communication, on a grand style of speaking and writing (indeed, even of listening) that transcends common day-to-day speech" (p. 202). This is in contrast to American negotiators, who use plain and technically oriented language that focuses on the bottom line. The different manner in which cultures express thoughts, concepts, and ideas requires negotiators to do a great deal of clarifying to be sure about the meaning of messages.

Studies of speech patterns also show a difference in the way thoughts and feelings are shared in negotiation. Spanish negotiators interrupt their counterparts five times more often than American negotiators do (Fant, 1989). North American and Western European negotiators value sequential, ordered discussion of issues. One person speaks at a time. In contrast, in many Latin American, Arab, and African cultures, ideas will be presented simultaneously in overlapping conversations.

Cultures vary widely in their use of nonverbal behavior. Strong eye contact communicates strength and honesty in Western cultures yet may be interpreted as aggressiveness or disrespect in Eastern cultures. Russian negotiators use less direct eye contact than members of other cultures and ask more questions than counterparts (Graham, 1996). Like the Russian negotiators, Japanese negotiators use less eye contact during negotiations and allow long, silent pauses during discussions. Both the Japanese and Chinese negotiators avoid directly saying "no" and also strategically use periods of silence. Africans use a lot of eye contact when speaking and very little while listening. Arabs engage in long, sustained eye contact to demonstrate interest and to assess the honesty of their counterpart. In the United States, smiles generally communicate agreement and affirmation. In Latin America, Japan, or Caribbean cultures, negotiators may smile to show respect but in actuality have a great deal of anger or disagreement.

Interdependence

Few symbols described the interdependence of the world's nations better than the towers of the World Trade Center in New York City. More than 425 businesses from 80 nations had offices in the towers before terrorists destroyed them on September 11, 2001. The global village has become a complex web of interdependence fostered by cultural exchange, treaties, and business relationships. The growth of communication technologies has created a world where villages in Africa have televisions and people with access to computers can speak with almost anyone in the world. The birth of the euro as a form of currency links nations of Europe together in a large financial network. Decisions made by one country affect the business and cultural affairs of other countries.

International negotiation often involves businesses with government processes. For example, in the church case described in Box 11.1, church leaders had to negotiate with both city and national officials to build their church. Commercial negotiation is often affected by security, foreign policy, and social issues of other countries. Phatak and Habib (1999) point out that "pervasive intrusion into the private affairs of companies is quite routine in most developing countries such as China, Indonesia, Egypt, and India" (p. 377).

Power

A fundamental dimension in cross-cultural negotiation is the distance of those who hold power from those who are affected by power. Hofstede (1980) describes the distance between the two groups as *power distance*. It accounts for a culture's orientation to authority, the importance it places on status, the way roles preserve superior-subordinate relationships, and the observance of class distinctions.

A high power distance (HPD) is demonstrated in negotiation in many ways. For example, Andersen and Bowman (1990) believe that the smiles used by East Asian negotiators project the kind of harmony subordinates are expected to maintain with superiors in East Asian cultures. Samovar and Porter (1997) explain that "cultures with high power differences will foster and encourage emotions that preserve status differences" (p. 251). Thus, subordinates are expected to express only positive emotions to superiors when disagreements occur.

Foster (1992) explains that HPD cultures are more paternalistic, place high value on protocol and status, favor centralized decision making, and respect hierarchy. Decisions are generally based on personal judgments of persons of authority, not necessarily on professional competency. Hofstede (1980) lists as nations with the highest HPD the Philippines, Mexico, Venezuela, India, and Yugoslavia.

In addition to France and India, nations of Latin America ranked high in HPD.

Low power distance (LPD) cultures, including the United States, view decision making and relationships from a more egalitarian perspective. Negotiators from LPD nations tend to be less formal and demonstrate less regard for status and protocol. During discussions, they downplay differences in rank to promote freer exchange of ideas. They may be less aware of their tone or volume of speech. Cordon and Yousef (1983) report that people from non-Western cultures view the tone of American speech as noisy, exaggerated, and childlike. Hofstede (1980) lists as the top five LPD nations Austria, Panama, Denmark, New Zealand, and Peru. The United States ranked 16th on the 53-nation list, with Great Britain close to the middle at 36th.

In many cultures, the effects of status and hierarchy extend to the role of gender in negotiations. Acuff (1997) states, "There are many countries where customs, attitudes, and religion are hostile to women in business and there is no question that international business negotiations are still dominated by men" (p. 62). For example, in Eastern Europe, Latin America, China, Spain, Germany, and many Middle Eastern countries, negotiations are primarily conducted by males. In North America, East Asia, Israel, and much of Western Europe, women negotiate with few barriers. Women can negotiate in almost any international setting as corporate executives, but they will face more challenges with cultures where chauvinism or machismo prevails.

Because each of the parties in an international negotiation represents a coalition, the negotiation processes may, at times, resemble labor-management negotiations, in which representatives from groups negotiate with representatives of other groups. As in labor negotiations, decision making may occur in public, but a great deal of the process is done in small groups outside the official meetings. Even after representatives reach an agreement, they must return to their own group to get ratification.

SUMMARY •

Although many generalities describe tendencies of decision makers or negotiators in different cultures, we must allow for a great deal of variation within each culture. For example, although some cultures, such as China, demonstrate high collectivistic tendencies, many individuals from China are highly individualistic. In our interview with Linda Putnam (see Chapter 5), she cautions, "Prescriptions do not work, nor always do essential beliefs about cultures. We're finding that while the study of high- and low-context cultures may help, negotiations depend on the dynamics of a particular duo or group." In addition, culture is dynamic and changing as world events change. Events within a culture can influence a negotiator's behavior at any given moment. When working with people from cultures different from our own, we need to possess a high level of adaptability and patience.

International, cross-cultural negotiation involves a great deal of sensitivity to many factors, including differences in communication and decision-making styles, orientations to power and group, the level of ambiguity in word choices or contract expectations, and the use of time during negotiations. Cultures approach problem-solving processes with different values for sharing information or authority. In addition, cultures contend with different levels and priorities of bureaucracy. The need for approvals by government officials can significantly slow business negotiations. When Eastern and Western nations must negotiate differences, Faure (1998) points out, "The crux of the matter, then, lies in negotiating the construction of the problem rather than its solution" (p. 143). The American priority for solutions will need to be tempered with Eastern needs for harmony at both the symbolic and group level.

To be successful in international negotiation, negotiators need to display a great deal of patience and adapt to the needs of the context. Some cultures require a long warmup for building trust and relationship, whereas others want to dispense with small talk and ceremony. A negotiator's orientation to power will influence his or her need for protocol and valuing of status. Negotiators from collectivistic nations will avoid direct confrontation and place a high priority on group approval for decisions. Nonverbal behaviors such as direct eye contact, loud volume, and fast rate of speech can create undesired perceptions of aggression or rudeness in some contexts. Graham (1993) emphasizes the importance of awareness and sensitivity in communication:

> The first step to improving the effectiveness and efficiency of cross cultural commercial transactions is to become aware that such differences lie not only in *what* is said (content) but in *how* it is said (linguistic structure and nonverbal behavior) and in the *social context* of the discussions. The initial goal should be to avoid misinterpreting or over interpreting the overt and subtle signals sent by our negotiating counterparts from other cultures. (p. 139)

Finally, signing a contract may indicate closure for a deal to most American negotiators, but this is not the case in other cultures. The concept of agreement differs across cultures. For example, the Japanese view a signed contract as a description of the relationship between parties. The Chinese view contracts as general principles that may be changed as conditions change. Copeland and Griggs (1993) warn, "The Arab might not fulfill an 'agreement' since a Westerner can mistakenly hear words of commitment when only politeness is intended" (p. 228). Negotiators need to know what agreement means to negotiators from other cultures.

PROFESSIONAL PROFILE

PETER ADLER, ●
**CONSULTANT, THE ACCORD GROUP,
AND PAST PRESIDENT OF THE SOCIETY
FOR PROFESSIONALS IN DISPUTE RESOLUTION**

Culture Braids Itself into Negotiation

Most of us are aware that culture can play a significant role in negotiations. In our newspapers, we read of difficulties in international negotiations related to differences in customs and language. At our workplaces, we find seminars on diversity, combined with an increased sensitivity to ethnic, religious, and gender subcultural differences. In community negotiations, we may be aware of differences in perspective among organizational cultures, be they governmental, corporate, or nonprofit. As we travel and do business in third-world cultures, we find that prices are sometimes negotiable; fixed prices are not nearly so common as they are in Europe, Canada, and the United States. Peter Adler is an expert on negotiations who has spent part of his career practicing, mediating, teaching about, and writing of intercultural differences.

In terms of concepts introduced in this chapter, Peter assists negotiations in which both high- and low-context cultures are at the table. In his practice, multiple parties come together for lengthy periods to solve complex problems. He finds dramatic cultural differences in negotiating styles and communication behavior when he assists negotiations between native Hawaiians and United States government officials. The impact of cultural differences varies across negotiations; sometimes differences are the subject of dispute, sometimes they are a subtext, and occasionally they have little effect relative to other variables.

Introduction to the Practitioner

Peter describes himself this way: "My specialty is negotiation and mediation: helping people with difficult, complex, sometimes dangerous, and always far-reaching discussions. I believe in Casey Stengle's [former New York Yankees manager] dictum: 'My job is to get everyone else to hit a home run.' When disentangling, way finding, and agreement making are at issue, bringing out everyone's best leadership is an imperative. I have a long background in convening, mediating, and helping people build constructive working relationships when they are involved in high-stakes conflict. I am keenly aware of the need for quality information. Most important, I love seeing people get unstuck and move forward in intelligent and graceful ways."

Peter Adler reports that his experience with culture and negotiation began in 1966 during his stint in the Peace Corps. Living and working in India, he was assigned to a small village in a poor, rural environment. Peter remembers, "For 2 years, I negotiated *everything*. I was organizing construction projects in a rural area. We were building small schools, roads, and wells. Negotiating was a constant part of what we did in that we had to provide supplies, materials, and workers all together on a project that had a completion date. My personal life also involved daily negotiation; going down to buy potatoes involved negotiating at the town market. There were no fixed prices. Suddenly, I found myself thrust into this high-context negotiation environment. It was instant immersion. It was baptism by fire."

Following his years in the Peace Corps, Peter went to graduate school, studying sociology and community development. His fieldwork in El Salvador again involved him in daily negotiations. After completing his PhD, Peter moved to Hawaii, where he became director of The Neighborhood Justice Center (now called the Mediation Centers of the Pacific).

In 1985, Peter left his position as Director of the Neighborhood Justice Center to work for the Supreme Court of Hawaii's Center for Alternative Dispute Resolution (ADR). In 1992, he joined the Accord Group, an international firm specializing in facilitation, mediation, planning, and problem solving. Typical issues in this work tend to be natural resources, the environment, and public policy. Peter's specialty is multiparty negotiation and problem solving. He has authored several books based on his expertise: *Oxtail Soup: For the Island Soul* (2001), and *Beyond Paradise* (1993), as well as numerous other professional and popular articles. Peter has held numerous offices, including president of the Society for Professionals in Dispute Resolution (now Association for Conflict Resolution).

Insights About Negotiation

Peter notes that there are many skills required of the negotiator who operates in an intercultural setting. When he trains and teaches negotiation skills, he bundles them into different packages. Peter offers this example: "There's a whole world of communication skills. Adept negotiators have a command of communication skills. This doesn't mean that they are highly verbal or articulate, but that they're able to clearly communicate their points and listen effectively to those with whom they are negotiating." In Peter's view, effective communication behaviors are one essential skill set.

The cognitive skill set is also important. Peters identifies insights and ideas as part of this package. In addition, "There are micro skills that have to do with managing tension and managing dilemmas in negotiation. There's a litany of different ideas about negotiation skills that have emerged in the last decade. I'm thinking of the differences between principled negotiation and positional bargaining. There are sets of skills that go along with those ideas, such as managing the differences between competition and cooperation." Negotiators who develop such skill sets become versatile in their ability to negotiate interculturally. Peter concludes that versatility is the most important trait of a successful negotiator.

Preparation for negotiation begins with the substantive research necessary to understand the issues involved. In Peter's opinion, "Skills are necessary but insufficient. You might be a great negotiator, but if you haven't done your homework, on the substantive end of things, you will get into a lot of trouble. You can't substitute negotiation skills for competence on the substantive side. Planning and the preparation are essential. I tell people to get clear on the numbers and the facts. Do the homework."

Peter uses the example of negotiation for a car purchase: "You must do the research on that car. What does a prospective deal look like from the other side? Try to understand everything you can about how they are going to be looking at you. The research should be producing some estimates about ranges. Interests, needs, and timing should be considered. You have to be clear about your own needs and interests. A big problem with interest-based bargaining occurs when people haven't thought through their own interests." Preparation requires the negotiator to consider his or her own interests as well as those of the other side. Then, important dynamics of the negotiation, such as a range of agreement and timing, should be considered. This research and planning should take place before the actual negotiation begins.

A typical intercultural negotiation for Peter is a case he worked on for a number of years involving the meeting of low- and high context cultures. The dispute, which occurred on the island of Hawaii in the Natural Area Reserves, concerned the hunting of feral pigs. Parties who wanted the pigs removed from the rainforest included the Audubon Society and the Sierra Club. They maintained that the pigs, which weighed 400 to 500 lbs., were severely damaging fragile parts of the rainforest. In contrast, the native Hawaiians revered the pigs and wanted them left undisturbed. The two sides were unable to agree so, eventually, an assisted negotiation or mediation was held to attempt to work out a plan.

Peter recalls, "A colleague and I spent almost 6 months working with both sides to try to resolve this conflict. Over and over again throughout the negotiation sessions, I could watch the different cultural perspectives and mindsets at work. Each party to the negotiation—environmental advocates, community members, government agencies and native Hawaiians—brought some version of an organizational culture to the table. For example, the government people came to the table with a version of a professional culture that values rules and regulations, with a backdrop of political and legal forces.

Whereas on the environmental side, there were a number of scientists who brought their organizational culture of science. Their way of perceiving the world values the distinction between what's factual and what's not factual, what's salient information and what is not. Finally, there's the native culture, based in rural perspectives and concerned with cultural revitalization. The pigs are hunted for food in subsistence communities, but they are also symbolic, cultural icons. The pig is one of many gods revered by the native people." The primary values of these different organizational cultures created a clash of perspectives that made intercultural negotiation particularly difficult.

There are also differences in the spoken traditions by which different cultures perform negotiation. Peter explains, "Native Hawaiians and Polynesians in general are great orators and storytellers. When they get into a negotiation session, they give long speeches and they talk loudly, they argue fiercely, and they come at negotiation with great passion and anger. Whereas the government agency representatives are speaking about what the law will and won't allow. They're talking as if the world is bounded by rules. The scientists are reading from scientific reports." It is not difficult to see how the three cultures fail to communicate effectively with one another, using their very different styles of presentation and language.

Such intercultural differences dictated a translator role for Peter and his colleague as neutrals attempting to facilitate this negotiation. He notes, "Our job was to slow down the talk, ensuring that the communication was actually heard, making sure that people were willing to tolerate a style of communication that was different than their own. We would coach people in front of each other and ask people from all sides to restate and summarize what the other person was trying to communicate. We were gatekeeping the discussion." Peter notes that there were 6 months of discussion, and certainly not all discussions were high intensity, high drama. However, the cultural issues threaded their way through all the conversations.

Eventually, the participants reached a set of 50 agreements that they forwarded to the legislature, the body that had originally set up the negotiation. These agreements stipulated that some areas would permit more pig hunting, whereas other areas would permit less hunting. Some community forestry councils were set up. These negotiated agreements were enacted into current policies.

Peter believes that successful negotiation depends on many factors. In his view, "In general, successful negotiation involves some version of communication and some version of problem solving. When you strip everything else away, people in a successful negotiation have communicated to one another, and some kind of problem solving has taken place. However fragile, however interim, however tentative, those are the two elements of successful negotiation." When the process works, people exchange messages, and they come to conclusions about the issues on the table.

The toughest challenges in negotiation may be traced to several origins. First, Peter identifies disputes that are largely value driven. Second, multiple parties make negotiations more complex and difficult. Peter explains, "The more parties there are, the more issues and values there are, the tougher it is to figure out a process that will yield an outcome that is satisfactory to all involved. For instance, I'm working on a case that involves the [U.S.] Army and the Army Corps of Engineers, as well as environmentalists. The case has to do with a training range where native Hawaiians want to close the Army down and get them out of this area that was historically important. The Army desperately needs a training area."

There are very sharp value questions suffusing this negotiation. The Army is trying to resolve the question, 'How can we minimize our live-fire impacts?' but the Hawaiians are asking, 'How do we get these lands back under our control?' These questions don't match; they reflect very different notions of what people hold dear. The toughest challenges occur when there are multiple parties negotiating many open-ended, unbounded value questions.

When negotiations break down, Peter observes, "People go home. Sometimes they go home and come back another day. Sometimes they don't. This is a hard question to answer generally, but I think there are lots of different ways in different cultures to say 'no.' When it's said with finality and the other person accepts it, then the negotiation is over. That can be done in a friendly way, it can be done in a harsh way, or it can be done in a way that leaves the door open. It can telegraph signals that the parties may talk again if someone different comes to the table. There are many feints and ploys that might take place. People may make demands that seemingly drive the other from the table, but it's only part of the negotiation dance. Negotiators must make their best estimate of the underlying meaning of these behaviors. When I say, 'That's my last offer,' how do you know whether or not I'm bluffing? We may walk away and later make phone calls that reestablish the negotiation. Negotiation breakdowns are so situational that it's very hard to respond generically."

Peter offers his response as a mediator to negotiation breakdowns. He explains, "I try not to prolong unproductive discussions. Timing is really critical in negotiations. There isn't one perfect time to end discussions. It depends on what the deadlines and the pressures are. I don't mean I slam the door prematurely, but I certainly don't want to prolong unproductive talk that may be just irritating people more. One of the things a mediator can do, if the parties trust you, is to flush out where the parties are and help them make a deal. I can sit with them in caucus and help them to achieve the greatest possible joint gains."

Contextual Differences

Peter reflects on the intercultural context. He muses, "I think culture is one of those things that braids itself into some negotiations. It becomes an important factor in some negotiations, a subtext in others, and virtually invisible in some. Sometimes culture is the primary element of a negotiation.

Sometimes there's a cultural etiquette of how to negotiate. Sometimes there's a cultural metagame. For instance, Indonesian corporate interests use a certain style of negotiation. The pattern is that they all bring in professional agent negotiators. The tendency is to bring in 'muscle,' such as four-star generals, to negotiate on their behalf. Then the other side brings in a five-star general. There's a lot of brute force to bring to bear. An American negotiator in Indonesia might not be aware of this pattern. A vice president who couldn't talk directly to his or her counterpart would be quite frustrated." Peter believes that culture is one of the threads running through negotiation that may or may not significantly affect the context. Typically, negotiators do not know how salient the cultural element will be until they are in a particular negotiation.

Changes and Conflicts

Peter doesn't see many new or emerging trends in intercultural negotiation. He feels that he may not be sufficiently conversant with the most recent literature to offer an opinion on this topic. He notes that there is more general awareness that culture is one of the lenses that we look through as we apprehend our reality. In this light, he finds the literature on high- and low-context cultures to be the most helpful. This body of knowledge helps us understand the forces that impinge on us and on our counterparts in negotiation.

The major topic of disagreement among practitioners that Peter notes has to do with the centrality of culture to negotiation. Peter says, "In a [1993] book called *Culture and Negotiation* [edited] by Guy Oliver Faure and Jeffry Z. Rubin, the debate is well framed. The authors take a series of international river cases. These are disputes over boundaries and water use in major rivers around the world. They examine the issue of how culture plays into the issues. One view is that when all these countries come to the table to negotiate, culture is really what's going on. The other view is that cultural differences sometimes impact international negotiations. Is culture an omnipresent element at the negotiation table? Or, is it more like birds flying into airplane engines—not a frequent occurrence, but devastating when it happens?"

However uncertain the resolution to this debate, it is certain that Peter Adler has contributed to the dialogue around cultural differences in negotiation. His trainings focus on the two skill sets of communication and problem solving. He cautions adequate preparation before negotiation, regardless of skill level. His consulting assists multiparty negotiations by operating as a cultural translator. He acknowledges the challenge of value clashes in multiparty negotiations but continues to consult and mediate in that arena. Through his scholarly experience, his leadership of the major professional organization in the arena of conflict management, and his active practice, Peter has developed and strengthened the work of negotiators who operate in an intercultural context.

PROFESSIONAL PROFILE

EDWARD KING, ●
SENIOR PROGRAM MANAGER, MCI WORLDCOM

Cultural Elements of International
Negotiations Are Absolutely Paramount

Imagine that your job is to put a system in place that will generate phone bills for 25 million customers. Normally, you would allow more than a year to get the job done but, under these specific circumstances, you are told to do it in 6 months. Oh, and, by the way, the company is in Brazil. This is the challenge that Edward King, a senior program manager for MCI WorldCom, faced when MCI bought a Brazilian telephone company.

In King's experience, the primary difference between United States and Brazilian cultures has to do with the importance of relationship to Brazilians. The skilled negotiator must take into account both personal and cultural values of other parties to the negotiation. In Brazil, differences in negotiating styles require negotiators to conduct more discussions before coming to the table. The practitioner also comments on the implications for negotiating across subcultures of United States organizations.

Introduction to the Practitioner

Ed is responsible for software development and implementation projects, and, although his title does not include the word "negotiation," he uses negotiation in most facets of his job. Ed spends three quarters of his time negotiating with other groups about content, schedule, and release dates of software products. He is also involved in the negotiation of contracts for software services, commercial software products, and general business activities. When he's not negotiating a contract or an agreement with another group, he is working with his own team members to achieve a common understanding of the task at hand and agreement about how to accomplish it. As for negotiation skills training, he explains, "I became involved with the negotiation aspects as a part of my job, with most of the training for this position being OTJ—on the job."

For 2 1/2 years, Ed commuted back and forth between Rio de Janeiro and Denver. When Ed and his colleagues first arrived in Rio de Janeiro, they had no prior experience in Brazil. They learned some things about Brazilian culture from travel books and brochures, but mostly they learned by developing relationships with their colleagues at work. Their business associates taught them aspects of the local culture that proved to be essential for successful negotiation. "There's the Brazilian culture to deal with, but also the local culture in Rio, called Carioca. People from Sao Paolo, called Paolistas, are very business driven—all business, all the time. Cariocas are really laid back. Getting into some of those subcultural elements is very important also. In Rio, people didn't want to work on the weekends, while, 200 miles away, 'yeah, sure man, no problem.'"

Ed believes that understanding and adapting to cultural differences is crucial, that the biggest challenge about international negotiation is bridging the cultural chasm. In his experience, Americans are very goal-oriented, focusing on the task more than on the relationship. In many other places, such as Japan and Brazil, you need to establish a relationship before you can conduct business. Ed explains, "So, we have very low-context people meeting very high-context people, and sometimes it's like putting hydrogen and oxygen together—boom." Thus, it is essential to take these differences into account. Ed points out, "If you are working in a very goal-oriented fashion, you may end up alienating the people that you have to agree with."

However, negotiating with people from another culture does not mean completely taking on their culture as one's own. The intercultural negotiator must persuade people to adopt new ideas and behaviors as well. In Brazil, Ed had to facilitate a change in the work culture from a government-owned monopoly to that of a private, entrepreneurial organization. To do this, he needed to find ways to persuade people to think and work in a different way than they were accustomed to so that project goals could be met. "The challenge here was to negotiate with the incumbent staff to work to our compressed deadlines," Ed says. "Because of the cultural differences in the way business in the United States and Brazil works, a lot of the 'standard' negotiation techniques to obtain buy-in and project progress did not work—they were simply ineffective." One technique that did work well was to discuss issues and work out differences with people individually before going into a meeting. Then, in the meeting, everyone was familiar with the topic and could ratify the solution that had been worked out beforehand.

Ed believes that team building is an important part of negotiating. "The team dynamics have to be established from inclusion right on up to ensuring the vision is set properly. After all, the two sides that are negotiating are the team that is going to make an agreement that is beneficial to both parties."

Insights About Negotiation

Before negotiation, Ed uses the following strategy: "I prepare by trying to find out what the values are of the other organization, to determine what drives it. Then, I consider the culture of the organization I'll be negotiating with; my intention is to get a glimpse of how things are done there. Next, I set out what the objective is and what the target of my negotiation is going to be, and then lay out a plan (as best I can) to manage the process towards that goal."

Ed believes it is essential to learn about the people you're going to be negotiating with, such as what their personal values are. This learning process can be very straightforward, and can be accomplished for the most part by relying on one's listening skills. "People love to talk about themselves, no matter who or where they are. The trick is to get the initial banter going and, once that is established, it will help to break down some of the psychological walls that get in the way of getting this information. Appropriate humor can help a lot to get this information and discussion going. Besides getting the information you will need to effectively negotiate, you are at the same time building the basis of the relationship that is needed to effectively work with others. The better the relationship, the better the information exchange."

In addition to asking people about themselves, Ed suggests finding some things you can safely joke about; for him, these included the Paolista versus Carioca lifestyle and his own mangling of the local language. He finds, "Through this process, people will open up to discuss who they are, what they do, their circumstances, job, the weather, sports, and just about anything—as long as it doesn't get into the touchy subjects (e.g., the volatile ones of politics and religion)." This background information is extremely valuable in planning an approach to the negotiation. It may require some time and research, but it provides the foundation for the negotiation.

It is also important to recognize that many places put more emphasis on hierarchy than does the United States. In these places, you need to start at the very top of the organization to get introductions and buy-in all the way down the reporting structure. Although senior executives may be far removed from the day-to-day business processes with which you are concerned, a personal referral from them may be essential to get the attention and cooperation of the people below them in the hierarchy.

For Ed, typical negotiation sessions begin with "the usual formalities, including business card exchanges. If I am running the negotiation, I may start out with a description of the problem to be solved by stating the need that will be fulfilled with the use of our services. If I am the recipient of the negotiation, I will have given an outline of the problem to be solved to the other side, letting them come up with the answers and approaches that need to be evaluated." From this point on, the focus is mainly on how to come to agreement to meet the business objectives. Very rarely do negotiations break down to the stage where one side will see the other side as unreasonable. Ed explains, "I work very hard to keep the parties together, and to time breaks strategically in the overall discussion." For example, if people's body language shows that they are disagreeing, Ed will call a break so that they can go meet informally with their colleagues and discuss their concerns. This saves the participants from having to call attention to their discomfort by asking for the time apart.

Contextual Differences

Both inside and outside formal negotiation sessions, Ed finds it important to remember that some cultures don't share information widely. In Brazil, he found that there was little information exchange among organizational "silos". Along the same lines, he found that workers did not maintain the overall vision of the project. Instead, they were satisfied to do a piece of the project without needing to understand how it fit into the whole. He felt he needed to pull them into the bigger picture for the project to be successful. Thus, to get coordinated cooperation, he started explaining to people how their tasks fit into the larger project.

International cultural differences are very tough to negotiate, and some business-to-business cultural differences in the United States can be just as challenging. Ed believes that it is important to pay attention to several levels of culture, both within the United States and internationally. There are country cultures, local subcultures, company cultures, and departmental cultures, to name a few. For example, he has found information technology (IT) departments to be similar around the world. As he puts it, "IT is IT all over." At the same time, he found noticeable differences in culture between the cities of Sao Paolo and Rio de Janeiro. Thus, the skillful negotiator must find out which cultural influences are at play in any given negotiation.

Negotiators need to recognize that different cultures negotiate differently. Ed describes some cultures as control-oriented, whereas others are role-oriented or goal-oriented. In a goal-oriented culture, such as an engineering group, it is usually appropriate to go directly to the person you need and work out what needs to be done. However, in a role-oriented culture, such as a hospital, it's necessary to work through the proper channels. In a control-oriented culture, you probably need to start at the top of the hierarchy and work your way to the people who will actually work with you on the solution. When you get to them, you'll have the authorization and credibility that you need.

Ed identifies several skills that intercultural negotiators need: "Often, the first approach does not work, so the ability to look through, evaluate, and obtain buy-in on alternatives in a real-time manner is a critical skill." Stamina and the ability to see things through are also essential; negotiators should not leave loose ends. Also, the ability to change one's communication style is critical—even to the point of learning a foreign language and customs.

Trying to adopt some of the local language and culture can be a tremendous help. In most places, Ed has found that if you make an attempt to use a few words of the local language, people will gladly take on the role of your teacher. This can really help to bridge the differences and start building relationships.

Changes and Conflicts

Ed has some other specific suggestions. One is related to gender: "Note that many countries are very macho. The role of women is not seen as that of a businessperson. If it is, the role of a woman in the foreign work environment may be stereotyped to an administrative, functional, individual contributor, or low-level manager—usually not one of a senior-level executive. Your negotiations may be queered by sending the wrong gender of person (at least initially) to do the negotiations. I know this isn't very politically correct, but remember that you are not dealing within the United States culture—you are a guest in someone else's country, and it is very important to respect the customs and culture of your hosts. To do differently will only make it more difficult."

Another suggestion focuses specifically on contracts. Ed warns that negotiators should "make sure the language in the contract is precise, and terms and conditions are set so that it's clear to both sides." Participants may not be aware that they understand things differently, so it is important to agree on the exact meaning of the terms of any contract. For example, negotiators should be specific about terms related to time—what does a business meeting at 10 a.m. mean? In the United States, if a meeting is scheduled to begin at 10, those who attend expect it to begin promptly. In Latin America, all the participants might be there by noon. U.S. culture is very time oriented; others may be less so.

For Ed King, understanding and adapting to cultural differences are essential parts of successful negotiation. And for Ed, everything involves negotiation. "It's just not limited to what we traditionally think of as negotiations, like contracts," he explains. "For example, in a goal-oriented work culture, the "currency" of the culture is information—information is power, and giving that information away may diminish your role or position relative to what is being done. Brought down to its lowest level, you have to negotiate—give and take—to get the information that you need to do your job effectively." In international business negotiation, the information needed includes both cultural and subcultural differences among negotiators. Possessing information about personal history and organizational goals enables Ed King to negotiate effectively, both at home and abroad.

CHAPTER **12**

INTEGRATING THE ART WITH THE SCIENCE OF NEGOTIATION

Summarizing the views of 25 practitioners from a variety of negotiation contexts is a daunting task. Some questions elicited insights specific to a practice or an area of conflict. Other questions elicited general information useful to both novice and experienced students of negotiation. To organize the insights of the practitioners, in this chapter, we compare their responses along seven dimensions: contextual differences, valued processes, important skills, barriers, professional differences, new directions, and changes that affect negotiations.

The practitioners varied in age, geographical location, professional orientation, and areas in which they practiced negotiation. Some of the practitioners negotiated for themselves, some facilitated negotiation, and others negotiated on behalf of a particular group. Although just a few of their insights may be generalized to the greater field of negotiation, we believe the combined education and experience of those interviewed provides a wealth of information for negotiation in the many contexts they represent.

PRACTITIONER PERSPECTIVES •
ON CONTEXTUAL FACTORS

Structure

Practitioners were asked in what way the context of their negotiations made a difference in their approaches. Probably the greatest differences relate to the scale of the negotiation. Where there are multiple issues and multiple stakeholders, negotiations tend to be more structured and procedures more formal. For instance, Bill Ury, cofounder of the Program on Negotiation at Harvard Law School, notes that international negotiations involve complex issues, cross-cultural issues, and large constituencies that do not have independent decision authority. Speaking of the same arena, MIT professor Larry Susskind reports, "When you take something that is bigger and more complex than a two-party negotiation and you overlay communication problems, you have compounding difficulties."

Negotiations do not need to be international to be large scale and complex. Wayne Carle, former superintendent of schools, finds teacher contract negotiations more formal and nit-picky than others he conducted as a public school administrator. Family mediator John Fiske and Larry Susskind note the public scrutiny of negotiations where governmental affairs are concerned, and the fact that enormous public pressures may be exerted on the negotiators. Commenting on leveraged buyout negotiations, investment firm chairman Joseph Rice makes the point that in this context, there are many complexities and a high amount of risk. Texas A & M professor Linda Putnam notes that systemic factors and regulations distinguish organizational negotiations from those in other contexts. Federal mediator Edward Selig explains that environmental disputes are especially complex because there is such a history of uncertain outcomes in litigation. Legal principles are still in a state of evolution, and cases as much as 50 years old introduce historical uncertainties. In additional, environmental negotiations are fraught with scientific and economic uncertainties, because experts are often divided on these topics.

Practitioners who specialize in multiparty negotiations mention one essential approach most often: making sure that all relevant stakeholders are included. Jesuit college president Fr. Charles Currie and Wayne Carle address the importance of the relationship between a constituency and its representative at the table. Susskind elaborates on how he assists stakeholder negotiators to deal internally with their own side or within their organizational group: "Parties must understand what their latitude is. What is their mandate? What is the scope of their authority? We help people prepare for negotiation by getting everyone in the group to enter into this prenegotiation assessment that will guide the one who will represent them. It's too late for the representative to come back later and tell everyone what assessment was underlying his or her approach."

Lawyers or representatives of constituencies are more likely to be the negotiators in multiparty negotiations. Susskind points out that the presence of a professional neutral complicates the process. Although the mediator may be helpful in moving the parties toward settlement, the mediator's goals are not always consistent with those of each party. Such agents have their own sets of goals as well as the ones that complement those of stakeholders. The presence of agents may add further obstacles to achieving resolution.

Union-management negotiators Linda Graves and Annie Hill report on the nature of labor-management negotiations based on their experiences across the table from each other. They find that anticipating the reaction of constituents not at the table (such as union members and boards of directors) is critically important. As Graves notes, "We have to keep in mind that everything we do at the table must be ratified outside." In their view, it would be hard to overcommunicate. Others representing constituencies in environmental and other multiparty negotiations are confronted with this same dynamic—the need to keep members informed.

In the corporate context, attorney James Freund advises, "Parties dealing through intermediaries such as mediators mustn't forget that they are still engaged in a negotiation. You should also give the mediator the factual and legal evidence to show your adversary why the mediator has come to this conclusion. In effect, you're urging the mediator to act as an agent of reality."

Norms and Values

Both Hill and Graves emphasize the importance of respect as a norm in negotiation settings if the negotiations are going to be productive. Graves states, "If you're going to respond, 'What you proposed was B.S.,' you might as well not be there.But if each side goes in [saying to themselves], 'Okay, we're going to get some things that we think are stupid, we are going to get some things that we probably can agree with,' then we can manage." Respect is an important norm for constructive communication in negotiations.

Some negotiators believe that agreement is harder to come by in their contexts because of the interaction of value differences. Judy Towers Reemstma, television documentary producer, says that there is somewhat less ability to compromise in video production (where journalistic standards are concerned) than there is in personal situations (where people can take turns or share something). ADR consultant Peter Adler, MCI program manager Edward King, and Larry Susskind point to intercultural differences in values, perspectives, and styles of communication. They believe the primary values of different organizational cultures create a clash of perspectives that makes negotiation in that context particularly difficult. Fr. Currie finds that in academic and religious negotiations, students and faculty have special sensitivities to justice issues: "Students especially are very easily disheartened when they perceive an injustice. They have such a keen sense of justice that sometimes makes it hard to get through to them." Value difficulties make finding common ground more problematic.

Adler points out that a clash of norms and values is inherent in cross-cultural negotiations. For example, Adler facilitated a negotiation regarding the hunting of feral pigs. Each of the groups who came to the negotiation, including environmental advocates, community members, government agencies, and native Hawaiians, held different values regarding information (what is fact and what is not?), the importance of pigs (revered as gods by some Hawaiians), and the way issues should be discussed (while scientists read from research reports, the Hawaiians engaged in long speeches at loud volume with great passion).

Relationship

The likelihood of an ongoing relationship is an important contextual variable. Mediator Marvin Johnson notes that the desire to preserve a continuing work relationship between colleagues or between employees and supervisors can be a significant factor in negotiations. Barbara Opotowsky, executive director of the New York City Bar Association, notes that it is the hope of ongoing relationships with consumers that motivates retail organizations to remedy complaints. Freund finds that mergers and acquisitions are often one-time disputes about money and that continuing relationships are seldom envisioned or desired.

Labor-management negotiations are characterized by other features. They depend on a shared understanding, such as a technological imperative for the business, to be successful. They depend on placing a value on continuing relationships. In Hill's words, "You need a strong relationship to work through the tough issues." In this context, negotiators don't necessarily like each other, but they must respect each other.

Third parties who assist interpersonal negotiations stress that their context involves long-term relationships, issues of high salience to all parties, and heightened emotionality. Family therapists Christie Coates and Marjorie Bribitzer allude to rich and complex interpersonal dynamics in the families they assist. There is also the issue of parties without highly developed negotiation skills. Nor do parties have the assistance of experienced professionals, since most interpersonal negotiations do not involve the presence of legal counsel. Speech Communication professor Sam Keltner observes, "Neighbors usually haven't had the experience of problem solving through give and take, generating options, and so on. And, of course, they get caught up in the emotion of the thing." In his EEO mediations, Johnson identifies heightened emotionality around feelings of discrimination. The importance of a job to economic security and personal identity virtually guarantees that negotiators will bring heightened emotionality to EEO negotiations.

Several practitioners report on the relationship between clients and their representatives. Fiske says that in municipal negotiations, making connections both with the public and with officials is vital. In his experience, "Through these connections, the negotiator achieves credibility, currency, status, influence. In concrete terms, when you call the town official, he returns your phone call." Selig finds that a typical aspect of his role is to bring rationality to the process. The client cannot be expected to do this, because, by definition, the client is outraged, hurt and/or insulted. Selig says that the client expects his or her attorney to "go and wipe the floor up with those guys!" The effective negotiator will plant doubt in the client's mind about how watertight the case is so that, as Selig says, "the client is softened up a bit for making concessions in the future." Relationships between stakeholders and their representatives must be thoughtful and balanced.

Communication

Coates observes that communication style is often a stumbling block in interpersonal disputes because people are unaware of how their style contributes to the problems that they have with others. In one case, Coates explained to a client, "Whenever you shake your finger in his face, you've lost him; he's gone." Coates adds that sometimes the clients communicate with such tense emotions that it prevents them from understanding the others' needs, articulating their own needs, or focusing on goals that may benefit the family. Communication that calms down these initial intense emotions becomes a priority of negotiating in interpersonal contexts.

In organizational discussions, Hill finds that "some people come in with big chips on their shoulders, so everything they present is said in an angry, antagonistic way. . . . What I see is that, for the most part, the people who get listened to are people who can present their positions in logical order, respectfully and calmly. People who are nasty and mean get attention for a short time, and then people close their ears." Fr. Currie makes a similar point in his assessment that, too often, parties lose their civility: "Parties take nonnegotiable stances. Everything that they believe is right, and everything that you believe is wrong."

But Freund points out that communication can become difficult after distrust grows to the point that "the arteries harden." Parties will take positions that they don't really believe in. Keltner explains, "A major difficulty is that people don't know how to talk to each other about problems. They tend to figure that their solution or position is the most practical one." The inability to approach a problem with civility may reach an extreme, as pointed out by Opotowsky in consumer negotiations: "There are people who make careers out of disputes. They are so personally angry at how they have been treated that it's very hard to resolve the dispute. They have ceased to be realistic. They want someone to be hung by their fingernails because they treated them so badly."

AES Director Robert Waterman believes that negotiations should begin with a lot of "informal talking . . . where ideas are offered in draft form. . . . What I'm trying to do is get them in the position where they're selling me on why I should do the project." Putnam agrees. Some needs will conflict, she says, "so you need to understand them before you get into the negotiation."

Adler explains that differences in communication styles pose a significant challenge in cross-cultural negotiations. People may be less tolerant of styles that differ from their own. Style can vary from intensely passionate and loud to technical and subdued. He explains, "Our job was to slow down the talk, ensuring that the communication was actually heard, making sure that people were willing to tolerate a style of communication that was different than their own."

Interdependence

In organizations, Putnam observes that "no one is operating on an island; no group, no sets of individuals, are independent. . . . For instance, there are policies about hiring practices that impact relations across units." It's critical to understand systemic forces and the interrelationship between departments and project needs and the mission of the organization. It's important to understand how each decision and each project affects others. Putnam explains that "the skilled negotiator makes that inferential leap, understanding how the connection operates, and articulates how this project contributes to the . . . mission."

Rice concurs. In his analysis of an IBM negotiation he facilitated, Rice concluded that it was hard to anticipate all of the interrelationships involving supply contracts, purchase contracts, legal questions of ownership of intellectual property, and how the smaller parts of the company can be affected by decisions of the parent company.

Freund finds that interdependence in contract negotiations is almost always about money: "It may masquerade in many different ways, and it may look as if there are many different issues, but most disputes come down to money." Negotiations in these contexts are not about relationship as much as they are about "racking up a disputed amount of money." Thus, Freund recommends looking for the overlap of interests, which becomes the zone of agreement. Waterman agrees that overlapping interests or needs serves as the place for interdependence: "Think of the two parties involved as two circles that represent their various needs. There is probably a bit of overlap at the beginning of the negotiation, since they found each other in the first place. The negotiator's job is to bring those circles into greater overlap."

Power

Issues of power and authority are addressed in the prenegotiation phase. Putnam asks about the other parties, "Can they make a decision then and there?" Some parties don't like to admit that they don't have authority, a problem that can delay negotiations. Putnam adds, "So it's critical to understand where they fit in a larger hierarchy, and what are the sets of relationships around decision processes." Waterman agrees; discerning where power lies between the parties is an important priority in negotiation. He recommends involving different authority levels in the negotiation processes. During the early stages of negotiating a contract, consultants must make sure that the executive decision makers are on board. Later, those negotiating the contract should involve employees who will actually be implementing the changes to achieve their buy-in. Within organizations, clear definitions of authority drive negotiation strategy.

Hill explains that in labor-management bargaining, parties occasionally exercise power from a distributive negotiation perspective. They expect one side to win and the other to lose. Parties feel the need to use power to demonstrate control or to make a symbolic point. Graves agrees. She describes how union and management in one negotiation disagreed about who ran the business. According to Graves, the union "had to show some muscle, regardless of what was on the table."

● NEGOTIATION PROCESSES

Prior to negotiation, several practitioners suggest that the first question that should be asked is whether such a process is possible. Rice sees the most basic act as "determining whether the buyer and seller have an overlapping range of opportunity." Speaking more plainly, Graves advises that we must first "determine whether there can be compromises, or whether the two sides are so far apart that you'll never reach an agreement." In family therapy, Bribitzer finds, "In order to be successful, all participants must share the belief that . . . a middle ground exists, and all must benefit from finding it." Selig notes that in environmental negotiations, one of the first questions is whether opponents truly want to negotiate or are just trying to discover your case. In his experience, "They pretend to be negotiating in order to discover your case, to smoke you out, but when push comes to shove, they are not interested in working out a settlement." The first priority of negotiators is to determine if there are sufficient interests (economic or relational) to be gained, identity needs to be achieved, or pressures creating a need to talk. Establishing the need to negotiate is an important first step.

After it is determined that negotiation is a possibility, many negotiators emphasize the skills discussed in Chapter 4 under the "Prenegotiation" heading. Susskind asserts, "The prenegotiation phase is probably the most important phase of any in a negotiation." Studying the issues and understanding one's own positions and those of the other side must precede successful negotiation. Practitioners involved in negotiations of the following types—organizational (Putnam, Waterman, Rice, Graves, Hill, and Reemstma), multiparty (Susskind, Coulson, Freeman, and Roisman), and intercultural (Ury, King, and Adler)—are especially likely to emphasize the importance of coming to the table well informed. In the words of Elaine Freeman, founder and executive director of the ETV Endowment of South Carolina, Inc., "The ability to analyze what the other side wants is vital." Travel agency owner Christine Beard says, "Make sure you have all the facts. I document everything." Adler advises, "You can't substitute negotiation skills for competence on the substantive side. Planning and the preparation are essential. I tell people to get clear on the numbers and the facts. Do the homework." Preparation matters, whether the facts are dollars, deadlines, or emotions. Bribitzer prepares for family negotiations by putting herself in the role of each member to understand what emotions are driving them. Then, she asks what aspects of the family's system "have caused it to become stuck in the current impasse."

Putnam elucidates the processes of prenegotiation. She recommends that each party understand what the issues are and the multiple ways of defining those issues because "research shows that when there are multiple interpretations of what the situation is, success is more likely." An understanding of needs and priorities is built through consulting with those involved.

Setting goals for negotiation and appreciating those of the other side are important to negotiation success. Waterman holds that "the number one skill is knowing yourself and your organization well enough." The second most important skill he names is developing a realistic understanding of the other party's needs and wants. The top negotiation skill in Ury's view is related: "If I had to pick a single skill, it would be the ability to put yourself in the other side's shoes and see the situation the way they see it." The capacity for empathy is essential to understanding the position and interests of the other.

Putnam specifies setting goals called "target and resistance points. Targets are what you can live with reasonably. . . . Resistance points . . . are your essential economic or resource needs; you must clearly understand what you can't relinquish and still accomplish your goals." Ury advises using adequate preparation time to "think through the interests behind your positions. What are the intangible motivations, such as resources or security, that drive your positions? Rank your interests. What are the interests of the other side?" Susskind offers a similar list. Both men underscore the importance of analyzing your BATNA (Best Alternative to a Negotiated Agreement) and the BATNAs of the others in your negotiation. Parties should be clear about their own goals and try to discern those of the other side.

When the issues of all stakeholders have been identified and explored, it is important to build factual arguments that will convince other stakeholders of the validity of one's cause. Clear communication in terms of reasoning and explanation become essential tools for this phase of negotiation. Susskind assists clients in framing arguments so that others have a basis for agreeing with what's being proposed. Selig believes that the effective environmental negotiator compellingly argues the strengths of the case. As a union representative, Hill speaks of "being able to sell your issues—not only with passion but also with facts. This is true whether I'm selling to members and leaders of the union or to representatives of the company." Careful analysis provides the framework for an effective case presentation.

Practitioners who negotiate for others have advice about offering options. Fr. Currie, Selig, Fiske, Freund, and others stress the importance of approaching resolution creatively. First, creativity is helpful in finding the common ground. In Fiske's words, "The effective negotiator has the ability to see that folks who demand very different things actually have a lot in common. Parties tend to focus on what divides them and must be constantly reminded that they share certain values and interests. An effective negotiator knows that common ground requires repeated emphasis."

Even when common ground is elusive, a creative approach helps in generating options and creating value. Freund explains that because litigation is always a threat in business mediations, the two sides are unlikely to share information with each other. Therefore, "It behooves the mediator to generate the options, see the avenues for creativity, and create value." Selig values imagination and finds that a creative third party comes up with options and solutions that parties may have missed. Finally, creativity is useful in designing the process that best fits a particular dispute or set of disputants.

Several practitioners comment on the importance of the terms of settlement. First, written agreements must be specific and clearly understood by all. Second, they should contain provisions for revision and consequences for abrogation. Finally, they must be consistent with organizational policies, government regulations, and applicable laws.

● QUALITIES AND SKILLS OF NEGOTIATORS

Good analysis is complemented by good communication skills. Many practitioners commented about the importance of listening to understand the views of others. King makes the connection between listening and gathering information about others' personal values; Reemstma captures the situation in organizations, where professionals "like to think they are in total control, but in fact there are layers of people" who review and pass judgment on new programs. Listening also helps us receive and use feedback from important others. In the view of management representative Graves, "Good listening is the skill most critical to the practice of labor negotiations." Putnam explains that listening for what isn't said is also a useful skill. She says, "Active listening is important, so you're listening for what's not being said, along with statements about what you think this means, so that parties can operate from meaning and interpretation levels, not just levels of language."

Putnam finds that in organizations, "persuasive skills are critical, because the negotiator needs to be able to articulate a position and support it." She discusses how organizational leaders translate needs and goals into bottom lines—that is, analyzing where the organization is going and how a negotiator's goals fit into its mission. In Russel Turbeville's work as district attorney for consumer fraud, "We have to come in and show that the business didn't fail—it was murdered. And, we have to convince 12 people of this beyond a reasonable doubt." Building a persuasive case demonstrates to a jury the defendant's intent to defraud.

Bribitzer thinks about what questions or statements might expand a family member's perspective of the conflict or, conversely, what language might cause them to be defensive. Keltner observes that an effective negotiator demonstrates skills of "listening, reframing, summarizing, feedback, developing empathy with the parties, et al." Putnam names reframing as the most important skill a negotiator can possess.

Flexibility is an important perspective to bring to negotiation. Coulson, Roisman, and Opotowsky speak about the importance of going into a negotiation with a give-and-take mindset. They make the point that a successful negotiator draws a clear distinction between what is wanted and what is possible. Opotowsky warns that the consumer must "be prepared for some back and forth, some give-and-take." Putnam asserts that firmness on ends and flexibility on means are the keys to negotiation success. Waterman approaches negotiation informally. He avoids polished analysis and presentations—"the rougher, the better," he advises. This approach invites participation from those who must approve the final document.

The ability to control emotions is a commonly noted communication skill. Former American Arbitration president Robert Coulson advises, "Don't be distracted by emotions. . . . Control of emotions and clear thinking are critical skills regardless of context." Rice finds that success depends on the ability to handle the negotiation process in a way "that doesn't allow the process to become inflamed." Selig subscribes to the *Getting to Yes* principle of being tough on the problem but easy on the people. His philosophy is to maintain friendly relations with even the most deadly adversary. Opotowsky advises that consumer disputes "are not about you personally, or about the other party personally—it's about the dispute. The more the consumer's ego is involved, the harder it is to solve the problem." Freeman says it simply: "Don't be hotheaded."

In contrast, Beard says that travelers may find themselves with more leverage through the display of immature behavior. In airports, emotional extremes may work to one's advantage when other approaches to negotiation have failed. In her experience, "It's the squeaky wheel that gets the grease. Instead of being proactive about a travel-related problem, customers who turn into obnoxious complainers usually get their way. Sometimes, tears help." Every good rule has its exception.

There are certain personal qualities that practitioners highlight. For instance, many negotiators speak of patience, others of perseverance, noting that negotiations can seem to go on interminably and, often, it is the party with physical and mental endurance who prevails. King advises that stamina is required for intercultural negotiations. Ury explains the value of patience: "Negotiation takes time; it takes more time than you'd think to build the relationships that are essential to a negotiation based on the kind of trust that allows you to explore a problem in depth." The majority of negotiators note the importance of respecting one's opponent and/or one's clients.

Carle and many others call for good judgment and fairness. Many practitioners mention the importance of being a trustworthy person. Fiske believes that negotiators must project "honesty and the motivation to achieve a fair solution. Those at the table and their constituents must believe that the negotiator has integrity." Coates notes that none of us are without bias, but the effective negotiator recognizes his or her biases and does not allow them to interfere. She calls on mediators to "uphold the basic ethical standards . . . of confidentiality and impartiality and neutrality." Freund goes one step further, pointing out that "one side may be very appealing in its presentation and the other side may be boorish, but you can't let that affect your judgment. Second, you not only have to *be* fair-minded, you have to *appear* fair-minded. These two things are not always the same and are not always so simple." Negotiators may manifest mature behavior in a variety of ways.

In addition, multiparty mediators add other skills to the traditional list. Susskind notes that it is often important to be able to work as a team member. Mediators must be able to deal with the media and possess documenting skills, such as how to report and make sense of what the parties are discussing. Freund believes a business mediator needs a sense of how a dispute might fare in court, because every dispute is mediated against the backdrop of possible litigation. In his experience, an attorney's ability to forecast probable legal outcomes is extremely useful in mediating business disputes. Selig agrees: "The first skill in environmental negotiations is knowing the law." Christine Coates and Marvin Johnson believe that mediators must know the law pertinent to their subject areas but do not need to be attorneys to be effective.

Some suggestions were mentioned by only one interviewee but are worth repeating. For instance, Ury suggests rehearsing for an important negotiation, putting yourself in the role of responder, to better assess the strength of your approach. Fr. Currie believes in giving thought to a neutral location and providing a climate that is comfortable and congenial. Reemstma notes she makes a practice of reserving her resistance to feedback to a few important instances; this builds her credibility so that, when she does insist on her view, she has more leverage. King suggests finding some things that negotiators can safely joke about. Turbeville offers a list of ways consumers can avoid being scammed in negotiations with con artists, beginning with "if it sounds too good to be true, it probably is." Waterman finds a low-key style is most effective in negotiating with clients in the business setting. In his experience, "it often works better to appear to be a little bit harmless and stupid, rather than to come on too strong."

NEGOTIATION BARRIERS •

There is universal agreement that multiple parties at the table render negotiation more difficult. Putnam finds that "it's more difficult to find the good for the whole when there are many stakeholders. More and more negotiations involve multiple parties." Waterman also names the challenge of negotiating with "many constituent groups." Susskind considers multiparty international disputes the most challenging, noting "enormous problems with communication, with understanding what's being said, what's involved."

Ury believes that the most important question for negotiators to address is how to respond to these multiparty disputes. He observes, "There is room for innovation, for new techniques and methodologies. We're in the beginning of the challenge that faces all of humanity: How do we learn to collectively make decisions together when we have all these differences?"

Some interviewees put challenging issues at the top of their list. For instance, Rice mentions that there are situations in his practice when "both parties have very legitimate claims to [a] single asset. This can be a very long, involved, and demanding process, and one that has in it the seeds for very contentious negotiation." Turbeville notes that white-collar crime is more complex than other areas of prosecution. Selig lists many difficult aspects of environmental issues, such as contradictions between state and federal laws and disagreements among experts about the significance and the costs of environmental problems. Adler and King speak of the difficulties in intercultural negotiations when values clash. Carle labels such challenges in school administration "deep ideological splits."

Having a history of conflict often makes negotiations more difficult in that the residue from past conflicts (antecedents) colors present negotiations. Putnam asserts that many organizational negotiators face the challenge of latent and recurring conflict. In EEO negotiations, Johnson reports considerable challenge where "the hurt has been going on for a long time," especially when that hurt derives from a perceived lack of respect or recognition. Susskind finds the challenge of "a long history of hostility and mistrust" characteristic of his international work. Issues complicate negotiation when they are complex, uncertain, value laden, and marked by a history of conflict.

Other practitioners feature more personal challenges: parties who are unwilling, unable, or conniving. For attorney Anthony Roisman and Linda Graves, a lack of personal integrity on the part of other negotiators produces the worst possible scenario. Reemstma says the time she feels "really *skunked*" in negotiation is when someone wants to make changes that misrepresent the facts in her film. Faithfulness to the facts of the story is a nonnegotiable issue for her. For Fiske, being stereotyped and attacked by the very folks he is trying to reconcile is frustrating. The behavior of opponents can present considerable challenge. Parties who are not capable of negotiating competently for themselves are a special challenge for those who assist interpersonal negotiations. For example, Bribitzer explains that a therapist has trouble helping families negotiate with teens when the parents have not resolved their own power struggles.

In divorce negotiations, Coates is challenged by clients who need psychological or mental health intervention. At other times, she may work with parties who are operating out of extreme anger or fear: "They are really not able to understand what the other needs; sometimes, they are not even able to articulate their own needs." For Keltner, the most challenging negotiations are those where the neighbors hold deep emotional involvement. The deeper the emotional involvement, the more difficult it is for negotiators to maneuver—for instance, "in cases which involve their families, where there's heavy money involved, personal pride is threatened, or long-standing traditions are challenged." Powerful emotional attachments prevent both negotiators and those who would assist them from using effective processes.

Others encounter the loss of emotional control in organizational settings. Freund finds his toughest challenge in mediating a *business divorce,* a term he gives to the dissolution of a partnership. He recalls, "It involves emotions stronger than those in a typical business dispute. The bitterness of a failed partnership is like the bitterness that follows a failed marriage." Selig and Roisman find they cannot be successful for clients whose motives are vindictive. Selig explains, "When you have a client who needs to establish that he is right, to protect his injured ego, to teach the other guy a lesson, it [negotiation] won't work." Parties who demand revenge or retribution are a challenge.

Parties who have emotional control but closed minds are also difficult to deal with. Johnson finds that "when they [negotiators] don't try to see the other person's point of view, when they're not willing to consider that they may have overlooked something, it's very tough." He senses trouble when he hears someone say, "It's the principle of the thing." Selig agrees, listing the frustration of assisting parties who "turn deaf ears to factual presentations." Neutral third parties cannot assist disputants who are unwilling to take a realistic stance with regard to their cases.

The con artist is a special case of personal challenge. The victims believe that they are negotiating in good faith. The con artist builds a relationship with the intended victims, persuading them to trust him. According to Turbeville, "The con man comes up to you and says, 'I like you. Let me help you.' And he intentionally fosters a relationship of trust so he can screw you to the wall like a molly bolt. That's his psyche." This is a negotiation in the mind of the victim only.

The con artist is a challenge for the prosecution also. Our system of English common law is based on identification of the culprit. In telemarketing and Internet fraud, there is little possibility of identification. In addition, many state laws are written to reflect a laissez-faire attitude toward business regulation. Legislatures respond to those who lobby and contribute to political campaigns. Business participates in this way; consumers do not. Both consumers and consumer fraud agencies are sorely challenged when it comes to consumer crime.

Some barriers related to process include conflict styles, hidden agendas, or the need for a mediator. Styles of conflict management vary from extremely competitive to quite collaborative. For Carle, adversarial relationships are challenging: "Unless administrators, school boards, teachers, and parents can build and maintain collaborative relationships, not much is accomplished." Labor-management negotiators also note the difference that a more adversarial process makes in their ability to come to agreement.

Putnam comments on the difficulties in negotiation when there are hidden agendas. In her experience, "When behaviors aren't consistent, or there isn't a standard of trust, you get a sense that the bargaining is about something else, not the issues on the table." In EEO mediations, Johnson sometimes finds that the official complaint is only the tip of the iceberg. Negotiators sometimes must look more deeply than the official agenda.

In Freund's opinion, mediation is the toughest of all negotiations because parties to mediation haven't been able to resolve the disputes on their own—if they could have done so, they wouldn't be needing a third-party neutral. One of Ury's frustrations in violent international conflicts is that they might have been resolved with the help of others from the international community. He notes that these conflicts don't arise suddenly; there are usually stages of escalation and the possibility that early intervention may stem the violence. In his view, "We need to spend a lot more time figuring out how to use negotiation to prevent wars rather than using negotiation just to end wars."

PROFESSIONAL DIFFERENCES: ● TRADITIONAL TOPICS OF DEBATE

One of the classic debates among negotiators is how directive or nondirective to be. Fiske and Carle, working in public negotiations, note differences of opinion about how much formal authority to invoke. Some negotiators are more likely to use force and regulatory power, whereas others favor the development of more voluntary compliance whenever possible. Opotowsky notes disagreement about the use of informal methods to resolve disputes. She leans "toward informal dispute resolution generally, not just for consumer disputes. I think that we litigate far too much." The majority of practitioners agree.

Coates finds herself less directive in family negotiations than in other kinds of legal cases. Bribitzer reports, "Therapists sometimes differ about the extent to which the neutral should be directing clients toward specific negotiation outcomes. Don't see yourself as the negotiator; see yourself as the mentor of others learning to negotiate." Operating in the workplace, Johnson labels himself "more facilitative than evaluative." There's an ongoing debate between those who espouse the directive approach and those who prefer a facilitative approach.

In contrast to the nondirective approach of Coates, Bribitzer and Johnson, Freund concludes, "The neutral has to be very activist and very judgmental." In his business setting, the neutral bridges the gap between negotiators who are stuck; both parties are negotiating with the neutral. Because of the level of distrust between parties, it is very difficult for them to make offers to each other with any hope of success. As the negotiation proceeds, the neutral not only enlarges the pie but also looks for innovative ways to carve it up. Although the *Getting to Yes* model portrays the neutral as more facilitative, Freund observes that the activist neutral typifies negotiation in corporate settings.

Opotowsky notices a difference between consumers in the business and personal context. For instance, she relates, "When my organization makes a purchase from another organization, negotiations regarding repairs or returns are rather impersonal. When individuals are involved, there is often more impact for the consumer. When something goes wrong, it really hurts their lives."

The interviewees also have differing views on the familiar debate regarding how knowledgeable a third party must be about content to be able to assist those in conflict. Several attorneys (Selig, Turbeville, and Freund) see their knowledge of the law as a vital skill in their ability to assist with negotiations. With regard to the substance of the dispute, Susskind's position is, "There are some who say that content knowledge isn't important, but I don't buy it. The more you understand content, the better you can assist people." Others are less likely to feel that a great amount of content knowledge is required. Keltner says, "My position is, if you are skilled in the process, it isn't necessary for you to be a specialist in the content." Rice believes he learned most of what he needed to know about business negotiating on the job. Practitioners interviewed in this book represent the range of traditional positions of this debate.

Finally, some of the interviewees touched on another debate—what the goal of negotiation should be. Should it be a deal? Should it be transformative? Freund and Susskind take a problem-solving stance. Freund maintains that fairness is an elusive concept, whereas satisfaction is a realistic goal. In Susskind's opinion, "The notion that I'm going to make them [the parties] into better people is manipulative and self-serving. It makes me very uneasy that people might define the work we do as somehow surreptitiously seeking to change parties without their knowledge." There is a stark difference between those who see the purpose of facilitated negotiation as problem solving and those who believe it should be transformative (for a discussion of transformation theory, see Chapter 3).

Putnam calls attention to areas of negotiation where scholars and practitioners have done little research and more is needed. She mentions the study of women in negotiation, because "women do not fit the scripted models [of negotiation] very well." There is also a need to study negotiation ethics, because what is ethical and appropriate in negotiation varies greatly across organizations. She finds that there is disagreement in the field about the role of relationships in negotiation. She notes that research shows that "no matter how skilled the negotiators or how perfect the processes they engage in, the outcomes are bombarded by relational problems." Finally, the old thinking that emotions in negotiation are bad needs revision. She says that emotions are clues as to when outside help is needed. They may signal when negotiators need to reframe issues.

Both Adler and Ury speak to the disputes about the interaction of culture and negotiation. Ury explains, "Some hold that culture is not that important a variable. Others believe that it's absolutely critical—that without understanding culture, you can't understand negotiation." Adler similarly finds that the major topic of disagreement among practitioners has to do with the centrality of culture to negotiation.

NEW DIRECTIONS ●

The growth of negotiation as a field was the change most often mentioned by those profiled. Sometimes practitioners profiled in this book made significant contributions to the field. For instance, Ury, Coulson, Susskind, and Keltner published the first books that might be technically termed ADR (alternative dispute resolution) books. Ury and Susskind are among the cofounders of the Program on Negotiation at Harvard Law School. Along with Coulson, Keltner, and others, they were instrumental in organizing and leading the Society for Professionals in Dispute Resolution, now the Association for Conflict Resolution. Commenting on the field of negotiation, several interviewees mentioned the fact that the negotiation profession is growing, drawing people from law, social work, and other fields.

The academic study of negotiation has also expanded. There are an increasing number of courses in dispute resolution and conflict management that include negotiation theory and practice as important components. Selig mentions the increase in law school courses that teach negotiation generally and environmental negotiation specifically. Ury informs us that cross-cultural negotiations have been the focus of recent research. Susskind points out a focus on the added complexity of multiparty negotiation, a recognition that "it's not a difference in degree, it's a difference in kind." Again, a number of practitioners, such as Johnson, Keltner, Putnam, Susskind, and Ury, are leaders in academic growth and development.

Some practitioners note the growing interest of the public in the problem-solving approach to negotiation. According to Selig, "Court after court is now setting up multidoor models, where cases come in and a case coordinator looks them over and determines which ones might be mediated. States are setting up offices of dispute resolution, and there are United States district court panels that can be called upon to assist settlement." Ury and Susskind note the public's increased attention to multiparty negotiation.

Carle wonders "how to inject civility into a process based on adversarial relationships."

Fiske finds that municipalities are becoming more aware of the need to prepare for demonstrations, including the possibility of negotiation between the city and the demonstrators. Keltner notes the growing number of communities that have adopted neighborhood mediation services. Johnson comments on the growing use of ADR in federal employment disputes. The spread of negotiated problem solving in recent years has been notable.

As principled negotiation becomes more widely recognized as an option, some processes are hybrids of competition and collaboration. Coates explains that new processes have evolved from the increased use of mediated negotiations. "What I see that is new is some hybrid processes that have grown out of mediations that failed. For instance, for the high-conflict couple who is not able to move on, mediation alone is not enough." Coates mentions parenting coordination, case management through coordinating among professionals involved, med-arb (where the parties agree in the beginning that the mediator will make decisions if they cannot), and special masters who do intensive work with families over time.

● CHANGES THAT AFFECT NEGOTIATION

Changes in the broader business context have influenced the practice of negotiation both positively and negatively. Rice finds that the recent surge in global competition has driven more business sales and has stimulated more mergers and acquisitions. His practice has grown into European markets as a result. Beard notes many consolidations in the travel business. Adler notices a growing awareness among negotiators of the significance of both national and organizational cultural differences in resolving disputes.

In contrast, other practitioners have experienced negative effects on their negotiations. For instance, Hill finds that "the speed of changes, turnover related to mergers, and the corporate giants which emerge make relationship across the labor-management divide rather problematical." In agreement, Bob Waterman notes that the dot-com frenzy of the 1990s and the demise of long-term relationships between negotiators changed for the worse the character of business negotiations.

Other negative changes include the injection of new stakeholders whose interests may not include collaboration. Carle points out that teacher contract negotiations often involve the use of professionals who may be "disconnected from the reality of schools" or who may focus on economic interests at the expense of community interests or educational outcomes. Additionally, issues that once were negotiated by professionals in education now become the subject of public debate by politicians. Negotiation separated from healthy relationships becomes adversarial and challenging.

Most negative of all, Turbeville notes that "the future looks bright for con men." A laissez-faire legal posture, loopholes in existing law, and consumers negotiating at a distance make it difficult for law enforcement to prosecute crooks. The power of the computer mouse will produce more and more fraud in the marketplace. As Turbeville observes, "Internet markets are still developing, evolving, and changing so fast that it's difficult to set up any kind of regulations or standards."

Susskind believes that the use of the Internet for negotiation is a con job by the insurance industry: "People have been conned into believing that the negotiation done by a machine is more fair. The fact is, you can insert any bias you want into a computer program." He is also negative about the usefulness of online negotiation services. In his opinion, "They are going to fail. We know that when people are not face to face, they ask for more, resist more, and are less oriented toward effective problem solving. So, while we might think we are gaining in efficiency by not spending money and time in face-to-face communication, we are in fact going to produce inferior results."

Ury agrees about the effect of the Internet on the practice of negotiation: "There is emerging interest in the effect of the Internet on negotiations. How does the Internet change negotiations? . . . There's a lot of richness that will be lost on the Internet, even when it goes to video." However, he finds that the most interesting question in the Internet debate is not whether or not to employ it in negotiation but "What negotiation functions can be usefully conducted over the Internet?" Finally, there's an expectation of speed connected with the Internet. Ury asks, "How do we line this up with the time that's required for successful negotiation?"

SUMMARY •

The art and science of negotiation will forever be an important skill for the development of human civilization. In addition to the familiar use of negotiation in business and international relations, negotiation serves as a communication process for building relationships, establishing and revising norms for behavior, and facilitating understanding in interpersonal and community relationships. Negotiation is an alternative to demanding or forcing as a form of persuasion for overcoming resistance. Principled processes for negotiation offer parties the opportunity to establish, refine, or affirm identities as well as to deal constructively with cultural change.

The abilities and skills identified by both theory and practitioners as important for negotiators are equally important in other areas of life: listening, questioning, summarizing, reframing, being flexible, managing emotion, and being patient. Negotiation favors ethical communication reflected in behaviors regarded as possessing integrity, honesty, good judgment, and standards of fairness. Practitioners point out that negotiation will be difficult in contexts where parties practice unethical tactics. Con artists who engage in fraud and biased Internet programs create inequities in agreements. Some factors—such as closed minds, a history of recurring conflict, or emotion-laden issues—present substantial barriers for negotiated agreements.

As the world becomes more complex and integrated, the processes of negotiation become more essential. Blended families, organizations encountering change, communities dealing with diversity, and nations working together to prevent violence require negotiations that will promote understanding and common ground. Safety, economic well-being, and peace will be a function of our ability to work together. As we move deeper into the 21st century, a time of both possibilities and perils, negotiation is no longer a choice—it has become a necessity, a way of life.

REFERENCES

Acuff, F. I.. (1997). *You can negotiate anything with anyone anywhere around the world*. New York: American Management Association.

Adler, N. J. (1986). *International dimensions of organizational behavior*. Boston: PWS-Kent.

Adler, N. J., Graham, J. L., & Gehrke, T.S. (1987). Business negotiations in Canada, Mexico, and the United States. *Journal of Business Research, 15*, 411-429.

Adler, P. S. (1993). *Beyond paradise: Encounters in Hawaii where the tour bus never runs.* Woodbridge, CT: Ox Bow Press.

Adler, P. S. (2001). *Oxtail soup: For the island soul.* Woodbridge, CT: Ox Bow Press.

Adler, R. S., Rosen, B., & Silverstein, E. M. (1998). Emotions in negotiation: How to manage fear and anger. *Negotiation Journal, 14*(2), 161-179.

Allred, K. G. (2000). Anger and retaliation in conflict: The role of attribution. In M. Deutsch & P. T. Coleman (Eds.), *The handbook of conflict resolution: Theory and practice* (pp. 236-255). San Francisco: Jossey-Bass.

Amy, D. (1987). *The politics of environmental mediation*. New York: Columbia.

Andersen, P. A. (1985). Nonverbal immediacy in interpersonal communication. In A. O. Siegman & S. Feldstein (Eds.), *Multichannel integrations of nonverbal behavior* (pp. 1-36). Hillsdale, NJ: Lawrence Erlbaum.

Andersen, P. A., & Bowman, L. (1990). Positions of power: Nonverbal influences in organizational communication. In J. A. DeVito & M. L. Hecht (Eds.), *The nonverbal reader* (pp. 391-411). Prospect Heights, IL: Waveland Press.

Antonioni, D. (1998). Relationship between the big five personality factors and conflict management styles. *International Journal of Conflict Management, 9*(4), 336-355.

Axelrod, R. (1984). *The evolution of cooperation*. New York: Basic Books.

Axtell, J. (1999). The first consumer revolution. In L. B. Glickman (Ed.), *Consumer society in American history* (pp. 85-99). Ithaca, NY: Cornell University Press.

Badham, J. (Director). (1983). *War Games* [motion picture]. United States: Metro Goldwyn Mayer.

Baker, J. (1995). *The politics of diplomacy: Revolution, war, and peace, 1989-1992*. New York: Putnam.

Bales, R. F., & Cohen, S. P. (1979). *Symlog: A system for multiple level observation of group*. New York: Free Press.

Barlow, J., & Moller, C. (1996). *A complaint is a gift*. San Francisco: Berrett-Koehler.

Baum, L. F. (1900). *The wonderful world of Oz*. New York: George M. Hill.

Bazerman, M. H. (1983). Negotiator judgment. *American Behavioral Scientist, 27*, 211-228.

Bazerman, M. H. (1991). Negotiator judgment: A critical look at the rationality assumption. In J. W. Breslin & J. Z. Rubin (Eds.), *Negotiation theory and practice* (pp. 197-209). Cambridge, MA: The Program on Negotiation at Harvard Law School.

Bazerman, M. H., & Neale, M. A. (1992). *Negotiating rationally*. New York: Free Press.

Bell, D. V. (1995). Negotiation in the workplace: The view from a political linguist. In A. Firth (Ed.), *The discourse of negotiation: Studies of language in the workplace* (pp. 41-81). Oxford, UK: Pergamon.

Bell, N. (1999). Alternative theories of power. In L. Kurtz (Ed.), *Encyclopedia of violence, peace and conflict: Vol. 3* (pp. 99-106). San Diego, CA: Academic Press.

Belli, M., & Wilkinson, A. P. (1987). *Everybody's guide to the law*. New York: Harper & Row.

Bingham, G. (1986). *Resolving environmental disputes*. Washington, DC: Conservation Foundation.

Blake, R. R., & Mouton, J. S. (1984). *Solving costly organizational conflicts*. San Francisco: Jossey-Bass.

Blake, R. R., & Mouton, J. S. (1985). *The managerial grid III: The key to leadership effectiveness*. Houston, TX: Gulf.

Bredenberg, J. (Ed.). (1997). *Beat the system: 1200 tips for coming out on top in every deal and transaction*. New York: Berkley.

Breen, T. H. (1999). Narrative of commercial life: Consumption, ideology, and community on the eve of the American Revolution. In L. B. Glickman (Ed.), *Consumer society in American history: A reader* (pp. 100-129). Ithaca, NY: Cornell University Press.

Brett, J. M., & Okumura, T. (1998). Inter- and intracultural negotiation: U.S. and Japanese negotiations. *Academy of Management Journal, 5,* 495-510.

Brett, J. F., Pinkley, R. L., & Jackofsky, E. F. (1996). Alternatives to having a BATNA in dyadic negotiations: The influence of goals, self-efficacy and alternatives on negotiated outcomes. *International Journal of Conflict Management, 7*(2), 121-138.

Brooks, M. (Director). (1968). *The Producers* [motion picture]. United States: Metro Goldwyn Mayer.

Brown, B. R. (1977). Face-saving and face-restoration in negotiation. In D. Druckman (Ed.), *Negotiations: Social-psychological perspectives* (pp. 275-299). Beverly Hills, CA: Sage.

Brudney, J. L. (1990). *Fostering volunteer programs in the public sector*. San Francisco: Jossey-Bass.

Burger, W. E.(1985). Using arbitration to achieve justice. *Arbitration Journal, 40*(4), 3-6.

Burke, P. J., & Franzoi, S. L. (1988). Studying situations and identities using experimental sampling methodology. *American Sociological Review, 53,* 559-568.

Burton, J. (1979). *Deviance, terrorism and war*. New York: St. Martin's.

Bush, R. A. (1996). What do we need a mediator for? Mediation's value added for negotiators. *Ohio State Journal of Dispute Resolution, 12*(1), 1-36.

Bush, R. A., & Folger, J. P. (1994). *The promise of mediation*. San Francisco: Jossey-Bass.

Cairns, L. (1996). *Negotiating in the workplace*. Chicago: Pluto.

Calhoun, P., & Smith, W. P. (1999). Integrative bargaining: Does gender make a difference? *International Journal of Conflict Management, 10*(3), 203-224.

Callaway, M. R., & Esser, J. K. (1984). Groupthink: Effects of cohesiveness and problem-solving procedures on group decision making. *Social Behavior and Personality, 12,* 157-164.

Cantrill, H. (1967). A fresh look at human design. In J. F. Bugental (Ed.), *Challenges of humanistic psychology* (pp. 14-17). New York: McGraw-Hill.

Carbaugh, D. (1985). Cultural communication and organizing. In W. Gudykunst, L. Stewart, & S. Ting-Toomey (Eds.), *Communication, cultural and organizational processes* (pp. 30-47). Beverly Hills, CA: Sage.

Carnevale, P. J., O'Conner, K. M., & McCuster, C. (1993). Time pressure in negotiation and mediation. In O. Svenson & A. J. Maule (Eds.), *Time pressure and stress in human judgment and decision making* (pp. 117-126). New York: Plenum.

Carpenter, S. L., & Kennedy, W. J. D. (1988). *Managing public disputes*. San Francisco: Jossey-Bass.

Chasin, R., & Herzig, M. (1988). Correcting misperceptions in Soviet-American relations. *Journal of Humanistic Psychology, 28*(3), 88-97.

Cialdini, R. B. (1993). *Influence: The psychology of persuasion*. New York: Quill William Morrow.

Cloke, K., & Goldsmith, J. (2000). *Resolving conflicts at work*. San Francisco: Jossey-Bass.

Cohen, H. (1980). *You can negotiate anything*. Secaucus, NJ: Lyle Stuart.

Coleman, P. T., & Deutsch, M. (2000). Some guidelines for developing a creative approach to conflict. In M. Deutsch & P. T. Coleman (Eds.), *The handbook of conflict resolution: Theory and practice* (pp. 355-365). San Francisco: Jossey-Bass.

Cooley, J. W., & Lubert, S. (1997). *Arbitration advocacy*. South Bend, IN: National Institute for Trial Advocacy.

Copeland, L., & Griggs, L. (1993). Negotiation: How to win in foreign negotiations. In S. C. Currall, D. Geddes, S. M. Schmidt, & A. Hockner (Eds.), *Power and negotiation in organizations* (pp. 215-231). Dubuque, IA: Kendall/Hunt.

Cordon, J. C., & Jousef, F. (1983). *An introduction to intercultural communication*. Indianapolis, IN: Bobbs-Merrill.

Coser, L. A. (1957). Social conflict and social change. *British Journal of Sociology, 8*(3), 197-207.

Coulson, R. (1968). *How to stay out of court*. New York: Crown Publishers.

Coulson, R. (1980). *Business arbitration: What you need to know*. New York: American Arbitration Association.

Coulson, R. (1987). *Business mediation: What you need to know*. New York: American Arbitration Association.

Craver, C. B. (1993). Negotiation techniques. In S. C. Currall, D. Geddes, S. M. Schmidt, & A. Hockner (Eds.), *Power and negotiation in organizations* (pp. 297-304). Dubuque, IA: Kendall/Hunt.

Crawley, J. (1995). *Constructive conflict management: Managing to make a difference*. London: Nicolas Brealey.

Crowfoot, J. E., & Wondolleck, J. M. (1990). *Environmental disputes: Community involvement in conflict resolution*. Washington, DC: Island.

Dallinger, J. M., & Hample, D. (1995). Personalizing and managing conflict. *International Journal of Conflict Management, 6*(3), 273-289.

Daly, J. P. (1991). The effects of anger on negotiations over mergers and acquisitions. *Negotiation Journal, 7*(1), 621-633.

Daniels, T. D., Spiker, B. K., & Papa, M. J. (1997). *Perspectives on organizational communication*. Madison, WI: Brown & Benchmark.

Davis, A. M. (1991). Follett and facts: Timely advice. *Negotiation Journal, 7*(2), 131-138.

Dawson, R. (1999). *Secrets of power negotiating*. Franklin Lakes, NJ: Career.

Deaux, K. (1987). Putting gender into context: An interactive model of gender-related behavior. *Psychological Review, 94*(3), 369-389.

DeBono, E. (1973). *Lateral thinking*. New York: Harper & Row.

Deetz, S. (2001). *Transforming communication, transforming business*. Cresskill, NJ: Hampton.

DePaulo, P. J. (1992). Applications of nonverbal behavior research in marketing and management. In R. S. Feldman (Ed.), *Applications of nonverbal behavior theories and research* (pp. 63-87). Hillsdale, NJ: Lawrence Erlbaum.

Deutsch, M. (1971). Conflict and its resolution. In C. G. Smith (Ed.), *Conflict resolution: Contributions of the behavioral sciences* (pp. 36-57). Notre Dame, IN: University of Notre Dame Press.

Deutsch, M. (1991). Subjective features of conflict resolution. In R. Vayrynen (Ed.). *New directions in conflict theory* (pp. 27-43). London: Sage.

Deutsch, M. (2000). Cooperation and competition. In M. Deutsch & P. T. Coleman (Eds.), *The handbook of conflict resolution: Theory and practice* (pp. 21-40). San Francisco: Jossey-Bass.

Devine, P. G., Sedikides, C., & Fuhrman, R. W. (1989). Goals in information processing: A case of anticipated interaction. *Journal of Personality and Social Psychology, 56,* 680-690.

Diekmann, K. A. (1997). Implicit justification and self-serving group allocations. *Journal of Organizational Behavior, 18,* 3-16.

Donahue, W. A., & Cai, D. A. (1999). History of interpersonal conflict. In L. Kurtz (Ed.), *Encyclopedia of violence, peace and conflict: Vol. 2* (pp. 257-267). San Diego, CA: Academic Press.

Donnellon, A., & Kolb, D. (1997). Constructive for whom? The fate of diversity disputes in organizations. In C. DeDreu & E. Van deVliert (Eds.), *Using conflict in organizations* (pp. 161-176). Thousand Oaks, CA: Sage.

Dukes, E. F. (1996). *Resolving public conflict*. New York: St. Martin's.

Dyer, J. H. (2000). *Collaborative advantage: Winning through extended enterprise supplier networks*. New York: Oxford University.

Eagly, A. (1987). *Sex differences in social behavior: A social role interpretation*. Hillsdale, NJ: Lawrence Erlbaum.

Edlund, A., & Svenson, O. (1993). Judgments and decision making under time pressure: Studies and findings. In O. Svenson & A. J. Maule (Eds.), *Time pressure and stress in human judgment and decision making* (pp. 27-40). New York: Plenum.

Ellinor, L., & Gerard, G. (1998). *Dialogue: Creating and sustaining collaborative partnerships at work*. New York: John Wiley.

Engel, J. F., Blackwell, R. D., & Miniard, R. N. (1995). *Consumer behavior*. Fort Worth, TX: Dryden.

Ethics at issue in trade missions. (2001, April 15). *Denver Post*, p. B1.

Fant, L. (1989). Cultural mismatch in conversation: Spanish and Scandanavian communication behavior in negotiation. *Hermes Journal of Linguistics, 3,* 247-265.

Faure, G. O. (1998). Negotiation: The Chinese concept. *Negotiation Journal, 14*(2), 137-148.

Faure, G. O., & Rubin, J. Z. (Eds.). (1993). *Culture and negotiation: The resolution of water disputes*. Newbury Park, CA: Sage.

Federal Trade Commission, Identity Theft Data Clearinghouse. (n.d.) *Identity theft victim complaint data: Figures and trends on identity theft November 1999 through June 2001.* Retrieved May 18, 2002, from www.consumer.gov/idtheft/charts/01-06c.pdf

Fine, M. G. (1991). New voices in the workplace: Research directions in multicultural communication. *Journal of Business Communication, 23,* 259-275.

Fisher, R. (1990). Needs theory, social identity and conflict. In J. Burton (Ed.), *Conflict: Human needs theory* (pp. 89-112). New York: St. Martin's.

Fisher, R. (1991a). Beyond yes. In J. W. Breslin & J. Z. Rubin (Eds.), *Negotiating theory and practice* (pp. 123-126). Cambridge, MA: The Program on Negotiation at Harvard Law School.

Fisher, R. (1991b). Negotiating power: Getting and using influence. In J. W. Breslin & J. Z. Rubin (Eds.), *Negotiating theory and practice* (pp. 127-140). Cambridge, MA: The Program on Negotiation at Harvard Law School.

Fisher, R. (2000). Intergroup conflict. In M. Deutsch & P. T. Coleman (Eds), *The handbook of conflict resolution: Theory and practice* (pp. 166-184). San Francisco: Jossey-Bass.

Fisher, R., & Davis, W. H. (1987). Six basic interpersonal skills for a negotiator's repertoire. *Negotiation Journal, 4,* 117-122.

Fisher, R., & Ertel, D. (1995). *Getting ready to negotiate: The getting to yes workbook*. New York: Penguin.

Fisher, R., & Ury, W. (1978). *International mediation: A working guide*. Cambridge, MA: Harvard Negotiation Project.

Fisher, R., & Ury, W. (1981). *Getting to yes* (B. Patton, Ed.). Boston: Houghton-Mifflin.

Fisher, R., Ury, W., & Patton, B. (1991). *Getting to yes* (2nd edition). Boston: Houghton-Mifflin.

Fisher, R., Ury, W., & Patton, B. (1993). Negotiation power: Ingredients in an ability to influence the other side. In L. Hall (Ed.), *Negotiation: Strategies for mutual gain.* (pp. 3-13). Newbury Park, CA: Sage.

Fiske, S. T., & Taylor, S. E. (1984). *Social cognition*. New York: Random House.

Foa, U. G. (1961). Convergences in the analysis of the structure of interpersonal behavior. *Psychological Review, 68,* 341-363.

Fodor, E. M., & Smith, T. (1982). The power motive as an influence on group decision making. *Journal of Personality and Social Psychology, 42,* 178-185.

Folger, J. P., Poole, M. S., & Stutman, R. K. (1993). *Working through conflict: Strategies for relationships, groups, and organizations*. New York: HarperCollins.

Follett, M. (1995). *The prophetic management*. Boston: Harvard Business School Press.

Foster, D. A. (1992). *Bargaining across cultures*. New York: McGraw-Hill.

Freund, J. (1990). *Advise and invent: The lawyer as counselor-strategist*. Englewood Cliffs, NJ: Prentice Hall Law & Business.

Freund, J. (1993). *Smart negotiating: How to make good deals in the real world*. New York: Simon & Schuster.

Freund, J. (1994). *The neutral negotiator: Why and how mediation can work to resolve dollar disputes*. Englewood Cliffs, NJ: Prentice Hall Law & Business.

Freund, J. (1997, February). Anatomy of a split-up: Mediating a business divorce. *The Business Lawyer* (Vol. 52, No. 2). Section of Business Law, American Bar Association, University of Maryland School of Law.

Friedeman, R. A., & Shapiro, D. L. (1999). Deception and mutual gains bargaining: Are they mutually exclusive? *Negotiation Journal, 11*(3), 243-253.

Friedman, M. (1999). *Consumer boycotts: Effecting change through the marketplace and the media*. New York: Routledge.

Froman, L. A., & Cohen, M. D. (1970). Compromise and logroll: Comparing the efficiency of two bargaining processes. *Behavioral Science, 15,* 180-183.

Frye, R. & Stritch, T. (1964). Effect of timed vs. non-timed discussion upon measure of influence and change in small groups. *Journal of Social Psychology, 63,* 139-143.

Fulmer, W. E., & Goodwin, J. S. (1994). So you want to be a superior service provider? Start by answering your mail. *Business Horizons, 37*(6), 23-27.

Gibbons, P., Bradac, J. J., & Busch, J. D. (1992). The role of language in negotiations: Threats and promises. In L. L. Putnam & M. E. Roloff (Eds.), *Communication and negotiation* (pp. 156-175). Newbury Park, CA: Sage.

Gilkey, R. W., & Greenhalgh, L. (1991). The role of personality in successful negotiation. In J. W. Breslin & J. Z. Rubin (Eds.), *Negotiation theory and practice* (pp. 279-290). Cambridge, MA: The Program on Negotiation at Harvard Law School.

Ginsberg, T. (2000, August 3). They only looked disorganized. *Philadelphia Inquirer,* p. AA 08.

Gorbachev, M. (2001, April 17). Speech given at the Peter Lowe's Success 2001 Seminar, Denver, Colorado.

Gotbaum, V. (1999). *Negotiating in the real world: Getting the deal you want*. New York: Simon & Schuster.

Gottman, J. M. (1979). *Marital interaction: Experimental investigations*. New York: Academic Press.

Gottman, J. M. (1994). *What predicts divorce? The relationship between marital processes and marital outcomes*. Hillsdale, NJ: Lawrence Erlbaum.

Gottman, J., Notarius, C., Gonso, J., & Markman, H. (1976). *A couple's guide to communication*. Champaign, IL: Research.

Gottman, J. M., & Silver, N. (1999). *The seven principles for making marriage work*. New York: Three Rivers.

Graham, J. L. (1981). A hidden cause of America's trade deficit with Japan. *Columbia Journal of World Business, 16,* 5-15.

Graham, J. L. (1993). The Japanese style: Characteristics of a distinct approach. *Negotiation Journal, 9*(2), 123-140.

Graham, J. L. (1996). Vis-à-vis international business negotiations. In P. Ghauri & J. Usunier (Eds.), *International business negotiations* (pp. 69-90). Oxford, UK: Pergamon.

Graham, J. L., Mintu, A. T., & Rodgers, W. (1994). Explorations of negotiation behaviors in ten foreign countries using a model developed in the United States. *Management Science, 40*(1), 72-95.

Green, M. (1998). *The consumer bible.* New York: Workman.

Greenhalgh, L., & Chapman, D. I. (1997). Relationships between disputants: An analysis of their characteristics and impact. In S. E. Gleason (Ed.), *Workplace dispute resolution* (pp. 203-229). East Lansing: Michigan State University.

Griffin, T., & Daggett, W. R. (1990). *The global negotiator: Building strong business relationships anywhere in the world.* New York: Harper.

Gross, M. A., & Guerrero, L. K. (2000). Managing conflict appropriately and effectively: An application of the competency model to Rahim's organizational conflict styles. *International Journal of Conflict Management, 11*(3), 200-226.

Gruner, S. (1998, May). Have fun, make money. *Inc,* p. 123.

Grzelak, J. L. (1982). Preferences and cognitive processes in interdependent situations: A theoretical analysis of cooperation. In V. J. Derlega & J. Grzelak (Eds.), *Cooperation and helping behavior: Theories and research* (pp. 95-122). New York: Academic Press.

Hall, C. L. (Director), & Zaillian, S. (Director). (1998). *A Civil Action* [motion picture]. United States: Touchstone Pictures.

Hall, E. T. (1976). *Beyond culture.* Garden City, NY: Anchor.

Hall, E. T. (1983). *The dance of life: The other dimension of time.* New York: Anchor.

Halpern, J. J., & Parks, J. M. (1996). Vive la difference: Differences between males and females in process and outcomes in low-conflict negotiation. *International Journal of Conflict Management, 7*(1), 45-70.

Hample, D., & Dallinger, J. M. (1995). A Lewinian perspective on taking conflict personally: Revision, refinement and validation of the instrument. *Communication Quarterly, 43,* 297-319.

Hampson, F. O. & Hart, M. (1995). *Multilateral negotiations: Lessons from arms control, trade and the environment.* Baltimore, MD: Johns Hopkins University.

Hargrove, R. A. (1998). *Mastering the art of creative collaboration.* New York: McGraw-Hill.

Harinck, F., Carsten, K., DeDreu, W., & Van Vianen, E. M. (2000). The impact of conflict issues on fixed-pie perceptions, problem solving, and integrative outcomes in negotiation. *Organizational Behavior and Human Decision Processes, 81*(2), 329-358.

Harr, J. (1995). *A civil action.* New York: Vintage Books.

Harris, J. C. (1896). *Uncle Remus.* New York: D. Appleton-Century.

Harris, P. P., & Moran, R. T. (1996). *Managing cultural differences.* Houston, TX: Gulf.

Hastorf, A. H. & Cantril, C. (1954). They saw a game: A case study. *Journal of Abnormal and Social Psychology, 49,* 129-134.

Hershey, P., Blanchard, K. H., & Johnson, D. E. (1996). *Management of organizational behavior.* Upper Saddle River, NJ: Prentice Hall.

Hicks, T. (2001). Another look at identity-based conflict: The roots of conflict in the psychology of consciousness. *Negotiation Journal, 17*(1), 35-45.

Hill, G. (Director). (1973). *The Sting* [motion picture]. United States: Universal Studios.

Hobson, C. A. (1999). E-Negotiations: Creating a framework for online commercial negotiations. *Negotiation Journal, 15*(3), 201-218.

Hofstede, G. (1980). *Culture's consequences*. Beverly Hills, CA: Sage.

Howard, C., & Meltzer, M. (2000). *Get Clark smart: The ultimate guide for the savvy consumer*. Marietta: Longstreet Press.

Howe, R. (1963). *The miracle of dialogue*. New York: Seabury.

Ilke, E. C. (1968). Negotiation. In D. Sills (Ed.), *International encyclopedia of the social sciences: Vol. 2*. New York: Macmillan.

In the end, the customer is always right. (1995, June 14). *New York Times*, pp. B1-B2.

Innes, J. G. (1999). Evaluating consensus building. In L. Susskind, S. McKearnan, & J. Thomas-Larmer (Eds.), *The consensus building handbook: A comprehensive guide to reaching agreement* (pp. 631-683). Thousand Oaks, CA: Sage.

Isenhart, M., & Spangle, M. (2000). *Collaborative approaches to resolving conflict*. Thousand Oaks, CA: Sage.

Jandt, F., & Pederson, P. (1994). Indigenous mediation strategies in the Asia-Pacific region. *Aspire Newsletter, 4*(1), 10-11.

Janosik, R. J. (1991). Rethinking the culture-negotiation link. In J. W. Breslin & J. Z. Rubin (Eds.), *Negotiation theory and practice* (pp. 235-246). Cambridge, MA: The Program on Negotiation at Harvard Law School.

Janis, I. L. (1989). *Crucial decisions: Leadership in policymaking and crisis management*. Boston: Houghton Mifflin.

J. D. Edwards. (2001). [Corporate document on negotiation training.] Denver, CO: Author.

Johnson, D., Johnson, R., & Tjosvold, D. (2000). Constructive controversy: The value of intellectual opposition. In M. Deutsch & P. T. Coleman (Eds.), *The handbook of conflict resolution: Theory and practice* (pp. 65-85). San Francisco: Jossey-Bass.

Jones, T. S., & Bodtker, A. (2001). Mediating with heart in mind: Addressing emotion in mediation practice. *Negotiation Journal, 17*(3), 217-244.

Kahneman, D. (1992). Reference points, anchors, norms, and mixed feelings. *Organizational Behavior and Human Decision Processes, 51,* 296-312.

Kale, S. (1996). How national culture, organizational culture, and personality impact buyer-seller interactions. In P. Ghauri & J. Usunier (Eds.), *International business negotiations* (pp. 21-38). Oxford, UK: Pergamon.

Karras, C. (1970). *The negotiating game*. New York: Thomas Crowell.

Keiser, T. C. (1999). Negotiating with a customer you can't afford to lose. In R. J. Lewicki, D. M. Saunders, & J. W. Minton (Eds.), *Negotiation: Readings, exercises, and cases* (pp. 412-420). New York: McGraw-Hill.

Keltner, J. S. (1994). *The management of struggle: Elements of dispute resolution through negotiation, mediation and arbitration*. Cresskill, NJ: Hampton.

Keltner, J. S. (1995). From mild disagreement to war: The struggle spectrum. In J. Stewart (Ed.), *Bridges not walls* (pp. 317-333). New York: McGraw-Hill.

Kemp, K. E., & Smith, W. P. (1994). Information exchange, toughness and integrative bargaining: The roles of explicit cues and perspective taking. *International Journal of Conflict Management, 5*(1), 5-21.

Kettering Foundation. (1991). *Citizen and politics: A view from Main Street America* (Report prepared by the Harwood Group; Document No. 1498). Dayton, Ohio: Author.

Kimmel, M. J., Pruitt, D. G., Magenau, J. M., Konar-Goldband, E., & Carnevale, P. (1980). Effects of trust, aspiration, and gender on negotiation tactics. *Journal of Personality and Social Psychology, 38,* 9-23.

Kimmel, P. P. (2000). Culture and conflict. In M. Deutsch & P. T. Coleman (Eds.), *The handbook of conflict resolution: Theory and practice* (pp. 453-474). San Francisco: Jossey-Bass.

Kochan, T. A., & Verma, A. (1983). Negotiation in organizations: Blending industrial relations and organizational behavior approaches. In M. Bazerman & R. Lewicki (Eds.), *Negotiating in organizations* (pp. 13-32). Beverly Hills, CA: Sage.

Koh, T. B. (1996). American strengths and weaknesses. *International Negotiation, 1,* 313-317.

Kolb, D. (1993). Her place at the table: Gender and negotiation. In L. Hall (Ed.), Negotiation: *Strategies for mutual gain* (pp. 138-150). Newbury Park, CA: Sage.

Kolb, D. M., & Putnam, L. L. (1992). Introduction: The dialectic of disputing. In D. M. Kolb & J. M. Bartunek (Eds.), *Hidden conflict in organizations* (pp 1-31). Newbury Park, CA: Sage.

Kolb, D. M., & Williams, J. (2000). *The shadow negotiation: How women can master the hidden agendas that determine bargaining success.* New York: Simon & Schuster.

Koren, L., & Goodman, P. (1991). *The haggler's handbook.* New York: W. W. Norton.

Kotter, J. (1985). *Power and Influence.* New York: Free Press.

Kramer, R. M., & Messick, D. M. (1995). *Negotiation as a social process.* Thousand Oaks, CA: Sage.

Krauss, R. M. & Morsella, E. (2000). Communication and conflict. In M. Deutsch & P. T. Coleman (Eds.), *The handbook of conflict resolution: Theory and practice* (pp. 131-143). San Francisco: Jossey-Bass.

Kressel, K. (2000). Mediation. In M. Deutsch & P. T. Coleman (Eds.), *The handbook of conflict resolution: Theory and practice* (pp. 522-545). San Francisco: Jossey-Bass.

Kriesberg, L. (1998). *Constructive conflict.* Lanham, MD: Rowman & Littlefield.

Kriesberg. L. (1999). Conflict transformation. In L. Kurtz (Ed.), *Encyclopedia of violence, peace and conflict: Vol. 1* (pp. 413-425). San Diego, CA: Academic Press.

Kriesberg, L., Northrup, T. A., & Thorson, S. J. (Eds.), (1989). *Intractable conflicts and their transformation.* Syracuse, NY: Syracuse University.

Kurtzberg, T., & Medvec, V. H. (1999). Can we negotiate and still be friends? *Negotiation Journal, 15*(4), 355-362.

Lax, D., & Sebenius, J. (1986). *The manager as negotiator: Bargaining for cooperation and competitive gain.* New York: Free Press.

Lax, D. A., & Sebenius, J. K. (1991a). The power of alternatives on the limits to negotiation. In J. W. Breslin & J. Z. Rubin (Eds.), *Negotiation theory and practice* (pp. 97-113). Cambridge, MA: The Program on Negotiation at Harvard Law School.

Lax, D. A., & Sebenius, J. K. (1991b). Interests: The measure of negotiation. In J. W. Breslin & J. Z. Rubin (Eds.), *Negotiation theory and practice* (pp. 161-180). Cambridge, MA: The Program on Negotiation at Harvard Law School.

Leana, C. R. (1985). A partial test of Janis' groupthink model: Effects of group cohesiveness and leader behavior on defective decision making. *Journal of Management, 11,* 5-17.

Lebow, R. N. (1996). *The art of bargaining.* Baltimore, MD: Johns Hopkins University.

Lee, H. O., & Rogan, R. G. (1991). A cross-cultural comparison of organizational conflict management behavior. *International Journal of Conflict Management, 2,* 181-199.

Lehrman, C. K. (1997, November). Border wars. *Today's Homeowner, 93*, pp. 52-56.

LePoole, S. (1989, October). Negotiating with Clint Eastwood in Brussels. *Management Review*, pp. 58-60.

Lewicki, R. J., Hiam, A., & Olander, K. W. (1996). *Think before you speak: The complete guide to strategic negotiation.* New York: John Wiley.

Lewicki, R. J., & Litterer, J. A. (1985). *Negotiation.* Homewood, IL: Irwin.

Lewicki, R. J., & Robinson, R. (1998). Ethical and unethical bargaining tactics: An empirical study. *Journal of Business Ethics, 17,* 665-682.

Lewicki, R. J., & Wiethoff, C. (2000). Trust, trust development, and trust repair. In M. Deutsch & P. T. Coleman (Eds.), *The handbook of conflict resolution: Theory and practice* (pp. 86-107). San Francisco: Jossey-Bass.

Lewin, K. (1951). *Field theory and social science*. New York: Harper Brothers.

Lewin, K. (1997). *Resolving social conflict and field theory in social science*. Washington, DC: American Psychological Association.

Lim, S. A., & Murninghan, J. K. (1994). Phases, deadlines, and the bargaining process. *Organizational Behavior and Human Decision Processes, 58,* 153-171.

Lowenstein, G. F., Thompson, L., & Bazerman, M. H. (1989). Social utility and decision making in interpersonal contexts. *Journal of Personality and Social Psychology, 57,* 426-441.

Lytle, A. L., Brett, J. M., & Shapiro, D. L. (1999). The strategic use of interests, rights and power to resolve disputes. *Negotiation Journal, 15*(1), 31-52.

Maney, A., & Bykerk, L. (1994). *Consumer politics: Protecting public interests on Capitol Hill*. Westport, CT: Greenwood.

Mannix, E. A., Thompson, L. L., & Bazerman, M. H. (1989). Negotiation in small groups. *Journal of Applied Psychology, 74,* 508-517.

Marriage counselors see new directions (2000, June 30). *Denver Rocky Mountain News,* p. 16A.

Marrow, A. J. (1969). *The practical theorist*. New York: Basic Books.

Marsick, V. J., & Sauquet, A. (2000). Learning through reflection. In M. Deutsch & P. T. Coleman (Eds.), *The handbook of conflict resolution* (pp. 382-400). San Francisco: Jossey-Bass.

Maslow, A. (1954). *Motivation and personality*. New York: Harper & Row.

Mayer, B. (2000). *The dynamics of conflict resolution*. San Francisco: Jossey-Bass.

McCall, G. J., & Simmons, J. L. (1978). *Identities and interactions*. New York: Free Press.

McCrae, B. (1998). *Negotiating and influencing skills: The art of creating and claiming value*. Thousand Oaks, CA: Sage.

McKearnan, S., & Fairman, D. (1999). Producing consensus. In L. Susskind, S. McKearnan, & J. Thomas-Larmer (Eds.), *The consensus building handbook: A comprehensive guide for reaching agreement* (pp. 325-374). Thousand Oaks, CA: Sage.

McKersie, R. B. (1999). Agency in the context of labor negotiations. In R. H. Mnookin & L. E. Susskind (Eds.), *Negotiating on behalf of others* (pp. 181-195). Thousand Oaks, CA: Sage.

Mead, G. H. (1934). *Mind, self, and society*. Chicago: University of Chicago.

Melandro, L. A., & Barker, L. L. (1983). *Nonverbal communication*. New York: Random House.

Menkel-Meadow, C. (2001). Negotiating with lawyers, men, and things: The contextual approach still matters. *Negotiation Journal, 17*(3), 257-294.

Miller, G. (2001). *The career coach: Winning strategies for getting ahead in today's job market*. New York: Doubleday.

Miller, R., & Jentz, G. (1993). *Fundamentals of business law*. Minneapolis, MN: West.

Mischel, W., & DeSmet, A. L. (2000). Self-regulation in the service of conflict resolution. In M. Deutsch & P. T. Coleman (Eds.), *The handbook of conflict resolution: Theory and practice* (pp. 256-276). San Francisco: Jossey-Bass.

Mitchell, S. (1998). *American attitudes: Who thinks what about the issues that shape our lives*. Ithaca, NY: New Strategist Publications.

Mnookin, R. H., Peppet, S. R., & Tulumello, A. S. (2000). *Beyond winning: Negotiating to create value in deals and disputes*. Cambridge, MA: Belknap.

Moore, C. W. (1996). The mediation process. San Francisco: Jossey-Bass.

Morrison, T., Conaway, W. A., & Borden, G. A. (1994). *Kiss, bow, or shake hands: How to do business in sixty countries*. Holbrook, MA: Bob Adams.

Moyers, B. (Producer) and Reemstma, J. T. (Producer). (1983). *People like us* [videotape]. United States: (CBS Reports/CBS News, 555 West 57th St., New York, NY, 10019).

Moyers, B. (Producer) and Reemstma, J. T. (Producer). (1993). *Healing and the mind* [videotape]. United States: (Public Affairs Television, 450 W. 33rd St., New York, NY, 10001).

Murninghan, J. K., Babcock, L., Thompson, L., & Pillutla, M. (1999). The information dilemma in negotiations: Effects of experience, incentives, and integrative potential. *International Journal of Conflict Management, 10*(4), 313-339.

Nader, R., & Smith, W. (1995). *The frugal shopper*. Washington, DC: Center for Study of Responsive Law.

Nauta, A., & Sanders, K. (2000). Interdepartmental negotiation behavior in manufacturing organizations. *International Journal of Conflict Management, 11*(2), 135-161.

Neale, M. A., & Bazerman, M. H. (1991). *Cognition and rationality in negotiation*. New York: Free Press.

Neale, M. A., & Bazerman, M. H. (1993). Negotiating rationally: The power and impact of the negotiator's frame. In S. C. Currall, D. Geddes, S. M. Schmidt, & A. Hockner (Eds.), *Power and negotiation in organizations* (pp. 197-204). Dubuque, IA: Kendell/Hunt.

Neu, J. (1988). Conversation structure: An explanation of bargaining behavior in negotiations. *Management Communication Quarterly, 2,* 23-45.

Ng, J., & Ang, S. (1999). Attribution bias: Challenges, issues and strategies for mediation. *Mediation Quarterly, 16*(4), 377-387.

Nierenberg, G.I. (1968). *The art of negotiating: Psychological strategies for gaining advantageous bargains*. New York: Barnes and Noble.

Nierenberg, G. I., & Calero, H. (1971). *How to read a person like a book*. New York: Cornerstone library.

Nyerges, J. (1991). Ten commandments for a negotiation. In J. W. Breslin & J. Z. Rubin (Eds.), *Negotiation theory and practice* (pp. 187-193). Cambridge, MA: The Program on Negotiation at Harvard Law School.

Opotow, S. (2000). Aggression and violence. In M. Deutsch & P. T. Coleman (Eds.), *The handbook of conflict resolution: Theory and practice* (pp. 403-427). San Francisco: Jossey-Bass.

Papa, M. J., & Canary, D. J. (1995). Conflict in organizations: A competence-based perspective. In A. M. Nicotera (Ed.), *Conflict in organizations: Communicative processes* (pp. 153-179). Albany: State University of New York.

Papa, M. J., & Pood, E. A. (1988). Coorientational accuracy and differentiation in the management of conflict. *Communication Research, 15,* 400-425.

Parkhe, A. (1991). Interfirm diversity, organizational learning and longevity in global strategic alliances. *Journal of International Business Studies, 22,* 579-601.

Patton, B. (1984). *On teaching negotiation*. Unpublished manuscript. Cambridge, MA: The Program on Negotiation at Harvard Law School.

Peters, T. J., & Waterman, R. (1982.) *In search of excellence*. New York: Harper & Row.

Phatak, A. V., & Habib, M. M. (1999). The dynamics of international business negotiations. In R. J. Lewicki, D. M. Saunders, & J. W. Minton (Eds.), *Negotiations: Readings, exercises, and cases* (pp. 373-397). Boston: Irwin/McGraw-Hill.

Pinkley, R. A., Neale, M. A., & Bennett, R. J. (1994). The impact of alternatives to settlement in dyadic negotiations. *Organizational Behavior and Human Decision Processes, 57,* 97-116.

Podestra, D. (1987, June 8). The terrible toll of human hatred: Wars may come and go, but ethnic rivalries are forever. *The Washington Post National Weekly Edition*, pp. 9-10.

Pohlman, R. A., & Gardiner, G. S. (2000). *Values driven management: How to create and maximize values over time for organizational success.* New York: Amacom.

Pollan, S., & Levine, M. (1994). *The total negotiator.* New York: Avon Books.

Poole, M. S. (1991). Procedures for managing meetings: Social and technological innovation. In R. A. Swanson & B. O. Knapp (Eds.), *Innovative meeting management* (pp. 53-109). Austin, TX: 3M Meeting Management Institute.

Potapchuk, W. R. (1995). A comparison of consensus and voting in public decision making: A response. *Negotiation Journal, 11*(1), 55-59.

Pouliot, J. S. (1999, April). Eight steps to success in negotiating. *Nation's Business, 87*(4), 40-42.

Prather, H., & Prather, G. (1990). How to resolve issues unmemorably. In J. Stewart (Ed.), *Bridges not walls* (pp. 348-356). New York: McGraw-Hill.

Pruitt, D. G. (1995). Process and outcome in community mediation. *Negotiation Journal, 11*(4), 365-377.

Pruitt, D. G., & Carnevale, P. J. (1993). *Negotiation in social conflict.* Buckingham: Open University Press.

Pruitt, D. G., Carnevale, P. J., Ben-Yoan, O., Nochajski, T. K., & Van Slyck, M. (1983). Incentives for cooperation in integrative bargaining. In R. Tietz (Ed.), *Aspiration levels in bargaining and economic decision making* (pp. 22-34). Berlin: Springer.

Pruitt, D. G., Carnevale, P. J., Forcey, B., & Van Slyck, M. (1986). Gender effects in negotiation: Constituent surveillance and contentious behavior. *Journal of Experimental Social Psychology, 22,* 264-275.

Pruitt, D. G., & Johnson, D. R. (1970). Mediation as a way to aid face saving in negotiation. *Journal for Personality and Social Psychology, 4,* 239-246.

Pruitt, D. G., & Lewis, S. (1975). Development of integrative solutions in bilateral negotiation. *Journal of Personality and Social Psychology, 3,* 621-633.

Pruitt, D. G., Parker, J. C., & Mikolic, J. M. (1997). Escalation as a reaction to persistent annoyance. *International Journal of Conflict Management, 8*(3), 252-270.

Putnam, L. L. (1994). Challenging the assumptions of traditional approaches to negotiation. *Negotiation Journal, 10,* 337-346.

Putnam, L. (1997). Productive conflict: Negotiation as implicit coordination. In C. DeDreu & E. Van deVliert (Eds.), *Using conflict in organizations* (pp. 147-160). Thousand Oaks, CA: Sage.

Putnam, L. (2001). Language and dialectical tensions in negotiations. Message posted to www.kommunicationsforum.dk/litterature/putnamart.htm and retrieved November 14, 2001.

Putnam, L., & Holmes, M. (1992). Frame, reframing, and issue development. In L. L. Putnam & M. E. Roloff (Eds.), *Communication perspectives in negotiation* (pp. 128-155). Newbury Park, CA: Sage.

Putnam, L. L., & Jones, T. S. (1982). The role of communication in bargaining. *Human Communication Research, 8,* 262-280.

Putnam, L. L., & Kolb, D. K. (2000). Rethinking negotiation: Feminist views of communication and exchange. In P. M. Buzzanell (Ed.), *Rethinking organizational and managerial communication from feminist perspectives* (pp. 76-104). Thousand Oaks, CA: Sage.

Putnam, L., & Roloff, M. E. (Eds.). (1992a). *Communication and negotiation* (Vol. 20, Sage Annual Review Series). Newbury Park, CA: Sage.

Putnam, L., & Roloff, M. E. (1992b). Communication perspectives on negotiation. In L. Putnam & M. E. Roloff (Eds.), *Communication and negotiation* (pp. 1-20). Newbury Park, CA: Sage.

Pye, L. (1986). The China trade: Making the deal. *Harvard Business Review, 46*(4), 74-84.

Russell, J. (1998, March). The neighbor. *Good Housekeeping*, pp. 96-99, 145.

Quattrone, G. A., & Tversky, A. (1988). Contrasting rational and psychological analysis of political choices. *American Political Science Review, 82,* 719-736.

Rackham, N. (1985). The behavior of successful negotiators. In R. Lewicki & J. Letterer (Eds.), *Negotiation: Readings, exercises and cases* (pp. 45-57). Homewood, IL: Irwin.

Raiffa, H. (1982). The art and science of negotiation. Cambridge, MA: Harvard University Press.

Raisch, W. (2001). *The e-marketplace: Strategies for success in B2B e-commerce.* New York: McGraw-Hill.

Reemstma, J. T. (Producer). (1980). *What shall we do about mother?* [videotape]. United States: (CBS Reports/CBS News, 555 West 57th St., New York, NY, 10019).

Richardson, L. F. (1967). *Arms and insecurity*. Chicago: Quadrangle.

Richmond, Y., & Gestrin, P. (1998). *Africa: Intercultural insights*. Yartmouth, ME: Intercultural.

Roloff, M. E., & Dailey, W. O. (1987, May). *The effects of alternatives to reaching agreements on the development of integrative solutions to problems: The debilitating side effects of shared BATNA.* Paper presented at the Conflict Intervention Perspectives on Process, Temple University, Philadelphia, Pennsylvania.

Roloff, M. E., Paulson, G. D., & Volbrecht, J. (1998). The interpretation of coercive communication: The effects of mode of influence, powerful speech, and speaker authority. *International Journal of Conflict Management, 9*(2), 139-161.

Ross, L., & Stillinger, C. (1991). Barriers to conflict resolution. *Negotiation Journal, 7*(4), 389-404.

Rubin, J. Z., Pruitt, D. G., & Kim, S. H. (1994). *Social conflict: Escalation, stalemate and settlement*. New York: McGraw-Hill.

Rubin, J. Z., & Zartman, I. W. (1995). Asymmetrical negotiations: Some survey results that may surprise. *Negotiation Journal, 11*(4), 349-364.

Ruch, W. V. (1989). *International handbook of corporate communications.* Jefferson, NC: McFarland.

Rutheford, R. (1998). *How to get from no to go*. Boulder: Hayden Alexander.

Saavedra, P., & Kwun, S. (2000). Affective states in job characteristics. *Journal of Organizational Behavior, 21,* 131-146.

Samovar, L. A., & Porter, R. E. (1997). *Intercultural communication*. Belmont, CA: Wadsworth.

Samuelson, W. E. (1995). Computer-aided negotiation and economic analysis. *Negotiation Journal, 11*(2), 135-144.

Sandler, C. (1998). *Secrets of the savvy consumer*. Paramas, NJ: Prentice Hall.

Saner, R. (2000). *The expert negotiator*. The Hague: Kluner Law International.

Schaffzin, N. (1997). *Negotiate smart: The secrets of successful negotiation*. New York: Random House.

Schuster, C., & Copeland, M. (1986). Cross-cultural communication: Issues and implications. In P. Ghauri & J. Usunier (Eds.), *International Business Negotiations* (pp. 131-152). Oxford, UK: Pergamon.

Schweitzer, M. E., & Croson, R. (1999). Curtailing deception: The impact of direct questions on lies and omissions. *International Journal of Conflict Management, 10*(3), 225-248.

Shapiro, R. M., & Jankowski, M. A. (1998). *The power of nice*. New York: John Wiley.

Shell, G. R. (1999). *Bargaining for advantage: Negotiation strategies for reasonable people*. New York: Viking.

Siegel, J., Dubrovsky, V., Kiesler, S., & McGuire, T. W. (1986). Group processes in computer-mediated communication. *Organizational Behavior and Human Decision Processes, 37,* 157-187.

Sillars, A. L. (1981). Attributions and interpersonal conflict resolution. In J. H. Harvey, W. J. Ickes, & R. F. Kidd (Eds.), *New directions in attribution research: Vol. 3* (pp. 279-305). Mahwah, NJ: Lawrence Erlbaum.

Sillars, A. L., Colett, S., Perry, D., & Rogers, M. (1982). Coding conflict tactics. *Human Communication Research, 9,* 83-95.

Silverman, R. E., & Dunham, K. J. (2000, July 16). Even in hot job market, candidates strike out. *Rocky Mountain News,* p. J1.

Singer, L. (1994). *Settling disputes: Conflict resolution in business, families, and the legal system.* Boulder, CO: Westwood.

Singh, J. (1990). A typology of consumer dissatisfaction response styles. *Journal of Retailing, 66*(1), 57-99.

Sites, P. (1990). Needs as analogies of emotions. In J. Burton (Ed.) *Conflict: Human needs theory* (pp. 7-33). New York: St. Martin's.

Skopec, E. W., & Kiely, L. S. (1994). *Everything's negotiable . . . when you know how to play the game.* New York: American Management Association.

Soderbergh, S. (Director). (2000). *Erin Brockovich* [motion picture]. United States: Universal Studios.

Sonnenfeldt, H. (1986). Soviet negotiating concept and style. In L. Sloss & M. Davis (Eds.), *A game for high stakes: Lesson learned in negotiating with the Soviet Union* (pp. 21-33). Cambridge, MA: Ballinger.

Spangle, M., & Moorhead, J. (1998). *Interpersonal communication in organizational settings.* Dubuque, IA: Kendall/Hunt.

Spector, B. (2001). Transboundary disputes: Keeping backyards clean. In I. W. Zartman (Ed.), *Preventive negotiation: Avoiding conflict escalation* (pp. 205-226). Lanham, MD: Rowman & Littlefield.

Spinotti, D. (Director), and Mann, M. (Director). (1999). *The Insider* [motion picture]. United States: Touchstone Pictures.

Spitzberg, B. H, Canary, D. J., & Cupach, W. R. (1994). A competence-based approach to the study of interpersonal conflict. In D. D. Cahn (Ed.), *Conflict in personal relationships* (pp. 183-202). Hillsdale, NJ: Lawrence Erlbaum.

Stark, P. R. (1994). *It's negotiable: The how to handbook of win/win tactics.* San Diego, CA: Pfeiffer & Company.

Stein, J. G. (1989). Getting to the table: The triggers, stages, functions, and consequences of prenegotiation. *International Journal of Conflict Management, 44,* 423-430.

Straus, D. (1993). Facilitated collaborative problem solving and process management. In L. Hall (Ed.), *Negotiation: Strategies for mutual gain* (pp. 28-40). Newbury Park, CA: Sage.

Strutton, D., Pelton, L. E., & Lumpkin, J. R. (1993). The influence of psychological climate on conflict resolution strategies in franchise relationships. *Journal of the Academy of Marketing Science, 21,* 207-215.

Stryker, S. (1980). *Symbolic interactionism: A social structural version.* Menlo Park: Benjamin Cummings.

Stuhlmacher, A. F., Gillespie, T. L., and Champagne, M. V. (1998). The impact of time pressure in negotiation: A meta-analysis. *International Journal of Conflict Management, 9*(2), 97-116.

Susskind, L., Chayes, A., & Martinez, J. (1996). Parallel informal negotiation: A new kind of international dialogue. *Negotiation Journal, 12*(1), 19-29.

Susskind, L., & Cruikshank, J. (1987). *Breaking the impasse: Consensual approaches to resolving public disputes.* New York: Basic Books.

Tannen, E. (1994). *Gender and discourse.* New York: Oxford Books.

Thomas, J. C. (1995). *Public participation in public decisions.* San Francisco: Jossey-Bass.

Thompson, L. (1990a). An examination of naive and experienced negotiations. *Journal of Personality and Social Psychology, 259,* 82-90.

Thompson, L. (1990b). Negotiation behavior and outcomes: Empirical evidence and theoretical issues. *Psychological Bulletin, 108*(3), 515-532.

Thompson, L., & Hrebec, D. (1996). Lose-lose agreements in implementation decision making. *Psychological Bulletin, 120,* 396-409.

Thompson, L., & Lowenstein, G. (1992). Egocentric interpretations of fairness and interpersonal conflict. *Organizational Behavior and Decision Processes, 51,* 176-197.

Thompson, L., & Nadler, J. (2000). Judgmental biases in conflict resolution and how to overcome them. In M. Deutsch & P. T. Coleman (Eds.), *The handbook of conflict resolution: Theory and practice* (pp. 213-235). San Francisco: Jossey-Bass.

Thompson, L., Peterson, E., & Kray, L. (1995). Social context in negotiation. In R. M. Kramer & D. M. Messick (Eds.), *Negotiation as a social process* (pp. 5-36). Thousand Oaks, CA: Sage.

Tidwell, A. C. (1998). *Conflict resolved: A critical assessment of conflict resolution.* New York: Pinter.

Tjosvold, D., Johnson, D. W., & Fabrey, L. J. (1980). Effects of controversy and defensiveness on cognitive perspective taking. *Psychological Reports, 47,* 1043-1053.

Touval, S. (1989). Multilateral negotiation: An analytic approach. *Negotiation Journal, 5*(2), 162-163.

Tracy, B. (2000). *The 100 absolutely unbreakable laws of business success.* San Francisco: Barrett-Koehler.

Tripp, T. M., Sondak, H., & Bies, R. J. (1995). Justice as rationality: A relational perspective on fairness in negotiations. In R. J. Bies, R. J. Lewicki, & B. H. Sheppard (Eds.), *Research on negotiations in organizations: Volume 5* (pp. 45-64). Greenwich, CT: JAL Press.

Tung, R. L. (1996). Managing in Asia. In P. D. Joynt & M. Warner (Eds.), *Managing across cultures: Issues and perspectives* (pp. 369-381). London: Routledge.

Turner, M. E., & Pratkanis, A. R. (1997). Mitigating groupthink by stimulating constructive conflict. In C. DeDreu & E. Van DeVliert (Eds.), *Using conflict in organizations* (pp. 53-71). London: Sage.

Tversky, A., & Kahneman, D. (1981). The framing of decisions and the psychology of choices. *Sciences, 211,* 453-458.

Uhland, V. (1999, May 30). Negotiating the raise. *Rocky Mountain News,* pp. J1-J2.

Ury, W. (1991). *Getting past no: Dealing with difficult people.* New York: Bantam Books.

Ury, W. (1999). *Getting to peace.* New York: Viking.

Ury, W., Brett, J. M., & Goldberg, S. B. (1988). *Getting disputes resolved: Designing systems to cut the costs of conflict.* San Francisco: Jossey-Bass.

Usunier, J. (1996a). Cultural aspects of international business negotiations. In P. Ghauri & J. Usunier (Eds.), *International business negotiations* (pp. 93-118). Oxford, UK: Pergamon.

Usunier, J. (1996b).The role of time in international business negotiations. In P. Ghauri & J. Usunier (Eds.), *International business negotiations* (pp. 153-172). Oxford, UK: Pergamon.

Vayrynen, R. (Ed.), (1991). *New directions in conflict theory: Conflict resolution and conflict transformation.* London: Sage.

Waldman, S. (1999). The tyranny of choice. In L. B. Glickman (Ed.), *Consumer society in American history: A reader* (pp. 359-366). Ithaca, NY: Cornell University Press.

Walton, R., Cutcher-Gershenfeld, J. E., & McKersie, R. (1994). *Strategic negotiations: A theory of change in labor-management relations.* Boston: Harvard Business School Press.

Walton, R., & McKersie, R. (1965). *A behavioral theory of labor negotiations: An analysis of a social interaction system*. Ithaca, NY: ILR Press.

Waterman, R. (1987). *The renewal factor: How the best get and keep the competitive edge*. New York: Bantam Books.

Waterman, R. (1990). *Adhocracy: The power to change*. Knoxville, TN: Whittle Direct Books.

Waterman, R. (1994). *What America does right: Learning from companies that put people first*. New York: Norton.

Watkins, M. (1999). Negotiating in a complex world. *Negotiation Journal, 15*(3), 245-270.

Watkins, M. (2001). Principles of persuasion. *Negotiation Journal, 17*(2), 115-137.

Watkins, M., & Rosegrant, S. (1996). Sources of power in coalition building. *Negotiation Journal, 12*(1), 47-68.

Weiner, M., & Mehrabian, A. (1968). *Language within language: Immediacy, a channel in verbal communication*. New York: Appleton-Century-Crofts.

Wheeler, M. (1995). Computers and negotiation: Backing into the future. *Negotiation Journal, 11*(2), 169-176.

White, J. J. (1984). The pros and cons of getting to yes. *Journal of Legal Education, 34,* 115-124.

Williams, G. (1992). Style and effectiveness in negotiation. In L. Hall (Ed), *Negotiation: strategies for mutual gain* (pp. 151-176). Newbury Park, CA: Sage.

Williams, T. D., Drake, M., & Moran, J. (1993). Complaint behavior, price paid, and the store patronized. *Internal Journal of Retail and Distribution Management, 21*(5), 9.

Wilmot, W. (1987). *Dyadic communication*. New York: Random House.

Wish, M., & Kaplan, S. (1977). Toward an implicit theory of interpersonal communication. *Sociometry, 40,* 234-246.

Wokutch, R. E. & Carson, T. L. (1993). The ethics and profitability of bluffing in business. In R. J. Wewicki, J. M. Litterer, D. M. Saunders, & J. W. Minton (Eds.), *Negotiation* (pp, 499-504). Burr Ridge, IL: Irwin.

Wycoff, J. (1986). *Mindmapping*. New York: Berkley.

Yerby, J., Buerkel-Rothfuss, N., & Bochner, A. P. (1990). *Understanding family communication*. Scottsdale, AZ: Gorsuch Scarisbrick.

Zadney, J., & Gerard, H. B. (1974). Attributed intentions and inferential selectivity. *Journal of Experimental Social Psychology, 10,* 34-52.

Zartman, I. W. (1976). Introduction. In I. W. Zartman (Ed.), *The 50% solution* (pp. 2-41). New Haven, CT: Yale.

Zartman, I. W. (1989). Prenegotiation: Phases and functions. *International Journal of Conflict Management, 44,* 237-253.

Zartman, I. W. (2001). Preventive negotiation: Setting the stage. In I. W. Zartman (Ed.), *Preventive negotiation: Avoiding conflict escalation* (pp. 1-18). Lanham, MD: Rowman & Littlefield.

Zartman, I. W., & Berman, M. (1982). *The practical negotiator*. New Haven, CT: Yale University.

ABOUT THOSE PROFILED

Peter Adler, PhD, is a partner in The Accord Group, LLC, an international firm specializing in facilitation, mediation, planning, and problem solving. He is a former Peace Corps volunteer and Outward Bound instructor. Peter has served in executive positions with the Hawaii Justice Foundation (1992 to present), The Hawaii Supreme Court's Center for Alternative Dispute Resolution (1985 to 1992), and the Neighborhood Justice Center (1979 to 1985). His specialty is multiparty negotiation and problem solving. He is past president of the Society for Professionals in Dispute Resolution (now the Association for Conflict Resolution). Peter is the author of *Oxtail Soup: For the Island Soul* (2001) and *Beyond Paradise* (1993), and numerous other professional and popular articles.

Christine Beard, owner of Absolute Travel and Tours, has worked in the travel industry for 25 years. She worked for different travel agencies in Houston, Texas, before opening her own agency 15 years ago. Her agency is part of a consortium of other travel agencies. The majority of her agency's business consists of corporate travel.

Marjorie Bribitzer, ACSW, LCSW, graduated with her MSW in 1987 from the Catholic University of America, where she specialized in Family and Children's Services. Over the course of her career, she has practiced as a family and individual therapist in various mental health settings, where she teaches negotiation skills as one of the tools useful to families in turmoil. She has published on the topic of home-based, family-centered intervention. Since 1995, she has worked with families in her private practice in Hampstead, North Carolina.

Wayne Carle, PhD, retired in 1997 as superintendent of the Jefferson County school district in Colorado, one of the largest public school districts in the country. He spent 45 years in education, primarily in administration. Before his last post, he had been professor in the Education department at the University of Colorado at Denver; vice president of Texas Southern University in Houston; Superintendent of Schools in Dayton, Ohio, and Hammond, Indiana; and Assistant State Superintendent of Public Instruction in Ohio. Carle's special interests in education include administrative teams, choice and charter schools, civility, finance, nonviolence, planning and budgeting, policy development, school public relations, teacher preparation, technology, and values. He is involved in many volunteer activities, including A Season for Nonviolence Rocky Mountain Alliance Board of Directors.

Christine A. Coates, MEd, JD, an experienced family law attorney, now emphasizes ADR in domestic relations. She is an active member of the Colorado Bar Association (CBA), where she serves as a member of the board of governors, as well as on numerous committees. Coates was named the CBA's Outstanding Young Lawyer in 1986. She was honored by the Colorado Council of Mediators and Mediation Organizations as the 1996 Mediator of the Year and was recognized by Voices for Children (CASA) for her advocacy for children that same year. She received the 1999 community service award from the Boulder Interdisciplinary Committee on child custody. Coates is a frequent lecturer on family law, professionalism, and dispute resolution options.

Robert Coulson, JD, was president of the American Arbitration Association from 1972 until 1994. He was also a member of the Council of the American Bar Association's Section on Dispute Resolution and a Director of the Fund of Modern Courts. Before joining the American Arbitration Association in 1963 as executive vice president, Coulson practiced law in New York City. He has written and lectured extensively on the settlement of disputes. He is a graduate of Yale University and Harvard Law School. Coulson is the author of *How to Stay Out of Court* (1968), *Business Mediation: What You Need to Know* (1987), and *Business Arbitration: What You Need to Know* (1980).

Rev. (Fr.) Charles L. Currie, S. J. has been involved with higher education for the Jesuit order since the 1950s. He has been twice a college president (Wheeling Jesuit College [now a university], 1972 to 1982, and Xavier University, 1982 to 1986) and currently oversees an association of 28 colleges and universities. In addition to his many other professional accomplishments, Rev. Currie also serves as assistant for higher education to the Maryland Province Provincial, with particular responsibility for the five Maryland Province institutions of higher education: Georgetown University, Loyola College, St. Joseph's University, Scranton University, and Wheeling Jesuit University.

John A. Fiske, JD, has been concentrating in family law and mediation with the law firm of Healy, Fiske, Woodbury, and Richmond in Cambridge, Massachusetts. By 2001, he had mediated about 1,700 divorces, separations, premarital agreements, and contracts to help couples stay married. Fiske has been active in promoting mediation in New England and nationally. He was the first Assistant Corporation Counsel for the City of Boston. He has written extensively about family mediation and trains mediators through his partnership, Divorce Mediation Training Associate.

Elaine Taylor Freeman is the founder and executive director of ETV Endowment of South Carolina, Inc., a nonprofit and membership organization in support of the South Carolina Educational Television and Radio

(SC ETV). She has also served since 1982 as the Executive Director of S. C. Educational Communications, a production affiliate of the ETV Endowment. Freeman has held numerous other directorships, such as for public utilities and banks. She has been trustee and board member for many nonprofit organizations, including the South Carolina Independent Colleges Foundation. She has been honored with several honorary degrees and awards, such as the Governor's Award in the Humanities in 1998.

James C. Freund, JD, was a senior partner at the New York law firm of Skadden, Arps, Slate, Meagher & Flom. Before his retirement, he was a prominent negotiator in many of the corporate takeover battles of the 1980s. In recent years, Freund has helped clients resolve business disputes through negotiation and has served as both a mediator and an arbitrator. Freund teaches negotiating at Fordham University School of Law. In addition to authoring six books, he has written numerous articles. In 1999, he created and narrated a six-hour Practicing Law Institute video course. He currently writes "Sage Advice," a regular column for the *New York Law Journal.*

Karen Graves is a recently retired management negotiator for Qwest.

Annie Hill is a union negotiator for Qwest.

Marvin E. Johnson, JD, is a nationally recognized mediator, arbitrator, and trainer with more than 25 years of dispute resolution experience. He is the founder and director of the Center for Alternative Dispute Resolution and previously was an associate professor at Bowie State University. Johnson has worked for the Department of Labor, the Federal Labor Relations Authority, the Federal Mediation and Conciliation Service, and the National Academy of Conciliators. As a consultant, Johnson serves as a mediator, an arbitrator, a fact-finder, and a facilitator in hundreds of public and private disputes. He provides dispute resolution training, and he lectures and writes extensively on the subject of conflict management. Former President Bill Clinton appointed Johnson to the Federal Service Impasses Panel in 1999 and to the Foreign Service Impasse Disputes Panel in 2000.

John William ("Sam") Keltner, PhD, is a professor emeritus from Oregon State University, Department of Speech Communication. Among other courses, Keltner taught graduate seminars on mediation and dispute resolution, collective bargaining, and arbitration. He has published widely in the ADR field. He served as mediation commissioner, training officer, and WAE mediator for the Federal Mediation and Conciliation Service from 1958 to 1970. Keltner is a charter member of the Society for Professionals in Dispute Resolution; he has held numerous offices in that organization. He was a mediation trainer, president of the board of directors, and volunteer mediator for the Community Mediation and Dispute Resolution Service of Oregon from 1989 to 1997.

Edward King has spent the last 25 years in the high-tech environment in a variety of computer- and software-related positions. For the last seven years, he has focused on global programs and project management. Currently, he is a senior program manager for MCI WorldCom Joint Venture System Support, based in Brazil. King is a graduate of Regis University in Denver, where he doubled majored in computer science and management. His MBA is also from Regis.

Barbara Berger Opotowsky served as assistant commissioner of the New York City Department of Consumer Affairs from 1974 to 1978. Later, she was the president of the Better Business Bureau (BBB) of Metropolitan New York. Currently, Opotowsky is the executive director of the Association of the Bar of the City of New York. She serves as chair of the New York State Bar Association Committee on Regulatory Reform, chair of the Association of the Bar of the City of New York Committee on Consumer Affairs, and chair of the Committee on Women in the Profession.

Linda L. Putnam, PhD, is professor of Organizational Communication in the Department of Speech Communication at Texas A & M University and director of the Program on Conflict and Dispute Resolution in the George Bush School of Government and Public Service. Her current research interests include negotiation and organizational conflict, metaphors of organizational communication, and language analysis in organizations. Her numerous publication credits include coediting *Communication and Negotiation* (1992a) and authoring the chapter "Productive conflict: Negotiation as implicit coordination" in *Using Conflict in Organizations* (1997). She has published many articles and is the recipient of awards such as the Distinguished Scholar Award from the National Communication Association.

Judy Towers Reemstma produces documentaries for television. From 1961 to 1978, she worked for CBS News. She produced television documentaries and series with Walter Cronkite, Bill Moyers, and Charles Kuralt. Later, she became an independent producer. Her documentaries cover a broad spectrum of topics, such as campaign finance, emerging nations, and heath issues. Reemstma graduated from Wellesley College and has been the recipient of numerous awards for her work, including three Emmys.

Joseph L. Rice III, JD, is the chairman of Gibbons, Green and Rice, Inc., a private investment firm headquartered in New York City. He graduated from Williams College in 1954. Following graduation, he enlisted in the United States Marine Corps and served as a lieutenant from 1954 to 1957. He returned to Harvard Law School, graduating in 1960. Rice practiced law with Sullivan & Cromwell in New York City from 1960 to 1966 before joining Laird Incorporated, an investment banking firm. He founded Gibbons, Green & Rice, a management buyout firm, in 1969, and Clayton, Dubillier & Rice in 1978. Rice is also a member of the Boards of Trustees of the Manhattan Institute, INSEAD'S International Council, and The Chase Manhattan

Corporation – National Advisory Board. He is a Director of ITALTEL SpA, Remington Arms Company, and Uniroyal Holdings, Inc.

Anthony Roisman, JD, is of counsel to Hershenson, Carter, Scott and McGee in Norwich, Vermont. He is a graduate of Dartmouth (cum laude, 1960) and Harvard Law School (LLB, 1963). Roisman has been involved in the litigation of environmental and radiation issues before the federal district courts and federal agencies since 1969. He has been lead counsel or co-lead counsel in several landmark environmental cases, including Calvert Cliffs Coordinating Committee v. U.S. Atomic Energy Commission (1971) and Anderson v. W.R. Grace (settled in 1986). He was senior staff attorney for the Natural Resources Defense Council (1977 to 1979), the chief of the Hazardous Waste Section and special litigator for Hazardous Waste in the Lands and Natural Resources Division of the U.S. Department of Justice (1979 to 1982), and executive director of Trial Lawyers for Public Justice (1982 to 1987). He is adjunct professor of Environmental Studies at Dartmouth College.

Edward Selig, JD, practiced law for 30 years in various public and private settings before embarking on his current career as a mediator of legal disputes. In affiliation with JAMS Endispute, the United States District Court for Massachusetts, and the Massachusetts Office of Dispute Resolution, he has mediated cases involving environmental, commercial, and land use issues. He also holds appointments as visiting lecturer in environmental law at Harvard University School of Public Health and at the Metropolitan College of Boston University.

Lawrence Susskind, PhD, Ford Professor of Urban and Environmental Planning, has been on the faculty in the Department of Urban Studies and Planning at MIT for 30 years. He is one of the country's most experienced public and environmental dispute mediators and a leading figure in the dispute resolution field. He has served as court-appointed special master, trainer, and a mediator for neighborhood, municipal, state, and national agencies and organizations in North America, Europe, and the Far East. He is founder and president of the Consensus Building Institute, a not-for-profit that provides mediation and dispute system design services to public and private clients worldwide.

Russel Turbeville, JD, is a native Houstonian who attended the University of Houston for undergraduate studies and law school. He began his legal-field employment as an assistant district attorney in 1974, left the office briefly in 1980, returned and was assigned to the consumer fraud unit, where he's been ever since. Over the years, he has investigated or supervised the investigation of more than 20,000 complaints, resulting in somewhere between 1,000 and 2,000 criminal fraud cases being filed. He has personally tried more than 100 felony fraud trials during that period. He has authored several fraud bills, a few of which have actually been enacted into law in Texas. He has spoken at numerous law seminars on the topic of fraud, including the

National Association of Securities Administrators (NAASA) and the National Association of Certified Fraud Examiners.

William Ury is cofounder of the Program on Negotiation at Harvard Law School, where he directs the Project on Preventing War. His books include *Getting to Yes* (1991, with Roger Fisher and Bruce Patton), *Getting Past No*, and *Getting to Peace*. For the last two decades, he has worked as a third party and mediator in conflicts ranging from union-management strikes to ethnic wars in the Balkans and the former Soviet Union. He also participated in the creation of nuclear risk reduction centers in Washington and Moscow, serving as consultant to the White House Crisis Management Center. Trained as an anthropologist, he received his BA from Yale and his MA and PhD from Harvard University.

Robert H. Waterman, Jr. is best known as the coauthor of *In Search of Excellence*. Since that book's publication in 1982, he has written three other books: *The Renewal Factor: How the Best Get and Keep the Competitive Edge* (1987), *Adhocracy: The Power to Change* (1990), and *What America Does Right: Learning From Companies That Put People First* (1994). When he's not writing, Mr. Waterman keeps busy putting his words into practice. He spent 21 years at McKinsey and Company, Inc., serving in or managing offices in San Francisco, Japan, and Australia. He is a founding director of the AES, Inc., now the world's largest independent power producer. He has a BS in Geophysical Engineering from the Colorado School of Mines and an MBA from Stanford University. Outside his business role, he paints in watercolor and oil.

INDEX

ABOUT THE AUTHORS

For more than two decades, **Michael Spangle**, PhD, has provided training or consulting for a wide variety of organizations including J.D. Edwards, Time/Warner, IBM, Inflow Inc., the U.S. Department of Health and Human Services, the National Association of Realtors, and the U.S. Navy, as well as schools, churches, and hospitals. He served as Director of Graduate Studies in Applied Communication and Alternative Dispute Resolution at the University of Denver and Director of Faculty and Curriculum for the School of Professional Studies at Regis University. In addition to obtaining a PhD in Speech Communication from the University of Denver, he completed an MS in Education from Kearney State College and an MDiv from Luther Theological Seminary. He teaches university courses in negotiation, mediation, conflict management, team communication, and leadership. He is coauthor of two other books, including *Interpersonal Communication in Organizational Settings* (1998; written with Jacqueline Moorhead).

Myra Warren Isenhart, PhD, teaches, writes, and consults about topics in organizational communication. Currently a faculty member at the University of Denver, she has also served on faculties at the University of Colorado at Denver and St. Thomas Theological Seminary. Her master's degree and PhD are in Human Communication. She is a speaker and author on conflict management in the workplace. She has published articles in communication journals and coauthored *Collaborative Approaches to Resolving Conflict* (2000), also written with Michael Spangle and published by Sage. Her client base is broad, with concentrations in health care, software development, and government. In addition, she serves on several nonprofit boards.